The Political Economy of International Financial Crisis

The Political Economy of International Financial Crisis

Interest Groups, Ideologies, and Institutions

Edited by Shale Horowitz and Uk Heo

ROWMAN & LITTLEFIELD PUBLISHERS, INC.
Lanham • Boulder • New York • Oxford

332.042
P769

ROWMAN & LITTLEFIELD PUBLISHERS, INC.

Published in the United States of America
by Rowman & Littlefield Publishers, Inc.
4720 Boston Way, Lanham, Maryland 20706
http://www.rowmanlittlefield.com

12 Hid's Copse Road
Cumnor Hill, Oxford OX2 9JJ, England

British Library Cataloguing in Publication Information Available

Library of Congress Cataloging-in-Publication Data

The political economy of international financial crisis : interest groups, ideologies, and
institutions / edited by Shale Horowitz and Uk Heo.
    p. cm.
    Includes bibliographical references and index.
    ISBN 0-7425-0132-9 (cloth : alk. paper)—ISBN 0-7425-0133-7 (pbk. : alk. paper)
    1. International finance. 2. Pressure groups. I. Horowitz, Shale Asher. II. Heo, Uk,
    1962–
HG3881 .P6518 2000
332'.042—dc21

00-057585

Contents

Figures and Tables

FIGURES

TABLES

I

Introduction, Theoretical Overview, and Economic Background

Explaining Precrisis Policies and Postcrisis Responses: Coalitions and Institutions in East Asia, Latin America, and Eastern Europe

Shale Horowitz and Uk Heo

The international financial crisis of 1997–1999 commands attention as the most important international economic event since the oil shocks of the 1970s and the subsequent debt crisis. Its unfamiliar character reflects an increasingly liberalized world economy. Unlike previous postwar crises, this one originated in fast-growing Southeast and East Asia, revealing the first major signs of weakness in what had seemed an inexorable march toward U.S. and European levels of wealth and power. As the crisis spread more widely through the developing world, policy makers faced their first major test in a world of rapidly expanding international trade and large, volatile international capital flows.

In fact, the crisis was preceded by chronic difficulties in Japan, the second largest economy in the world and by far the most important in Asia. The collapse of real estate and stock price bubbles had left the Japanese financial sector with massive bad loan problems—far in excess of those associated, for example, with the U.S. savings and loan crisis. The larger Asian crisis began with a run on Thailand's currency, and then spread throughout Southeast and East Asia. However, some economies—such as those of Taiwan, Singapore, the Philippines, Hong Kong, and China—were much less strongly affected. Similarly, when the crisis spread to other parts of the world, the impact was highly uneven. In Latin America, Brazil and to a lesser extent Argentina were more heavily affected than Mexico. Among the postcommunist countries, Russia was more heavily affected than Poland and Hungary, while the crisis in the Czech Republic began prior to the Asian crisis.

Most attention has focused on explaining why the crisis occurred, and particularly on identifying the optimal economic policy response to the crisis. Discussion of the causes of the crisis has looked at internal sources of deteriorating

economic performance and has asked whether the crisis reached artificial proportions due to increasingly large and volatile international capital flows. Discussion of optimal policy responses has examined issues such as the merits of
fixed as opposed to flexible exchange rate regimes, the extent to which devaluation should be utilized instead of macroeconomic stringency, and whether and
how foreign exchange controls should be used.[1]

In contrast, this volume focuses on political explanations of economic policies
and institutional changes as they actually occurred: What explains precrisis
choices of economic policy regimes? What explains economic policy responses
to the crisis? What explains whether and how the crisis precipitated changes in
political institutions? These issues are examined through a broad array of case
studies of mostly middle-income developing countries,[2] from a number of different regions, with a wide range of initial economic and institutional conditions,
and with a wide range of policy and institutional outcomes.

Although often starting from highly interventionist initial conditions, precrisis policy trends were strongly liberalizing. With some notable exceptions,
this continues to be true for the policy responses to the crisis. Our explanation
for this policy trend looks at coalitions of economic interest groups and types
of political institutions. Our first main question asks, *what kinds of interest
group coalitions have supported the liberalizing policy trends of the recent
past and present?* Today the more important developing countries either are
democracies or are in the process of becoming democracies. Economic policies in democracies are directly subject to the voting and lobbying pressures
of economic interest groups. Our claim is that explanations of policy in
democracies must look not only at the more highly concentrated and organized
industries directly involved in the international economy but also at the more
dispersed middle and working classes in the domestically oriented service sector. In particular, we argue that it is difficult to explain the general liberalizing
policy trend before and after the crisis without reference to these dispersed interest groups. In this context we argue that ideologically colored interpretations of past experience play an important role in increasing or decreasing dispersed interest group support for policies primarily benefiting concentrated
interest groups. Such considerations are also relevant to explaining policy stability and change in authoritarian regimes, although their political rules and
processes are less transparent.

In authoritarian regimes, economic policy making is often more insulated from
interest group pressures; and in "developmental" authoritarian regimes, such in-
sulation has often been joined with technocratic economic management aimed at
achieving rapid economic growth. Our second main question is, *how do transitions to democracy affect policy in what were once developmental authoritarian
regimes?* Here our claim is that, contrary to much received wisdom, new democracies are not likely to break decisively with policies that have been successful in
producing high rates of economic growth.

Both old and new democracies are likely to learn from recent experiences in which policy makers—whether democratic or authoritarian—ignored the long-term costs of distorting and inflationary policies. Again, we claim that this capacity to conserve past achievements and learn from past mistakes must refer to dispersed as well as concentrated economic interest groups.

Our third main question asks, *how are precrisis policies and postcrisis responses affected by variation in the forms of democratic political institutions?* We argue that varieties of executive and legislative institutions and party systems that concentrate power are more likely to be responsive to changes in dispersed interest group preferences. On the other hand, legislative and executive institutions and party systems that disperse power are more likely to allow narrowly based, well-organized interest groups to block or dilute threatening policy changes.

WHAT IS BEING EXPLAINED

We are interested in providing political explanations of (1) foreign economic policy regimes adopted both prior to and in response to the crisis, and (2) any crisis-induced changes in political institutions.[3] These outcomes are defined broadly. "Foreign economic policy regimes" include trade policies and capital market regulations, as well as related fiscal, monetary, banking sector, regulatory, and exchange rate policies. "Political institutions" refer primarily to (1) formal executive and legislative institutions, including economic regulatory bodies such as executive branch ministries and central banks, and (2) electoral rules and party systems. However, a full understanding of such institutions must often address the formal and informal ways in which economic policy makers and technocrats may be insulated from popular and interest group pressures, and animated by guiding political and economic ideologies.

HOW IT IS BEING EXPLAINED

Explanations of continuity and change in economic policy and political institutions begin by looking at internal economic structure and the associated pattern of concentrated, highly organized interest group cleavages, and at political institutions that mediate such interest group pressures. These factors in themselves often appear to offer incomplete explanations. In such cases the authors show that pivotal roles are often played by more dispersed, weakly organized interest groups and by political leadership. The preferences of the more dispersed, weakly organized interest groups are based on interpretations of recent experiences with one or more of the rival policy regimes being touted by competing political movements. Such interpretations often reflect ideologies specific to the histories of the various regions and countries.

DEMAND SIDE: ECONOMIC INTEREST GROUPS AND COALITIONS

The place of the various important economic interest groups within a country's
economic structure is the basic determinant of such groups' economic policy
preferences. The most well-organized economic interest groups relative to their
shares of the workforce are likely to be more "concentrated" in a number of complementary ways. They are likely to use more specific capital to produce relatively homogeneous products more subject to national and international competition, and to be concentrated in large units of production, often located in
relatively close proximity to one another. Industries using more specific capital to
produce more homogeneous products are more likely to be affected strongly and
similarly by various policies, and hence have a stronger incentive to organize collectively. Industries concentrated in large units of production and located close together are likely to have lower costs of organization. Other things being equal,
such concentrated interest groups are likely to enjoy organizational advantages
over more dispersed interest groups in influencing the policy-making process.

Concentrated interest groups are disproportionately located in the part of the
economy directly exposed to international trade. This "traded" sector is most
strongly affected by international trade and financial policies that alter the (relative) prices of its products. The traded sector includes almost all manufacturing
and agriculture, but only a small part of the service sector. Dispersed interest
groups are located disproportionately in the part of the economy not directly
exposed to international trade. This "nontraded" sector is usually more weakly affected by trade and financial policies that alter the prices of traded sector products. Nontraded sector interests are more weakly and indirectly affected by international trade and financial policies, through their impact on consumer goods
prices and on monetary and fiscal policies and economic growth. The nontraded
sector includes most of the service sector, and its most important strata are the
more skilled middle classes and the more unskilled working classes. A similar
analysis applies to subsidies dispensed to concentrated interest groups through
policies such as preferential access to bank credit and regulatory privileges. Such
policies also affect dispersed interest groups more weakly and indirectly, through
their impact on consumer goods prices and on monetary and fiscal policies and
economic growth. It should also be noted that there are important concentrated
interest groups within the nontraded sector, for example, in local financial services, utilities, and government.

All of these interest groups can be expected to form or join political coalitions
to pursue their preferred economic policy options. In the case of dispersed interest groups, such mobilization is likely to be weaker and more unstable. Again, this
is because trade, macroeconomic, banking sector, and other policies benefiting
concentrated, especially traded sector interest groups, typically have a weaker,
more indirect effect on the incomes of dispersed nontraded sector groups—with
many of the costs in particular being incurred in the longer run. Dispersed inter-

est group preferences toward such policies are likely to be more unstable in two ways. Such preferences are more likely to be independently influenced by ideologies that misrepresent, minimize, or exaggerate the long-term consequences of policies primarily benefiting concentrated interest groups. Similarly, such preferences are more subject to change as experience with the long-term consequences of these policies accumulates.

The most stable coalitions are likely to form where groups can agree on a coherent set of the more consequential policies. We argue that changes in dispersed interest group preferences are an important source of significant change in economic policy-making coalitions. In the recent, liberalizing period examined in this volume, they are by far the most important source.

SUPPLY SIDE: POLITICAL INSTITUTIONS AND LEADERSHIP

Political institutions determine the extent to which the government is formally and informally accountable to economic interest groups, as well as the specific manner in which economic policies are chosen and implemented. Authoritarian regimes are more likely to exclude some important interest groups from the political process while privileging others. Similar but weaker effects may result from variation in the form of democratic political institutions. Given our emphasis on the potentially pivotal role of dispersed interest groups, we emphasize the ways in which political institutions may limit or enhance their influence relative to that of concentrated interest groups. In authoritarian regimes, this is likely to depend on the importance attributed to cultivating mass legitimacy relative to patron–client relationships with concentrated interest groups. In democratic regimes, institutions that concentrate power are less likely to allow concentrated interest groups to block threatening policy changes. Within the constraints imposed by supporting coalitions and political institutions, leaders in positions of discretionary power may sometimes exert important independent influences on policy and institutional outcomes.

THE INTERNATIONAL CONTEXT: GEOPOLITICS, THE INTERNATIONAL ECONOMY, AND IDEOLOGICAL TRENDS

Our explanations of policy outcomes in particular countries focus on internal economic structure and interest group coalitions, political institutions, and often ideology and leadership. These primary factors are discussed at greater length below. Here it should be noted that these internal factors operate in the context of international military, economic, and ideological "boundary conditions." There may be military interests in restricting or developing international trade and investment relations with other countries. With the end of the Cold

War, however, military interests have tended to become less influential. The trade and investment policies of the countries with the largest economies have a dramatic effect on the opportunities available through integration with the international economy. For example, if the most important economies have relatively "open" policies, the potential gains and losses associated with different international trade and financial policies are much larger. International ideological influences are likely to have an impact that reinforces tendencies toward "openness" or "closure" of the international economy. When the international economy is relatively open, ideologies that emphasize the benefits to be gained from international economic integration are liable to be more influential. When the international economy is relatively closed, ideologies that emphasize desirable consequences of protectionism and state intervention are liable to be more influential. In the 1980s and 1990s, the international trends have been toward increasing economic openness, as well as toward increasing ideological confidence in the superior performance of more open economies. A related source of international influence is the presence of regional models functioning as attractive (or unattractive) exemplars of alternative policy paths.

Especially in an era of increasing openness, another way in which international ideological trends are likely to be influential is through international economic organizations, particularly the International Monetary Fund (IMF). Although IMF policies must be broadly consistent with the national policy preferences of the major developed country donors, the general guiding principles and specific contents of IMF loan programs have changed dramatically over time, following ideological trends in the economics profession. Particularly insofar as the IMF's conditional lending programs have an impact on the confidence of domestic and international investors, the principles and contents of IMF programs may have a significant impact on the policy and institutional outcomes in particular countries.[4]

PLAN OF THE VOLUME

The following theoretical chapter sets out in more detail how the present emphasis on dispersed interest groups fits into the existing international political economy literature. Dispersed interest groups are considered along with concentrated interest groups as elements of coalitions supporting rival economic policies. Political institutions are discussed in terms of how they affect the mobilization and influence of rival interest group coalitions.

Subsequent chapters apply the framework to a sequence of case studies drawn from different regions. The regional groupings are not accidental. The Southeast and East Asian countries are typically liberalizing from a starting point of export-oriented but still interventionist policy regimes. The Latin American countries, and still more so the postcommunist countries, are liberalizing from a baseline of more inwardly oriented, interventionist policy regimes. It is shown that these starting points affect the cleavage line between status quo and liberalizing coalitions in predictable ways, in terms of dispersed as well as concentrated interest groups. On the other hand, ideological influences on dispersed interest group preferences and mobilization are to varying degrees historically specific.

SUMMARY OF CASE STUDIES

In the East Asian democracies, especially in South Korea, Thailand, and Japan,[5] the case studies find broad evidence of dispersed interest group support for liberalizing policies. Such policies were expected to correct the excesses of heavily subsidized, export-led industrialization policies perceived to be at the root of the financial crisis. In particular, there was broad dispersed interest group support for cutting back the state-backed or state-tolerated financial sector bias that extended large soft credits to concentrated business groups with personal or political connections to the big commercial banks. It should be noted, however, that dispersed interest groups also sought to preserve the elements of previous policy regimes they associated with their economies' tremendous growth records in recent decades—for example, macroeconomic stability, integration into the international economy, and extensive state investment in infrastructure and education.

These dispersed interest group demands were not always quickly or fully accommodated by democratic political systems. In particular, countries with more divided democratic political institutions have tended to respond more slowly and indecisively. This could be because there were multiple formal parties in the ruling coalition, as in Thailand, or multiple informal factions within the dominant party, as in Japan. Such divisions provided greater scope for concentrated interest groups benefiting from status quo policies to block proposed reforms. There was a faster, more decisive response in South Korea, where the president led a ruling coalition of only two parties following the crisis. There were significant financial sector reforms in all three of these cases, although they occurred much more promptly in South Korea. These involved creation of stronger and more independent bank regulatory bodies and extensive privatization of state-rehabilitated banks (especially to foreign banks expected to follow more neutral, cautious lending practices). In South Korea, the dominant export-oriented conglomerates were for the first time forced toward restructuring their over-diversified investments and over-leveraged financial structures. In Japan, the central bank was also made independent from the Ministry of Finance. It is also noteworthy that in Thailand and Japan reforms of political institutions were broadly supported and implemented because policy making was perceived to be sluggish and too beholden to concentrated interest groups. These institutional reforms were aimed at creating party systems that would be more responsive to dispersed interest groups, although it remains to be seen whether and how much this will happen.

In Taiwan, dispersed interest groups also supported broadly liberal policies.[6] However, by contrast with the other East Asian cases, concentrated interest groups were weak and not strongly favored by policy to begin with. Continued strong economic performance created strong, dispersed interest group support for continued economic policy management by executive branch technocrats. These legendarily cautious technocrats chose to scale back recent financial liberalization measures that they perceived to create an unacceptable risk to their "rock-solid" macroeconomic fundamentals. Because of the success of the mainlander-dominated state's economic policy, there is no mainlander–islander split over economic policy. As the chapter points out, this is no accident. If the mainlander-dominated state had built up a much larger mainlander–controlled concentrated interest group patronage network, there would have been ideologically enhanced hostility to its excesses among the numerically dominant islander dispersed interest groups. On the other hand, islander-controlled concentrated interest groups would have been a political threat during the long period of mainlander-based authoritarian rule. Thus the mainlander–islander ethnic cleavage is at the root of concentrated interest group weakness in Taiwan.

In the East Asian cases under authoritarian rule, Malaysia and Indonesia,[7] there were strong initial financial sector, trade, investment, regulatory, and other policy biases favoring concentrated interest groups with close connections to ruling elites. However, in Malaysia these groups were associated with a mass-mobilizing ruling party legitimized by its pursuit of distributive justice for the dominant ethnic group, whereas in Indonesia they were much more narrowly and illegitimately based on connections with the ruler's family and friends. In Malaysia, the ethnic cleavage made the majority Malay population hostile to liberalizing policies that would dismantle state-sponsored patronage networks designed to empower Malays, even though such policies benefited only a relatively small Malay urban elite. As a result, Malaysia's leader, Mahathir Mohamad, was able to use state bailouts and temporary exchange controls to protect the ruling party-sponsored big business networks, with broad support from dispersed interest groups of Malay ethnicity, especially peasants and unorganized urban labor. This is an important example of how ideology can help shape dispersed interest group preferences, in this case making ethnic Malays presumptively hostile to certain liberalization policies because they were perceived to be likely to benefit the Chinese minority and foreigners at the expense of the Malay majority.

In Indonesia, the blatantly corrupt policies of the long-ruling dictator, Suharto, and his family-dominated patronage networks, along with their close association to the small but economically dominant Chinese minority, made the regime's legitimacy dependent on continued rapid economic growth. When this growth faltered and Suharto failed to respond with a decisive, stabilizing policy response — whether of the "Malaysian" or "IMF" type — popular frustrations boiled over and the military withdrew its support. In the ensuing period leading up to elections, Suharto's lame duck successor was also unable to adopt a coherent policy response.

In these authoritarian cases, of course, there was stronger institutional autonomy than in the democracies. However, such autonomy could be used indecisively and incoherently (Suharto) as well as decisively and more coherently (Mahathir), and it tended to be shaped by considerations of concentrated and dispersed interest group support that are more explicit in democracies. Economic policies proved to be most sustainable where any benefits provided to concentrated interest groups could be reconciled with ongoing dispersed interest group support. Otherwise, regime survival and policy continuity is reduced to depending on the threat to use force—which, as the Indonesia example shows, is a risky proposition.

Moving to the Latin American cases, Mexico, Argentina, and Brazil,[8] there is a clear pattern of sustained liberalization policies despite economic difficulties. In all three cases, the key dispersed interest group basis of the enduring shift away from protectionist, interventionist ("populist") policies has been increasing defection of urban unorganized labor and small peasants or rural poor to the liberalizing coalition. These traditional, dispersed interest group components of populist coalitions were reacting against the increasingly disastrous economic results of populist policies, and thus they supported macroeconomic austerity, trade liberalization, privatization of state enterprises, and various other structural reforms. In Mexico, election year politics and a poorly managed financial liberalization effort produced a deep devaluation, a banking crisis, and a crushing recession in 1994. Yet there was no lasting reaction among the pivotal dispersed interest groups against the liberalizing policy trend, and the resulting policy orthodoxy played an important role in insulating Mexico from the 1997–1999 crisis. Brazil and to a lesser extent Argentina experienced significant recessions in 1998–1999 but nevertheless stayed the course of liberalization. In each case, dispersed interest groups' memories of failed populist policies were still fresh, and improved liberalizing programs were perceived to offer superior prospects. To the extent that past support from these groups for populist policies was ideologically based on their purported benefits for the poor in general, disillusion with the policies would be expected to have a correspondingly strong effect in reverse.

As in East Asia, there is also a pattern of divided political institutions impeding reform efforts. Reform has been implemented most thoroughly, if not always most competently, in Mexico, while the president of the ruling Partido Revolucionario Institutional retained authoritarian powers. However, reform has sometimes been slowed, as in the postcrisis restructuring of the banking system, by the legislative divisions produced by Mexico's democratization process. Argentina's relatively concentrated institutional powers also facilitated decisive reforms under Carlos Ménem. On the other hand, the repeated legislative setbacks to liberalization efforts in Brazil, most recently under Fernando Cardoso's government, can be attributed to Brazil's notoriously balkanized party system and strong provincial governments. However, it is worth noting that the failure of Brazil's exchange rate peg due to failed fiscal reform efforts and the associated recession did not result in a populist reaction by dispersed interest groups.

It is also worth noting that there were efforts to reform political institutions associated with past and present policy failures. In both Argentina and Brazil, constitutional amendments lengthening the terms of reformist presidents were aimed at strengthening executives thought to be more accountable to dispersed interest groups. In Mexico, reforms of political institutions perceived to have inadequately restrained populist excesses were part of the same process. In Mexico's case, this meant division rather than concentration of power, not only through democratization but also through changes in the electoral system and creation of an independent central bank. This was because unrestrained presidential powers were associated with the populist excesses of 1976 and 1982. In all three cases, free trade agreements and, at various times, fixed exchange rates were also utilized as institutional commitments to market reform.

Among the postcommunist cases, liberalization efforts were clearly more aggressive and complete in Poland, Hungary, and the Czech Republic than in Russia.[9] In all four cases, urban dispersed interest groups, the middle classes and unorganized labor, were the core of the liberalizing coalition. In Poland, Hungary, and the Czech Republic, these dispersed interest groups backed initial postcommunist liberalization more strongly. They also maintained such support more doggedly in the face of difficult transitional recessions and subsequent international financial weakness (Hungary, 1993–1995) or crisis (Czech Republic, 1996–1999). There appears to be a strongly ideological component to this variation. Although dispersed interest groups were and are significant long-term beneficiaries of market reforms in highly distorted economies, this is true everywhere and cannot explain variation in such support. In Poland, Hungary, and the Czech Republic postcommunist economic reform was a component of larger national revival movements, aimed at restoring political and cultural autonomy and economic potential taken to have been set back by the externally imposed Soviet system. This type of ideological impetus was much weaker in Russia because the Soviet system was homegrown and because Russian national pride was strongly tied to the advance of Soviet power.

Variation in concentration of institutional political power within these postcommunist democracies does not appear to have played a significant role where, as in Poland, Hungary, and the Czech Republic, there was a strong dispersed interest group consensus in favor of market reform to begin with. Thus Poland's high degree of institutional and party fragmentation was not a significant drag on reform efforts in relative terms. On the other hand, institutional dispersion of political power appears to have played a more important role where dispersed interest support for market reform was shakier, as in Russia. Here a very strong presidency at first had the effect of compromising market reform efforts in a manner that contributed to subsequent economic malaise and crisis. Although this produced a political backlash among urban dispersed interest groups, these swing voters did not shift their preferences toward communist-type policies. In fact, they did not usually see a clearly desirable alternative and so were increasingly willing to support charismatic leaders without clear policy platforms. As a result, the backlash against Yeltsin's compromised market reforms was limited, and significant policy changes could be blocked using the presidency's substantial powers.

In short, we find dispersed interest groups to have been a potentially pivotal force for liberalization across case studies in all three regions, despite their diversity of initial conditions. In the democratic cases, we also find that institutional dispersion of political power offered concentrated interest groups greater scope for blocking or compromising liberalizing reform efforts.

NOTES

1. For an analysis of how international financial crisis affects real economies and a discussion of the IMF response, see W. Max Corden, in chapter 3 of this volume, "The World Financial Crisis: Are the IMF Prescriptions Right?" For a sampling of the literature, see Feldstein 1998, Fischer 1998, Krugman 1999, Radelet and Sachs 1998, and the exhaustive compilation on Nouriel Roubini's Web site, <http://www.stern.nyu.edu/~nroubini/asia/asiahomepage.html>.

2. 1995 per capita gross national products at purchasing power parity for the case study countries, with the United States at 100, were as follows: Indonesia 14.1, the Russian Federation 16.6, Brazil 20.0, Poland 20.0, Mexico 23.7, Hungary 23.8, Thailand 28.0, Argentina 30.8, Malaysia 33.4, the Czech Republic 36.2, South Korea 42.4, and Japan 82.0. A comparable estimate for Taiwan is unavailable, but its level is presumably somewhat higher than that of South Korea. World Bank 1997, 214–15.

3. A close precedent is the work of Stephan Haggard and his associates: Haggard 1990, Haggard and Kaufman 1992b, and Haggard and Webb 1994.

4. For a discussion, see W. Max Corden in chapter 3 of this volume. The IMF plays a particularly visible role in Kimberly Niles's analysis of Indonesia in chapter 6.

5. See chapter 8 by Uk Heo (South Korea), chapter 4 by James LoGerfo and Gabriella Montinola (Thailand), and chapter 7 by Eric Browne and Sunwoong Kim (Japan).

6. See chapter 9 by Alexander Tan.

7. See chapter 5 by A. Maria Toyoda (Malaysia) and chapter 6 by Kimberly Niles (Indonesia).

8. See chapter 10 by Aldo Flores Quiroga (Mexico), chapter 11 by Jeffrey Cason (Brazil), and chapter 12 by Walter Molano (Argentina).

9. See chapter 13 by Shale Horowitz (Poland, Hungary, and the Czech Republic) and chapter 14 by Peter Rutland (Russia).

We thank Professor Mark Tessler and the University of Wisconsin–Milwaukee's Center for International Education for supporting this collective project.

(Asia, L. America,
CEEC)

2

The Persistent Liberalizing Trend in Foreign Economic Policies: The Role of Dispersed Interest Groups, Policy Legacies, and Ideologies

Shale Horowitz

For

019 P33 050

The theoretical focus in this volume is on two classic issues in the political economy literature. Political explanations of economic policies have traditionally referred to the economic interest group coalitions that form for and against particular policies and to the institutional conditions that restrict or amplify the influence of various groups and offer leaders varying means of choosing and implementing policies.

ECONOMIC INTEREST GROUP COALITIONS

Theories about the influence of economic interest groups on foreign economic policy have had an understandable tendency to focus on homogeneous and relatively concentrated producer groups in the parts of the economy directly exposed to international trade and investment. These "concentrated" interest groups are mainly exporting sectors benefiting from access to markets abroad or import-competing sectors suffering from the home market inroads of more competitive foreign firms.[1] They also include banks, suppliers, and distributors with close links to such traded sector producers, as well as banks, utilities, and other non-traded sector producers vulnerable to competition through direct foreign investment. Since such "concentrated" interest groups are more strongly affected by international economic policy choices, they are likely to mobilize more effectively and to have a disproportionate influence on policy outcomes.[2]

However, the position taken in this volume is that the largest interest groups in the part of the economy not directly exposed to international trade—the

15

"nontraded sector"—often must also be discussed to provide an adequate explanation of foreign economic policy outcomes. The two largest nontraded sector groups are the middle classes and unorganized labor in the mostly nontraded, mainly urban, service industries.[3] The service sector often employs the majority of the workforce in middle-income countries, and well over half in high-income countries.

These two "dispersed" nontraded sector interest groups can be an important component of an adequate explanation of foreign economic policy outcomes for three reasons. First, the numerical weight of the "dispersed" groups gives them considerable power and influence in all but the most authoritarian regimes.[4] In democracies, the direct voting impact of the middle classes and unorganized labor in the service sector is clear. However, even authoritarian regimes—whether without democratic institutions or with restricted democratic institutions—are often concerned about maintaining political support among such a large subset of the population.

A second point concerns linkages between foreign economic policies and other economic policies. True, dispersed interest groups are typically less concerned than concentrated interest groups with international trade and investment policies. However, the latter are often linked with other economic policies—particularly fiscal, monetary, banking sector, and exchange rate policies with strong redistributive and economic performance effects—which more directly affect the interests of dispersed interest groups.[5] Liberalizing trade and investment policies are often linked with some combination of the following: reductions in fiscal subsidies and social welfare benefits, cutbacks in government-backed distribution of "soft" credits,[6] an end to inflationary monetary policy financing of fiscal deficits, and stronger currencies. On the other hand, more restrictive trade and investment policies are often linked with more generous redistributive fiscal policies and soft bank credits, or at least with maintenance of existing redistributive policies. These in turn are associated with high inflation and ongoing currency depreciation.

The middle classes are likely to oppose large-scale redistributive social welfare policies. They are also likely to oppose the inflationary consequences of soft credit expansions and of increased fiscal deficits, particularly as experience with such long-term consequences accumulates. Even unorganized labor, despite being a beneficiary of broad redistributive transfers, will increasingly oppose any significant inflationary consequences—particularly if, as is common, most of the fiscal and credit transfers are siphoned off by concentrated interest groups and bureaucratic intermediaries.

The third reason has to do with the extent to which dispersed interest groups are less strongly affected, and hence more weakly mobilized, than concentrated interest groups. The more restrictive the existing trade and investment policies, and the larger the proposed changes in trade and investment policies, the larger the possible impact on the incomes of dispersed interest groups. Thus, in more "closed" economies, and in economies debating fundamental changes in trade and investment policies, dispersed interest groups should be more strongly mobilized.[7] Similarly, the smaller the economy, the more consequential are trade and investment policy changes, and the greater the incentive for dispersed interest groups to mobilize.

DISPERSED INTEREST GROUPS AND IDEOLOGY

It is also worth making another point about dispersed interest groups. To the extent that the incomes of dispersed interest groups are less directly, less immediately, and less strongly affected by international economic policies, these groups are more likely than concentrated interest groups to be independently influenced by ideology. General, worldwide ideologies justifying more closed or more open international economic policies have already been mentioned in chapter 1. Apart from these, ideologies specific to the particular histories of countries and regions can have "elective affinities"—not strictly implying but being more or less compatible—with more closed and interventionist or more open and neutral international economic policies. Important examples are Latin American "populism" and some variants of Eastern European postcommunist nationalism and East Asian nationalism.

Latin American "populism" has traditionally rallied support based on ideology as well as economic interests. Visions of increased equality in societies traditionally dominated by landed elites were used to justify more extensive redistributive fiscal policies, and resentments against foreign, especially U.S. power and interference, were used to justify more restrictive international trade and investment policies. This ideology broadened the appeal of populist policies beyond those most directly interested in economic terms, particularly into the middle classes; and it deepened the appeal of populist policies among those groups it sought to benefit most directly. The persistent weakening of the appeal of populist ideologies, under the impact of the relatively poor performance of economies governed by populist policies, should have a corresponding impact on the strength of the coalition supporting these policies.

In much of postcommunist Eastern Europe, the self-sufficient planned economies of the communist period are associated with an externally imposed setback to national development. Therefore ideologies of national autonomy and renewal lend additional support to liberalizing international trade and investment policies, particularly among the dispersed interest groups that ordinarily have smaller stakes in such policies. On the other hand, Malay or bumiputera ethnic nationalism in Malaysia strengthens preferences for interventionist policies designed to modify free market outcomes perceived to sustain the economic advantages of the Chinese minority. Thus, not only are dispersed interest groups often unduly neglected in explaining demand for international economic policies, but they are also more likely than concentrated interest groups to have their mobilization and even their preferences influenced by ideologies.

POLITICAL INSTITUTIONS

Another classic issue in the political economy literature is how political institutions affect economic policy making. There are many important theoretical issues on this institutional "supply side" of economic policy making. Because of its contemporary relevance, we are particularly interested in how economic policy making is influenced by the difference between "developmental" authoritarianism and democracy, and by transition from developmental authoritarianism to democracy.[8] A developmental authoritarianism is here characterized broadly as a ruling regime that bases its legitimacy heavily on economic performance, and that attempts to maintain large supporting interest group coalitions despite the lack of unrestricted electoral competition. Of the case studies in this volume, Japan, South Korea, Thailand, Argentina, Brazil, the Czech Republic, Hungary and Poland are examples of democracies, Malaysia and Suharto's Indonesia are developmental authoritarianisms, and post-Suharto Indonesia, Taiwan, Mexico, and Russia are examples of democracies in transition.[9]

The political economy literature points to at least two important effects of regime type on foreign economic policy. First, elections make policy makers directly accountable to all adult citizens. Second, elections introduce short-term political feasibility constraints, which may make it necessary for policies to aim at producing faster results, and to be implemented more effectively, than would otherwise be necessary. Such constraints will be more likely to influence policy choices and policy implementation, the larger and the more likely are the changes in economic policies at stake as a result of election outcomes.[10] By contrast, authoritarian regimes do not have such constraints. Where such regimes are not likely to share the interests of broad sectors of society, this would often be expected to produce policies quite damaging to long-term economic performance. However, developmental authoritarianisms can in principal use freedom from short-term political constraints to more efficiently pursue their long-term economic growth objectives. The prospect of elections often leads incumbent governments to interfere with the autonomy of economic policy-making technocrats in central banks, finance ministries, and other economic agencies. In the literature on the political economy of East Asia in particular, there is a long and influential strand of argument that such autonomous technocrats have often been an important source of pragmatic, but generally market-oriented economic policies.[11] To the extent that shorter-term electoral constraints become binding and technocratic autonomy is disrupted, one might expect less decisive, less coherent and more poorly implemented policies.

However, as will become clear, not all democracies are shortsighted, and developmental authoritarianisms often impose highly distortionary policies on their technocrats. The case studies support the following explanations of variations across countries having the same regime type. Democracies are more likely not to impose short-term constraints on newly developing policy regimes where the primary alternatives have been discredited in recent experience. Similarly, they are more likely not to disrupt the preexisting policy regime where the latter has performed well in recent experience. Nontraded sector groups are likely to be pivotal in providing such short-term forbearance. On the other hand, developmental authoritarian regimes are more likely to compromise their long-term growth objectives where they possess strong political or personal links to concentrated interest groups benefiting from distorting policies.

Another important issue is how policy is affected by variation in the form of democratic political institutions. My approach to this issue is to ask how particular executive and legislative institutions and party systems facilitate or block often-changing interest group coalitions from implementing their policy preferences. In keeping with the emphasis on the potentially pivotal importance of dispersed interest groups, I follow the recent literature arguing that institutions that increase the number of "veto players" are more likely to give concentrated interest groups the power to block threatening policy changes. Veto players can be multiplied, for example, by the existence of strong presidencies alongside legislatures, by bicameral or multicameral legislatures, by proportional representation electoral systems (especially those with low thresholds for party representation), and by weak intraparty discipline.[12]

INTERNATIONAL FINANCIAL CRISES: POLICY-RELATED CAUSES AND POLICY RESPONSES

Before attempting to explain the precrisis policy regimes and the economic policy and institutional responses to the international financial crisis of 1997–1999, I shall briefly review the range of economic policy choices to be explained.

What exactly is an "international financial crisis"? It is defined as a sudden, large decline in international competitiveness, as measured on the current and capital accounts, such that large economic policy adjustments are necessary to restore a country's external financial balance. The current account measures the net balance of international payments for goods and services and returns on past investments in a given period (usually a year). The capital account measures the net balance of international payments for new investments made in a given period (usually a year). Apart from any adjustments to central bank reserves of foreign currencies, the net balances on the current and capital accounts must offset each other in a given period. Countries experiencing sudden declines in net earnings on the current and capital accounts must somehow offset these changes to maintain external balance. This must be done with policies that increase inflows on the current and/or capital accounts, or policies that decrease outflows, or both.

The contributors to this volume do not attempt to offer comprehensive economic explanations of why crises did or did not occur in particular countries or why some affected countries recovered faster than others. They attempt to explain precrisis foreign economic policies, as well as policy and institutional responses to the crisis. It is difficult to understand responses without understanding how precrisis policies contributed to the crisis. What types of precrisis policies tended to contribute most significantly? Broadly, they were policies that tended to increase domestic prices and/or reduce domestic productivity, with corresponding effects on the expectations of domestic and foreign investors. Such policies were pursued to widely varying degrees in different countries. Important culprits include (1) large fiscal deficits, with a corresponding risk of inflationary monetary financing; (2) significant expansions of bank credit, with a corresponding risk of increasing bad loan burdens and banking crises; and (3) increased amounts of public and/or private debt financed by foreign borrowing, much of it short-term and often facilitated by overvalued, fixed exchange rates.

Once a crisis occurs, adjustments can take a number of nonexclusive forms. Some reduce the relative prices of domestic goods and services and domestic assets, thus tending to improve performance on both the current and capital accounts. The most important policies of this type are (1) allowing currency devaluation and (2) imposing more restrictive monetary and fiscal policies. Another important type of response is (3) raising trade barriers and imposing or tightening exchange controls. Higher trade barriers, by increasing the relative prices of foreign goods and services, may improve the current account. Exchange controls, by restricting capital outflows, may improve the capital account.[13] Yet another type of response is (4) instituting "structural" reforms of the internal economy. This typically involves reductions in subsidies (including soft credit), regulations and corrupt practices, thereby increasing economic efficiency. Although any increase in efficiency would be expected to significantly affect performance on the current account only over the longer run, any resulting favorable effects on investor expectations can immediately improve performance on the capital account.

INTEREST GROUP PREFERENCES AND RESULTING CLEAVAGE PATTERNS OVER POLICY CHOICES

Interest Group Preferences

To understand "demand side" coalition formation by economic interest groups, it is necessary to first understand the economic policy preferences of "concentrated" and "dispersed" interest groups.

First consider precrisis policies. Large fiscal deficits are favored by the main net recipients of the more significant transfer payments, and they are opposed by the largest net contributors. Concentrated interest groups are often important net recipients. Among dispersed interest groups, the middle classes typically favor greater fiscal restraint. Unorganized labor tends to favor transfers if it is a large net recipient. But this support is weaker when transfers primarily benefit concentrated interest groups and state employees. And support can turn to opposition if transfers not only favor other groups but also have inflationary and other negative consequences for general economic performance. The main beneficiaries and supporters of politically sanctioned soft credit are typically concentrated interest groups. The main opposition is likely to come from those denied credit and those suffering from the general economic consequences of banking crises and poor capital allocation. However, the latter groups are generally more dispersed and slower to mobilize. Fixed exchange rates are typically used as a commitment against future inflation. Thus they often reflect efforts by dispersed interest groups and excluded concentrated interest groups to stop large fiscal deficits and politically directed credit expansions that have hurt general economic performance in the past.

Precrisis fiscal, banking, and exchange rate policies that contribute to the outbreak of crises are also often linked politically to other policies. In particular, the concentrated interest groups that tend to benefit from fiscal and credit expansions often benefit from restrictive trade policies. These concentrated interest groups may include not only import-competing sectors that suffer from international competition but also exporting sectors that depend heavily on protected domestic markets. On the other hand, the dispersed interest groups, particularly the middle classes, that oppose such expansionary fiscal and monetary policies also tend to oppose restrictive trade policies. They are typically joined by the more competitive exporting sectors. These sectors would not lose significant domestic market share under free trade, and they are more concerned about protecting the long-term growth prospects of the domestic economy and maintaining access to lucrative foreign markets. Although unorganized urban labor in the service sector loses from restrictive trade policies, these losses can be offset by large fiscal transfers. Hence it is not uncommon for concentrated traded sector interest groups to attempt to exchange expanded fiscal transfers to unorganized labor for the latter's support of restrictive trade policies and directed credit policies.

Among the possible policy responses to international financial crisis, the most dramatic contrast is between responses that emphasize some mix of devaluation, macroeconomic stringency, and structural reforms, and those that rely more heavily on increased trade barriers and exchange controls. Use of increased trade barriers and exchange controls is typically designed to avoid macroeconomic stringency and structural reforms that strike at preexisting fiscal, monetary, and regulatory policies. Consider first the concentrated interest groups in the traded sector. In many cases, the import-competing sectors benefiting from protection are also the main beneficiaries of directed credit and regulatory policies, so that exporting sectors would be expected to oppose both policies. This, for example, has often been the case in "populist" economic policy regimes in Latin America. However, there are also many cases where trade protection and directed credit and regulatory policies also significantly benefit exporting sectors. This has often been the case for the "developmental" economic policy regimes common in East Asia.

To the extent that there is also a trade-off between reliance on devaluation and reliance on macroeconomic, particularly monetary stringency, both import-competing and exporting sectors can ordinarily be expected to prefer devaluation. Devaluation increases competitiveness vis-à-vis foreign competitors without necessarily pushing the economy into recession, and, unless firms have borrowed directly and extensively in foreign currencies, it tends to reduce debt burdens. On the other hand, the banking sector may be more hostile toward devaluation, particularly where it has borrowed in foreign currencies to lend in the domestic currency.

In all of these cases, the picture of coalition formation is incomplete without a discussion of the preferences and mobilization of dispersed interest groups. As discussed, there are many circumstances under which these large groups can be expected to become more mobilized. What are their policy preferences? These groups are concentrated in the service sector, and hence they benefit as consumers from free trade and investment. Thus it is often argued that they can be expected to prefer devaluation and macroeconomic, particularly monetary, stringency to increased trade barriers and exchange controls. Similarly, it is often argued that they should prefer macroeconomic stringency to devaluation, since devaluation reduces the prices of nontraded goods relative to traded goods.

However, in both cases the purported preference depends on a trade-off in which higher long-term benefits and lower long-term costs outweigh any benefits from minimizing short-term costs—particularly those avoided by postponing the often severe recessions that result from devaluation and, above all, from macroeconomic stringency. But what if there is little recent experience with the longer-term costs (in higher inflation, reduced efficiency, and more volatile and anemic long-term growth rates) of avoiding contractionary policies (especially fiscal and monetary stringency) through recourse to increased trade barriers and exchange controls or larger devaluations? In that case, the short-term recession likely to be associated with reliance on macroeconomic stringency is likely to loom larger.[14] This is particularly likely to be true for unorganized urban labor. And it is even more likely to be true if macroeconomic stringency includes significant cuts in income-based social welfare programs aimed primarily at unorganized labor. Without recent experience of the long-term costs of postponing adjustment, and a reinforcing ideological climate drawing attention to them, unorganized labor and the middle classes in the nontraded, mostly service sector are more likely to support restrictive trade and investment policies and/or larger devaluations in order to avoid the short-term pain associated with monetary and fiscal stringency. However, these groups are likely to turn against these policies as experience and ideological developments intensify awareness of their long-term costs.

Four Basic Types of Cleavage Patterns over Policy Choices

Regarding concentrated traded sector interest groups, I have distinguished between cases in which trade, credit, and fiscal policies are targeted more exclusively at import-competing sectors and cases in which they also embrace exporting sectors. For dispersed, nontraded sector interest groups, I have distinguished between cases of less or more experience with the long-term costs of trade and investment restrictions, large fiscal deficits, extensive soft lending, and higher inflation. These two distinctions give rise to four basic types of cleavages over *postcrisis* policies, which are shown in table 2.1. It should be noted that trade policy subsidies have tended to be more heavily supplemented by fiscal subsidies in Latin America and by credit subsidies in East Asia. Reasons for losses of investor confidence and postcrisis adjustment requirements tended to be correspondingly different.

These cleavages are similar to those to be expected on precrisis policies. They are the same for the traded sector groups. They are the same for unorganized labor, if significant fiscal transfers are part of the precrisis policy package. Again, this has been the case in Latin America more often than in East Asia. Otherwise, unorganized labor can be expected to oppose trade and credit policies and fiscal subsidies that primarily benefit concentrated interest groups. Similarly, the middle class will be more uniformly opposed to the precrisis trade, credit, and fiscal subsidies of populist or developmental policy regimes. The difference between the precrisis and postcrisis situations is that the short-term negative economic impact of eliminating these restrictions and subsidies becomes larger once the crisis is under way, which potentially makes a difference for nontraded sector groups that at all times gain less from such policies.

This predicted pattern of interest group preferences offers predictions about not only coalition and cleavage patterns but also, potentially, policy outcomes. In the case studies that are examined in this volume, recent experience with the costs of maintaining or extending trade, credit, and fiscal subsidy policies in order to postpone painful short-term adjustments appears to be an important source of variation in outcomes. And it correctly predicts the changing character of cleavage patterns and the ascendance of "liberal" coalitions in both Latin America and East Asia.[15] The basic theoretical point here is that it seems difficult to explain the neoliberal policy shifts in Latin America and East Asia without making reference to "dispersed" interest groups and the reasons for their changing preferences and mobilization.

Table 2.1   Four Types of Interest Group Cleavages over Postcrisis Policy Responses

	Concentrated Interest Groups: Initial Protection and Subsidies Primarily Benefit Import-Competing Sector	*Concentrated Interest Groups:* Initial Protection and Subsidies Benefit Exporting and Import-Competing Sector
Dispersed Interest Groups: Little Recent Experience with Costs of Protection and Subsidies	*Populist Coalition:* Import-Competing Sectors, Unorganized Urban Labor and Much of the Middle Class *vs.* *Liberal Coalition:* Exporting Sectors, Much of the Middle Class (*Historical Example:* "Populist" Latin America)	*Developmental Coalition:* Import-Competing and Exporting Sectors, Unorganized Urban Labor and Much of the Middle Class *vs.* *Liberal Coalition:* Much of the Middle Class (*Historical Example:* "Technocratic-Developmental" East Asia)
Dispersed Interest Groups: Extensive Recent Experience with Costs of Protection and Subsidies	*Populist Coalition:* Import-Competing Sectors, Much Unorganized Urban Labor *vs.* *Liberal Coalition:* Exporting Sectors, Middle Class and Much Unorganized Labor (*Historical Example:* More Recent, Liberalizing Latin America)	*Developmental Coalition:* Import-Competing and Exporting Sectors, Much Unorganized Urban Labor *vs.* *Liberal Coalition:* Middle Class and Much Unorganized Labor (*Historical Example:* More Recent, Liberalizing East Asia)

Note: "Protection" refers to restraints on domestic as well as foreign competition. "Subsidies" refer to direct fiscal subsidies as well as indirect subsidies through government-backed provision of soft credit.

Agriculture

There are two more theoretical issues that must be discussed before more empirically precise expectations of coalition and cleavage patterns can be advanced for each of the three regions to be examined in the case studies. The first issue concerns the preferences of the agricultural sector. In principle, agriculture is either an exporting or an import-competing sector, with corresponding policy preferences—based primarily on whether the country in question is relatively abundant or scarce in land.[16] However, there are a couple of important complications, deriving from past political efforts to react to the uniquely large character of the agricultural sector as a group producing relatively homogeneous products.

First, it is possible for institutional transformations to transform potentially net-exporting agricultural sectors in land-abundant countries into import-competing or only marginally exporting sectors. Where this is so (among the case studies due to collectivization in Russia)[17] one would expect these sectors to have preferences like those of import-competing sectors. A second and more generally relevant complication arises from the large size and relative homogeneity— usually one of smallholders—of most agricultural sectors.[18] These agricultural sectors are typically so large and so potentially pivotal politically that all coalitions competing for majority status promise to protect and subsidize them. This typically leads to quotas and price supports that render agriculture a nontraded rather than a traded sector—albeit a nontraded sector subsidized in its productive capacity.[19] In these cases, agriculture is not likely to be wedded either to an interventionist coalition (such as import-competing or heavily subsidized exporting sectors) or to a liberal coalition (such as relatively unsubsidized exporting sectors). Its economic position being insulated from international competition, it will choose coalitions in a manner closer to dispersed interest groups; its position being a relatively protected one, it will tend to choose more like the middle classes than like unorganized labor for as long as its subsidies are unquestioned. Agricultural sectors of this subsidized, nontraded type exist in all of the Southeast and East Asian cases, in most of Brazilian agriculture, and in the dominant ejido sector in Mexico. However, they are not dominant in Argentina, where agriculture is heavily export dependent, or in Russia and most of Eastern Europe, where the huge subsidies of the Soviet era have been dramatically reduced and agricultural incomes have come under heavy pressure.

Dispersed Interest Groups and Country-Specific Ideologies

A second important issue concerns the effects of country-specific ideologies on the preferences of dispersed interest groups. Again, since the economic interests of the two main dispersed groups are not usually as strongly affected by foreign economic policies as those of concentrated interest groups, these groups are likely to be more easily swayed by specific ideologies that have elective affinities with certain policy choices. Such ideologies would be expected to be particularly important in periods in which there is little experience of the costs of postponing adjustment of destabilizing trade, credit, and fiscal policies.

As mentioned in chapter 1, in Latin America the historical dominance of landed elites and the regional power and influence of the United States and other foreign powers gave special appeal to "populist" interventionist economic policies. This was particularly significant not just among unorganized urban labor, which "populism" appealed to directly, but also to significant subsets of the middle classes. Therefore, the decline of this ideology's credibility as a result of poor economic performance can be expected to reinforce the effect of "learning" about the long-term effects of policies on the preferences of unorganized labor and the middle classes.

Among the former Soviet bloc countries with widely held ideologies of national renewal, which view the Soviet period as an externally imposed deviation from a promising precommunist past, market-oriented reforms held a special appeal. This is true not only among the urban middle classes, who could be expected to benefit most from the market transition, but also among significant subsets of unorganized labor.

It is an interesting question whether anticommunist nationalisms in much of East Asia exerted a similar effect on dispersed interest groups, leading them to accept subsidies to concentrated interest groups toward which they might otherwise be hostile. With the collapse of the Soviet Union and the recent signs of domestic corruption and economic mismanagement, any such influence would be expected to be wearing off. If this were so, the effect on dispersed interest group support for the "developmental" coalitions in East Asia would be analogous to the effect of the decline of populist ideologies in Latin America (though presumably weaker, given East Asia's relatively strong economic performance). Of course, no "wearing off" would be predicted for Taiwan, given the continued high levels of tension with an increasingly powerful China. But a similar effect may have been exerted by the rising "islander" identity over against the "mainlander" character of the Kuomintang ruling elite. And not surprisingly, Malaysia's politically salient ethnic divisions have weakened a liberalizing coalition easily branded as a threat to the progress of the majority bumiputera (i.e., as "excessively" Chinese and foreign).

Regionally Specific Cleavage Patterns

It is now possible to present more fully specified expectations of postcrisis cleavages for the three main regions from which the case studies are drawn. Relative to table 2.1, figure 2.1 adds agriculture and ideological factors, as well as a distinct cleavage pattern for Eastern Europe. However, it presents "old regime" interventionist coalitions, that is, coalitions prior to dispersed interest group "learning." Such learning is a result of experience with long-term costs of postponing adjustment policies and of the associated effect on regionally specific ideologies. Figure 2.2 presents "liberal" adjustment coalitions, also adding agriculture and ideological factors, and an Eastern European cleavage. These coalitions reflect dispersed interest group "learning."

As already noted, trade, credit, and fiscal subsidies benefiting particular traded sectors typically benefit both capital and labor in the given sectors; thus the distinction between exporting and import-competing industry. However, policies sometimes target the capital or the labor side more heavily in these traded industries, and such policies may divide organized capital from organized labor in the traded sectors. Hence, the organized capital–organized labor cleavage is an alternative decomposition of the traded sector. In figures 2.1 and 2.2, solid arrows indicate more complete inclusion in the coalition than dashed arrows. Little or no inclusion is indicated by the absence of an arrow.

Figure 2.1 Prelearning, "Old Regime" Interventionist Coalitions

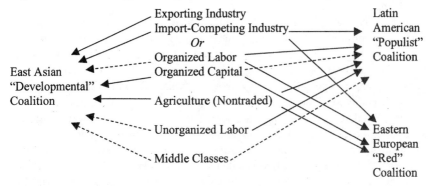

Note: Solid arrows indicate more complete inclusion than dashed arrows. No arrow indicates little or no inclusion.

Figure 2.2 Postlearning, "Liberal" Adjustment Coalitions

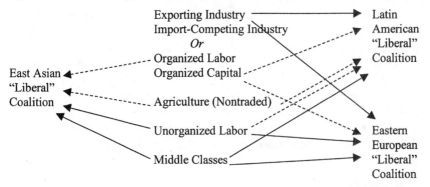

Note: Solid arrows indicate more complete inclusion than dashed arrows. No arrow indicates little or no inclusion.

East Asia

For the East Asian "developmental" coalition, figure 2.1 differs from table 2.1 in that agriculture is explicitly included, and organized labor (typically concentrated in the traded sector) and unorganized labor (concentrated in the nontraded, mostly service sector) are partially excluded. In these countries, agriculture is insulated from international market pressures by quotas and price supports and is thus a nontraded sector. Although it is a sector subsidized by the old regime, it has such political importance that its subsidized, nontraded status is not threatened by neoliberal adjustment policies and the associated coalition. After learning about the long-term costs of avoiding macroeconomic and (in nonagricultural sectors) "structural" adjustments (fig. 2.2), much of this sector is liable to defect to the neo-liberal coalition. This is even more true for the middle classes, which are not benefiting from large subsidies.

As already noted, organized labor in the traded sector would ordinarily be expected to support the old interventionist policy regime as a direct beneficiary of protection and other subsidies; and unorganized labor can initially be expected to emphasize short-term over long-term costs in choosing adjustment policies. However, these expectations are somewhat weakened in the East Asian cases by the typically antilabor bias of the old regimes. These regimes have typically restricted and repressed organized labor, and they have emphasized national security and economic growth over social welfarist ideologies. Thus liberal adjustment policies tend to involve cutting back credit subsidies and imposing structural reforms. Fiscal deficits tended to be small to begin with, and typically no large cuts were contemplated in broad-based fiscal transfers. Hence, in figure 2.1, significant proportions of organized and unorganized labor are initially likely to be more hostile to incumbent regimes and more likely to desert them in times of economic troubles in order to advance democratization and social welfare policies in the future.

After some learning about the long-term effects of postponing macroeconomic and structural adjustment policies (fig. 2.2), the liberal coalition is likely to have attracted not only most of the middle classes and much of agriculture but also an increased portion of unorganized labor. Again, organized labor—while still likely to be hostile to liberal macroeconomic and structural policies—is not likely to offer its wholehearted support to the maintenance of the old policy regime.[20] Because there is no reformist majority without the urban middle classes and the agricultural sector, there is no majority available to move beyond liberal reforms to offer more generous redistributive policies to unorganized labor.[21]

Latin America

For the Latin American interventionist coalition, figure 2.1 differs from table 2.1 in that agriculture is explicitly included. In Brazil and Mexico most agriculture is a subsidized nontraded sector, so that in these cases agriculture should have preferences similar to the East Asian cases—initially friendly to the old interventionist regime (fig. 2.1) but then subject to partial defection with learning about long-term costs (fig. 2.2). Again, Brazil and Mexico also have significant exporting subsectors, which would never be expected to be included in populist coalitions. Agriculture would be entirely excluded from the interventionist coalition if, as in Argentina, it is heavily export dependent.

Unorganized labor is initially likely to be very favorably disposed toward the interventionist policy regime because of the fiscal and ideological prolabor bias of populism. As already discussed, populist ideology should also have an initial appeal among the middle class (fig.2.1). The implication is that learning about the effects of postponing macroeconomic and structural adjustments is likely to hit the interventionist coalition particularly strongly on the side of unorganized labor and the middle class (fig. 2.2). In Brazil and Mexico, this is likely to be supplemented by partial defection of the larger, inwardly oriented part of the agricultural sector. Because of the crucial importance of unorganized labor to the Latin American neoliberal coalition, neoliberal reform in these cases would be expected to leave relatively untouched broader redistributive policies aimed at the poor generally and focus instead on eliminating fiscal, credit, and regulatory subsidies to concentrated interest groups.[22]

Eastern Europe

From an interest group perspective, the Eastern European "red," or planned, type of interventionist old regime can be viewed as an extreme form of a protected and subsidized market regime of the populist type. There are virtually no exporting sectors left; import-competing sectors tend to be highly inefficient and overbuilt; and agriculture is given a highly inefficient collective organization but then is heavily subsidized to compensate. Compared to similarly developed market economies, all of these ordinarily "traded" sectors are larger and the service sector smaller.

Although the initial revolution was carried out in the name of labor, poor long-term performance is likely to have led most less heavily subsidized unorganized labor to defect from the "red" coalition and be favorably disposed toward market reform (fig. 2.2). The same poor long-term performance is likely to have entirely alienated the middle classes in the service sector. Thus postcommunist market transition policies are expected to be spearheaded by the middle classes and unorganized labor. In the initial stage of market reform, the hitherto underbuilt service sectors will grow rapidly, as will new exporting sectors, at the expense of the old "import-competing" sectors (including agriculture). To the extent that the new market reforms experience adjustment difficulties and international financial crises at later stages, the alliance for continued rapid adjustment will include the new exporting sectors, the middle classes, and much unorganized labor. The alliance for resistance to further adjustment will include the residual import-competing sectors (including agriculture) and more hard-hit unorganized labor.

Across this set of cases, there is likely to be significant variation in nationalist ideologies. Countries strongly viewing the communist period as a foreign-imposed setback to precommunist achievements are more likely to support more aggressive initial market reforms and more aggressive adjustment policies in the face of any later-stage deteriorations of international competitiveness. As discussed, given the nature of groups' direct economic interests, such nationalist ideologies are likely to have the greatest impact on unorganized labor and the middle classes. For the cases discussed below, this implies that support for more aggressive initial reform and subsequent adjustments is likely to be stronger in Poland, Hungary, and the Czech Republic than in Russia.

Thus in Poland, Hungary, and the Czech Republic, unorganized labor is expected to start and remain more firmly in the liberal camp than in Russia. (Figures 2.1 and 2.2 depict Poland, Hungary, and the Czech Republic. For Russia, the main difference is that figure 2.2 would show a dashed line for unorganized labor.) There is no learning effect on dispersed interest groups depicted for these postcommunist countries. This is because "learning" is already reflected in figure 2.1 in the weak dispersed interest group support for the Soviet-era "red" coalition.[23]

POLITICAL INSTITUTIONS: DEMOCRACY AND ITS INSTITUTIONAL VARIETIES, DEVELOPMENTAL AUTHORITARIANISM, AND TRANSITION TO DEMOCRACY

I first examine how the difference between democracy and authoritarianism would be expected to affect precrisis policies and postcrisis responses. For democracies, I survey the likely consequences of variation in the form of democratic political institutions. Among authoritarian regimes, we focus on developmental authoritarianisms that base their legitimacy largely on their economic management and development records. This type of authoritarian regime typically cultivates broad supporting interest group coalitions and often possesses limited forms of democratic political institutions. We conclude by discussing the likely consequences of transition to democracy.

Democracies

Democracies are typically viewed as governments whose policies are driven by politicians' efforts to represent the interests of coalitions necessary to reelect themselves and their parties. As already discussed, there is a tradition that focuses on coalitions of concentrated interest groups, arguing that dispersed interest groups do not have sufficient incentive to mobilize. I argue that they often do and that this should be the more true the more the policies being chosen are expected to have a significant effect on general economic performance.

I have already argued that dispersed interest groups can be expected to go through some learning about the long-term consequences of postponing macroeconomic and structural adjustments. This position corresponds to an intermediate position in the theoretical debate on how voters as economic agents react to economic policies.[24] One extreme position is that voters can always be fooled by relatively favorable short-term results, regardless of the predictable long-term consequences of achieving such short-term results. In this case, democracies would be expected to experience increases in distorting subsidies and higher inflation in the run-up to elections. Similarly, insofar as recession clouds future election prospects, democracies should also show a greater tendency to postpone macroeconomic and structural adjustment to economic crises. This "myopic expectations" model cannot explain the varying extent of crisis-inducing policies, either across countries or within the same countries across time. Similarly, it cannot explain variation in policy responses to such crises, either across countries or across time. The opposite, "rational expectations," model is that voters always know precisely what the long-term consequences of different policies are and always factor these into their voting decisions in the short run. Compared to the myopic expectations approach, this rational expectations approach predicts less frequent crisis-inducing policies and more rapidly resolved crisis-and-adjustment phases. But it also cannot explain variation across countries and time.

The "learned expectations" position taken here, in which long-term consequences are increasingly taken into account the more certainly they are anticipated,[25] has the merit of being able to explain variation across countries and time. Moreover, it also implies an approach to explaining how quickly such learning takes place. Like the rational expectations approach, it emphasizes that, other things being equal, agents that bear more of the long-term costs are more likely to mobilize against the relevant policies. However, it points to at least two possible sources of variation in the speed with which long-term costs are taken into account. As mentioned above, these sources are past experience of bearing these costs and ideological predispositions to identify and more highly assess such costs. Hence, apart from differences deriving from the sizes and preferences of economic interest groups, variation in frequency and severity of crisis-inducing policies and in macroeconomic and structural adjustment to such crises should also be explained by past experience with such cycles and relevant ideological biases. And again, extent of past experience and nature of ideological bias would be expected to have the biggest impact on the preferences and degree of political mobilization of dispersed interest groups.

In terms of succession of opposition governments under democratic rules, the more well-established democracies examined in this volume are Japan, South Korea, Thailand, Argentina, Brazil, Poland, Hungary, and the Czech Republic. Over time we would expect to see increasing awareness of the long-term costs of any distortionary subsidies and inflationary macroeconomic policies, and hence less frequent crisis-inducing policies and more rapid macroeconomic and structural adjustment. Such learning is particularly evident where, as in Argentina and Brazil, more myopic policies were pursued in recent memory. The pivotal "learners" in these cases have come from dispersed interest groups—unorganized labor, the middle classes, and the nontraded agricultural sector. In the East Asian cases, learning appears to have been slowed by the generally favorable growth records of the recent past. In other words, strong growth records make dispersed interest groups slower to demand reform of credit subsidies and other distorting policies as long as any economic setbacks are resolved with reasonable dispatch.

Variation in the initial emphasis placed on long-term costs and benefits might be explained by the larger size of sectors economically predisposed to join liberal coalitions or by ideological predispositions. To begin with, the Eastern European democracies appear to have been less myopic than the Latin American ones. Variation in the size of liberally disposed sectors does not seem a promising explanation, given the huge size of the uncompetitive traded sector and the somewhat smaller size of the nontraded sector in Eastern Europe at the time of transition from communism.[26] On the other hand, Latin American populisms did incorporate nearsighted policy biases, and Eastern European anticommunist nationalisms, farsighted policy biases.[27] The typically export-oriented but still protectionist and heavily subsidized policy regimes of East Asia were more commonly initiated under authoritarian rule.

There is a large literature on the effect of different types of democratic political institutions.[28] However, with notable exceptions such as Rogowski (1987) and Haggard and Kaufman (1992b), this literature has not usually focused on economic policy as the dependent variable. It is worth summarizing here how the literature meshes with the present emphasis on the distinction between concentrated and dispersed interest groups, and on the pivotal role of dispersed interest groups in explaining major changes of foreign economic policy regimes. The main institutional implication of this emphasis is that large policy reversals under democracy will often depend on reliable representation of dispersed interest groups. By definition, all democracies allow dispersed interest groups the potential to make their huge numbers felt. However, such representation is more reliable when concentrated interest groups with status quo policy preferences cannot easily block policy changes during periodic surges of dispersed interest group mobilization.

In the most general terms, the point can be stated in terms of Tsebelis's (1995) veto players framework. The larger the number of veto players and the larger the difference in preferences between such veto players,[29] the more likely that status quo–oriented concentrated interest groups will possess veto power. A particular example of political institutions that tend to constrain concentrated interest group influence are systems dominated by two "catch-all" parties. Haggard and Kaufman (1992b) argue that such catch-all party systems have better records of avoiding highly distortionary policies and better records of correcting such policies once they produce economic difficulties. Some support for these arguments is provided by the cases of Thailand and Brazil. Here large numbers of veto players, in the form of multiparty coalitions, appear to have contributed to policy rigidity despite reformist mobilization by dispersed interest groups. LoGerfo and Montinola, discussing Thailand in chapter 4, show how repeated efforts to control credit subsidies were blocked by the strong influence of the financial sector and its allied enterprises. Cason, discussing Brazil in chapter 11, shows how repeated efforts to scale back fiscal subsidies have been blocked by the strong influence of concentrated beneficiaries. However, it should be emphasized that many different institutional setups can strongly represent dispersed interest groups and restrain concentrated interest group influence. For example, presidencies are broadly elected and hence would be expected to more strongly reflect dispersed interest group preferences. Proportional representation electoral systems should be more likely to amplify the influence of concentrated interest groups. However, this need not be the case if the parties with veto power are more strongly constituted on broad ideological rather than narrow interest group lines.

It is important to make another point in this context. The capacity of concentrated interest groups to use institutional advantages to block reform may backfire. It may only intensify dispersed interest group reformism and mobilization, resulting in more decisive and sustained reforms once the concentrated interest groups' veto power is broken. On the other hand, the veto power of concentrated interest groups may take a more insidious form. It may only partially block reform but in the process undermine its effectiveness and thus match the old discredit of the status quo with a new discredit of reform. A similar outcome may occur if the liberal coalition implements reform incompetently and/or in a highly corrupt fashion. In such cases, dispersed interest groups' willingness to continue to support liberalization and to sustain a high level of mobilization is likely to depend on the extent to which interventionist alternatives have been discredited by past experience and ideology.[30]

Developmental Authoritarianisms

By definition, authoritarian regimes do not have to worry about short-term electoral constraints. This is a source of policy-making autonomy. It can be an advantage relative to democracy if authoritarian regimes prefer to maximize long-term economic growth. Such regimes can even ignore majority preferences for long periods of time—although they are usually aware that this is politically risky and therefore attempt to maintain large supporting coalitions. Autonomy can be a disadvantage if such regimes prefer to maximize the power and wealth of selected elites and a privileged set of concentrated interest groups. Relative to broadly accountable democracies, highly autonomous authoritarian regimes would be expected to produce a wider variety of economic policies, and hence a wider variety of growth performances. However, authoritarian regimes are not always highly autonomous. To the extent they are not, there may be important informal constraints on their policies.

Suppose we assume developmental authoritarianisms that maximize long-term growth. Such regimes would be expected to be able to use their relative autonomy to outperform democracies, minimizing distortionary subsidies and regulations and inflationary macroeconomic policies, and more rapidly correcting macroeconomic and structural sources of deteriorations in international competitiveness. It has long been emphasized that the more successful empirical examples of such regimes have tended to set up economic regulatory institutions (central banks, finance ministries, etc.) dominated by technocrats and empowered to pragmatically vary economic policy with a view toward maintaining long-term economic performance.[31] However, it should also be emphasized that such regimes are typically concerned about maintaining a high degree of legitimacy among what they regard as crucial interest group constituencies—so that the interests of such constituencies tend to act as constraints on the autonomy of the technocrats. Variation in the nature of such supporting constituencies is a key source of policy variation across such developmental authoritarian regimes. In this sense, their policies can be expected to show similarities to those of democratic governments with similar interest group bases of support—with the difference that the constraints would not be expected to be as closely correlated with election cycles as they sometimes are in democracies. To the extent that authoritarian rulers are more autonomous relative to such supporting coalitions, leadership preferences and competence are likely to loom larger in forming policy.

The developmental authoritarian cases examined in this volume are Malaysia and Suharto-era Indonesia. In past crises, developmental authoritarian regimes have often shown the potential for pragmatic policy adjustments that attempt to maintain healthy fundamentals, while still minimizing large-scale economic instability. In response to the present crisis, such a pragmatic balancing act is evident in China's hesitant restructuring of the inefficient, heavily indebted state sector portion of industry. However, during the present crisis, Malaysia and Suharto's Indonesia show the importance of coalitions and leadership in such autonomous regimes. The desire to minimize short-term political instability, as well as to protect heavily subsidized elites and sectors allied with the regime, can lead authoritarian leaders to constrain their economic technocrats. This can lead to more myopic policies (i.e., to avoidance of macroeconomic and structural adjustment despite significant long-term losses in international competitiveness).[32] In both cases, supporting coalitions imposed only limited constraints, within which relatively autonomous leaders made policy. Such leaders were capable of resisting liberalizing coalitions strengthened by changing preferences and heightened mobilization. But the two examples also reveal the high volatility of policy outcomes that can result (MacIntyre 1999a). Suharto's Indonesia in particular shows that, within the subset of policies aimed at protecting allied elites and sectors, autonomous authoritarianism also carries the risk of less coherent policy making.

Transition to Democracy

What occurs during the transition from developmental authoritarianism to democracy? Supposedly, in the run-up to the first elections, electoral constraints should kick in. There should be a relative deemphasis on long-term costs and benefits of alternative policies, and a corresponding reduction in the autonomy of economic technocrats. There should be similar new constraints on policy responses to any deterioration in international competitiveness. Here it is argued that the factors determining the extent of these changes should be the same factors that determine the influence of long-term costs and benefits in more established democracies. What are the interest groups' bases of the main policy alternatives? Particularly for dispersed interest groups, how do past experience and ideology influence the emphasis placed on long-term costs and benefits? To the extent that dispersion of institutional power and/or poor leadership block or distort policy implementation, what sort of staying power do past experience and ideology impart to the preferences and mobilization of pivotal dispersed interest groups?

The transitional cases examined in these pages are post-Suharto Indonesia, Taiwan, Mexico, and Russia.[33] There is evidence of new electoral constraints producing more myopic and less coherent economic policies in post-Suharto Indonesia, Mexico, and Russia—although not in Taiwan. Tarred with Suharto's excesses and facing elections almost immediately, the Habibie government did not feel strong enough to ruthlessly impose adjustment policies that would initially be expected to deepen the postcrisis recession. In Mexico during the run-up to the 1994 elections, an otherwise careful economic technocracy sacrificed macroeconomic stability to avoid a preelection recession. In Russia, Yeltsin has repeatedly compromised the integrity and public image of market reforms in order to avoid personal association with painful policies and to obtain short-term support from interest group factions opposed or at best indifferent to reform. This has been particularly noticeable prior to presidential elections. In Taiwan, by contrast, technocrats characteristically designed and executed a combination of liberal and interventionist adjustments, which maintained the preexisting austere economic policy regime while minimizing short-term disruptions.

Among the cases in which electoral constraints weakened liberalizing reforms, liberalizing reforms are likely to persist in Indonesia and Mexico. This is already evident in Mexico from the 2000 elections. The PRI government anticipated being punished immediately for a repetition of the pre-1994 election policies and so has maintained strict fiscal and monetary discipline, which helped Mexico emerge relatively unscathed from the 1997–1999 crisis. This policy correction was made likely by the resilient level of public support for the PRI and for the market-oriented Partido Acción Nacional opposition party in the painful aftermath of the 1994 crisis. On the other hand, liberal reforms are most likely to have been set back for longer in Russia.

Contributors to this volume argue that dispersed interest group preferences, driven by past experience with competing policy regimes, provide the most plausible explanation for this variation in the context of transitional democracy. In Taiwan, the economic policy record of the old authoritarian regime has probably been unmatched in its efficiency and in the limited scope of its corruption. Thus it makes sense that there has been a consensus during democratic transition on maintaining the old economic policy regime, including the autonomy of the technocrats. The opposition has thus focused its appeal on other issues, such as Taiwan's politico-legal status vis-à-vis the mainland. In Mexico, the absence of a stronger backlash benefiting the center–left Partido de la Revólución Democrática must be largely attributed to strong dispersed interest group memories of the negative long-term consequences of the populist policies pursued during the 1970s and early 1980s—prior to the liberalizing reforms initiated by the de la Madrid administration (1982–1988). In post-Suharto Indonesia, reform is likely to proceed for two reasons. Suharto's corruption and incompetent management of the 1997–1999 crisis have discredited the trade, financial, and regulatory subsidies benefiting his close allies. On the other hand, Indonesia's high growth rate since the move to export-oriented policies continues to limit support for the more inward-looking, interventionist alternatives associated with Indonesia's earlier history. In Russia, Yeltsin has managed to strongly discredit market reform policies. However, it is still worth noting that he has managed to win two presidential elections amid the constant economic difficulties since 1991 and that the more radical interventionist alternatives are still strongly discredited. This explains why Russia is most likely to be ruled next by a nonideological, more charismatically based set of parties and leaders. But why has Yeltsin been able to attract comparatively strong support until recently, and why is the Communist opposition still relatively discredited? Again, this must be largely attributed to negative memories of economic and other conditions under communism, particularly among the middle classes and unorganized labor in the more services-oriented big cities.

CONCLUSION

In this chapter I have attempted to develop the existing theoretical literature in two main ways, above all showing how large changes in foreign economic policy regimes often cannot be understood without examining the role played by dispersed interest groups in forming and sustaining coalitions. I have argued that the preferences and mobilization of such dispersed interest groups are highly dependent on recent experiences with alternative policy regimes and on ideologies. Second, I have attempted to show that this view of the role of dispersed interest groups nicely supplements existing efforts to understand the policy consequences of democratic and authoritarian political regimes, and of the different varieties of democratic political institutions.

NOTES

1. The approach taken here is that foreign economic policies have the greatest impact on sectors rather than factors, that is, on both capital (including management and more skilled labor) and labor in particular traded sector industries rather than on labor or capital as wholes across all sectors. This corresponds to the assumption that there are high costs to labor and capital mobility, so that a changing product price feeds back to the in-

comes of labor and capital in the particular product sector, but not, in the short run, to the incomes of capital or labor in other sectors. (On the other hand, if mobility is assumed to be costless, then capital earns the same rate of return and labor the same wage across all sectors.) Thus my assumption is that capital and labor in given sectors share trade policy preferences and that capital across sectors and labor across sectors do not. See Dixit and Norman 1980, 86–87, 102–10, and the discussion and evidence in Frey 1984, chap. 2, and Magee, Brock, and Young 1989, chap. 7. For political economy applications sharing the present assumptions, see Frieden 1991 and Gourevitch 1989. For a work assuming more rapid mobility of factors of production, see Rogowski 1989. An additional point is worth noting here. The high mobility assumption has the merit of including all sectors of the economy in the analysis. The low mobility assumption excludes the nontraded sector. The political role of this sector must then somehow be theoretically reintegrated.

2. This is implied by the highly influential work of Olson (1965). Traded sector groups also tend to be organized in larger units of production located in closer proximity to one another and to produce relatively homogeneous products. Such groups tend to have organizational advantages over groups in smaller units of production that are more far-flung, producing more heterogeneous products.

3. Organized labor tends to be heavily concentrated in traded sector manufacturing and in the public sector.

4. Among the case studies, the service sector shares of the workforce in 1990 were as follows: Japan 59 percent, Argentina 56, Brazil 54, Malaysia 50, Mexico 48, Hungary 47, South Korea 47, Czech Republic 44, Russia 44, Poland 37, Indonesia 29, and Thailand 22 (World Bank 1997, 220–21). The shares have risen since 1990, although uniformly updated data is not yet available.

5. Arguments of this type occur in works such as Frieden 1991, Gerschenkron 1989, and Gourevitch 1986.

6. Soft credits are those extended in the presence of higher risk, weaker collateral and/or lower rates of interest, relative to terms that would prevail in competitive financial markets. They are typically extended to clients with personal or political connections, usually encouraged by explicit or implicit government guarantees to prevent banks from failing, and often publicly endorsed by the government as part of an official economic development strategy.

7. An early argument along these lines is Becker 1983.

8. For examples of work emphasizing the effects of different types of democratic political institutions, see Haggard and Kaufman 1992a and 1992b, Rogowski 1987, Stepan and Skach 1993, and Tsebelis 1995.

9. The distinction between established democracies and regimes in transition to democracy is not cut and dried. It is commonly argued that democracies are consolidated when there is a solid majority that does not consider any other type of regime to be a legitimate alternative. It has also been argued that this must also be true for political players with the capacity to mount coups, such as the armed forces and powerful party organizations. The dividing line used above is the simpler one of whether the first democratic government has been peacefully succeeded by an opposition-led government according to democratic rules. Thus, after the crisis periods examined here, peaceful and democratic power transfers occurred in Taiwan and Mexico, and arguably also in Russia. For our purposes, it will be seen that the most important issue is whether the experience of a previous authoritarian regime is close enough to strongly influence policy preferences and

assessments of performance under democracy. In this sense, all the democracies except Japan have a relatively recent history of authoritarianism. Some developmental authoritarianisms have of course relied much more heavily upon force to maintain their power. However, with the accession of Gorbachev, even the Soviet regime became increasingly concerned with building broad supporting coalitions.

10. For surveys of this literature, see Persson and Tabellini 1990, Persson and Tabellini 1994, and Przeworski and Limongi 1993.

11. For example, see Deyo 1987 and World Bank 1993.

12. Tsebelis 1995 also notes that veto players are more likely to block policy change when their preferences are more divergent.

13. But adverse responses to both increased trade barriers and tightened capital controls are to be expected. Any retaliatory increases in foreign trade barriers will worsen the current account balance, and declining investor confidence and corresponding reductions in capital inflows will worsen the capital account. The net effects can be difficult to predict.

14. Przeworski 1991, chap. 4, argues that this is the more typical preference. There is a similar trade-off between devaluation and exchange controls. If there is little recent experience with the distortionary and discriminatory consequences of exchange controls, the immediate price increases associated with devaluation may loom larger.

15. Such coalitions are also often termed "neoliberal."

16. The most common measure of relative land abundance is the ratio of cropland (thousands of square kilometers) to population (millions). For the case studies, the land-labor ratios are as follows: Russian Federation 9.22, Argentina 7.97, Hungary 4.92, Poland 3.89, Malaysia 3.77, Thailand 3.61, Czech Republic 3.37, Brazil 3.21, Mexico 2.77, Indonesia 1.68, South Korea 0.46, Japan 0.36. Roughly, the Russian Federation and Argentina should be considered highly land abundant; Indonesia, South Korea, and Japan, highly land scarce. Cropland is as of 1994, and population as of 1995. Figures are calculated from World Bank 1997, 214–15, 230–321.

17. Collectivization also occurred in the Czech Republic (formerly part of Czechoslovakia) and Hungary, and to a very limited extent in Poland. A partial collectivization has also transformed most of Mexican agriculture. But these countries are not highly land abundant and hence are not potentially large net exporters of agricultural goods.

18. As of 1990, agriculture's share of the workforce was as follows: Japan 7 percent, Czech Republic 11, Argentina 12, Russian Federation 14, Hungary 15, South Korea 18, Brazil 23, Malaysia 27, Poland 27, Mexico 28, Indonesia 57, and Thailand 64. World Bank 1997, 220–21.

19. However, generally import-competing agricultures may have significant net-exporting subsectors. Among the case studies, this is true for Brazil and Mexico.

20. For Japan, exporting sectors are mostly relatively mature and not dependent on trade, credit, and fiscal subsidies, and hence should be more firmly in the liberal camp.

21. For case studies, see the discussions by James LoGerfo and Gabriella Montinola on Thailand (chapter 4), A. Maria Toyoda on Malaysia (chapter 5), Kimberly Niles on Indonesia (chapter 6), Eric Browne and Sunwoong Kim on Japan (chapter 7), Uk Heo on South Korea (chapter 8), and Alexander Tan on Taiwan (chapter 9).

22. For applications, see the discussions by Aldo Flores Quiroga on Mexico (chapter 10), Jeffrey Cason on Brazil (chapter 11), and Walter Molano on Argentina (chapter 12).

23. For applications, see the discussions by this writer on Poland, Hungary, and the Czech Republic (chapter 13) and by Peter Rutland on the Russian Federation (chapter 14).

24. See note 10.

25. This is similar to the position taken, for example, by Leijonhufvud 1981.

26. See note 4.

27. See the discussions in this volume by LoGerfo and Montinola on Thailand (chapter 4), Browne and Kim on Japan (chapter 7), Heo on South Korea (chapter 8), Cason on Brazil (chapter 11), Molano on Argentina (chapter 12), and this writer on Poland, Hungary, and the Czech Republic (chapter 13).

28. See note 8; see also MacIntyre 1999a.

29. Tsebelis also generalizes the analysis to include the internal makeup of veto players (i.e., the number of internal veto players and their differences in preferences).

30. Striking examples of such situations are analyzed in Flores Quiroga's chapter 10 on Mexico, this writer's chapter 13 on Poland, Hungary, and the Czech Republic, and in Rutland's chapter 14 on Russia.

31. See note 11.

32. See the discussions in this volume by Toyoda on Malaysia (chapter 5) and Niles on Indonesia (chapter 6).

33. See Niles on Indonesia (chapter 6), Tan on Taiwan (chapter 9), Flores Quiroga on Mexico (chapter 10), and Rutland on Russia (chapter 14). Again, after the period examined in this volume, Taiwan, Mexico, and arguably also Russia experienced peaceful and democratic transfers of power.

3

The World Financial Crisis: Are the IMF Prescriptions Right?

W. Max Corden

Given that a financial crisis in the capital and foreign exchange markets, caused by a sudden loss of confidence, has taken place, how are the effects transmitted to the real economy? Why must such a crisis cause a recession or even a depression? How can such transmission to the real economy be avoided or at least minimized? Surely it is not inevitable that workers and poor people should suffer so much from financial mistakes, whatever they are, nor that there should be such a large loss of national output owing to unemployment and excess capacity caused by lack of demand.

These issues are particularly relevant for the East Asian countries affected by the crisis, on which this chapter mainly focuses. It must be said from the beginning that there are no simple answers to these questions. There has not been any obvious "easy" way out, and certainly not one that can do without the International Monetary Fund (IMF). Furthermore, the IMF has not been unambigously "right" or "wrong." It is now probably mostly right with its prescriptions and conditions. But it went off the rails at the beginning, in 1997, though it went gradually back on again, being flexible. Some criticisms seem justified and will be discussed below. It is particularly important to stress the trade-offs involved in policy decisions. One should have no sympathy for oversimplifications that give only one side of an argument. But one main point will also be stressed. Keynesian analysis and a classic textbook Keynesian remedy for a recession—the use of expansionary fiscal policy—have been highly relevant for this particular crisis.

Discussions of the Asian crisis include three distinct issues. First, what were the reasons for the crisis? This has been the focus of much academic discussion.

Second, how can such a crisis be avoided, or its effects moderated, in the future? Right from the beginning this has been the principal focus of IMF attention. Here the concern is with the third issue, namely, the transmission of the financial crisis to the real economy, and how the adverse effects on the real economy—on output, employment, and the standard of living—can be avoided or minimized.

A principal theme of this chapter is that when a decline in demand originates in the private sector, a fiscal contraction should be avoided; insofar as financing is available, a fiscal expansion, designed to offset to some extent the decline in demand, is desirable. This is an argument that has seemed very appropriate for the East Asian crisis countries—Malaysia, South Korea, Indonesia, and Thailand—because they have records of conservative fiscal policies and because the crisis that hit them was in no way connected with expansionary fiscal policies and foreign borrowing by governments. In these cases the original prescriptions of the IMF can be criticized, though, as the crisis evolved, IMF prescriptions changed, recognizing the need for some fiscal ease. In the case of Indonesia, indeed, by 1998 the IMF programs allowed for very substantial fiscal deficits. The problems connected with fiscal expansion are analyzed at length in this chapter. But there are other countries where the argument for fiscal expansion does not hold at all. The crises in Russia and Brazil were essentially caused by large and prolonged budget deficits, leading to unsustainable domestic and foreign borrowing. The principal need was for fiscal contraction, not expansion. This was unavoidable. In these cases a failure to reduce budget deficits would have an adverse effect on investor confidence and thus intensify the crisis. Indeed, it was this failure that played a major role in setting off their crises.

A principal feature of the crises that occurred in all the East Asian countries, as well as Mexico, Russia, and Brazil, was that markets forced the abandonment of fixed, or nearly fixed, exchange rates. The values of the various currencies then plummeted. This had one favorable effect, though it has been an effect that operated only with a lag. It made exports more competitive and thus stimulated a growth in exports—greatly in some cases, notably South Korea, and more slowly in others. Such an expansion of exports helps to reduce the current account deficit—which is necessary when capital inflow has declined or even turned into capital outflow. It also provides a stimulus for domestic output and employment, hence offsetting the adverse effects of the decline in investment demand resulting from the loss of confidence that created the crisis. The export growth also offsets, at least to an extent, the decline in demand that would result from fiscal contraction in those countries, for example Brazil, where such contraction was needed. In the case of the East Asian countries, it meant that the necessary fiscal expansion could be temporary.

But the drastic depreciations of exchange rates that resulted in all cases also had an immediate adverse effect in all those countries where private borrowers—whether banks, finance companies, or ordinary corporations—had borrowed abroad, incurring debts denominated in foreign currencies (mostly in dollars). The value of these debts measured in terms of domestic currencies rose. This had a devastating effect on their financial sectors, adding to the difficulties that resulted from the initial euphoria-induced overborrowing, and from the recession. The domestic financial crises then intensified their recessions.

An important issue is the kind of monetary policy that should be followed when the exchange rate depreciates massively and there is a recession. Tight monetary policy, involving a rise in interest rates, would help to maintain exchange rates, or at least moderate the exchange rate depreciations by making it more attractive to hold the countries' currencies. In the East Asian cases this was desirable because the exchange rate depreciations had clearly overshot and thus led to the severe financial problems just mentioned. This matter is further discussed below. But whether it was sensible in Brazil and Russia to try to maintain exchange rates before the crisis with the help of very high interest rates—even when the need for depreciation was very apparent—is more questionable. The other side of the argument is that higher domestic interest rates are likely to intensify the recessions. In the East Asian cases, there was a clear trade-off between the favorable exchange rate effects and the adverse recession effects of the tight monetary policies recommended by the IMF. An issue touched on below is whether it is feasible and desirable to impose some kind of exchange controls that break the link between domestic interest rates and the exchange rate, thus allowing greater monetary expansion than otherwise.

The issues are complex, as are the assessments of IMF recommendations and conditions. They are further discussed, especially with reference to the examples of Thailand and South Korea, in the remainder of this chapter.

A SIMPLE KEYNESIAN DEMAND STORY

It is elementary Keynesian economics that one needs to recall here. There was a private sector investment boom, partially financed from domestic savings and partially from foreign capital inflow. For whatever reason, expectations of future profitability of investments changed. There was a growing realization of problems—growing excess capacity, rising costs, and declining export prices. So capital inflow stopped, and there was some outflow as well. Short-term loans could no longer be refinanced. There has thus been a decline in lending, both domestic and foreign. Hence investment (i.e., spending by business) has declined. We know that in the case of recent events such a decline has been drastic. Such a decline can also come about when there is no capital inflow initially but all investment is domestically financed.

To give concreteness to such a story, let me quote figures for Thailand. These are IMF estimates or projections. Gross fixed investment rose 6 percent in 1996 (having risen much more in earlier years), fell 16 percent in 1997, and was expected to fall a further 24 percent in 1998.

Thus aggregate demand declined and a severe recession (even depression) resulted. There was a big turnaround in particular parts of the economy, notably building and construction. Loss-making firms dismissed workers. The story started with a decline in investment, but the effects were supplemented by the familiar Keynesian multiplier, which leads to a fall in consumer spending. In Thailand the consumption decline is expected to be 8 percent in 1998.

And there is more. One must not forget the Keynesian "accelerator." This is a secondary effect on investment caused by the recession. Reduced profitability caused by the recession affected both internal funds available for investment and expected future profitability. In other words, the story started with a primary decline in investment, which brought about a recession, which in turn brought about a further decline in investment, which in turn intensified the recession. Hence there was a severe fall in aggregate demand. All this is a textbook story, often forgotten but a good description of what actually happened.

It is worth stressing that "fundamentals" may explain and even justify, at least in part, the initial decline in investment. But the decline in consumption and the secondary decline in investment are explained by the recession which—as I shall argue—is not necessarily an inevitable part of the story.

We have here the typical story of the end of a boom that, in its last stages, had a good deal of euphoria in it. The ending can be seen in the sudden declines in growth rates. High positive growth rates have actually turned into highly negative ones. Thus the growth rate of real Gross Domestic Product (GDP) of Thailand was 5.5 percent in 1996—and higher in earlier years—and was projected at minus 7 percent or so for 1998.

It is not very surprising that imports have declined and thus current accounts have improved. This is the inevitable result first of the initial decline in investment spending and then of the recession. The deeper the recession, the more imports will decline. In the case of Thailand, in 1998 Thai imports in dollars are expected to be 70 percent or so of their 1997 value. In 1996 the Thai current account deficit was 8 percent of GDP, and for 1998 a 7 percent surplus is projected.

From the point of view of the balance of payments, the process is thus self-correcting. Initially a current account deficit—huge in the case of Thailand—was financed by capital inflow. Then capital inflow stops, and there is some outflow, so the current account deficit has to turn into a surplus, which it does. But the self-correcting process is brought about at great cost, namely, a major recession. It is surely no achievement to bring about a balance-of-payments improvement in this way.

In the absence of policy changes, there will eventually be a recovery. This will depend on the recovery of private sector demand, above all, investment spending. It may take years, as debts are worked off or written down, the financial sector is cleaned up, excess capacity is gradually reduced, and the confidence of domestic and foreign investors is restored. For the moment I leave aside the role of exports and the exchange rate. I shall discuss this in detail below, as it is crucial. If—in the absence of policy changes—a decision is made to wait for the restoration of confidence, a lengthy recession may ensue.

THE KEYNESIAN SOLUTION

Apart from doing nothing, there are, in principle, two policy approaches. The first is to implement policies that would restore the confidence of private investors, so that lenders will be prepared to lend and borrowers to borrow again. (In the language of Keynesian economics, the aim is then to shift the marginal efficiency of capital schedule—which refers to expectations of profitability—to the right.) This need to restore confidence has clearly been the primary emphasis of IMF programs and of recommendations coming from Washington and, more generally, from people in the financial sector.

The second approach is to compensate for the initial decline in private investment with a fiscal expansion requiring deficit finance. In this case the private investment decline itself is accepted as inevitable and not quickly reversible, either because it would be difficult and would take a long time to reverse or because it was to a considerable extent a justified decline based on fundamentals, such as the emergence of excess capacity in fields where much of the investment had taken place (e.g., real estate, electronics manufacture, and motor car production). Compensation through fiscal expansion would take the form of increased government expenditures, such as expenditures on infrastructure projects, which would create demand for some of the building and construction firms that will have lost business owing to the end of the private building boom. It would also include reduced taxes, increased transfers, and subsidies that would boost private incomes and hence consumption. Sufficient fiscal expansion, if initiated in time, can avoid a recession completely.

At least that is the simple textbook Keynesian argument. Actually there are serious difficulties and possible objections to this proposal, which I shall discuss systematically below. But first let me continue with this line of thought.

Public funds are required to recapitalize domestic banks because of the problems of the financial sector, which I shall also discuss below. Banks need to be recapitalized so that they are able to lend again. Since some part of the decline in aggregate demand will have been caused not by the factors I have already described but by the inability of domestic firms to borrow from domestic banks because of the latter's financial difficulties, restoring the capital of the banks would boost spending. But the effect of such recapitalization on aggregate demand should not be overstated. Not all these funds will lead to extra spending; a good part will simply strengthen the banks' reserves.

A recession will naturally lead to an increase in a fiscal deficit or reduced surplus. A recession reduces incomes and thus tax revenue declines—whether from income tax, corporate tax, or taxes on imports—even when tax rates stay constant. One should not make the mistake of treating an increase in a fiscal deficit as necessarily an indication of fiscal expansion. It is a natural tendency in all countries for a fiscal deficit to increase in a recession and decline in a boom. This is the familiar "automatic stabilizer." For this reason the Organization for Economic Cooperation and Development calculates "fiscal impulse" measures to distinguish the genuinely expansionary or contractionary effects of fiscal policy changes from the automatic or endogenous effects on the deficit.

If fiscal policy is directed toward avoiding such an endogenous increase in a fiscal deficit by reducing government spending, then it is adding to the decline in aggregate demand and thus intensifying the recession. That is exactly what happened in the beginning of the Great Depression in the United States. A genuine fiscal expansion requires the deficit to actually be greater than would result from the automatic stabilizer.

Let me now look at IMF "conditionality" on fiscal policy. What conditions has the IMF attached to its emergency loans? I have come to the conclusion that initially the IMF went off the rails. Apparently it required fiscal contractions from affected countries. Probably the concern was with fiscal discipline. But Thailand, Indonesia, and Korea all have excellent fiscal policy records over long periods. While it could be argued that government-directed bank credits to favored borrowers should really have been items in their budgets—hence making their fiscal positions look not so good—in general they have not had problems of fiscal discipline, unlike Latin American or African countries, not to speak of Russia. Whenever fiscal problems have emerged, they have dealt with them remarkably quickly.

But the IMF staff are quick learners and the organization is flexible. Hence conditions regarding fiscal policy have been modified as the economies deteriorated. After criticisms and experience—and after urgings from the governments concerned—the programs were adjusted, notably in the case of Indonesia. Whether the adjustments have been sufficient, time will tell. But there is no doubt that they have been too late to avoid serious recessions. Fiscal policy works with a lag, and the aim must be to anticipate the recession, not to react once the recession is well under way.

Now let me give some figures. Thailand's overall public sector balance in 1996 was actually a surplus of 2.7 percent of GDP. This clearly reflects the automatic stabilizer operating in a boom. It turned into a 2 percent of GDP deficit in 1997 and (at the time of this writing), a 3 percent forecast deficit in 1998. I am sure this 1998 projected fiscal deficit figure is less than would result from the automatic stabilizer alone, so that it embodies some predicted fiscal contraction. In the case of Indonesia the IMF had to reverse course, as by the middle of 1998 there was an unavoidable huge deficit. According to the June 24, 1998, modification of Indonesia's IMF program, the fiscal deficit was projected to be 8.5 percent of GDP in 1998–1999. Most of this (7.5 percent of GDP) was accounted for by the social safety net program.

The aim of Keynesian countercyclical fiscal policy is to maintain, as far as possible, the overall level of output, or perhaps output per capita, that is, to avoid a major domestic recession. But it would not solve all problems. The pattern of output would inevitably have to shift, so that there would have to be some reallocation of labor: some activities would inevitably decline while others (resulting from fiscal expansion) would grow faster than otherwise. And this process itself would generate transitional unemployment and pain for some sectors of the community. A completely smooth adjustment would be impossible.

PROBLEMS OF FISCAL EXPANSION

Any serious discussion of the issues must face up to the arguments against fiscal expansion. Critics of the IMF cannot ignore the fact that there are problems with, and possible obstacles to, the Keynesian approach. Clearly, initially, the IMF gave these heavy weight. I shall now discuss a number of these problems.

Deficit Financing

First, the main problem is that deficits need to be financed. If such a Keynesian fiscal expansion policy were followed, the current account would no longer improve automatically as a result of the self-correcting process described above. If the import content of higher government expenditure were less than the import content in private investment spending that it replaced—as is possible if the public spending increase is well designed—there might be some improvement. But a current account deficit would continue and, with the drying up of private sector funds, it would have to be financed. And it is here that the IMF comes in and that the limits to fiscal expansion are set. At this stage I am still assuming that there is no change in exports, a matter to which I return later.

The role of the IMF is to help countries over temporary difficulties. Eventually exports should increase and there may also be some economizing on imports and import substitution. This would be brought about by currency depreciation. I shall come to that subject below. In the intervening period, which could be several years, fiscal expansion would maintain domestic employment and incomes. As exports increase, the fiscal expansion should be gradually reversed. The role of the IMF would be to finance current account deficits during that intervening period. Because of gradual export expansion, these deficits would be declining and eventually a current account surplus (which would allow for some repayment of debt) would be attained. The aim of such a policy is to avoid the pain of a deep recession.

This is the proper role of the IMF: to avoid severe effects on the people of the country. It is an alternative role to lending the country money so that it can bail out some or all of the country's short-term foreign creditors. The role of the IMF in financing "bailouts" has, of course, been important, and I shall return to it later. But it is a major feature of the Keynesian way of avoiding or moderating a recession that IMF financial support would not be used for bailouts.

If a recession were avoided, the decline in taxation revenues that would result from a recessionary decline in incomes would also be avoided. It follows that some part of increased government expenditures would actually come back into public coffers in the form of revenue that would otherwise be lost. There would no longer be an automatic stabilizer that increased the fiscal deficit. This has to be taken into account when the financing implications of a fiscal expansion are calculated.

It bears repeating that the limits to temporary fiscal expansion and hence temporarily continuing current account deficits are set by the availability of IMF (and other) finance. The IMF plays a crucial role, so that some IMF conditions would have to be accepted.

Market Expectations

Second, it has been said that expansionary fiscal policies would have an adverse effect on market expectations. Since the whole focus of the IMF, of the U.S. Treasury, and of financial market commentators was initially on restoring market confidence, this concern may have weighed a great deal. Fiscal expansion, it might be said, is an indication of loss of fiscal discipline and suggests the likelihood that deficits that could not be bond-financed or IMF-financed would be monetized. Hence exchange rates would depreciate even more, foreign creditors would be even more reluctant to refinance or reschedule debts, and there would be even more capital flight.

The "market" has indeed been obsessed with fiscal deficits, based on Latin American experience. But such a concern about fiscal discipline is simply not justified in the case of Thailand, Indonesia, and Korea, in view of their excellent long-term records. It should be the role of the IMF to educate markets on this matter and to explain the need for temporary fiscal expansion. Incidentally, Radelet and Sachs (1998) have argued that when IMF programs in early 1998 switched to lessen the fiscal contraction (i.e., to allow for increased deficits), the exchange rates appreciated rather than depreciated. Thus it appears that the market did not view such fiscal policy shifts in an expansionary direction adversely.

Foreign Financing

Third, another problem, one that is all too familiar, is that the IMF makes loans, not gifts. Let us assume that foreign financing, through the IMF or otherwise, is available. A fiscal deficit will increase the public debt and hence the obligation to raise taxes later to pay for debt service (i.e., for interest and eventual repayments) if the debt cannot be refinanced. In the precrisis period there was a current account deficit that was financed by private debt accumulation; now it will be replaced by a current account deficit financed by growing public debt accumulation. For this reason, the fiscal deficit—or at least its growth relative to GDP—should be temporary. It is relevant here that the overall debt/GDP ratios of most of the affected countries (other than Indonesia, at least) have not been high; the problem has been the high ratios of short-term debt relative to foreign exchange reserves. Hence, as nations, they have had liquidity rather than solvency problems.

To some extent the fiscal deficit could be financed from domestic savings—the same savings that had previously contributed to financing the domestic private sector boom. To that extent, there is less need for foreign funds. If foreign funds are insufficient for financing desirable fiscal expansion, it may then be necessary to ensure through various restrictions that private domestic savings do not all go abroad or are discouraged from doing so. This would, in effect, be an indirect way of taxing domestic savings. At this point I can thus see a case for temporary controls on capital outflows. But the obligation to raise taxes in the future to pay interest on the public debt, and possibly repay it eventually, would remain.

False Expectations

Fourth, the fiscal expansion should be temporary, until the private sector revives and, above all, until export expansion fills the required gap in demand for labor and domestic inputs. But for political reasons it may be difficult to reverse the process, especially in the case of subsidies. Hence it would be a good idea to build in "sunset clauses" to ensure that subsidies, for example, are known to be temporary and false expectations of permanence are not created. Infrastructure projects should be of the kind that can be completed within three years or so.

There may also be inevitable delays in getting various projects started. Much hinges on the efficiency of the bureaucratic system. What this means is that substantial and timely fiscal expansion may be quite difficult. But it is clear that, at the minimum, in the kind of situation that the Asian countries faced in the latter part of 1997 and early 1998, policies of actual fiscal contraction should not be imposed.

Effects on the Private Sector

Fifth, it might be asked whether a fiscal expansion would not slow up a private sector revival by drawing resources into the public sector and into consumer spending (owing to subsidies or tax cuts). There are clearly two opposing effects here. On the one hand, maintaining aggregate demand would prevent the secondary decline in private investment that would result from a recession. In other words, it would prevent the Keynesian downward accelerator from doing its negative work. In this case, the more government spending, the more private investment. On the other hand, as more resources are drawn into the public sector or into satisfying consumer demand (owing to subsidies and tax cuts), there will be a slower transfer of labor into exports as the exchange rate depreciation does its work of making exporting more profitable. For this very reason, the fiscal expansion must be gradually reversed. Clearly, the more unemployment there is, the lower wages will be and hence the lower labor costs for exporting, and the easier it will be for expanding exporters to obtain labor. This point is important, but one must ask: does a country really need a massive recession to generate an export boom?

The Need for Safeguards

Finally, any large increases in public expenditure provide the opportunity for misspending and corruption. I need not elaborate on this here. It is thus inevitable that the IMF, with World Bank support, has to set conditions on how the funds for which it provides the finance are to be spent. This fairly detailed "conditionality" is actually the situation now. Expenditure increases should be focused on financing public investment projects with sound long-term value, on subsidies targeted to soften the impact of the crisis on the poor, and on recapitalizing well-managed banks, but not so as to lead to capital flight. In the case of Indonesia, the enforcement of such conditions is clearly a difficult problem.

THE EXCHANGE RATE AND THE HOPED-FOR EXPORT BOOM

The massive depreciations of the currencies should, in due course, lead to increased exports. To that extent the depreciations are to be welcomed. There should be an export-led recovery. This is what one would normally expect and what happened in Mexico after its 1994–1995 crisis. But, inevitably, such an effect will be lagged, so that in the interim an IMF-financed fiscal expansion is required if a recession is to be avoided.

Eventually the current account and the recession problem should both be overcome without necessarily any fiscal expansion relative to the initial situation. It is standard theory that if a country has a current account deficit that has to be eliminated, and if a constant overall level of employment is to be maintained ("internal balance"), there must be both a decline in total domestic spending ("absorption") and a switching of foreign and domestic spending toward home-produced goods. The decline in absorption is brought about by the decline in investment demand that started off the whole story, while real depreciation brings about "switching." All this may seem too easy and neat. Hence it must be remembered that the export boom combined with the decline in investment demand would inevitably involve a reallocation of resources, with gainers and losers.

Here I must note that, so far, there seems to be little sign of the beginning of a real export boom. I shall come back to this important and disturbing matter shortly. It certainly calls for explanation. The steep depreciations have greatly raised the domestic currency (baht, rupiah, won) costs of imports and thus are likely to induce the economizing of imports. In fact, a depreciation is the equivalent of a uniform tariff. It must lead to some import substitution. Also, it would reduce the adverse current account effects of an aggregate demand expansion that would be brought about by a fiscal expansion. All this is highly desirable because it reinforces the effect of an export boom and reduces the financing requirement of a given fiscal expansion. At the same time, insofar as imports are essential— either basic foods or inputs for domestic production—the scope for reducing them, at least in the short term, is limited.

It might also be observed that the steep depreciations make it unnecessary to impose import restrictions or raise tariffs. From a long-term point of view such measures would, in any case, be undesirable. But a case for temporary tariffs could be made if the exchange rate had to stay fixed. Yet what need is there for higher or new tariffs (or for quantitative import restrictions) when a depreciation produces the equivalent of a very high uniform tariff? In the case of Thailand, a depreciation that reduced the value of the baht from 24.5 to the dollar to 41 to the dollar is the equivalent of a 67 percent uniform tariff.

Another important point is that domestic inflation must not fully offset the favorable competitive effects of the depreciations. There will only be an export boom and some switching away from imports if there is not just a nominal but also a real depreciation. In the case of Mexico, there was considerable offsetting in 1995, though significant real depreciation remained. This is unlikely to be a problem in the Asian countries with their excellent anti-inflation histories.

Of course, domestic prices of imports and of home-produced goods with a significant import content will rise as a result of the depreciations, and hence the cost of living will rise. In that sense there is inevitably a period of consumer price inflation as domestic prices adjust to the steep depreciations. This is very noticeable in Indonesia. But what counts for the export boom and the switching effect is not the change in the overall price level but rather the change in relative prices: domestic prices of exports and imports must rise relative to wages and to prices of nontraded goods. If wages rise to the same extent as the domestic prices of exports, there will be no cost advantage leading to an export boom. But, to repeat, I do not have the impression that this is a problem in Asia. In the case of Thailand, the inflation rate in 1997 was only 5.6 percent and for 1998 is expected to be 10.5 percent, which is still very low.

What are the present and prospective obstacles to an export boom? First, a rise in the volume of exports is likely to be accompanied temporarily by a fall in their dollar prices, owing to the depreciations. It takes time for prices to adjust. This is the well-known "J-curve" effect. Second, dollar prices may need to fall for countries to be able to expand international sales of those particular exports where they have significant shares in world markets. Both these factors are now evident in Korea and Thailand: Korean export volume has risen, as also have Thai agricultural exports, but dollar prices have fallen significantly. Third, world market conditions are not favorable because of the slump in Japan, the yen depreciation (affecting Korea), the fall in oil prices (affecting Indonesia), and excess capacity in the electronics and other markets. Fourth, there is the danger of a protectionist reaction in the United States and Europe when Korean exports finally expand on a large scale. Export expansions by Thailand, Indonesia, and Malaysia are less likely to generate reactions of this kind because these countries are generally still "small fish" in world markets.

Let me elaborate on this protectionist issue. It would be outrageous—but not surprising—if the United States and Europe responded with antidumping duties on the grounds that these Asian exports are produced with cheap labor or benefit from excessively depreciated exchange rates. If the United States and Europe are not willing to supply extra loans either through the private capital market or through the IMF, then they must allow Korea to finance its desired imports with increased exports. In other words, they will have to buy either Korea's bonds or its goods. If neither bonds nor goods are bought in sufficient quantities, Korea would have to reduce its imports, thus hurting exporters in the United States and Europe.

Finally, the most severe and immediate obstacle to an export expansion in Indonesia, and possibly also in the other countries, is the problem of trade credit. Potential exporters cannot obtain trade credit, without which they cannot purchase the imported inputs necessary for exports. I come back to this crucial problem later.

BIG PROBLEMS CREATED BY EXCESSIVE EXCHANGE RATE DEPRECIATIONS

It is clear that for all the countries a significant real depreciation has been necessary, at the minimum to generate current account balance combined with "internal balance," and in the longer run to generate a surplus so as to allow for some repayment of debt. But the depreciations overshot initially and are probably still higher than necessary (certainly in the case of Indonesia). Even if they are necessary, they have several adverse effects that have dominated discussion.

First, they have adverse effects on consumers of imports and producers who depend on imported inputs. Both social and production problems result. This is very evident in Indonesia, and it is one reason why the IMF has focused on the restoration of confidence designed to moderate the depreciations.

Second, banks, nonbank financial intermediaries, and corporations borrowed short-term in dollar-denominated form (or in yen) and failed to hedge their debts. Steep depreciations then raised their domestic currency foreign liabilities to unsustainable levels and, in effect, bankrupted them. This is the most serious effect of exchange rate overshooting. Bankrupt banks are unable to lend. This then adds to the deflationary consequences of the financial panic. I return to this issue below. The IMF has correctly focused on this problem.

Here, let me add one thought. It is said that banks and other firms borrowed unhedged in dollars (or yen) because they expected the fixed exchange rate regimes to last. In effect they were misled by the promises of governments to maintain exchange rates fixed. But here it must be added that they chose to borrow in foreign currency rather than baht, rupiah, or won because dollar and yen interest rates were significantly lower. But why were they lower? The answer is that "the market" did allow for the possibility of devaluation or depreciation of the baht, rupiah, and won. It was only a possibility, but because the exchange rates were not fixed with absolute certainty, interest rates payable by the same borrower were higher in baht, rupiah, or won than in dollars. Unless the borrowers who chose to borrow in dollars and benefit from the lower interest rates knew less than "the market," they simply gambled on the maintenance of fixed rates, and lost.

Third, a matter of much controversy has been interest rate policy. Lower interest rates stimulate domestic demand and can reduce bankruptcies of banks and firms. On the other hand, lower interest rates are also likely to lead to more capital outflow and hence depreciation. From the point of view of a domestic firm, there is a crucial trade-off. A lower interest rate will reduce the cost of domestic borrowing and, indeed (insofar as it avoids bankruptcies of banks), makes it possible to borrow, while a higher interest rate will (or may) appreciate the exchange rate and thus reduce the domestic currency value of foreign debt and thus the cost of debt service. Some firms will benefit from lower interest rates and some from higher interest rates, depending on the extent of their foreign debt and their current need for new domestic borrowing or refinancing. Korean firms have had particularly high (and excessive) ratios of debt to equity and hence would suffer greatly from increased interest rates.

A crucial issue is to what extent a higher interest rate does actually succeed in moderating the exchange rate depreciation. The IMF has focused on this exchange-rate effect of interest rate policy, and its conditions have called for high interest rates. A high interest rate policy seemed to work in Mexico, and possibly it worked in Thailand and Korea, helping to explain the rebound of their currency values in early 1998. On the other hand, there is no doubt that high interest rates add to the domestic deflationary effect, and this has been the basis of serious criticism of the IMF. But it should be clear that there is a trade-off, and one should not just look at one side of the story. In a serious slump I am inclined to give the domestic demand factor priority. It may be desirable to impose some controls to discourage the outflow of capital when the interest rate is reduced. This is a large subject, with the usual pros and cons, that I cannot pursue here. At the same time, because there is indeed a trade-off, there is all the more reason to make use of fiscal policy, and not just monetary policy, to maintain or restore domestic demand.

One paradoxical possibility, which is not at all unrealistic, is possibly borne out by recent events, and goes against the IMF approach, should also be noted.

Higher interest rates may actually lead to more, rather than less, depreciation. The higher the interest rate, the deeper the recession. The deeper the recession, the more numerous domestic bankruptcies and the greater social unrest. And the more of these domestic troubles, the more adverse will be market expectations about the ability of the government to cope, to maintain some stability, and to bring about reforms. And the more adverse these expectations, the more the exchange rate will depreciate.

THE DOMESTIC FINANCIAL BREAKDOWN

I come now to the third way in which the initial financial and currency crisis was transmitted to the real economies of the countries concerned (the first being through the Keynesian demand process and the second through the exchange rate). There has resulted a breakdown of the domestic banking system; the banks have become bankrupt, with a drastic rise in the domestic currency values of their foreign liabilities and fall in the values of their domestic assets. Hence the banks have been unable to lend.

The domestic financial sector crisis has three distinct causes. First, there were the excessive or unwise investments and loans that resulted from the euphoric stage of the investment and borrowing boom. These would inevitably have led to some crisis, though not necessarily as severe as the one that actually took place. Second, there were the effects of the recession, and, third, the effects of the massive depreciations in raising the domestic currency values of the foreign liabilities of banks and other financial intermediaries, as well as some of their customers. The large number of nonperforming loans on the books of banks before the currency crisis struck indicates the importance of the first cause. If more Keynesian fiscal policies had been followed, the second cause would not have operated; and if the foreign exchange market had not gone to such extremes, the third cause would have been less severe. Added to this were certain inadequacies in the financial systems and in the laws—lack of transparency, absence of bankruptcy procedures, and so on. These have been much written about and have been the focus of IMF reforms. These inadequacies have made the countries more vulnerable to the various shocks. I will not go into detail here as this aspect goes beyond the scope of this chapter. On all this, see Goldstein (1998). Here I only want to note how the domestic financial crisis relates to transmission to the real economy.

There are actually two main points. One is that banks were bankrupted and thus were unable to lend. Firms have been unable to obtain credit. For Keynesian reasons outlined earlier, the demand for credit for production for the home market would have declined in any case. In addition there was thus a restriction on the supply of credit, which further created difficulties for firms and reduced total spending. It is possible that this has been a more binding constraint than the reduction in demand for credit. We have thus an additional explanation for the decline in aggregate demand and the recession, quite distinct from the Keynesian story. Correctly, the need to clean up and recapitalize the banks has been seen as a priority task by the IMF.

The other point—which is of extreme importance—is that trade credit for exporting has become hard to get or completely unavailable (especially in Indonesia). This is a large subject of its own and I refer to it only briefly. I know that Singapore has tried to help Indonesia here, but there have been difficulties. One wonders why foreign banks cannot fill the gap. One answer is that they do not have the detailed knowledge and contacts to be able to select creditworthy firms efficiently. They would have to use reliable local banks as agents. But another answer suggests that the obstacle to the provisions of trade credit is not just in the financial sector. The potential exporting firms themselves are in many cases in debt to foreign creditors, having borrowed, like the banks, in dollar- or yen-denominated form. Hence they have been unable to meet their debt-service obligations and thus are not creditworthy for new loans. If there were proper bankruptcy procedures that subordinated old debt to new trade-credit debt, they would become creditworthy. Hence there is a desperate need to organize such procedures, and action along these lines is now under way.

DO THE CRITICS OF THE IMF HAVE A CASE?

There are three main plausible criticisms of the IMF, and I consider arguments for and against them. In most cases the critics do have a case, but they usually ignore the other side—the trade-offs. A particularly clear and thorough exposition of the IMF point of view can be found in Fischer (1998).

Fiscal Policy

The first instinct of the IMF was for fiscal tightening. It ignored the good fiscal policies of the Asian governments. Obviously this was inappropriate and was proven to be so, given the deep slumps that developed. Subsequently the IMF modified its conditions and has—with a lag and after some criticisms—shown itself to be flexible. As is clear from what I said earlier, here is my main criticism.

But there are limits to fiscal expansion that are set by the funds available to the IMF. Furthermore, to some extent, the pressure to use these funds to bail out foreign creditors, rather than maintain domestic demand, came from the countries themselves.

Interest Rate Policy

Initially the IMF wanted high interest rates, if only for a limited period. The aim was to reverse some of the excessive depreciations that had such harmful effects on the balance sheets of domestic financial intermediaries and companies that had borrowed in dollars. This view was based on Mexican experience as well as well-known general principles. In Mexico interest rates fell after six months or so. There was talk of restoring confidence.

It seems that the exchange rate response did come in Thailand and Korea, though not Indonesia. But, arguably, the IMF underrated the adverse effects domestically of high interest rates. In any case there is a trade-off, and it cannot be ignored. Interest rate policy was thus a matter of judgment.

Inappropriate Bailouts

Here is the principal criticism coming from the U.S. Congress and right-wing opponents of the IMF in the United States. I can be brief here, as this has been much discussed. IMF funds have been used to bail out foreign lenders, primarily international banks, who lent short term and should have known the risks. The use of IMF and supplementary funds for bailing out international banks that had lent to Korean conglomerates (*chaebols*) was the reason for the large funds required in the Korean case.

There are actually two distinct criticisms here. The first is the common one, namely, that such bailouts create moral hazard, encouraging risky lending in the future. It was argued that the Mexican bailout had set a bad example. The second is the one I wish to emphasize; it follows from my earlier discussion. There is a better use for the limited funds available, namely, to finance short-term budget deficits required to avoid or minimize recessions.

But there is much to be said on the other side and, in fairness, I must say it. Contrary to what some U.S. right-wingers have been saying, governments were not bailed out but suffered severely. Nor were equity investors bailed out. Furthermore, subsequently, especially in the case of Korea, there were debt renegotiations that led to agreed reschedulings by international banks. With hindsight, these should have been initiated earlier, following the example of the 1982 debt crisis. Additionally, the mechanisms for negotiated reschedulings, and (in the case of Indonesia) the necessary information, were not easily available.

At the time of the sudden Korean crisis, it was thought that a quick response in helping Korea pay off foreign short-term creditors was needed to avoid contagion spreading worldwide. This was surely a legitimate motive of the IMF, given its international responsibilities. On the other hand, it clearly increased moral hazard in the future. On balance, I think there was a policy failure in not acting more quickly to organize reschedulings.

Another point in defense of the IMF is that governments themselves were keen to avoid default in order to preserve access to the capital market later. The initiatives for bailouts of foreign creditors came (as I understand it) primarily from the Asian governments motivated—to some extent—by this consideration. There is, again, the example of Mexico to consider. There was certainly a big bailout in that case, with no defaults or forced reschedulings. The result was that after one year capital inflow resumed.

It could be argued that in the future the Asian countries, with their high saving ratios, have no need to borrow internationally other than in the form of direct investment. They should not rely on short-term borrowing nor possibly even on long-term debt. Hence less emphasis need be placed on the potential of accessing the international capital market for short-term funds in the future. In any case, they should reschedule any short-term debts in a crisis, if necessary, unilaterally. Yet here there is also another side. It is exactly in a crisis—for example, one caused by a sharp deterioration in the terms of trade or by a political transition—that short-term borrowing is needed. If enough funds are not available from the IMF or if the IMF is too slow to act, the private capital market will have to come to the rescue. For this reason, there is much to be said for trying to preserve a reputation for not defaulting or rescheduling unilaterally.

Too Many Conditions

Some conditions are not needed for dealing with the crisis. The reforms proposed and required by the IMF may be good in themselves, and even reduce vulnerability in a future crisis. But the "Christmas tree" approach (hanging numerous conditions on the tree of conditionality) confuses the market and makes it more difficult to obtain agreement with governments. Measures to reduce cronyism, abolish monopolies, and improve "governance" in Indonesia come under this heading, as do, rather obviously, requirements of further trade liberalization or opening up the country to foreign takeovers. A strong, persuasive argument for this criticism is made by Feldstein (1998), and it is widely voiced in the Asian countries themselves.

Initially there was a tendency by the IMF to overreach in this respect. These kinds of reforms are in general desirable, but in some cases it is questionable whether a crisis is the time to implement them. Furthermore, strong long-term conditionality was justified for countries in Africa and Latin America that had a long history of low economic performance, but it is more questionable for Asian countries in which the overall growth performance has, on balance, been impressive. After all, Korea has been set up as a model for so many other developing countries. The IMF should distinguish recommendations or advice from actual conditions for obtaining emergency loans.

But there is at least one argument on the other side, and I record it for completeness. The United States and other countries that in effect underwrite the IMF or even supplement its funds cannot be expected to provide emergency loans to countries in which the funds would be wasted or misused owing to monopolies, cronyism, and so on. Surely, it might be said that all details about uses of the funds are relevant. But this cannot possibly justify some conditions.

On this matter, I have carefully gone through the Korean government's Letter of Intent of May 1998, which lists the conditions to which the government has agreed in order to gain access to IMF funds. It lists many conditions that appear appropriate. But then there are others about which one must surely wonder. There are various items concerning capital account liberalization that I discuss below. In addition there are the following: fully liberalize rules on takeovers of nonstrategic corporations by foreign investors. Phase out the import diversification program (i.e., liberalize imports further). Permit foreigners to engage in various services (security dealings, insurance, leasing, and other property-related business).

Overstatement of Structural Problems

The IMF overemphasized at the beginning, and possibly even now, the supposed structural causes of the crisis, when the severity of the crisis is explained by pre-existing euphoria followed by market panic. These structural features—for example, inadequacies of corporate governance, lack of transparency, corruption, closeness of government and business (called cronyism now)—have existed for many years and did not stand in the way of the Asian economies' successes. Admittedly, they increased the countries' vulnerability to crises, and reforms are certainly needed. As Radelet and Sachs (1998) have pointed out, the net result of that emphasis was that market expectations were affected adversely—or even more adversely than otherwise—and the market was confused by this emphasis, since the various structural reforms that were set as conditions should not necessarily be needed to restore confidence.

Would it not have been better to try to calm markets by emphasizing the positive features of these economies? Korea, in particular, had a liquidity problem because of excessive short-term borrowing but surely in a long-run sense was solvent and hence able to pay debt service provided short-term debts were rescheduled. In 1996 its ratio of total external debt to GDP was only 22 percent. I have found this criticism convincing, even though there were plenty of things wrong in these countries that should, in an ideal world, be put right.

Pushing for Further Capital Market Liberalization

Before the crisis the IMF was urging further liberalization of capital flows and, in particular, further opening up by countries to foreign direct investment. Since the crisis, it has been stressed that such opening should be carefully staged and should only take place provided appropriate prudential and other arrangements are in place. Probably the IMF position has been changing, since—as already noted—the staff of the IMF are quick learners. But as Rodrik (1998) and others have pointed out, a push for further opening up hardly makes sense at a time when the disadvantages of international borrowing—especially short-term borrowing—have become dramatically clear. One need hardly add that there are also obvious advantages of capital market opening, which I shall not go into here, and not all borrowing ends in crises.

Foreign direct investment flows have been far more stable than short-term flows, and fluctuations in direct investment have not been causes of the crisis. Extra direct investment into banking would definitely help in dealing with the effects of the crisis by helping to recapitalize banks and by making them more efficient as well as less dependent purely on local conditions. But foreign direct investment into other areas raises many issues—including nationalistic or xenophobic resistance to it for historical reasons—that are not closely connected with the crisis and its solutions, and thus not really relevant here. It is not sensible that IMF crisis programs include conditions that require further opening to such direct investment.

It is worth looking closely at the Korean letter of intent referred to above. It lists the conditions subject to which Korea gets emergency loans from the IMF. My first reaction was some surprise. Among other items, there are the following. (1) Reviewing all remaining restrictions on corporate foreign borrowing, including short-term borrowing. (2) Abolishing restrictions on foreign ownership of land and real estate. (3) Permitting equity investment in nonlisted companies. (4) Eliminating aggregate ceiling on foreign investment in Korean equities.

Requirements (2) to (4) may or may not be beneficial for Korea if implemented, though it is hard to see how they would either help to resolve the crisis or prevent a future one. It is item (1) which—if I have interpreted it correctly—amazes me. The crisis in Korea essentially resulted from excessive short-term international borrowing by Korean *chaebols* (conglomerates) or by Korean banks that then on-lent to the *chaebols*. Their ratios of debt to equity, especially short-term debt, were far too high. This is well known. The remaining restrictions cannot have been very effective, but if this condition means that they should possibly be removed, then I am at least surprised. But perhaps a review implies a possibility of tightening restrictions?

Pursuit of U.S. Interest

Certain conditions in the Korean program (and possibly in others)—notably those summarized above—clearly reflect the interests of U.S. exporters, investors, and especially financial firms. They have been clamoring to get into the somewhat restricted Korean market. These proposals have thus become suspect. Perhaps their implementation would actually be in the Korean interest (which, from a long-term point of view certainly applies to further trade liberalization and probably also to allowing more equity investment), but they should then take the form of advice and not "conditionality."

One might also reflect whether it is really in the long-term U.S. interest that such conditions are included in programs when they might intensify anti-Americanism. It will be a subject for Ph.D. dissertations in future years to discover the political and decision-making processes behind these conditions. One has to remember that the IMF is governed by its executive board, not by its staff. The governments are the owners of the IMF, and the largest owner is the United States.

I believe in always putting forward the other side, so perhaps one could make the following realistic argument in favor of these conditions. Korea has depended on U.S. financial support and hence congressional approval, so it is only realistic for it to accept measures that favor U.S. interest groups that will help Korea get these funds. One must remember the dramatic emergency situation at the end of 1997, and the size of the funds required for Korea. Korea had no choice but to accept IMF conditions, and the IMF had no choice but to try and please these U.S. interest groups in view of its dependence on Congress for new funding. A matter of political realism!

THE SHORT TERM VERSUS THE LONG TERM

Initially, the IMF was focused on the medium and long term, meaning a period of three years or more. It wanted to get the fundamentals right, to bring about structural reforms in the financial and corporate sectors, and to maintain the cautious fiscal and monetary policies that have served the Asian countries so well in the past. It wanted to reduce the vulnerabilities of the countries to a future crisis, and perhaps avoid one altogether. It wanted to make resource allocation more efficient. It was much concerned with restoring confidence in the markets, so that capital inflow and investment would resume and exchange rates would rebound. But all this would inevitably take time.

I believe that if the current IMF conditions and recommendations, as well as World Bank advice, are followed and the countries can survive the short term, they are likely to be better off than otherwise; they will be more prepared to deal with future shocks and surprises—for example, by having proper bankruptcy laws and arrangements for rescheduling debt. One can have doubts about some of the IMF conditions, but broadly this is true. This does not mean that there would not be shocks again and that the IMF (or anyone else) will ever forecast such shocks adequately.

The problem is the "short term," which currently looks like lasting more than three years, possibly much longer. Everything hinges on when the export boom— if there is going to be one—begins. The issue is how short the short term will be. The political and social consequences of a prolonged and severe recession can in themselves damage the long term, affecting attitudes toward markets, leading to increased xenophobia, and to a reversion to inward-looking policies.

Yet short-term remedies that can moderate or avoid a prolonged recession are not easy. Restoring the availability of credit by cleaning up the banking system (a need much emphasized by the IMF) takes time. Lowering interest rates involves the trade-off I have discussed. Thus the main way of moderating or avoiding deep recession in the short run is through Keynesian fiscal policy. And the limits here are set by the availability of finance. At the minimum, the limited funds available from the IMF and from IMF-dominated packages (including World Bank, Asian Development Fund, and supplementary funds from the United States, Japan, and other countries) should be used not for rescuing foreign creditors—nor for financing capital flight—but for financing compensating fiscal expansion.

CONCLUSION

It is obvious to me that the IMF is needed, desperately needed, in situations like the Asian crisis. There is no need to establish a new organization, and it would be foolish—as some U.S. right-wingers propose—to abolish it. The IMF should be provided with adequate resources to cope with major crises. These resources should not be used primarily to rescue international banks and other financial institutions—nor the owners and managers of domestic institutions in crisis countries—but to provide temporary relief to allow for necessary adjustments without major recessions or adverse effects on the mass of the population, and especially the poorest. Of course, funds will inevitably be limited.

The Asian crisis, by comparison with the 1982 world debt crisis, the 1994 Mexican crisis, the 1998 Russian crisis, and the 1999 Brazilian crisis, has been unique. It involved almost wholly private sector borrowing and lending. And it affected countries whose economic histories since the 1960s have been exceptional success stories. This uniqueness may explain why IMF advice and "conditionality" in the early stages of the crisis have not been as defensible as in the other crises episodes listed above. But, as I have stressed, there are indeed difficult trade-offs.

II

Southeast Asia Comparative Case Studies

4

Thailand: Episodic Reform, Regulatory Incapacity, and Financial Crisis

James LoGerfo and Gabriella R. Montinola

After committing over $23 billion in forward markets to defend the *baht*, on July 2, 1997, the Bank of Thailand surrendered and watched helplessly as the currency plummeted in value by nearly 20 percent. The Thai stock market staged a brief rally on the news of the float, but then turned south and closed the year with a loss of over 50 percent. How did Thailand, apparently one of the most successful "emerging markets" in the early 1990s, end up in 1997 with a melting currency, a collapsing equity market, and an economy sustained only by an IMF life support program?

Initial explanations have tended to lay the blame for the recent crisis on the adoption of inappropriate macroeconomic and financial sector policies.[1] In particular, they fault the government's commitment to maintaining a pegged exchange rate while liberalizing the capital account and the government's implicit guarantee to bail out ailing financial institutions. The pegged exchange rate was detrimental because it minimized currency risk and encouraged financial actors to borrow and lend in foreign currencies more than they otherwise would have. The currency peg also left the government with fewer tools with which to control the money supply once capital started flowing into the country. The guarantee to bail out financial firms contributed to the crisis by minimizing the expected costs of poor investments, thereby encouraging excessively risky behavior.

We do not dispute these economic explanations; indeed, we show in this chapter that the recent experience of Thailand is consistent with them. However, we analyze not only the recent financial crisis but also one that occurred during 1983–1986, and we find that the earlier crisis occurred under significantly different macroeconomic circumstances. We find that common to both the 1983–1986 and 1997 crises is a factor not sufficiently emphasized in other works: the Thai state's lack of capacity in financial sector supervision. We suggest that this weakness was the crucial condition underlying both crises.

Why has the Thai state, so highly praised for its performance in other economic realms, failed so miserably in the realm of financial oversight? We suggest that the inconsistency in Thai officials' capabilities was the result of an often contested yet relatively stable bargain between established financial industry actors and a succession of political leaders. This bargain gave technocrats relative autonomy in areas such as interest and exchange rate policy. But it provided them with little effective power to regulate the financial sector, despite an increasingly strong legal basis to do so. We show below that both the 1983–1986 and 1997 crises resulted from a typical pattern of conflict between entrenched firms, on one hand, and technocrats backed by reformist political leaders, on the other, as the former sought to evade financial sector supervision with the support of their political patrons, and the latter attempted to bypass dominant financial actors in order to foster an industry that would better serve the country's developmental needs.

This repetitive pattern of outcomes occurred because the Thai state has been more permeable to the influence of concentrated interest groups than to dispersed interest groups, especially when highly lucrative, particularistic goods are at stake. Pressures on the state apparatus to bend rules for favored clients have persisted regardless of political regime. Mobilization against powerful financial actors by dispersed interest groups has been episodic and insufficient to generate comprehensive reform and sustained financial sector supervision. Factionalism within the armed forces and a fragmented political system has meant, under both authoritarian and democratic rule, a concentrated social force such as finance capital has been able to advance its interests to the detriment of more diffuse groups.

ECONOMIC POLICIES LEADING TO THE 1997 COLLAPSE OF THE *BAHT*

Poor macroeconomic policy was a crucial part of the 1997 financial crisis, and arguably the most damaging policy was liberalization of the capital account through the creation of the Bangkok International Banking Facility (BIBF). The BIBF was an offshore banking facility proposed by the Bank of Thailand (BOT) as a response to changes in the country's domestic and international political economy. The facility opened the floodgates to a river of foreign capital that too liberally watered the projects of local entrepreneurs, ultimately drowning the currency and the overall economy. Understanding the crisis thus requires analyzing the origins of the BIBF, the context in which it emerged, and its impact on the financial system and the economy.

The creation of an offshore banking facility was formally proposed by the BOT in 1990 as conflicts in Indochina appeared to be moving toward a peaceful resolution (*Nukul Commission Report* [hereafter *NCR*] 13; *Bangkok Bank Monthly*

Review [hereafter *BBMR*] November 1992, 8).[2] The Soviet Union had been scaling back assistance to Vietnam and Laos, its client states in Southeast Asia. This had the secondary effect of undermining Vietnam's ability to prop up the embattled regime it had installed in Cambodia. In need of external support, and aware of the relative success of economic liberalization in China under Deng Xiaoping, Vietnam, Laos, and Cambodia began to loosen socialist controls and open up to foreign capital. Meanwhile, Burma, which was on the verge of economic collapse in 1988, initiated a similar program of reform.

Located in the center of the Southeast Asian mainland and economically more developed than its neighbors, Thailand saw an opportunity to play the regional economic hegemon and to channel foreign capital into the newly liberalizing economies. Accordingly, the incumbent Chatchai administration launched a program "to turn battlefields into marketplaces" and deepen Thailand's trade, investment, and diplomatic ties with Burma and Indochina (*BBMR*, April 1989, 172–175). The BIBF was proposed in part to advance Thailand's bid for regional economic hegemony as these public and private sector initiatives were under way.

Meanwhile, fueled by surging exports and huge capital inflows, the Thai economy had been growing rapidly in the second half of the 1980s (see table 4.1). Runaway growth, however, placed tremendous strains on Thailand's long-neglected physical and human infrastructure (*BBMR*, April 1989, 155–165). The vast improvements necessary, estimated in 1992 to reach 7 trillion *baht*, would somehow have to be financed (*Far Eastern Economic Review* [hereafter *FEER*], 9 July 1992, 49). Domestic resources appeared insufficient to finance so many large projects. Concern at the BOT over continued access to foreign finance to underwrite such highly capital-intensive infrastructure projects was a second factor motivating the establishment of the BIBF (*BBMR*, November 1992, 8).[3]

Thus in the context of the times, the creation of an offshore banking facility appeared to make sense. The BIBF would resolve two pressing issues with a single stroke: it would ensure continued access to foreign capital to fund future economic growth, and it would enable Thailand to become the financial hub for mainland Southeast Asia. But given the state of Thailand's asset markets and financial system in the late 1980s, the wisdom of capital market liberalization was less clear. The financial system was just recovering from the severe crisis of 1983–1986. The booming economy helped restore tattered balance sheets, but a number of financial institutions remained weak. Aggressive bank and finance company lending in the context of full-throttle economic growth and ample liquidity was inflating a bubble in the real estate market. Stock market manipulation was rampant. Disaster in the early 1990s was averted more by luck than by skill. An economic slowdown in 1991 due to the Gulf War and a recession in the developed world cooled the feverish pace of property construction, allowing demand to begin catching up with supply. However, problems of massive overbuilding in the real estate sector, ballooning levels of nonperforming loans held by banks and finance companies, and

Table 4.1   Key Indicators of the Thai Economy, 1970–1996

Year	GDP Growth	DFI (US$m)	Exports (US$m)	External Debt/ GDP	Inflation	Current Account/ GDP	Exchange Rate	Budget Deficit/ GDP
1970	6.6	48	710	10.6	0.8	−3.5	20.9	—
1971	5.0	39	827	10.8	0.4	−2.4	20.9	—
1972	4.1	68	1039	11.2	4.8	−0.6	20.9	−4.8
1973	9.9	77	1527	8.5	15.6	−0.4	20.6	−3.2
1974	4.4	189	2402	8.5	24.3	−0.6	20.4	0.1
1975	4.8	22	2162	9.1	5.3	−4.1	20.4	−2.0
1976	9.4	79	2950	9.5	3.8	−2.6	20.4	−4.9
1977	9.9	106	3451	11.7	7.6	−5.5	20.4	−3.2
1978	10.4	50	3996	12.6	7.9	−4.8	20.3	−3.6
1979	5.3	51	5207	16.0	9.9	−7.6	20.4	−3.7
1980	4.8	187	6369	21.1	19.7	−6.4	20.5	−4.9
1981	6.3	288	6849	25.1	12.7	−7.4	21.7	−3.6
1982	4.1	189	6797	28.3	5.2	−2.8	23.0	−6.5
1983	7.3	348	6275	28.1	3.8	−7.3	23.0	−4.0
1984	7.1	400	7279	31.0	0.9	−5.1	23.5	−3.5
1985	3.5	162	7056	39.2	2.4	−4.1	27.1	−5.4
1986	4.9	261	8786	38.3	1.9	0.6	26.3	−4.5
1987	9.5	182	11629	35.8	2.5	−0.7	25.7	−2.3
1988	13.2	1081	15902	28.9	3.8	−2.8	25.3	0.7
1989	12.2	1726	19976	26.8	5.4	−3.7	25.7	2.9
1990	10.0	2302	23002	29.2	6.0	−6.0	25.6	4.5
1991	8.6	1847	28324	33.8	5.7	−7.7	25.3	4.7
1992	8.2	1979	34473	33.7	4.1	−5.7	25.5	4.2
1993	8.6	—	—	40.8	3.4	−5.1	25.5	2.6
1994	8.9	—	—	42.6	5.1	−5.6	25.1	2.1
1995	8.7	—	—	47.8	5.8	−8.1	25.2	2.0
1996	5.5	—	—	47.7	5.9	−8.1	25.6	2.6

Sources: Corbett and Vines 1998; Jansen 1997, 114; Parnell 1996, 35–36.

excessive stock market speculation would soon return with a vengeance once the spigot of foreign capital had been opened by the BIBF.

The government officially announced the establishment of the BIBF in September 1992, and the facility opened for business in March 1993. The central bank granted BIBF licenses to forty-seven banks: all fifteen of Thailand's domestic commercial banks, twelve of the fourteen foreign banks operating in Thailand at that time, and twenty new foreign institutions. Tax incentives offered to the forty-seven banks included a cut in the corporate tax rate from 30 percent to 10 percent, a reduction in the withholding tax on foreign-currency loans to Thai customers from 15 percent to 10 percent ("out-in" transactions), and a complete exemption from withholding taxes on foreign-currency loans to clients outside

Thailand ("out-out" transactions). The BOT thus structured the tax regime to encourage out-out transactions, in accordance with their goal of using the BIBF first and foremost to position Thailand at the center of regional capital flows rather than to bring in foreign capital for local needs. Nonetheless, at the facility's inauguration in 1993, observers were predicting that the vast majority of the overseas loans would be extended to Thai customers.

Overseas borrowing had increased significantly in the late 1970s and early 1980s, but it was the Thai state, not the private sector, that incurred this debt. By 1989, the level of foreign debt to GDP was still manageable at 27 percent (see table 4.1), and a substantial share was owed by the public sector (Dixon 1996, 32–37; Akrasanee et al. 1993, 43). With capital account liberalization, Thai corporations quickly tapped into new sources of capital overseas, issuing dollar-denominated bonds and taking out low-interest foreign currency loans to pay off higher-interest lines of credit extended by domestic commercial banks. Faced with this increased competition, domestic banks came under pressure to borrow from the BIBF themselves to lower their own cost of capital and bring down their lending rates (*FEER*, 18 November 1993, 92). The result was an explosion of private-sector foreign debt. In March 1994, one year after its inauguration, BIBF loans stood at 263 billion *baht*, or about $11 billion at prevailing exchange rates. By March 1996 total BIBF loans had nearly quadrupled to about $43 billion.[4] Much of the foreign debt was short-term in nature, and a large share was channeled to the property sector.

Flush with cheap credit, real estate developers built new residential and commercial space at a furious pace, adding a huge volume of new supply to a property market that was still struggling to absorb the construction binge of the late 1980s. Less than two years after the creation of the BIBF, the property market was glutted. The oversupply constricted cash flows even as interest rates began rising in 1995. Finance companies were especially aggressive in granting loans to the real estate sector. They underwrote many real estate projects, and when excess supply and climbing interest rates left property developers struggling to make interest payments to domestic banks, finance companies provided developers with working capital loans. By the middle of 1996, 24 percent of loans granted by finance companies were held by real estate developers, and 13 percent of all loans made by banks and finance companies combined were real estate credits (Cristensen and Bamrungchatudorn 1996).[5]

The flood of capital washing in and the economic growth that came in its wake initially papered over weaknesses in the financial system, such as the loose lending practices of numerous financial institutions, their tendency to overlend to the real estate sector, and the central bank's seeming inability to exercise effective regulatory control. However, the problems of one particular bank, the Bangkok Bank of Commerce (BBC), could not be brushed under the carpet. A BOT examination of BBC books in 1991 revealed nonperforming loans of 18.2 billion *baht*, or 26.7 percent of total assets, far worse than the banking industry average of 7.4

percent. The BOT immediately ordered a capital increase of 800 million *baht* to be carried out in 1992 and required the BBC to draw up a plan for further increases through 1994. The modest sanctions imposed on the BBC did nothing to discourage bank management from excessively risky lending; the bank's nonperforming loans continued to mount. Moreover, the apparent commitment of BOT officials to propping up extremely weak institutions created a moral hazard problem.[6] Assuming they had little to lose should their investments fail, other financial actors began to engage in riskier behavior than they would have without the government's implicit guarantee to bail them out.

Serious strains on the system from capital account liberalization first became evident in the realm of monetary policy. The central bank fought valiantly to maintain control over the money supply as foreign capital poured in (and sometimes fled back out), but the paucity of instruments available made an already difficult task nearly impossible. Determined to maintain a fixed exchange rate, the BOT began conducting open-market operations to sterilize inflows and prevent the *baht* from appreciating (*FEER Asia 1995 Yearbook,* 217). The operations failed to control the growth of the money supply, so the central bank began to raise interest rates. But higher interest rates in the absence of a foreign exchange rate adjustment had the perverse effect of attracting yet more yield-hungry overseas capital. Upward pressure on the level of inflation continued, and the current account deficit in 1995 and 1996 ballooned to an unsustainable 8 percent.

The BOT's commitment to an exchange rate of about 25 *baht* to the dollar had another perverse effect; it created a second moral hazard problem that contributed to the crisis. The perception of a virtual absence of currency risk, founded on the *baht*'s nominal stability since 1985 (see table 4.1) and the government's strong fiscal and foreign reserves positions, invited private actors to ignore the risks of borrowing or lending in foreign currencies.

To make matters worse, the economy began to slow in 1996, dragged down by a weakening export sector. A cyclical decline in global demand for electronic products contributed to Thailand's weak export performance. Rising real wages in the country's labor-intensive industries and increased competition for export markets from other developing countries undercut Thailand's position in areas of traditional strength, such as textiles, garments, and footwear, while progress up the value chain faltered (Doner and Ramsay 1999).

Thailand's deteriorating fundamentals started attracting the international financial community's attention in 1996. Moody's downgraded Thai sovereign debt due to the country's persistently high current account deficits, and the first speculative attacks on the *baht* occurred late that year. The financial system began to collapse in the first half of 1997, dragged down by the weight of excessive foreign debt, failing property developers, and a slowing economy. The first visible crack appeared in February 1997, when Somprasong Land missed payment on a Eurobond issue. Many financial institutions, including Finance One, Thailand's largest finance company, soon started slipping into the vortex. Regulatory authorities scurried to arrange a rescue, but to no avail. Officials spent 400 billion *baht* in the first six months of 1997 trying to prop up failing banks and finance companies.

Meanwhile, the buzzards circled. Speculators launched attacks on the currency, betting that the yawning current account deficit, the crumbling financial system, and the weakening economy would ultimately undermine the state's ability to defend the *baht*. They were right. On July 2, 1997, after committing nearly all of the country's foreign currency reserves in an attempt to maintain the currency, and with the central bank nearly broke from the effort to prop up bankrupt financial institutions, BOT officials finally waved the white flag and floated the *baht*. The devaluation that quickly ensued pushed many financial institutions, already saddled with shaky dollar-denominated loans, into insolvency.

Summing up, then, the crisis was in part the result of the policy to launch the BIBF in the context of a pegged exchange rate. Had the BOT allowed the currency to float while it was liberalizing the capital account, imbalances may well have emerged, but the kind of meltdown that occurred in 1997 might have been avoided. With a floating exchange rate, the inrush of foreign capital, which was creating strong demand for *baht*, would have driven up the value of the local currency. If monetary authorities had permitted the appreciation to occur, exports would have become less competitive, imports would have increased, the economy would have slowed, the demand for credit would have declined, and the attractiveness of Thailand to foreign actors with capital to lend or invest would have diminished. At least until 1995, however, monetary authorities appeared to agree that the country should maintain the *baht*'s peg. They believed that a stable *baht* was a necessary condition for investment and for the continued success of the country's export-oriented strategy. They were also concerned that a strong *baht* would alter the structure of imports from that of raw materials and capital goods to consumer goods, creating a consumption pattern similar to that of Mexico before its 1994 crisis.[7]

The essentially dollar-pegged currency, together with the state's support of the clearly failing BBC and its apparent willingness to turn a blind eye to violations at numerous other financial institutions, created perverse incentives that contributed to the crisis. The pegged exchange rate minimized currency risk and resulted in unprecedented levels of foreign borrowing and significant distortions in asset markets. Supporting the BBC encouraged other bankers to follow suit and engage in progressively risky behavior. But neither the launching of the BIBF nor the commitment to a pegged exchange rate and support of the BBC were sufficient conditions for the crisis. Throughout the early 1990s, Thai macroeconomic authorities were well aware of the potential for excessively risky lending that their policies could generate. As we show below, they attempted to minimize the negative consequences of these policies through credit limits and increased capital requirements, but to little avail. If the BOT had been able to enforce its supervisory powers over the financial sector, the crisis may have been averted or significantly mitigated.

THE CRUCIAL CONDITION UNDERLYING THE CRISIS:
LACK OF STATE CAPACITY

Thai authorities' inability to supervise the financial industry was evident in the period leading up to the 1997 collapse of the *baht*. In 1993, the Bank of Thailand set stringent limits on the growth of credit to the real estate sector (*BBMR,* December 1993, 20; *FEER,* 17 August 1995, 51). While commercial banks exercised some restraint in this area, finance companies virtually threw money at the property sector. In 1993–1995, real estate loans grew by annual rates of roughly 35–45 percent. In 1994, the BOT set a target of 21 percent for consumer loan growth. By July 1994, however, outstanding loans were already up 24 percent (*FEER Asia 1995 Yearbook,* 218; *FEER,* 6 October 1994, 76). The central bank also imposed restrictions on overall growth of credit, but these were violated as well. In the first seven months of 1995, commercial bank credit was up 30 percent year-over-year, well in excess of the BOT's 24 percent limit (*FEER,* 28 September 1995, 71). Finally, in 1995, the BOT introduced measures to slow the inflow of foreign funds, but once again to no avail (*FEER Asia 1996 Yearbook,* 218). The value of BIBF loans more than doubled in 1995, increasing from 469 billion *baht* to 1.033 billion *baht.*[8]

The BOT not only failed to rein in credit growth but also had difficulty detecting or punishing more troubling violations. Senior management of major financial institutions engaged in a range of excessively risky and illegal practices, many of which came to light only after they had effectively run their companies into the ground. Massive malfeasance at the BBC, involving among others a number of members of Parliament, ended up costing the state 60 billion *baht* prior to the onset of the crisis (*Economist,* 15 August 1998, 55). Total bad debt held by the BBC at the time of its nationalization in 1998 reached 160 billion *baht* (*Bridge News,* 4 February 1999). At Finance One, once the nation's largest finance company, top executives were accused of misappropriating 2.1 billion *baht* from the company's coffers. Former managers at Sitca Investment Finance & Securities, another major finance company, apparently siphoned at least 2.26 billion *baht* out of the firm between 1994 and 1997. The Central Bank accused top executives of General Finance, one of whom was a commerce minister, of illegally granting loans totaling 338 million *baht* without sufficient collateral. It discovered more than one billion *baht* in damage arising from poor lending practices by company managers. Democrat Party MPs and their relatives were accused of obtaining improper loans from two other finance companies that were shut down for insolvency (*Bangkok Post,* 27 May, 21 August, 27 August, and 30 September 1998). The number and size of the improprieties, along with the central bank's difficulties enforcing credit growth limits, suggest that regulatory authorities were incapable of overseeing the financial sector.

An emphasis on the problem of financial sector supervision is also warranted when one considers Thailand's financial history. As mentioned earlier, the country had a financial crisis that started in 1983, less than a decade and a half before the 1997 debacle. This earlier crisis first materialized in the nonbank financial sector but soon spread to the banking sector. Fifteen finance companies were eventually shut down and another thirty-two companies were placed directly or indirectly under government control. Five banks, whose combined assets accounted for 25 percent of total commercial bank assets, required government support. Three of them were restructured by the government (Johnston 1991, 248–249).

Shortly before the 1980s crisis, several macroeconomic indicators were signaling problems as they did before the 1997 crisis. As table 4.1 shows, current account deficits rose to dangerous levels, growth faltered, and inflation increased rapidly. Moreover, although the country's exchange rate regime was amended a number of times during 1978–1984 (Warr and Nidhiprabha 1996, 85–86; *BBMR,* February 1979, 71–72), the changes were minor. The country effectively operated under a fixed exchange rate, as it did in the 1990s. Thus one might at first attribute the earlier crisis to the same macroeconomic policy errors that were made in the 1990s.

However, in contrast to the decade of seemingly relentless capital inflows before the 1997 crisis, the economy in the late 1970s and early 1980s alternated between periods of tight money conditions and excessive liquidity (Jansen 1997). Two years before finance companies started collapsing, inflation and the current account deficit had already started declining. Moreover, capital inflows as a percentage of GDP were also much lower in the 1980s than in the 1990s. Inflows peaked in 1980 at under 8 percent of GDP while inflows peaked in 1991 at close to 12 percent of GDP. Nor did the *baht* appreciate in real terms as markedly in the early 1980s as it did before the 1997 crisis. From 1976 to 1982, the real value of the *baht* appreciated by less than 5 percent. In contrast, the *baht* appreciated by almost 50 percent during 1985–1994. Thus the macroeconomic policy-induced crisis model, which attributes the 1997 debacle to the country's pegged exchange rate and monetary authorities' consequent loss of macroeconomic control, does not fit the 1980s crisis well. The country operated under an effectively fixed exchange regime, but authorities did not lose macroeconomic control.[9]

Moral hazards were also less likely culprits in the 1980s crisis. Although the country's exchange rate was effectively fixed, confidence in the government's ability to defend the *baht* could not have been a factor underpinning excessively risky foreign borrowing. Lack of confidence in the value of the *baht* was evident in public statements by bankers, early repayments of foreign currency-denominated loans, and periodically escalating risk premiums for forward exchange contracts (*FEER,* 21 September 1979, 100; 10 September 1982, 62; 25 April 1985, 95–98; *BBMR,* August 1981, 305–308). Bankers' concerns were not unfounded; the *baht* was devalued by almost 10 percent in 1981, prior to the crisis, and again by 15 percent in 1984 (Warr and Nidhiprabha 1996, 85–86). This can be contrasted with the long-standing stability of the *baht* prior to 1997 (see table 4.1). Also questionable is the notion that official guarantees to bail out every financial institution may have resulted in excessively risky lending because four years before the crisis, the government provided a clear signal that not all financial firms would be bailed out. In 1979, Raja Finance, a company whose stock was among the best sellers in the stock exchange, was liquidated by the BOT. Holders of Raja promissory notes were paid only 20 percent of their notes' face value (*BBMR,* December 1979, 448–457).

If macroeconomic policies and moral hazards were not substantial problems in the 1980s, what led to the crisis? An unfavorable external environment—an oil price shock, a decline in commodity prices, the global recession and consequent interest rate hikes—likely contributed to the failure of financial institutions (Johnston 1991; Nijithaworn and Weerakitpanich 1987; Leeahtam 1991, 22–23; Jansen 1997, 81). But further examination of the 1980s crisis points to a factor that was also present in the 1990s: lack of state capacity in the area of financial sector supervision.

The state's weakness vis-à-vis the financial industry was evident in its inability to effect genuine compliance with the 1979 Commercial Bank Act (CBA), which called for substantial capital divestiture to reduce concentration of ownership in the financial sector. Most banks had complied with the letter of the 1979 CBA by 1984, but many former shareholders avoided reduction in their control by using other people or their related firms to buy shares in the banks they originally controlled as individuals (Chaiyasoot 1993, 237–238; Cristensen et al. 1997).[10] And despite clear restrictions on lending to associated companies, most institutions that experienced difficulties were found to have lent heavily to related interests (*FEER,* 20 October 1983, 96–97; 13 September 1984, 67–68; 25 February 1988, 82; 22 January 1987).

In sum, external conditions may have contributed to the 1980s crisis, as inappropriate macroeconomic policies and moral hazards contributed to the 1997 debacle. But if the state had had the capacity to better regulate the financial industry, both crises could have been prevented. What explains this critical weakness within the Thai state? The issue is striking because Thai technocrats have been highly praised in the recent past for their policy performance. (See table 4.1 for indicators of Thailand's economic performance.) Scholars such as Muscat (1994), Campos and Root (1996), and Cristensen et al. (1997), to name just a few, argue that the Ministry of Finance (MOF) and the BOT engineered Thailand's stable macroeconomic environment, which was critical to its consistent growth rates over the past decades. The ostensible success of Thailand's restructuring efforts in the early 1980s is also often presented as a sign of Thai technocrats' competence and capacity. How could such respected macroeconomic managers have failed so miserably?

Not long after the 1997 collapse of the *baht,* the government appointed a commission headed by former BOT governor Nukul Prachuabmoh to determine the causes of the crisis. The commission laid a good deal of the blame on the decline in quality of BOT officials over the four or five years prior to the crisis (*NCR,* 169).[11] However, as we noted above, Thailand experienced a financial crisis in the early 1980s, when BOT officials and Thai monetary authorities in general appear to have been highly respected. This suggests that, even without deterioration of the quality of BOT officials, the 1990s crisis is likely to have occurred.

Doner and Laothamatas (1994, 445) provide a possible answer to the inconsistency between monetary authorities' apparent competence and recent weakness. They point out that the Thai government has been more successful in macroeconomic stabilization than in trade and sectoral reforms, and that this was due to an implicit bargain between state officials, politicians, and private sector actors. We suggest that the relationship between the state and finance industry is no different from that between the state and other economic sectors. That is, Thai officials often had the capacity to promote macroeconomic stability because it was a public good desired by the financial industry.[12] But they were weak in the area of financial sector supervision, where gains to financial actors were particularistic.

In the following section, we discuss the political and institutional factors that obstructed Thai monetary officials' ability to supervise the financial sector. We start with the legal bases of the government's authority over the financial sector. We then discuss the conditions that limited the government's attempts to ensure compliance.

EXPLANATION OF THE POLICY REGIME: POLITICAL INSTITUTIONS PERMEABLE TO CONCENTRATED INTEREST GROUPS

The government's authority to supervise the financial sector was first established with two laws: the Bank of Thailand Act, which created the central bank in 1942, and a Commercial Bank Act (CBA), adopted in 1945. The 1945 CBA was amended in 1962 to increase the government's power over banks. In 1972, Revolutionary Council Announcement 58 extended the government's authority to cover nonbank financial institutions (Bank of Thailand 1992, 99–100, 180). The legal bases for supervising commercial banks and finance companies have been strengthened over time, in large part due to financial crises. In 1979, after the collapse of Raja Finance, the government adopted a more comprehensive CBA (BE 2522). The act required dilution of any single individual's control over a bank, limited holdings of banks in other companies, imposed tighter restrictions on banks' transactions with their own directors, and increased penalties on interlocking directorships between banks. The 1979 CBA also gave BOT inspectors the right to enter a bank's premises when they suspected an offense, the right to demand cooperation from banks' external auditors, and the power to demand that a bank write off as worthless any assets that were found to be unrecoverable. The act also gave the MOF the authority to recommend that a bank either dismiss its directors or officers or see its license revoked. To strengthen the government's powers over the nonbank financial sector, a similarly comprehensive Act on the Undertaking of Finance Business, Securities Business, and Credit Foncier Business (BE 2522) was also enacted in 1979 (Johnston 1991, 252–253).

In the wake of the 1980s crisis, the regulatory framework was yet again strengthened through three emergency decrees (BE 2528, BE 2526, BE 2528) adopted from 1983–1985. The increasingly stringent regulations on financial institutions were designed primarily to ensure the stability of the banking system. Yet they failed to avert crises. Four years after the 1979 bank and finance company acts were passed, the financial sector was in serious distress, as already noted. And despite the government's substantial powers to intervene in the financial sector as specified in the 1983–1985 decrees, the 1997 crisis occurred. Before the last of the emergency decrees was passed in 1985, a BOT official remarked, "We could order a bank to improve on any shadowy operations; but if it refuses, there is nothing much we could do apart from imposing nominal fines. . . . The [present] law doesn't allow us to remove unqualified bank directors or senior executives" (*FEER,* 18 July 1985, 82–83).

In fact, the 1979 act specified that the MOF could use the threat to revoke a bank's license in order to effect removal of directors or officers. But neither the 1979 act nor its 1985 refinement has prevented banking crises. The power to revoke licenses or stop operations has tended to be implemented too late. When crises occurred, the immediate cause invariably included violation or evasion of extant regulations, in particular, rules against lending to related interests.

Financial authorities have had difficulty ensuring compliance with rules against "relationship banking" because they impair the interests of the most powerful actors in the sector: commercial banks. Most banks were established by Thai-Chinese business families to help finance their own trading operations, and they have become the cores of large conglomerates of nonfinancial concerns. In 1987, the Sophonpanich family of Bangkok Bank controlled forty-two domestic nonfinancial firms; the Lamsam of Thai Farmers Bank and the Tejapaibul family with majority stakes in three banks each controlled thirty-three nonfinancial firms (Akira 1989, 285–297).

The banking community has been able to resist complying with regulations inconsistent with its economic interests because of its privileged place in Thailand's political economy. This position is based on three interrelated conditions: (1) the structure of the financial system, (2) the concentration of assets and ownership within the banking sector, and (3) the presence of a strong representative organization, the Thai Bankers Association (TBA).

Although the Thai financial system consists of a wide range of financial institutions, it has long been dominated by the commercial banking sector. In 1970, commercial banks held 79.6 percent of total assets in the financial sector. In 1990, commercial banks still held a substantial 71.4 percent of total assets. The growth of nonbank financial companies did little to undermine the dominance of banks. Not long after the government began licensing companies in 1972, the industry had 114 finance and/or securities firms, but these companies held only 14 percent of total assets through the 1990s (Robinson 1991, 21; Chaiyasoot 1995, 166). For most of the period, growth of assets and deposits of commercial banks and finance companies was positively correlated, suggesting that the organized financial sector as a whole was tapping into funds previously held in unorganized money markets (Johnston 1991, 240–242). In addition, 40 percent of finance companies were backed by commercial banks (*BBMR,* November 1984, 440–449); and nineteen out of the top twenty finance companies in terms of assets were majority-owned by banks or families that owned banks (*Business in Thailand* [hereafter *BIT*], July 1974; Skully 1984, 329). By 1979, four families had shareholdings in 89 out of the 114 finance companies (Hewison 1989, 181). The establishment of the Stock Exchange of Thailand (SET) in 1975 also failed to challenge the primacy of commercial banks within the financial system. As late as 1986, banks mobilized 70.7 percent of total savings in the country, while the stock market mobilized only 8.6 percent (Chaiyasoot 1995, 165–166).

The banking community is powerful not only because most resources in the country are intermediated through commercial banks or their affiliated finance companies but also because assets and ownership within the sector, which includes twenty-nine banks, are highly concentrated. Since 1978, fourteen of the twenty-nine banks have been foreign-owned, but they have held only about 5 percent of total bank assets. Among the fifteen domestic banks, concentration is extremely high. Three banks, Bangkok Bank, Thai Farmers Bank, and Krung Thai Bank, have consistently topped the list, together accounting for 55–65 percent of total assets held by domestic banks.[13] Moreover, as mentioned above, despite the divestiture laws stipulated in the 1979 CBA, most banks continue to be controlled by one or a few families.

The concentrated nature of resources within the industry provides bank owners with substantial bargaining power vis-à-vis the government. This is particularly true when the government is most in need of funds, as in 1975–1987, when official concessional loans became scarce and the government began running fiscal deficits. Before 1975, 90 percent of all public and publicly guaranteed debt was financed with official development assistance. By 1980, that proportion had declined to 31 percent; and public debt had to be financed through commercial bank loans, bond market issues, and suppliers' credits at commercial rates (Jansen 1997, 63). In the 1979 draft budget, for example, 40 percent of the proposed borrowing was expected to come from domestic commercial banks (*FEER,* 1 September 1978, 79–80).

The fungibility of the banking community's resources has proven to be a great asset in the country's constantly changing political environment. In the last three decades, Thailand has seen at least seven regime changes:

- a military coup in 1971 followed by two years of military government
- a student-led revolt in 1973 followed by a caretaker government appointed by the king

- democratic rule from 1975 to 1976
- a return to military rule in 1976
- a military coup in 1977 followed by the establishment of a new set of military rulers
- a return to democratic rule in 1979
- a military coup in 1991 followed by a caretaker government appointed by the king
- a public uprising and democratic rule from 1992 to the present time

During periods of military dominance, the banking community protected its interests by accepting military officials as shareholders and/or directors. The officers who ruled from 1963 to 1973, Thanom Kittikachorn and Praphat Charusathian, were involved in 137 firms and had deposits of 151 million *baht* in commercial banks (Akira 1989, 263–264). Not only was Praphat named president of Bangkok Bank, the largest bank in all of Southeast Asia, but his family was a major shareholder in four banks, including Bangkok Bank. Before the 1973 revolution ushering in democratic rule, twelve out of the existing sixteen domestic banks had at least one military official on their board of directors. Eight banks had military officials as major shareholders. The armed forces itself held a majority of shares in the Thai Military Bank; the remaining 5,000 shares were distributed among personnel. In 1973, when democracy was installed, the need for military protection waned. As of December 1974, although eleven domestic banks still had at least one military official on its board of directors, only two banks aside from the Thai Military Bank had military officials as major shareholders (*BIT,* July 1974, April 1975).

During periods of democratic rule, banks protected their interests by supporting political parties and their politicians. In the first set of elections after the 1973 revolution, business groups in Bangkok supported three parties that ultimately dominated parliament: the Democrat Party, the Chart Thai Party, and the Social Action Party. Fifty-three percent of the executive committees of these three leading parties claimed business as their primary occupation (Laothamatas 1992a, 35). Boonchu Rojanastien, then executive vice president of Bangkok Bank and eventually president of Bangkok Bank and the Thai Bankers Association, supported Kukrit Pramoj, leader of the Social Action Party (SAP). Kukrit became prime minister in 1975 and appointed Boonchu finance minister. Boonchu himself ran for office as an SAP candidate in 1979 and was appointed deputy prime minister in charge of economic affairs. He was only one of a growing number of businessmen in political office, many of whom were financed by members of the banking community. In 1933–1969, 24 percent of the House of Representatives — the dominant legislative body — were businessmen.[14] This increased to an average of 43 percent during 1975–1992. Furthermore, the proportion of businessmen in cabinets increased from 11 percent under the military government during 1972–1973 to 73 percent in the democratic government of Chatichai Choonhaven during 1988–1991 (Phongpaichit and Baker 1995, 223, 339).

The small number of critical actors within the sector has made it relatively easy for banks to coordinate behavior. This coordination is enhanced by the presence of the Thai Bankers Association (TBA), established in 1958 as a forum for discussion among bankers and as the industry's agent in relations with the government. Since its establishment, the TBA has set standard rates for service charges and loans. It holds regular meetings with the BOT and MOF. It has lobbied strenuously on behalf of the industry and participated in shaping financial legislation.[15] The TBA was one of three business associations represented on the Joint Public Private Consultative Committee (JPPCC), an organization established by Prime Minister Prem Tinsulanonda in 1981. By 1991, the association had been represented on eighty-one government committees or subcommittees (Laothamatas 1992a, 39, 50; Laothamatas 1992b, 203; Warr and Nidhiprabha 1996, 40).

The 1962 CBA was drafted with input from the TBA. The law prohibited foreign banks then operating in Thailand from opening new branches (Bank of Thailand 1992, 176). In addition, the government unofficially granted one of the banking community's most important requests: a moratorium on new banks (Hewison 1989, 188; Johnston 1991, 238). Since the law was passed, different governments have floated the idea of opening new banks. Each time the idea surfaced, the TBA lobbied against it.

In 1972, the military government led by Thanom and Praphat considered the idea of licensing regional banks (*Monthly Bulletin,* February 1972, 9–14). The idea was proposed by Puey Ungpakorn, BOT governor from 1959 to 1971 (*FEER,* 27 May 1972, 37). It was quickly shelved. After the 1973 revolution, the interim government that replaced the military rulers considered granting new bank licenses. Banks were under attack from various social forces—students, academics, the urban middle class, and a few military leaders (*BIT,* April 1974, June 1974; Hewison 1989, 190; Ruangsan 1976). Finance and securities companies were licensed, but because they were restricted to specific types of transactions and could be controlled by banks, they did not threaten the dominant position of banks. In 1978, as the military government led by Kriangsak Chomanand was considering amendments to the 1962 CBA, it announced that new banks would be allowed when the CBA was settled. The idea was supported by major shareholders of nonbank affiliated finance companies hoping to receive bank licenses (*FEER,* 1 September 1978, 77–79). Again, the proposal died. In 1990, the democratic government under Prime Minister Chatchai Choonhaven raised the idea of granting existing finance companies the right to offer banking services. Twenty new foreign institutions were licensed to operate under the BIBF, but only as offshore lenders and not as real domestic banks. Finally, in 1994 the government of Chuan Leekphai announced plans to issue full banking licenses to five foreign banks and began urging finance companies to upgrade to full bank status (Phongpaichit and Baker 1998, 86). In the end, only one new bank, a German bank, was opened after 1962. It was licensed in 1978 in exchange for a license for Thai Farmers Bank to operate in Germany (Johnston 1991, 238).

The TBA has also been influential in legislation affecting development of finance companies and the SET. The organization was consulted when the law on finance companies was being drafted in 1971. Many banks set up finance companies to take advantage of the fact that the latter were allowed to charge higher interest rates than banks. One of the amendments to the 1962 CBA considered in 1978 would have reduced equity of banks in finance companies from 20 percent to 5 percent. The TBA lobbied to have the 5 percent rule applied only to new holdings (*FEER*, 1 September 1978, 76, 78–79). A compromise was reached: banks were allowed to hold up to 10 percent of shares in other companies. Ultimately, just as they evaded ownership provisions by using related firms, banking families found other means to maintain control of finance companies. In 1974, the caretaker government began considering revision of tax laws, in part to promote the SET to be inaugurated in 1975. The government introduced a bill that would impose a 10 percent tax on bank deposits. Bank deposits were at that time tax exempt; it was expected that the new tax would induce depositors to shift some of their funds to securities, dividends from which were not tax exempt. The new tax was finally adopted, but not until 1978 under the Kriangsak military government. Yet in 1979, under pressure from bankers, the same government lifted a 10 percent withholding tax then being levied on foreign loans (*FEER*, 28 August 1981, 75).

Thus the economic resources and organizational strength of the banking community as a whole, as well as its individual members, has allowed it to shape or evade legislation with relative impunity. It should be noted that banks evaded prudential guidelines to varying degrees, but they were not the only violators of regulations. Finance companies were as bad or worse in this regard. Although a number of banks suffered serious distress in the 1980s, most of the finance companies that collapsed were unrelated to banks (*BBMR*, November 1984, 440–449). As a result of the 1997 crisis, six banks have required government assistance, while fifty-eight finance companies have been shut down.

With the licensing of over one hundred finance and securities companies in the 1970s and the licensing of forty-seven banks to engage in offshore banking in 1993, the difficulties faced by supervisory authorities due to industry resistance were compounded by the increase in the number of institutions engaged in financial activity. Given their apparent inability to supervise industry actors, it is at first glance surprising that the authorities chose to license these additional institutions. However, this apparently irrational outcome reflected macroeconomic technocrats' efforts to foster a more competitive and efficient financial industry in the face of tacit resistance by an entrenched financial community attempting to protect its interests.

One of the issues uppermost in the minds of macroeconomic technocrats since the 1970s has been the availability and proper allocation of capital in order to sustain the country's development. Surveying the financial landscape through the years, Thai technocrats have tended to believe that the banking community never quite fulfilled the country's existing credit needs. In 1974, Finance Minister Sommai Huntrakul considered imposing legal controls to ensure extension of credit to priority sectors (*BIT,* July 1974, 9–10). In 1979, BOT governor Unakul Snoh asserted that

> left alone, financial institutions usually channel funds into sectors that promise the highest yield and the lowest risk. . . . The credit needs of agriculture, small business and industry, including a large number of traditional enterprises employing a large number of people, have to be met by non-institutional lenders with higher costs and limited availability. (*FEER*, 21 September 1979, 102–103)

As late as 1980, the agricultural sector was the country's main engine of growth and major source of government revenue (Dixon 1996, 29); 72 percent of export earnings came from primary products.[16] Yet loans to the agricultural sector in the early 1970s accounted for only 2–3 percent of total commercial bank credit. Most credits financed foreign trade and domestic distribution of imported manufactured goods (*Monthly Bulletin,* February 1972, December 1979).

By 1990, the structure of the economy had substantially changed. Industrial output accounted for 36 percent of GDP; manufactures accounted for 75 percent of exports (Phongpaichit and Baker 1995, 152, 160). And the lack of adequate infrastructure to sustain the country's growth was becoming painfully obvious. Although the share of commercial bank credits to manufacturing had slowly risen since 1970, only 26 percent flowed to manufacturing. Approximately 40 percent financed real estate, construction, and foreign and domestic commerce (Chaiyasoot 1993). As one analyst remarked, "No one wanted to upgrade textiles exports when more money could be made selling condominiums and betting in the stock market" (Phongpaichit and Baker 1998, 102). In fact, the BIBF was established in part to ensure access to foreign capital for the country's infrastructure needs.

To ensure availability of capital and its efficient allocation at the national level, Thai technocrats have advocated development of Thailand's financial industry by gradually increasing the number and types of institutions, as well as the types of financial instruments, available to those in need of capital. They have argued that a more competitive and diversified financial system would better serve the country's needs. In 1979, BOT governor Snoh expressed concern that "banks [were still] too much under the control of a limited number of families, and a limited number of people" (*FEER,* 21 September 1979, 102–103). In 1990, BOT governor Chawalit Thanachanan expressed similar views, advocating an upgrading of top-tier finance companies to banks. This would "heighten the competitiveness of the system, which is too low at present" (Muscat 1994, 308). In 1995, the finance minister stated that one of the ministry's major objectives was to liberalize the financial sector in order to destroy old monopolies (Phongpaichit and Baker 1998, 86). The technocrats' underlying belief in the allocative efficiency of competitive markets was borne of their common education; most had received degrees in economics from institutions in the United States or the United Kingdom (Muscat 1995, 119).

With the support of different groups and individuals, monetary authorities had the capacity to introduce competition into the banking sector at various points through time. In the 1970s, students were among the most active in calling for the dismantling of financial conglomerates. By then, the number of universities in Thailand had more than tripled, student enrollment had increased almost sevenfold, and many students were eager to contribute to debates over government policy. Influenced by Marxist ideas, students began to demonstrate against the lack of freedom of speech and association, the foreign presence in Thailand (especially that of the United States and Japan), and the role of the military in government. They also protested against the power of capitalism, most clearly embodied in the banking community. Their greatest victory was in organizing demonstrations, which at their height involved over 400,000 students, and which brought down the military regime in October 1973 (Phongpaichit and Baker 1995, 301–305). Sanya, the interim prime minister subsequently appointed by the king, appeared sympathetic to students' ideas on reform. Although the act recognizing finance companies was decreed under the military government in 1972, it was during Sanya's year and a half in office that ninety-five finance companies were licensed (*BIT*, April 1975, 101–104), and that the government first considered abolishing the tax exempt status of interest on bank deposits.

Monetary officials were also supported by farmers in their bid to induce competition in the financial sector in the 1970s. Commercial banks allocated relatively meager funds to agriculture. Farmers were often forced to borrow from the unorganized financial sector, which charged extremely high interest rates. Many farmers lost their land due to foreclosure on loans. After the 1973 revolution, farmers formed an organization, the Peasants Federation of Thailand (PFT), which eventually established branches in forty-one provinces (Phongpaichit and Baker 1995, 296–299). The PFT organized protests publicizing farmers' problems of debt, land loss, and rent extraction. In 1975, the democratic Kukrit government introduced a price support scheme for rice growers. The government also enacted legislation requiring banks to devote 5 percent of total loans to agriculture and setting credit allocation restrictions on banks that wanted to open new branches (*BIT,* July 1976, 120).

In addition to students and farmers, factions of the military not coopted by the banking community as well as some industrialists not affiliated with bank groups also supported monetary officials' moves to weaken the oligarchic power of bank groups in the 1970s. Indeed, they were often one and the same. Two leading military figures, Admiral Sangaad Chaloryu and General Yos Thepasdin, were on the board of a non–bank affiliated finance company, First Trust Company, expecting to receive full bank status in 1978 (*FEER,* 17 March 1978, 52–53). Likewise, then Major-General Chatchai Choonhavan had similar hopes for the finance company, Erawan Trust, of which he was a major shareholder (*FEER,* 1 September 1978, 76, 78–79). Even more threatening to banks was the group of junior officers known as the "Young Turks." The group provided the muscle for the 1977 coup that brought General Kriangsak to power and then engineered his replacement by supporting General Prem in 1979. In 1981, the Young Turks attempted to oust Prem, stating as one of their goals the nationalization of as much as 30 percent of bank shares (*FEER,* 17 April 1981, 20).

By the mid-1990s, the issue of market concentration in the financial industry was no longer a salient domestic political issue, in large part due to the economic boom that began in 1987. Students, who had been among the most vocal on the issue, were busy taking advantage of the new job opportunities created. Non–bank affiliated industrialists, as well as bank groups, scrambled for the opportunities opened up by the relatively low overseas interest rates, which generated substantial private capital inflows from 1985–1990 (Phongpaichit and Baker 1998, 79, 85). Democratization brought to power many politicians eager to capitalize on the boom through their ties to bank groups. Indeed, if technocrats were feeling any pressure in the late 1980s, it was from foreign interests prompting them to hasten trade and financial liberalization. In 1989, the United States withdrew Generalized System of Preferences status for six categories of goods from Thailand. In response to this and a General Agreements of Tariffs and Trade ruling in 1990, Thailand liberalized trade in tobacco (Leeahtam 1991, 105). To harmonize the country's financial structure with other members of the World Trade Organization, the Thai government committed the country to new foreign bank entry and other financial liberalization policies.[17]

Finally, while the banking community opposed the licensing of new banks, they did not oppose the licensing of different types of financial institutions and instruments through the years. Any opposition they may have had to the establishment of finance companies in 1972 was moderated by their ability to set up their own firms. Similarly, their concerns regarding the licensing of foreign banks to operate through the Bangkok International Banking Facility in 1992 were mitigated by continued restrictions on other foreign bank activities within the country, as well as by their ability to participate in the BIBF and to reap significant tax savings by shifting part of their loan portfolios over to the facility (*FEER,* 18 March 1993).

Unfortunately, while the support of these different groups enabled authorities to introduce some competition into the financial system, it was insufficient to ensure state capacity to regulate the sector. Indeed, it complicated the task. Competition in the financial sector is a double-edged sword. Coupled with adequate supervision, it can lead to a more efficient allocation of credit. But, as the experience of Thailand demonstrates, without a corresponding increase in the ability to supervise the sector, increasing the number of financial actors and instruments leads to excessively risky allocation of credit—a recipe for financial crisis.

AFTERMATH OF THE CRISIS: DISPERSED INTEREST GROUP
MOBILIZATION AND INCREMENTAL REFORM

The financial crisis had a profound political and economic impact. In the economic realm, the failed defense of the *baht* exhausted the foreign currency reserves of the central bank. This forced the government, led by Chawalit Yongchaiyudh at the outset of the crisis, to turn to the IMF for a rescue program in August 1997. The IMF put together a $17 billion loan package and imposed stringent monetary and fiscal requirements on Thailand in return for the assistance. Conditions included maintenance of a fiscal surplus and a restrictive monetary policy, financial sector restructuring, and privatization of state enterprises (*Bangkok Post*, 6 August 1997).[18]

Although in theory the content of Thai economic policy was largely determined by the IMF agreement, in reality, in Thailand as elsewhere, the speed and extent to which the terms of the program were actually implemented were often hotly contested. Shortly after the Chawalit government signed off on the IMF compact, it announced an increase in the excise tax on gas and oil, higher duties on imported luxury goods, and a severe budget cut, in order to maintain the 1 percent fiscal surplus mandated by the IMF. The excise tax hike was revoked after a massive public outcry. The Chawalit government also dragged its feet over the IMF-mandated closure of fifty-eight finance companies. Certain senators, themselves major debtors in danger of losing their businesses, managed to block passage of a new bankruptcy code until March 1999. Intensive lobbying by representatives of the fifty-eight suspended finance companies succeeded in delaying establishment of a Financial Restructuring Authority and an Asset Management Corporation to handle their bad debts. The government had difficulty forcing powerful commercial banks to write off loans. Because the state had already spent such vast sums trying to prop up the finance sector prior to the collapse of the *baht*, the parliamentary opposition denounced the use of public funds to recapitalize financial institutions or buy non-performing loans of ailing banks and finance companies. Meanwhile, politicians, academics, businesspeople, and labor leaders denounced the privatization of state enterprises and the opportunistic purchase of private assets by foreign "vulture capitalists."

As Chawalit waffled on reforms, criticism of his particular government was extended to the system in general. Chawalit's background as a former army general who used rural patron–client networks to secure political power marked him as the kind of classic machine-style politician that the middle class had come to oppose over the last fifteen years. His government came to be viewed as the embodiment of a corrupt political system that produced shortsighted leadership, allowing pursuit of private gain at the expense of the public good. Public protests calling for the promulgation of a new constitution, which had been in the works for over two years, began to grow. Thailand's deteriorating economy created a sense that sweeping political change was necessary, even among groups such as big business and the military that had in the past defended the existing order (*Bangkok Post,* 5 September 1997, 10 September 1997, 12 September 1997, 22 September 1997, 27 September 1997, 28 September 1997). Owners and managers of capital began to associate the economic crisis with the apparently dysfunctional political system and concluded that revival of the economy necessitated cleaner and more effective political institutions. The military, increasingly concerned about the potential for unrest as the political and economic situations deteriorated, viewed the passage of the proposed constitution as the best way to maintain stability and resuscitate the economy.

Under assault from nearly every direction, Chawalit and the conservatives in parliament relented, and on September 27, 1997, Thailand's sixteenth constitution became law. The new charter is the most liberal ever promulgated. It lays out a robust bill of rights for the individual; creates an administrative court and ombudsman's office; devolves power down to local government councils; and empowers individuals to sue the state, initiate national referendums, and petition for the investigation of government officials pursuant to removal from office. The new constitution is also designed to reduce political corruption by restructuring the electoral system,[19] removing responsibility for the conduct of elections from the Interior Ministry and assigning it to an independent election commission, requiring elected officials to disclose their personal wealth, and stipulating that cabinet ministers convicted of corruption resign from their seats in parliament.

Unfortunately for Chawalit, passage of the new constitution was insufficient to quell dissatisfaction with his government's mismanagement of the economic crisis. Demonstrators by the thousands continued to fill the streets demanding his resignation. A revolt in parliament soon succeeded in bringing down the government, and Chuan Leekphai became the country's twenty-first prime minister.

The new government, however, has been no more immune to the political effects of the economic crisis. The imploding economy pushed a range of social classes to mobilize in defense of their interests. Former employees of suspended finance companies took to the streets to demand either the reopening of their firms or government compensation. Workers staged protests against pay cuts, layoffs, and the privatization of state enterprises. A coalition of northeastern farmers organizations mobilized to demand debt relief on loans owed to the state-run Bank of Agriculture and Agricultural Cooperatives. They argued that if the government could spend 400 billion *baht* trying to rescue wobbly finance companies run by politically connected businesspeople, it could certainly grant forbearance to struggling farmers innocent of any responsibility for the economic crisis. Faced with the threat of mass rallies in Bangkok, the Chuan government quickly agreed to a one-year debt moratorium for 31,000 farmers.

Protests and minor compromises notwithstanding, Chuan has vigorously moved forward in implementation of the IMF program in order to restore domestic and international confidence. By July 1999, the Chuan government had shut down one bank and the fifty-eight suspended finance companies, intervened in or nationalized six banks and nine finance companies, and set up two types of capital support facilities to assist in the recapitalization of viable banks and finance companies (Baliño et al. 1999, 161, 167). In keeping with the IMF program, the government yet again strengthened the country's legal prudential framework and required remaining banks to recapitalize. The Chuan government also agreed to abolish the Financial Institutions Development Fund (FIDF), an entity within the BOT that had been set up in the wake of the 1983–1986 crisis to support weak finance companies and banks. Funds from the FIDF were used to prop up failing institutions prior to the collapse of the *baht*. The Nukul Commission, the task force created to investigate the causes of the crisis, argued that the implicit unlimited insurance provided by the FIDF had contributed to the crisis by minimizing credit risk and encouraging excessively risky lending (*NCR*, 146). In place of the FIDF, the government will set up an agency to provide limited deposit insurance. The limited insurance is expected to remind depositors of the risks involved in investing their funds in any one bank or finance company. Furthermore, the government streamlined the examination process at the BOT by assigning a single assistant governor sole responsibility for financial sector oversight (*Wall Street Journal,* 26 August, 1 September 1999).

As in past crises, mobilization of dispersed interest groups has produced a new round of financial reform legislation. Will these changes improve the state's capacity to supervise the financial sector? In the face of resistance from the finance industry, stronger prudential guidelines, abolition of the FIDF, and clarified responsibility for financial sector supervision is likely to improve its quality only marginally. But changes in the structure of the industry due to the crisis may actually make the BOT's task of supervising the sector less difficult in the future. Domestic banks now control only 39 percent of total assets; foreign banks now control 12 percent; and the state controls six commercial banks that account for 28 percent (Baliño et al. 1999, 167). The state is in the process of privatizing five of the six banks it now controls. But if the new owners do not have substantial related interests in the country, they may be more likely to implement rigorous due diligence procedures when allocating credit. This may reduce excessively risky lending to related interests, which has long been a weakness of Thai banks. Indeed, the need to recapitalize has already led two surviving domestic banks to accept foreign partners with limited directly related interests in Thailand. The Development Bank of Singapore now owns 53 percent of Thai Danu Bank, and the Dutch group, ABN-Amro, holds 75 percent of Bank of Asia. As one industry expert noted, "The whole control system is going to be put in place by the major shareholder. Thai Danu for example will now have Singaporean banking controls" (*Asian Business,* December 1998, 30). If, in fact, foreign-controlled banks exercise more self-governance in allocating credit because they have arms-length relationships with most Thai borrowers rather than directly related interests, then significant foreign ownership and control of financial institutions may serve as a substitute for the state's lack of regulatory capacity.[20] In effect, the crisis may finally accomplish what Thai technocrats have been advocating for the past three decades: dispersion of ownership, heightened competition in the financial sector, and more efficient and prudent allocation of credit.

CONCLUSION

Thailand's recent economic crisis has generally been attributed to misguided policies. As we have shown, there is considerable evidence that policy mistakes, specifically liberalization of the capital account in the context of a fixed exchange rate and implicit guarantees to bail out ailing institutions, played significant roles in the creation of the 1997 crisis. In addition, however, we highlighted the substantial role of poor financial sector supervision, a factor that has not been sufficiently emphasized by most other scholars. By analyzing not only the recent financial crisis but also that of 1983–1986, we show that Thailand experienced financial crises in times of both growth and austerity, rising and falling real exchange rates, open and restricted capital accounts, and higher and lower levels of moral hazard. Common to both the 1983–1986 and 1997 crises was inadequate policing of financial institutions, which occurred under both democratic and military-backed regimes. This deficient supervision was due to weakness of the Thai state in the face of an oligarchic and well-organized financial sector. As long as the Thai party system remains highly fragmented, the state is likely to remain weak vis-à-vis the financial sector. In this context, increased foreign control of commercial banks, occurring in the wake of the recent crisis, may be a more promising means of averting future banking crises than another round of regulatory reforms.

NOTES

1. See the Asian crisis web page of Nouriel Roubini, <http://www.stern.nyu.edu/~nroubini/asia/ AsiaHomepage.html>, for analyses of the crisis and related articles.
2. The idea of establishing Thailand as a regional financial center was first floated in the Sixth National Economic and Social Development Board Plan (1987–1991).
3. The Seventh National Economic and Social Development Board Plan (1992–1996) forecast an investment-savings gap of nearly 1 trillion *baht*. Thailand's status as an emerging regional financial center was expected to help attract overseas funds to meet that finance gap.
4. Analyst at W. I. Carr, interview by authors.
5. Real estate was not the only economic sector facing pressures from oversupply. Easy access to financing had also driven excessive investment in the automotive, steel bar, and petrochemicals industries (Doner and Ramsay 1999).
6. The term "moral hazard" was first coined by the insurance industry and refers to the tendency of people with insurance to engage in riskier behavior than they would if they did not have insurance.

7. Tarrin Nimmanhaeminda, currently finance minister of Thailand, finance minister when the BIBF was launched, Bangkok, November 4, 1997, interview by authors; and Pisit Leeahtam, currently deputy finance minister, former BOT official, interview by authors, Bangkok, October 22, 1997.

8. Analyst at W. I. Carr, interview by authors.

9. Thailand did not experience a loss of macroeconomic control in the 1980s, despite the country's effectively fixed exchange rate, in part because the government had more legal controls over the country's capital account and foreign exchange transactions. Moreover, fiscal adjustment was an effective instrument of monetary policy in the 1980s. More than half of inflows in the early 1980s was due to public sector borrowing. Most of the inflows were linked to expenditures on specific public investment projects and used immediately to pay for essential capital goods. They did not, therefore, have a direct impact on the monetary base. In contrast, the vast majority of capital inflows in the 1990s were private sector investments and short-term loans. Thus shelving government projects and public loans would have had little impact on the monetary base. Moreover, the government could not easily reduce spending. It had started running surpluses in 1988, and further austerity meant curtailing spending on crucial infrastructure projects (Warr and Nidhiprabha 1996, 170–73).

10. Akira (1989, 245–60) describes the steps that four families took to maintain control of their banks.

11. Siamwalla (1997, 8) marks the critical turning point as 1990, when Vijit Supinit was appointed BOT governor.

12. Cristensen et al. (1997, 369) note that leading enterprises and banks, the majority of which are owned by Thai-Chinese families, favored a stable macroeconomic environment.

13. Calculated from data provided in *BIT*, July 1976, 139, and Chaiyasoot 1993, 233.

14. Calculated from table 10.1, Background of Members of the Assembly, 1933–1992, in Phongpaichit and Baker (1995, 338); see also Laothamatas (1992a, 33) for similar data, albeit from 1933–1986. The Thai legislature is composed of two houses: a Senate whose members are appointed by the prime minister and a House of Representatives whose members are directly elected by the public. Constitutionally, the House is the more powerful body; the Senate's power lies mainly in delaying legislation. Thus, during democratic periods, legislation was the product of House representatives' preferences. During periods when the military was dominant, however, the Senate was stacked with military officers and exercised significant power.

15. Laothamatas (1992a, 140–41) states that the 1983 and 1985 banking legislation was written "without any consultation with the influential TBA." The laws were introduced as emergency decrees by the executive branch when Parliament was in recess. Emergency decrees are as effective as laws passed by the legislature, if they are not vetoed by Parliament when it reconvenes. Laothamatas notes that only the prime minister, minister of finance, deputy minister of finance, and BOT officials knew of the banking amendments before they were promulgated. As discussed, there is a pattern of reform efforts being initiated episodically in response to public pressure, in this case amid an economic crisis.

16. Calculated from table 2.1b in Dixon (1996, 36).

17. Pisit Leeahtam, currently deputy finance minister, interview by authors, Bangkok, October 22, 1997.

18. See also the letter dated December 8, 1997, submitted by Finance Minister Tarrin Nimmanhaeminda and Bank of Thailand governor Chaiyawat Wibulswasdi to Michel Camdessus, managing director of the International Monetary Fund, for the IMF board meeting.

19. Election rules under the new constitution have changed significantly. Senators will be elected rather than appointed. Provinces will be represented by one to eighteen senators, depending on population size. Voters will be allowed to choose as many Senate candidates as there are available seats. House districts that used to be represented by two to three members will be divided into single-member districts. In addition, one-fifth of the House will be elected by party under a proportional representation rule.

20. This is not a foregone conclusion. Foreign banks lent substantial amounts to Thai banks and companies. It is difficult to believe that they did not know about weaknesses in the financial system.

We thank the government officials, scholars and financial experts in Thailand interviewed for this project, and Richard Doner for his helpful comments on an earlier version of this chapter. Gabriella Montinola also thanks the Institute for Southeast Asian Studies (ISEAS), where she was a visiting fellow during the early stages of the project, and the University of California, Davis, for its financial support. The views expressed in the chapter are those of the authors and not necessarily those of individuals interviewed, ISEAS, or UC Davis.

5

Malaysia: Ethnic Cleavages and Controlled Liberalization

A. Maria Toyoda

Adoption of liberalizing economic policies, as many of the chapters in this volume suggest, can hinge on the mobilization of pivotal groups that are characterized by the dispersed rather than the concentrated nature of their interests. It is relatively easy to see how concentrated interest groups align in coalitions and mobilize for or against certain policy stances. It is much harder to see the effects that more dispersed groups have on policy outcomes. There are instances, though, when they become critical players in tilting the balance toward or away from policy reforms. However, even on these occasions, the alignment of economic interests for and against a given reform movement is only a necessary, and not a sufficient, condition of political success. This is especially evident when the demands of these groups are filtered through social and political institutions. In this chapter, we look at the case of Malaysia, a country that had been making steady progress toward liberalizing its financial system. But when struck by crisis, it resorted to a surprise strategy of closing its capital accounts. How is this response to be explained?

Malaysia's response to the crisis stands out. Most countries hit by the crisis took the IMF's advice and the IMF's money. Interest rates were raised and fiscal spending was cut to stem capital flight and control the extent of devaluation. Structural reforms were also part of the usual effort to restore investor confidence. Heavily indebted banks and firms were forced to restructure, restore competitiveness, and reassure investors that similar sources of competitive weakness would not develop in the future. But this is not what happened in Malaysia. Malaysia rejected IMF involvement and significantly delayed what few austerity measures it eventually imposed. Most noticeably, contrary to what had become "conventional" wisdom in international financial circles, Malaysia closed its capital accounts. Malaysia lowered rather than increased interest rates, using exchange controls to fend off attacks on its currency. Lower interest rates and in some cases bank bailouts and fiscal or quasi-fiscal subsidies were used to shore up debt-ridden corporations.

These policies were perceived by many Western observers to be economically irrational. Prime Minister Mahathir Mohamad's well-reported statements regarding the causes of financial crisis were mainly characterized as defiant, polemical, and even desperate. Mahathir cast his country as the victim of a range of supposed culprits, including financier George Soros, the International Monetary Fund, hedge fund managers, and Jews. His allegations were often delivered as rants that, by and large, were perceived by Western observers as displays of irrationality and desperation. Whatever the economic effectiveness of Mahathir's policies, his rhetorical excesses should not be allowed to obscure the domestic political calculations behind both his statements and his actions. In fact, Malaysia's methods of dealing with the crisis have been structured by long-standing political forces.

We can compare Malaysia's response to that of other, similarly affected countries, and to its own response to economic recession in the mid-1980s. Increasing financial internationalization is only one of the forces that structure the process of economic decision making, and it alone cannot explain variations in precrisis policies or postcrisis responses. Forces of a more enduring nature have helped to determine Malaysian economic policies. Most important has been the constant preoccupation with ethnic politics and Malaysian leaders' pursuit of national policies that aim to redistribute economic goods to the majority Malay population.

Interethnic violence in 1969 became the basis for an ambitious program of state intervention to boost the status of ethnic Malays. In response to economic difficulties in the mid-1980s, these policies were qualified and coupled with liberalization in order to preserve economic growth and broaden available economic opportunities. When similar economic difficulties developed in 1997, many assumed that Malaysia would respond by accelerating the process of liberalization. However, this did not happen because the ethnic cleavages that were responsible for the initial turn to state intervention also divided and weakened the usual dispersed interest group coalition favoring liberalization as a response to competitive difficulties. In East Asia, this liberalizing coalition of dispersed interest groups is drawn from the peasantry and from the middle classes and unorganized labor in the cities. However, in Malaysia the primarily Malay peasants and urban poor continued to be suspicious of liberalization. Liberalization most visibly benefited urban Chinese and foreigners, and it seemed to call into question the state's commitment to improving the lot of Malays. Hence the ethnic cleavage provided a mass base of support for policies to shore up the government-sponsored business networks whose competitive difficulties underlay the crisis. Even middle-class groups, which had most strongly supported the liberalization policies instituted in the mid-1980s, did not strongly oppose the government. The Chinese middle class feared a return of ethnic violence and hence acquiesced quietly. Even the new Malay middle class did not strongly dissent, because of its strong ties of identity and past association with the government's efforts to bolster the position of Malays. All this made exchange controls and government bailouts the safest way of maintaining political power as well as economic patronage, hence a politically irresistible formula.

OVERVIEW

The trend toward economic openness in Malaysia has been driven by both strong domestic interests and the international economic environment. Reliance on foreign investment increased considerably with the onset of recession in the mid-1980s. Upon realizing that the inefficient state sector had placed a heavy debt burden on the national economy, Malaysia's policy makers embarked on a gradual scheme of privatization and eased some of the rules guiding foreign direct investment, particularly in the exporting sector.

Though raw materials (palm and vegetable oils, timber, rubber, natural gas, and petroleum) continue to be important exports, the greatest gains have been made in manufacturing. Between 1990 and 1994, manufactured exports rose from 47.2 billion *ringgit*s to 120 billion *ringgit*s.[1] Within manufacturing, electrical machinery and electronic components, requiring relatively well-paid skilled and semiskilled labor, are the most important exports. The growth in such relatively capital-intensive ventures came largely through increased foreign investment. This came from Malaysia's regional neighbors, but particularly from Japan during the 1980s—most noticeably following the 1985 Plaza Accord, which led to a significant appreciation of the yen. From 1987, the bulk of Japanese investment went into manufacturing. The export-led strategy, phasing in economic openness amid rapid economic growth, did not have a straightforward liberalizing effect on the political constellation in the 1990s. This was because its effects were filtered through Malaysia's strong ethnic cleavages and ethnic-Malay affirmative action programs.

First, steady increases in employment in the higher-paying manufacturing sector (versus a decline over time in employment in agriculture, forestry, and fishery) have produced a new middle class. In the case of Malaysia, the benefits of economic reform have accrued more to skilled and semiskilled workers, than to unskilled labor and the peasants. Thus, despite the fact that all dispersed interest groups have benefited from liberalization and economic growth, the strong ethnic cleavage has tended to divide the different groups, primarily along ethnic lines. The Malay peasants and urban poor have tended to focus on the widening gap between themselves and the heavily Chinese and foreign elite and middle classes.

Second, since the liberalization of the mid-1980s, a more significant role is being played by Chinese capitalists, though they continue to partner frequently with Malay colleagues. Following the onset of Japan's recession, the year-on-year percentage increase in Japanese foreign direct investment in Malaysia dropped considerably. But by then, Malaysia was also receiving large capital injections from ethnic Chinese capitalists, both from Malaysia and abroad. The need to sustain levels of investment helps to explain why the response to economic crisis in the late 1990s differs considerably from the response to crisis in the 1980s. In the latter case the need to draw in additional Chinese investment meant drawing the Chinese back in politically as well. Though the Chinese remained cautious about their status in Malaysia, Chinese investment responded strongly to the significant shifts in the long-standing policies of affirmative action that had severely limited Chinese economic and political participation in the 1970s and 1980s. However, this modus vivendi with the Chinese does not extend to completely dismantling the government-sponsored business networks constructed to advance the position of Malays. The position of the Chinese remains dependent on Malay support, and the government realizes that the Chinese are in a weak position when it comes to offering political opposition.

Third, export-led economic growth meant restructuring and privatizing state-run corporations. This was an even more significant departure from the strategies pursued in the 1970s and 1980s. Below I explain how the New Economic Policy of the 1970s and 1980s, which was meant to increase Malay participation in business, was grounded in state firms. Its successor programs are somewhat less explicit in defining the role of state firms in the marketplace. However, the process of privatization took place in a context that still favored a strong developmental role for the state. As a result, it did not break up but rather enlarged and solidified the Malay business elite associated with the government.

Of the dispersed interest groups that might ordinarily be assumed to favor liberalization over policies primarily benefiting government-allied concentrated interest groups, few could truly be considered organized or even as having homogeneous interests in the Malaysian context. The middle classes, a relatively diffuse group, are ethnically divided. The Chinese are fragmented in their political and economic interests and their ethnic and linguistic identities. Those not closely associated with government business networks tend to support greater openness. Greater openness is also supported by segments of the new middle class Malay business elite—particularly those benefiting from partnerships with foreign investors. These middle-class groups create a momentum for economic reform that is very strong (Pasuk 1990, 92). However, this relatively significant middle-class support is balanced by ethnically charged alienation among the heavily Malay peasantry and urban poor. Thus, with the entry of crisis conditions, liberalizing policies were not strongly upheld by a strong coalition of dispersed interest groups.

In the sections below, I look at the context of ethnic politics, the construction of ruling party legitimacy, and how these factors affected economic policy. I also look at how economic trends in turn have affected ethnic politics and the role of the state. Finally, I argue that changes in these areas were not sufficient to overcome the strong ethnic cleavages that drove Malaysia's interventionist policies to begin with. This helps to explain Malaysia's response to the financial crisis of 1997.

THE UMNO'S INTERETHNIC POLITICS: STABILITY AND LEGITIMACY THROUGH ECONOMIC GROWTH, COOPTATION, AND REDISTRIBUTIVE POLICY

Even before the establishment of the Malay state, there had been great disparities between the political and economic circumstances of the federation's major ethnic groups. The Chinese had greater access to capital, business opportunities, and higher education. Members of the politically influential elite, however, tended to come from the majority Malay population. Prior to the 1970s, Malaysian politics operated under an official scheme of interethnic accommodation. The system resembled a consociational pattern of power sharing, characterized by elite accommodation in a "fragmented" society (Lijphart 1969). Consociationalism followed closely on the upheaval created by the postcolonial process of nation and state building, and the expulsion of Singapore from the Federation of Malaya in 1965. The system was seen by many of the state-building elite as the most workable way to establish some stability among the multitude of ethnic groups within the boundaries of the federation. What Lijphart would describe as a political grand coalition was formed by the three major ethnic groups within the federation: the Malays, the Chinese, and the Indians. These three major groups were represented by three parties, the dominant United Malays National Organization (UMNO), the Malayan Chinese Association (MCA), and the Malayan Indian Congress (MIC). Together these constituted the Alliance, or Barisan Nasional (BN). Throughout the 1960s, the Alliance dominated elections. But when its hold on power threatened to slip in 1969, the system of consociational politics met its demise.

The May Thirteenth Crisis of 1969 marks the end of consociationalism and the beginning of the Malay-dominated and Malay-centered politics that have characterized Malaysia for the past three decades. The riots of 13 May 1969 were sparked by large Alliance losses in the elections held in the peninsular area of the country. (Borneo elections were scheduled for a slightly later date.) The riots tipped the political scales away from official accommodation of different ethnic groups toward a system of concerted economic affirmative action for the Malays, to the disadvantage of other ethnic groups, particularly the Chinese.

The end of consociational politics heralded a sea change in the role of the state in economic affairs. In the early years of the federation, state intervention in resource distribution was mostly limited to improving conditions in the rural areas.

Private capital took the lead in investment and development (Khoo 1992). This relationship was turned on its head following the birth of the New Economic Policy (NEP), implemented in response to the May Thirteenth Crisis. The NEP ushered in a sustained period of state-led, state-dominated economic policy making. Throughout the 1970s and 1980s, private capital took a more secondary role, restricted by the priorities laid out by the Malaysian state. The NEP and the increasingly dominant nature of the state led to a heightened awareness and emphasis on communal politics.

One important point should be made here. The existence of interethnic disparities and cleavages should not be taken as evidence that there is a cohesive and monolithic character to intraethnic relations. While it is tempting to view the UMNO structure in corporatist terms, Malaysian ethnic politics before and after 1969 can best be described as fragmented, both in terms of inter- and intraethnic groupings. Among the Malays, government-connected elites and middle-class urban dwellers have benefited disproportionately, leaving peasants and the urban poor relatively disaffected and more subject to the appeals of the heavily Islamist opposition. Among the Chinese, there are at least nine different important linguistic divisions, and there are further subcultural groups within these divisions (Siow 1983). Consequently, Chinese support of the MCA and the Alliance is far from monolithic. Many Chinese have actively supported opposition parties such as the mainly Chinese Democratic Action People's Party (DAP), and even the mainly Malay and Islamic Gerakan. Among the Indians, linguistic, religious, and caste differences exert fragmenting pressure.

These differences have persisted over time. But as Malaysia developed economically during the 1970s and 1980s, the nature of the cleavages has been transformed in several ways. Some of these changes are a direct result of the NEP. There is now a solid and growing middle class, primarily urban Malay and Chinese, whose economic interests contrast even more sharply than before with Malays and non-Malay indigenous groups who mostly populate the rural areas.[2] There is also a small but influential class of "New Rich" entrepreneurs—also mostly Malay and Chinese—who have benefited enormously from privatization during the 1980s. The growth of the Islamic social movements have also served as a fragmenting rather than a unifyng force among Malays. The fissures emerged following the UMNO's effort during the 1970s to coopt the dakwah or Islamic social movement in order to quiet student activism (Crouch 1996; Means 1991; Shamsul 1994).[3] Another dividing factor is the split among Malays between hardcore followers of Islam and those who follow a more secular route. These divisions have been deepened by widening economic inequalities that developed as reforms took hold in the Malaysian economy during the 1980s.

The defining character of the NEP, implemented through several multiyear national plans, was that of ethnic economic restructuring in favor of the majority Malay, or Bumiputera, population.[4] Naturally, the range of new measures meant to give the Bumiputera an advantage over other ethnic groups met with opposition. But increasingly authoritarian control by the state over previously private transactions, and the lack of significant unity among any of the other important communal groups in Malaysia, meant that throughout the 1970s and 1980s Bumiputera politics would prevail.[5] The economic and political conditions created by the NEP are the contextual starting point for understanding the impact of international financial openness and financial crisis on Malaysia's domestic political economy.

BLURRING THE LINES BETWEEN THE STATE, THE MARKET, AND THE PARTY: THE UMNO'S BUSINESS CONNECTIONS

By many measures, the NEP was largely successful in meeting its goals of eradicating poverty, providing greater access to higher education for Malays, and increasing their economic participation. As Crouch (1996, 181) notes, "By 1990, Malaysia's class profile reflected its new status as an advanced middle-income country. At the same time the implementation of the NEP resulted in a sharp increase in Malay participation in both middle- and working-class occupations." The Malay government has, since making the transition from British rule, been involved in business and finance. But, as noted above, the process of bringing about significant change required stronger and more active state intervention in the economic affairs of the nation. Attempts had been made in the 1960s to develop a Malay business class, but until the inception of the NEP in 1969, these had been largely unsuccessful. The NEP period, therefore, marks a period of substantially increased state involvement.

The activities of the state during the NEP period have led to an increased blurring of the lines between the state, markets, and the dominant party, the UMNO, both during the NEP years and the subsequent years of gradual privatization. Even before the NEP, public enterprises were established to help mobilize resources to gain control of strategic segments of the Malaysian economy. But during the NEP, public enterprises became more politicized as a means for transferring resources to the Bumiputera. At the time, the ruling elite assumed (with some evidence) that the Bumiputera were not likely to save and accumulate capital for investment purposes. Public corporations and private companies with government connections served to create access points and incentives for Bumiputera participation in important sectors of the economy. Most of these corporations had ties back to the UMNO through its main investment arms, the largest being the Fleet Group Sdn Bhd and Hatibudi Nominees Sdn Bhd. Other important holding companies, such as Magnum and Multi-Purpose Holdings Bhd (MPHB), were associated with the MCA, and still others with the MIC. The range of businesses included lotteries and sweepstakes, sports and leisure clubs, textiles, heavy industry, and publishing.[6] Other methods, such as favorable pricing of shares in public corporations sold to Bumiputera, also helped to quickly boost their levels of ownership. But the sector of greatest importance, and hence the area of greatest state involvement, has been banking and finance.

According to Gomez and Jomo (1997, 62), the NEP period saw a huge transfer of banking assets into Bumiputera or government control, including many previously under Indian or Chinese control. Dominance over banks, in particular, meant greater control over other sectors that rely heavily on debt financing. "The importance of control of the banking sector in Malaysia's financial system cannot be overemphasized. . . . The banking industry alone accounted for over fifty-six percent of the total assets of the financial system at the end of 1990" (Gomez and Jomo 1997, 65).

The growing dominance and influence of the UMNO government in economic affairs came at substantial cost both in terms of the disadvantage to the non-Bumiputera population and the increasing incidence of corruption and scandal at the highest levels. These costs would persist through the 1980s and 1990s, contributing to the overall problem of the Malaysian and Asian financial crisis. Ties between politicians, cabinet members, and business leaders became progressively stronger as the effect of holding companies and interlocking ownership and management through stock swaps took hold, concentrating economic power in the hands of a few politically connected players.[7] For example, Peremba and Kumpulan Fima were two corporations set up to acquire assets on behalf of the Bumiputera. These companies were run, respectively, by Dain Zainuddin and Mahathir prior to their taking up political posts. When these two government companies were finally privatized in 1990, the bulk of the shares went to UMNO proxies (Gomez 1991). Today most cabinet members in Malaysia maintain strong business concerns of their own.

Combined with poor documentation and accounting methods, therefore, the opportunities for patronage and collusion have been plentiful. In 1993 an anticorruption investigation cleared the Energy, Telecommunications, and Posts Minister S. Samy Vellu, after it was disclosed that most of the 10 million shares floated during the privatization of Telekom Malaysia were allotted to companies linked to his family. Also in 1993, it was disclosed that a government trust set up to manage Bumiputera investment interests was purchasing golf courses and condominiums at highly inflated prices from private owners (*Far Eastern Economic Review*, 21 January 1993, 9 September 1993).

Among the non-Malays who participated in the patronage and collusion game were the wealthy Chinese, who saw an even greater need, after the NEP introduced greater uncertainties for them, to cooperate with the UMNO.[8] The most common form of cooperation involved "silent" Chinese capitalists who took on Malay partners as company directors. In the highest-profile cases, Chinese businessmen recruited Malay politicians as their partners. The quest for Malay patronage eventually drew many Chinese businessmen, and the MCA, into debilitating scandals.[9] It also served to further splinter the Chinese population, eliminating the possibility of unity against the NEP and the Bumiputera affirmative action programs. By and large, however, the need for Malay patronage to further Chinese business interests led the Chinese to hedge their interests by moving toward shorter-term investments and moving their capital abroad to other markets, such as Singapore.

By the 1980s, the NEP had helped to create additional fissures in the UMNO—leading to its eventual splintering—and in the Barisan Nasional alliance. The cultivation and concentration of patronage networks, as well as the distribution of government rents, led to greater stratification among Malaysia's business interests, intense factionalism within the UMNO ranks, and a split between those in the party who maintained a strong rural, grassroots base and those who generally supported concentrated urban business interests. This rural–urban cleavage was further complicated by the proliferating business interests in Kuala Lumpur. Other conflicts began to emerge among large private capital, government businesses, and medium-sized businesses. The ideological divide that had always existed within the party between more moderate and stricter Islamists was further deepened by these additional fissures.[10] The pressures within the UMNO continued to build during the mid-1980s, as Malaysia fell into economic recession and a banking crisis.

These forces for change in economic policy coincided with the emergence of a new class of business interests, outside of UMNO patronage networks, calling for greater economic openness. Chief among their demands was the relaxation of capital controls and Malay-centered ownership regulations, and greater access to foreign and Malay–Chinese capital. By the early 1980s, there was already a movement to reverse the earlier pattern of development through state enterprises. Public corporations had become the basis of contested policies. At first, there was limited acknowledgment that state enterprises were competing primarily with the most dynamic small- and medium-sized firms. The move toward privatization, therefore, was initially pursued as a temporary redistributive measure. But as foreign capital flowed in, primarily from Japan, privatization soon acquired greater momentum from a business perspective as well as a political one. (See table 5.1.)

FINANCIAL OPENNESS AND THE REEMERGENCE OF PRIVATE CHINESE CAPITAL

By the late 1980s—largely in response to NEP-related tensions that came to a head in response to the mid-1980s economic difficulties—Prime Minister Mahathir's vision of national development underwent important changes that translated into reforms in economic policy. Chief among the reforms was some relaxation of the principles behind the NEP, which expired in 1990, and its successor program, the new National Development Policy (NDP).[11] Linked to the NDP was Mahathir's longer-term perspective on national growth, Vision 2020. Vision 2020, in contrast to the NEP, downplayed the previous emphasis on communal

Table 5.1   Privatization Transactions in Malaysia, 1988–1997

Year	# of Trans-actions	Value ($USm)	Sectors
1988	1	16.0	manufacturing
1989	2	30.6	manufacturing, cement
1990	9	375.1	manufacturing, hotels, utilities, telecommunications, transportation, services
1991	6	387.4	cement, autos, shipping, telecommunications
1992	6	2883.4	airlines, autos, utilities, telecommunications
1993	5	2148.0	airlines, forestry, utilities, transportation, services
1994	2	798.0	airlines, petroleum
1995	7	2519.0	agriculture, utilities, manufacturing, shipping
1996	3	214.3	trading
1997	4	—	forestry, ports, railways, steel

Source: World Bank 1999.

politics and advocated greater interethnic business cooperation. Substantive policy changes included reversal of earlier promotion of state enterprises as the main instruments of redistribution from Chinese to Malays, and greater reliance on privately led growth and incentives to foreign direct investment. Other concerns were relieving hard-core poverty and developing Malaysia's human resources through an aggressive training and education program. One of the most important outcomes of reform was the UMNO's increasing accommodation of Chinese business interests. This acknowledged the growing importance of interethnic cooperation among the younger generation of Malay and Chinese. It led to a significant reentry of the Chinese into the Malaysian domestic economy, and a reversal of the capital flight that took place at the beginning of the NEP period. During the 1980s, Malaysia significantly opened its financial markets to foreign capital, driven partly by domestic demand and partly by continuing pressures from the open offshore *ringgit* market in Singapore.

Limits on foreign equity in manufacturing were also relaxed considerably. In 1975, only 27.5 percent of manufacturing projects involved foreign participation. But by 1989, this percentage increased to 73.9 percent. (See table 5.2.) At the same time, Bumiputera participation in the public sector rose substantially when compared to 1970, but leveled off in the 1990s (table 5.3). This demonstrates that NEP policies initially had the desired impact on ownership patterns but did not maintain that momentum.

The pivotal groups during this period of change were the rapidly rising urban middle classes, both Chinese and Malay. On the one hand, the Chinese, in particular, have favored privatization and financial liberalization because it releases some of the constraints placed on their capital by Malay-centric policies. The younger generation of rising Malay capitalists also favors the more robust and

Table 5.2 Equity Participation by Foreigners in Manufacturing Projects

Year	% Foreign Owned	Year	% Foreign Owned	Year	% Foreign Owned	Year	% Foreign Owned
1975	27.5	1979	39.5	1983	25.7	1987	49.1
1976	24.9	1980	32.9	1984	22.7	1988	57.9
1977	30.1	1981	29.0	1985	17.8	1989	73.9
1978	37.0	1982	27.5	1986	28.0	1990	64.3

Source: Yasuda 1991, 340–341.

Table 5.3 Shares of Foreign and Domestic Equity in Malaysian Publicly Held Companies

Year	Foreign	Non-Bumiputera	Bumiputera	Others
1970	63.3	32.3	2.4	2
1990	25.4	46.8	19.3	8.5
1995	27.7	43.4	20.6	8.3
1998	31.8	41.1	19.4	7.7

Source: Nikkei Weekly, 27 September 1999.

competitive business climate that economic openness fosters. On the other hand, traditional Malay oligopolists, and their long-term silent Chinese partners—who have benefited directly from the NEP and the elite networks that directly connect them to the Malay leadership—have resisted certain changes.

The priorities laid out in the NEP have shaped communal politics during the Mahathir years. But Mahathir and his close advisers are also aware that the relatively stable balance between Malaysia's major ethnic groups has been achieved at least partially through rapid economic growth. Thus the leadership's transformation of NEP into NDP and Vision 2020 also reflects a realization that the balance between ethnic groups and economic classes is a delicate one. Occasional, and lately more frequent, ethnic flare-ups in Indonesia have been potent reminders of this—in the unlikely event that memories of 1969 have faded. The recession and banking crisis of the mid-1980s thus intensified the pressure on the UMNO leadership to strengthen its support base beyond the urban business and (mostly unorganized) labor groups directly benefiting from government-controlled financial, business, and patronage networks.

Indeed, post-NEP policies have resulted in gradual shifts in the UMNO's support. The Chinese urban middle class, which traditionally supported opposition parties, started to increasingly support the UMNO following liberalizing measures. So did urban Malay small and medium-sized business owners, who benefited from privatization.[12] Far from dismantling the system of political patronage, privatization has offered additional opportunities to cultivate ties between ruling politicians and the business elite. Privatization has furthered the consolidation of business holdings among the politically connected. Access to the ownership opportunities created by privatizing corporations has been as politicized as the original process of establishing these government corporations. Rent-seeking activity in this quarter, and in others, continues among both Malay and Chinese businesspeople, to the benefit of the UMNO and individual UMNO leaders. Liberalization and relaxation of ownership requirements in the 1980s has helped stem disgruntlement among the Chinese and contributed to improved bilateral relations between Malaysia and China. Thus insider privatization combined with liberalization have helped to consolidate both Malay and Chinese middle class support behind the UMNO.

Rural groups and the urban poor, however, have become increasingly disaffected with the economic liberalization policies. These groups associate liberalizing policies with corruption and greater income disparities. At first sight, this is confusing. For these groups have been the broadest beneficiaries of wider access to new economic opportunities beyond UMNO networks—particularly by the flood of better-paying jobs in the new foreign-run, export-oriented enterprises. Here the ethnic cleavage has played the crucial role in altering perceptions. Because the largest and most visible benefits have gone to urban business elites and because Chinese and foreigners are among the most visible entrepeneurs, poorer rural and urban Malays tend to perceive liberalization as threatening the traditional NEP goal of bringing Malays up to Chinese levels of opportunity and wealth.

To summarize, in Malaysia the ethnic cleavage breaks up the usual dispersed interest group coalition in favor of liberalization, creating a powerful logic at the level of mass politics for protecting UMNO business networks. We can now trace this logic as it unfolded through the crisis.

EXPLAINING MALAYSIA'S RESPONSE TO THE 1997 CRISIS: USING ETHNIC POLITICS TO RECONCILE DISPERSED INTEREST GROUPS TO CONTINUED STATE SUBSIDY OF CONCENTRATED INTEREST GROUPS

In contrast to other Asian countries, Malaysia has not instituted further financial openness or institutional or regime change in response to its 1997 financial and economic crisis. Prime Minister Mahathir's reaction to the financial crisis has been defiant and isolationist. If anything, the crisis seems to have strengthened the hand of Malaysia's ruling elite, especially that of Mahathir. This is somewhat perplexing because the similar crisis of the mid-1980s was important in pushing Mahathir in the direction of liberalization and privatization. How is the contrasting response of the late 1990s to be explained? Why has the crisis not been the "trigger event" for change it has been elsewhere?

It is important to understand the strategic recovery policy and the accompanying rhetorical stances taken by the leadership as a political package consistent with the strong state policies responsible for the original development of the elite business networks. Exchange controls and state-directed fiscal and monetary policy subsidies are designed to protect the elite networks centered around the UMNO. The authority of the state was further underscored by its growing intolerance of opposing views. The Malaysian leadership had embarked on a series of legal and social measures to crack down on press freedoms and dissent even before the crisis, but the crisis period saw cases that were particularly high profile.[13] Continuity of the strong state image was also visible in Malaysia's rebuffing of international criticism of alleged human rights abuses and unconventional economic policies.

However, preserving UMNO business networks is not a sufficient explanation. It alone does not explain why these networks were compromised and broadened in response to the crisis of the mid-1980s. For Malaysia, the impact of the Asian financial crisis and its subsequent response were conditioned by the conflicts between the emerging and dynamic elements of its economy and the traditional problems of communal politics. In particular, the ethnic division has turned many poor rural and urban Malays who would ordinarily be favorably disposed toward breaking down heavily subsidized urban business networks into enemies of liberalization. Again, this is because urban groups, more heavily Chinese and foreign in composition, have been the most visible beneficiaries. Thus Mahathir's policies make eminent political sense, not only as a means of preserving the UMNO's business networks but also as a means to steal the thunder of the Malay opposition and shore up the UMNO's mass support base.

This is a delicate balancing act. Malaysian leaders are highly sensitive to the need to maintain national stability and unity, especially in view of the ethnic, political, and economic instability that has engulfed its similarly endowed neighbor, Indonesia. This is another key to understanding the political logic of Mahathir's response. It shores up UMNO business networks and Malay mass support but does not strongly alienate the urban middle-class groups outside the UMNO circle. The Chinese fear ethnic violence, and Mahathir is the devil they know. Mahathir's rhetoric carefully cultivates this modus vivendi. Mahathir's legitimacy had long relied on his ability to turn his confrontational stance against the West into a source of unity for Asians in general. Thus Mahathir carefully avoids a direct assault on Chinese interests. Instead, he underscores the distinctions he sees between the West and Asia. He appeals to South–South politics and actively seeks out venues (such as Namibia) for voicing the position of the developing countries as victims of Western "recolonization" (*New Straits Times,* 26 July 1998, 1).

Mahathir's policies have also proven acceptable to the broader Bumiputera urban middle classes. As Gomez notes,

The limited reformist orientation of the middle class may . . . be due to the fact that the access of most Bumiputeras to higher education has been facilitated by the award of state scholarships and the enforcement of ethnic quotas. [Also] much of the

Bumiputera middle class is either employed by the state or by public enterprises, and views [Mahathir's party, the United Malay National Organization (UMNO)] as the main means for their upward social mobility. Many Bumiputeras still conceive of UMNO and the state as protectors of their political and economic interests. (1999, 140)

CRISIS ONSET TO CRISIS PEAK

The late 1980s to mid-1990s were a period of recovery and restructuring for Malaysia's banks, which suffered a severe crisis from 1985 to 1988. This recovery was hastened and aided by rapid economic growth, an appreciating real estate market, and a rise in stock market investments. The IMF notes that during this period, the ratio of nonperforming loans to total lending fell from a crisis peak of 35 percent in 1987 to a respectable 3.6 percent in 1997 (Adams et al. 1998). By the time of the onset of the 1997 crisis, Malaysia had one of the healthier banking systems in the region—though nonperforming loans began to rise again in 1997. The economy in general had been experiencing a prolonged run of extremely high growth, at about 7–8 percent a year. Moreover, banking woes were probably less severe than those faced by other countries in the region—thanks, in part, to some prudent measures taken after the banking crisis in the 1980s by the central bank, Bank Negara.[14] Restrictions had been placed on foreign borrowing for the corporate and banking sectors. Whereas other countries in the region had to contend with substantial foreign exchange risks, Malaysia was less exposed and therefore had somewhat greater freedom in crafting its macroeconomic policies.

Nevertheless, there were still significant areas of vulnerability that exposed Malaysia to escalating problems once the currency and stock market speculative shocks began. To begin with, Malaysia at the time of crisis onset still had one of the highest domestic debt to GDP ratios in the world. About 90 percent of corporate debt was held by domestic banks. A significant portion of that figure represented exposure to real estate and stock market investments. Like banks in many other countries in the region, the highly leveraged position of Malaysian banks during the financial crisis would leave them with a raft of bad loans once asset values began to dive. That position was exacerbated by a growth rate of new loans to private businesses of almost 30 percent, especially by the smaller, second-tier banks. The IMF estimates that the private sector was leveraged in the amount of 163 percent of equity (Baliño et al. 1999, 132). The bad loan situation reached crisis proportions in early March 1998, when Bank Negara reported that four of Malaysia's largest financial institutions, including the prestigious Sime Darby Bhd's banking unit, were in need of fresh capital injections.

A second, related area of vulnerability in the banking system derives from the domination of conglomerates and the interlocking ownership of financial institutions and corporations. Analysts estimate that control over about one-fourth of the market capitalization in Malaysia is held by its top ten families (Iskander et al. 1999). While this is a modest figure in comparison to Indonesia, the lack of transparency and the paucity of minority shareholders' rights have tended to undermine investor confidence in Malaysia.

These long-standing patterns of capital formation and ownership were cited by many observers as being at the heart of Malaysia's vulnerability to regional crisis. But what really drew the world's attention to these patterns, and to Malaysia's particular role in the unfolding crisis, was Malaysia's imposition of capital controls on September 1, 1998. What follows is a brief chronology of the crisis and of the measures Bank Negara took leading up to the imposition of capital controls.

In March 1997, Bank Negara, sensitive to the danger of crisis, decided to restrict loans for property and stock market investments. Two months later, in May, the Asian financial crisis broke with massive speculation against the Thai *baht*. Two months after that, in July, Bank Negara began its long series of aggressive interventions, as the *ringgit* became victim to the kind of speculation that the *baht* suffered. Intervention this time could not prevent its fall. Around this time, Mahathir began to issue a series of provocative and now infamous statements, accusing George Soros, the Jews, currency traders, virtual reality (i.e., electronic financial transactions), and hedge fund managers of creating the crisis. As the *ringgit* continued falling, the Kuala Lumpur stock exchange experienced close to a 50 percent decline over the year, and additional bad news issued from South Korea and Japan. But Mahathir held firm in his national vision, forging ahead with several big-ticket prestige projects. These included the Petronas Twin Towers (the tallest buildings in the world at the time of writing); the construction of Asia's largest airport; a new administrative capital (Putrajaya); and the Multimedia Super Corridor, linking the new capital to a "Cyberjaya" at a cost of some \$40 billion.

By December, however, Mahathir's deputy, Anwar Ibrahim, began to voice concerns about the imperatives of economic nationalism embodied in these projects. He proposed an alternate direction, that is, a move toward austerity measures. In addition to suggestions that some of the prestige projects be postponed, Anwar's statement of austerity included warnings that there would be no bank bailouts, that big-ticket imports would be severely limited, and that there would be restrictions on certain types of investments. Enforcing these measures would have been politically difficult. Interest rates would rise as domestic investment and consumption slowed. Companies that were highly leveraged through bank loans would be hit by rapidly falling domestic sales, limited and more costly access to additional capital, and declining stock and property values, possibly facing bankruptcy as a result. Private corporate debt, in particular, posed the single largest threat to the banking sector. Without the safety net of a bailout, the banks would face failure, and heavily indebted UMNO-linked businesses would face loss of their equity. Most threatening of all to the UMNO-linked business elite was the possible end of Mahathir's Vision 2020 ideals and the accompanying rapid-growth strategies that had personally enriched them.

Thus it is hardly surprising that Anwar's austerity measures were not accept-able to them. However, it turned out that they were also unacceptable to Mahathir. Mahathir and Anwar diverged sharply in their preferred responses to the crisis. Anwar championed a liberal stance. He favored fiscal and monetary austerity, bank restructuring, and greater financial openness to bolster the confidence of in-ternational investors and hopefully reverse the outward flow of foreign capital. Mahathir, on the other hand, looked to a strong, interventionist state. He viewed the effects of international capital flows as the problem, not the solution. His so-lution rested primarily on domestically oriented macroeconomic policies that would defend the currency from foreign attacks and stop domestic deflationary pressures by making it extremely costly to pull capital out. As it soon turned out, Anwar's divergence from Mahathir was considered a serious enough threat to the prime minister's authority and governing philosophy that it would lead to Anwar's firing and eventual arrest and conviction on corruption and sexual mis-conduct charges. Other arrests of prominent Mahathir opponents followed. For example, Lim Guan Eng, deputy secretary general of the DAP, was convicted on charges of sedition.

Anwar's sacking occurred one day after the announcement of capital controls. The sweeping nature of the controls stunned many observers. The purpose of their imposition was to curb capital flight and end speculation against Malaysia's cur-rency. One element of the controls was to eliminate offshore *ringgit* transactions. (This caused great disruption in Singapore, where the majority of offshore *ringgit* transactions occur.) Another measure required that the proceeds from the sale of securities be deposited for one year in *ringgit* accounts, and that they were uncon-vertible. Domestic credit was denied to foreign banks and brokers. Most transfers required administrative approval. Outward investment exceeding limited amounts required approval. The only type of investment that was spared from these con-trols was foreign direct investment, which could be repatriated at any time (IMF 1998). These controls had still not been fully eased at the time of writing.

Throughout 1998, the stock market and the currency continued to suffer great volatility. Bank Negara's regular efforts to prop up the *ringgit* consistently met with failure. The largest blow in 1998 came from the disclosure of the liquidity problems facing the largest banks. Other ominous events put the financial crisis into Malaysia's larger, ethnically charged political context. Malaysia's neighbor to the south, Suharto's Indonesia, experienced violence as it entered into negoti-ations with the IMF over efforts to control the effects of a massive amount of bad private debt. Some of this violence spilled over into Malaysia as Indonesian refugees rioted in response to Malaysia's efforts to deport immigrants near Kuala Lumpur (Associated Press, 26 March 1998).

As already noted, the political climate in Kuala Lumpur, therefore, was over-all not one supportive of solutions calling for austerity, especially those imposed by foreigners. The national budget passed in October 1998 was far from austere. It called for even more deficit spending on infrastructure and the support of strategically important businesses such as construction, transportation, and tourism. Malaysia's second minister of finance, Dato' Mustapa Mohamed, justified the deficit spending as a measure to "strengthen the social safety net to protect the more vulnerable segments of society" (IMF 1998). This budget defied the trends elsewhere among the hardest-hit countries. But Malaysia, in contrast to those countries, was not accepting advice from the IMF or any other transnational organization. Defiance was also increasingly apparent as Mahathir publicly voiced concerns about political instability, especially as events unfolded in Indonesia. He was particularly angered by statements made by U.S. Vice President Albert Gore, who, at a November 1998 APEC meeting in Kuala Lumpur, obliquely suggested that student protests in Indonesia calling for government reform might find sympathy among some Malaysians.

The Mahathir-Anwar split and the long shadow of Indonesia's instability are the key to understanding Mahathir's turn toward exchange controls and domestic reflationary policies. Anwar began his career as a student leader appealing in Islamist terms to the Malay masses that benefited least from heavily urban growth. Mahathir coopted Anwar into the UMNO as a means of bolstering the support of these groups. Anwar correctly diagnosed UMNO patronage networks as an important economic obstacle to the further broadening of opportunities to the Malay masses. However, the very strength of the ethnic cleavage made the Malay rural and urban masses more likely to view liberalization policies as benefiting urban, heavily Chinese, and foreign elites. Hence Mahathir has been able to outflank Anwar politically on the mass level by championing an inwardly oriented policy response as a defense against "foreign" interests. That this could also be used to maintain UMNO business networks made it a "win-win" political strategy.

DID THE CONTROLS HELP OR HURT?

Was Malaysia's reaction the right one? We will not know in economic terms until the full implications of the financial crisis become clearer. However, there can be little doubt that Malaysia's policies were the right ones politically from Mahathir's point of view. During the recession of 1984–1985, capital controls seemed the only way to reconcile targeted exchange rates and domestic interest rates, in the absence of any other economic policy instruments (Fischer and Reisen 1993). But in the mid-1980s, these financial difficulties were a catalyst for greater liberalization. As we have seen, this logic no longer held in the 1990s. This is not only because of the short-term political instability that might explode in response to severe austerity policies. This was also true in the mid-1980s and was not inconsistent with further liberalization once the immediate crisis had passed. However, in the late 1990s further liberalization might mean a nearly complete dismantling of UMNO business networks. But this would be undesirable not only for the affected elites. It would also deprive the UMNO of the ethnic politics card it has so effectively used to appeal to the poor rural and urban Malays. Malaysia's domestic politics demanded this reconciliation of export-led growth and maintenance of UMNO business networks in the mid-1980s and demanded it again in the late 1990s.

Malaysia made mistakes in its handling of the crisis. It maintained a strong *ringgit* when it could have pursued more competitive exchange rates to encourage exports. Despite prudential measures and greater regulation, its banks did not learn the right lessons from the 1984–1985 crisis about excessive debt and over-commitment in property markets. Economic nationalism in the form of expensive prestige projects got the better part of Mahathir's judgment. And crony capitalism and the lack of corporate restructuring continued to maintain high barriers to entry in Malaysia's marketplace. But by 1999, Malaysia was on the path to recovery. Its currency has recovered somewhat, property prices have leveled off, progress has been made in restructuring the financial system, and foreign investment has once more begun to flow in. To the extent the ethnically charged interventionist policies have been and continue to be the key to the UMNO's mass Malay base as well as to its narrower business and patronage networks, the decision to pursue a strategy of economic nationalism seems to have paid off politically both before and after the crisis.

NOTES

This chapter is a revised version of a paper first published in 1998 as "The Asian Crisis: Is There a Way Out?" by the Institute of Southeast Asian Studies, Singapore. Reproduced here with permission of the publisher.

1. Figures are from the Malaysian Department of Statistics and were accessed through <http://www.jaring.my/isis/merc/gemc.html>.

2. These groups include the non-Malay Bumiputeras, the Orang Asli, or aboriginal communities of Peninsular Malaysia, and other indigenous groups in Sabah and Sarawak. There are also poor Chinese and Indian rural workers who have been overlooked by the NEP.

3. The UMNO passed restrictive legislation in the mid-1970s to stem the tide of student protest. Under the initiatives taken by then education minister Dr. Mahathir, university students were barred from holding public office or expressing support for any political party or union. Outright banning of student participation was complemented by other UMNO initiatives to "Islamicize" the nation and to coopt the positions held by religious organizations. The UMNO's Islamization plans were criticized by religious leaders who accused the government of deviation from strict Muslim practices. But the UMNO did succeed in coopting important Islamist leaders such as Anwar Ibrahim, who, until his arrest and conviction on charges of corruption and sexual misconduct in 1999, was generally thought to be Mahathir's eventual successor. We should note that scholars characterize the *dakwah* itself not as a monolithic movement but rather as the coming together of diverse groups, with varying degrees of emphasis on the fundamentals of Islam, united only by their rejection of Western ideals (Shamsul 1994).

4. Bumiputera, literally "sons of the soil," was a category eventually broadened to include indigenous non-Malay groups (Andaya and Andaya 1982, 302).

5. The kinds of measures that favor Bumiputera are widely catalogued elsewhere. Apart from the government's direct participation in business activity, the most important privileges given to Malays are special access to schooling (especially at the university level); preferential access to capital; and special rules that govern setting up businesses as Bumiputera or with Bumiputera participation, which are favorable in comparison to the rules governing businesses set up by non-Bumiputera.

6. Publishing and media, in particular, have been important business areas for the UMNO and its partners in the BN coalition. The UMNO-owned Fleet Group controls the *New Straits Times* as well as the top newspapers in the Malay and Chinese languages. The MCA and MIC own other papers, including Tamil-language publications.

7. The interlocking relationships and the corresponding UMNO and MCA cliques arising from these business groups are well documented by Gomez (1991, 1999).

8. The MCA, mostly through its MPBH investment company, had been responsible for raising most of the campaign funds for the Barisan Nasional (Gomez 1991, 48).

9. The deposit-taking cooperatives scandal of 1986 was the most serious one involving the MCA. This scandal involved twenty-four deposit-taking cooperatives that were overexposed in the property and development market. The exposé of the scandal came as a serious blow to both the MCA and the UMNO, coming as it did during an economic recession, on the heels of massive electoral losses for the MCA, and exacerbating internal succession struggles within the MCA. The deposit-taking scandal undermined MCA legitimacy in the late 1980s, and pulled support away from the Barisan Nasional. The Barisan would not regain this lost Chinese support until the UMNO began to ease economic policies in the 1990s to accommodate younger Chinese and Malay entrepreneurs.

10. As Crouch (1996), Khoo (1992), and Means (1991) argue, the UMNO split in 1990—into UMNO and Semangat 46—was the outcome of succession struggles (involving the nomination of Anwar as deputy party president), together with greater social stratification resulting from the NEP.

11. Upon the expiration of the NEP, controlling ownership of publicly listed companies by Bumiputera was about 19 percent, well short of the 30 percent target. The UMNO extended the program another ten years, renaming it the National Development Policy, or NDP, which at the time of writing, was set to expire in the year 2000. The NDP has not succeeded in moving Bumiputera ownership above the 20 percent level. For that reason, few believe that its expiration in 2000 would mean the end of Malaysia's affirmative action strategies.

12. Trade unions long ago ceased to have any influence in party politics.

13. Among the most prominent cases was that of Lim Guan Eng, deputy secretary-general of the opposition Democratic Action Party. After criticizing a prominent Malay politician accused of raping a teenage girl, he was jailed for eighteen months on charges of sedition (*Economist*, 29 August 1998, 17). Another well-publicized case involved a Canadian reporter sentenced to six weeks' imprisonment on charges of contempt of court after authoring an article critical of the handling of defamation suits in Malaysia (*New York Times Online*, 13 September 1999).

14. Important legislation was adopted, beginning with a new banking law in 1989. The legislation required greater prudential oversight, new regulations, and regular auditing with better accounting practices.

6

Indonesia: Cronyism, Economic Meltdown, and Political Stalemate

Kimberly J. Niles

E63. G21 010
053 F32 024

When Thailand devalued the *baht* in July 1997, most financial analysts expected the devaluation to have some short-term adverse effects in Indonesian markets, but few economic observers predicted the devastation to follow. It was initially believed that Indonesia's sound macroeconomic fundamentals and stable political leadership would enable the country to escape the crisis, as it had others in the past, relatively unscathed. Indeed, early reports praised Indonesian policy makers for their swift response to the initial currency pressures.[1] However, within a few months of allowing the Indonesian *rupiah* to float, the currency had lost more than 50 percent of its value.[2] Real GDP declined 13.7 percent in 1998, a truly severe contraction. Inflation reached 60 percent in Indonesia, while inflation in other Southeast Asian crisis countries was below 10 percent. The initial misreading of the situation was due to a failure to recognize the role of political actors and institutions in exacerbating the economic crisis, as well as subsequent recovery efforts.

International economic forces triggered the crisis in Indonesia, as in other neighboring countries, following Thailand's devaluation. The "herd mentality" of foreign investors who panicked and withdrew funds from Indonesia contributed substantially to the currency's collapse (Wade 1998). Although the Indonesian domestic economy had very weak financial regulation prior to July 1997, structural problems in the economy were similar in scope and degree to those of other Southeast Asian countries. In other words, the Indonesian economy did not appear to be any worse off than other Asian economies in 1997, though it was similarly vulnerable to sudden, large-scale capital outflows. As late as June 1997, the International Monetary Fund praised Indonesia for "prudent macroeconomic policies, high investment and savings rates, and reforms to liberalize markets"

(*Wall Street Journal,* 30 December 1997). Nonetheless, Indonesia was the hardest hit country at the height of the financial crisis and it continues to struggle at this time, while other economies are showing strong signs of recovery.

Political factors must be taken into account to explain the depths of Indonesia's despair. Latent opposition to the regime had built up incrementally during the 1990s. Yet, short of extreme unrest producing an abrupt change in regime, there were no institutional mechanisms to dissipate tensions. President Suharto stubbornly refused to plan for his eventual succession, political parties were ineffectual, and the military had become increasingly divided in the 1990s (Schwarz 2000). The situation changed when the economy contracted sharply and Suharto signaled his continued unwillingness to force close regime allies, including his own children, to accept their fair share of the burden of financial restructuring.[3] The regime had lost its main source of legitimation, broad-based economic growth. However, in the absence of mechanisms for societal groups to bring about political change within the existing institutional structure, President Suharto was reappointed unanimously in March 1998, even though the Indonesian public was quite unsatisfied with his performance.

Soon after reappointment to a seventh consecutive term as president, Suharto announced increases in gasoline prices and bus fares in accordance with the third IMF agreement. Such price hikes would mean that the poor and middle-income groups would face an undue burden. Long simmering political pressures exploded, leading to widespread rioting and demands for a democratic transition. The ensuing political instability exacerbated the panic of international investors, caused Indonesians of Chinese descent to flee the country, and ultimately led to Suharto's resignation on 21 May 1998. In the period of transition, interim president B. J. Habibie's close association with Suharto, as well as impending elections, prevented any coherent and credible policy response from developing.

How did economic and political decision making since the 1970s set the stage for Indonesia's recent turmoil and current stalemate? Following a discussion of precrisis economic liberalization reforms and political coalitions, this chapter will review the causes of the financial crisis that began in July 1997, including key responses by the governments of Suharto and his protege B. J. Habibie. What roles were played by interest group demands, patronage networks, and political institutions in explaining early policy responses to the financial crisis? How did political instability interfere with economic recovery efforts? Finally, why has Indonesia been the country hardest hit and slowest to recover in Southeast Asia?

ECONOMIC POLICY IN THE SUHARTO ERA: DEVELOPMENTALISM QUALIFIED BY CRONYISM

After Suharto came to power in October 1965, following an abortive leftist coup, government-sponsored efforts to purge Communist Party (PKI) sympathizers resulted in one of the bloodiest internal conflicts in modern history. The most common estimate is that over 500,000 people were murdered in a six-month period from 1965 to 1966.[4] Moreover, the Indonesian economy was in shambles as a result of the disastrous economic policies of the previous president, Sukarno. Inflation had reached 600 percent at times during the 1960s, and GDP per capita was still less than US$100 in 1970. Human development indicators were also quite low. In 1960, life expectancy was forty-one years, and 61 percent of the population was illiterate.[5] In short, there seemed to be little prospect for the rapid economic growth and political stability that was to follow.

What economic and political factors produced this dramatic turnaround? First, in order to stabilize the economy, Suharto sought the advice of a set of Western-educated economic technocrats, often referred to as the "Berkeley Mafia."[6] This group implemented fairly orthodox economic policies that brought down inflation and stimulated growth. Their policies, in combination with the Suharto regime's strong anticommunist stance, secured the resumption of aid from Western nations. During the late 1960s and early 1970s, the influence of these technocrats in setting and implementing policy goals was high. This was because the economic crisis of the Sukarno period had been severe, and restoring growth was crucial to the new regime's political survival.

Receipts from oil revenues accelerated the economic turnaround in the 1970s. As an oil exporter, Indonesia benefited from high prices and the government used these revenues to encourage economic development. With such a large windfall, there was little need to make the painful trade-offs faced by oil importers during the same period. In the Indonesian case, it was possible for the regime to provide benefits to broad segments of society (Liddle 1992).

With respect to trade policy, oil revenues allowed the government to encourage domestic industrialization through tariff and nontariff barriers without worrying about the need to be immediately competitive in international markets. Protectionist barriers allowed a small number of conglomerates to expand through rent-seeking activities. Licenses to import inputs for food processing or manufacturing, for example, were limited to close allies of the regime. With respect to fiscal policy, Indonesia has had an open capital account since 1970, but a handful of state banks dominated the banking sector.[7] These banks were largely used for patronage purposes, and the subsidized credit they provided was not available to wide sectors of society. Among the largest debtors to the state banks were Suharto's children and close associates (Pincus and Ramli 1998; *Wall Street Journal,* 14 July 1998).

Within the elite, the patronage-based nature of the regime was not overly controversial because Indonesia never had a landed oligarchy and the Dutch had not encouraged indigenous business activities. Following independence, many Dutch firms were nationalized, so an independent business class did not develop. Perhaps most importantly, the bureaucratic and military elite who might challenge President Suharto received material benefits in the form of licenses or access to capital that limited any potential conflicts. Military officers often ran state-owned enterprises, particularly in the oil and minerals sectors.

Outside the elite, agricultural policies benefited both small-scale farmers and urban consumers. Preventing a resurgence of rural political activism was a priority of the Suharto regime, given the high mobilization of the 1960s. With oil receipts, the government was able to design agricultural policies that provided subsidized credit to small-scale farmers, new types of rice varieties, and fertilizer for agricultural inputs. At the same time, the government stockpiled rice in order to keep the price paid by urban consumers stable and artificially low. Due to rapid GDP growth and fairly equitable agricultural policies, Indonesia probably experienced the greatest decline in absolute poverty of any country in the world during this period, from over 60 percent of the population in 1970 to less than 15 percent by 1996.[8] Both economic growth and declining poverty were important sources of regime legitimation.

The economic gains of the 1970s were associated with a period of state-led development, financed with revenue from natural resource-based extraction. The shift to greater openness in the 1980s was again the result of external economic factors, this time falling oil prices. The government needed to develop a non-oil export base after oil revenues had declined dramatically. The share of oil and gas exports plus aid inflows as a percentage of GDP had fallen from over 30 percent in 1981 to about 10 percent in 1986 (Pincus and Ramli 1998, figure 3). Yet, by the time oil prices collapsed in the mid-1980s, both strong macroeconomic fundamentals and the bases for sustained rural development were already in place.

In order to reduce state reliance on oil receipts, Suharto again turned to the economic technocrats, this time to design a series of policies to encourage manufacturing, including foreign investment in manufacturing. As a result of their policies, tariff barriers were lowered and special licensing arrangements were phased out in many sectors, though not in some key industries in which the president's children or Chinese conglomerates had a stake (*Far Eastern Economic Review* [*FEER*], 16 October 1997). In general, however, there was a shift toward market-driven mechanisms and reduced reliance on the state in the trade arena. The share of domestic manufacturing controlled by licenses dropped from 68 percent in 1986 to 33 percent in 1990 (Bresnan 1993). Between 1990 and 1997, the number of nontariff barriers fell from 1,000 to 200 and the average tariffs from 22 percent to under 12 percent (*FEER*, 16 October 1997).

The economic technocrats also liberalized the financial sector in the 1980s. These reforms were numerous (Cole and Slade 1996). A 1983 reform removed interest rate ceilings on state banks. The reforms of 1988 removed restrictions on new banks, allowed joint ventures between foreign and local banks, and lowered reserve requirements. State-owned enterprises were also permitted to deposit 50 percent of their funds with private banks, rather than exclusively with state banks. The overall effect of these reforms was to shift lending from state to private banks. The number of private banks rose from 108 in 1988 to 232 in 1993 (Radelet forthcoming), but the state-run banks remained more influential in Indonesia than elsewhere and the new private banks were grossly underregulated.

As financial liberalization took effect, the wealth of the president's children and close associates soared, since foreign and domestic firms alike sought to reduce risk in an uncertain legal environment through connections with presidential allies (Root 1996). While using personal connections for private gains was not a new feature of Indonesian business practices, and hardly unique among Asian countries, the level of these types of arrangements appeared to increase in the 1990s. One reason for the appearance of this sudden surge in cronyism is that after their special concessions to market oil for export became less profitable, the president's children began to engage in a broader range of business activities. Another reason is that several of the conglomerates began to list shares on the Jakarta Stock Exchange after 1988 in order to secure additional financing. An unintentional effect was that these listings enabled the public to get a clearer picture of the wealth of the top conglomerates.[9]

The pattern of reforms in the financial sector mirrored that of the trade sector. The implemented reforms were substantial but stopped short of challenging powerful vested interests. In trade policy, tariffs and quantitative restrictions were removed, but not in some key areas where patronage-based relationships took precedence. Regarding fiscal policy, the economic technocrats were unable to reform the patronage-based lending of the state banks. According to Pincus and Ramli (1998), the economic technocrats decided to open up the financial sector as an alternative way to increase competition when they were unable to reform the lending practices of the state banks.[10] The new private banks were grossly underregulated, however, and many conglomerates formed affiliations with private banks that allowed them to lend to related companies. In sum, the decision to liberalize the financial sector had two consequences. First, a series of reform measures left Indonesia with one of the least regulated financial sectors in the world and second, the reforms unintentionally limited the future ability of the technocrats to use monetary policy to adjust to adverse shocks (Pincus and Ramli 1998).

The Indonesian economy up to July 1997 could be characterized as one that had a long history of an open capital account and a heavily managed exchange rate pegged to the dollar, but little government oversight of banking and a lack of transparency in awarding contracts or supplying credit. While the macroeconomic situation was fairly strong, the financial sector was quite vulnerable to sudden capital outflows. Why were the economic technocrats able to liberalize certain industries but not others? Why did they allow the number of private banks to soar while even the state-controlled banks still lacked transparency and lent disproportionately to the president's family and close associates? In each case, liberalization was part of an effort by the technocrats to halt reliance on patronage connections as the main basis for trade and financial policy outcomes, but such reforms usually fell short of challenging powerful vested interests[11] and therefore had unintended consequences.

POLITICAL COALITIONS IN THE SUHARTO ERA: PATRONAGE NETWORKS AND CO-OPTED INTEREST GROUPS

Before addressing the economic and political devastation that took place in Indonesia subsequent to the Asian financial crisis, I shall examine the underlying coalitions that kept the regime in power for over thirty years. There is no doubt that Indonesia under Suharto was an authoritarian state. However, Suharto did not rule for thirty years exclusively by force. Within the regime, Suharto was skilled in balancing potential rivals in the military or bureaucratic elite, as well as rewarding those who were loyal to him personally. There is general agreement among scholars that Indonesia under Suharto was a highly centralized, patrimonial state characterized by vertical linkages between patrons and their clients (MacIntyre 1994). The military had a large role in politics under the *dwi fungsi* (dual functions) doctrine, which delegated to the military a formal role in both national defense and political affairs. This dual function legitimized the military's role in political affairs and social development. Many governorships and administrative posts in the outer islands were given to military officers.

Most scholars agree that the types of interest group demands which have played a prominent role in economic policy formation in other settings were not influential in Indonesia. In many East Asian states, developmental success has been attributed to governments that were autonomous or insulated from organized interest group pressures. In the Indonesian case, these pressure groups never matured in the first place, though the regime was certainly autonomous. Concentrated interest groups, such as trade associations, were either weak or politically vulnerable. According to Mackie (1999), "Social classes and interest groups based on the country's major industries or productive sectors have not developed as significant actors on the Indonesian political stage or discovered how to operate politically as pressure groups." The Indonesian Chamber of Commerce (KADIN) was not consulted prior to economic policy decisions (Root 1996). KADIN has usually been characterized as part of the corporatist structure of the regime and thus a tame institution.

Another potential source of interest group pressure, the ethnic Chinese business community, has always been vulnerable politically and has therefore kept a low profile in organizations such as KADIN (Mackie 1992). Suharto's ties to Chinese businessmen were controversial because the percentage of ethnic Chinese was smaller than in other countries in the region, while their wealth was great. The most commonly cited estimate is that ethnic Chinese made up only 3.5 percent of the Indonesian population but controlled 73 percent of the nonland wealth

(Government of Australia 1995). Ethnic Chinese businessmen controlled many of the top conglomerates, often in association with Suharto's children.

Although the Suharto regime did not face significant demands from concentrated interest groups, it remained permeable to personal appeals (MacIntyre 1994). The Chinese business community tended to make appeals for preferential policies on a personal basis, not as part of a larger organization. Although the Chinese business community was less socially integrated in Indonesia than in any other country in Southeast Asia, it was conspicuous in its attempts—along with the president's children—to reregulate the economy to secure cartels and special licensing arrangements from the government in such key sectors as plywood, cloves, wheat, and autos.[12]

The Suharto regime was not entirely insulated from societal pressures. Yet, due to the regime's willingness to resort to force, these pressures were weaker and erupted less frequently than in other contexts. Dispersed interest groups, such as small-scale farmers or workers in the urban informal sector, were subject to repression if they tried to organize. The only major challenge to the regime occurred in 1974, when a group of student leaders protested the growing presence of foreign firms in the economy (the "Malari Affair"). These activists were jailed, and further political rallies were banned on university campuses. Labor organization also remained very weak. The main labor union was part of the corporatist structure of the regime and was co-opted by the ruling party. Workers in coveted formal sector jobs were reluctant to risk losing their employment, given the poor prospects that the Suharto government would ever agree to their demands. Despite greater attempts to organize independent labor unions in the 1990s, the leaders of these movements usually ended up in prison (Hadiz 1994).

Moreover, Suharto had engineered a set of institutions that ensured his continued selection as president.[13] Suharto controlled well over half of the legislative assembly representatives who, in turn, then appointed him president (Boileau 1983; MacIntyre 1999a). Nor were opposition political parties a potential source for sweeping political change. Only two opposition parties were permitted by law after 1971. Both were depoliticized and quiescent (Liddle 1992).

In sum, the trade and financial liberalizations of the late 1980s were caused more by the external shock of declining oil revenues than demands from either concentrated or dispersed interest groups, or even opposition political parties. Although not driven by domestic demands, these liberalizations could nonetheless have increased the mobilization of different sectors of the economy and thus empowered them by 1997 to lobby for greater fairness in the distribution of gains. Yet the beneficiaries of liberalization were disproportionately the president's children and a few extremely wealthy Chinese businessmen associated with the president. The turnover of the top twenty conglomerates was equivalent to 22 percent of GDP in 1996 (EIU 1998). These twenty conglomerates usually had close ties to the regime that reflected personal relationships more than interest group pressure, in the sense that the term "concentrated interest groups" is generally meant to refer to lobbying and consultative activities on the part of a recognized group in a public arena prior to the formal decision-making process. In Indonesia, both concentrated and dispersed interest groups were still in a very weak position and unable to influence policy decisions.

Although neither concentrated nor dispersed interest groups had abandoned the regime prior to the financial crisis, cracks had begun to appear in the coalitional basis of support for Suharto in the 1990s. Societal anger over the concentration of wealth and lack of even minor democratic openings had escalated primarily over three events. First, in 1994, following a story in the widely respected *Tempo* news magazine that was unflattering to the Minister of Research and Technology, B. J. Habibie, the president closed down *Tempo* and two other newsmagazines. Second, the government overreacted to the slight rise in popular support for one of the two opposition parties, Megawati Sukarnoputri's secular-nationalist party (PDI), in the 1992 election. To prevent a further rise in support for the PDI in the 1997 election, Suharto engineered Megawati's ouster as PDI chairwoman in 1996. This ouster was widely perceived as unfair, and it convinced many Indonesians that the Suharto government was unwilling to allow even a gradual political opening through the electoral process. The July 1996 riots that followed in Jakarta were the worst in twenty years.[14] While the riots were blamed on student activists who had tried to form an alternative party (PRD), many Indonesians believed the military had staged the confrontation at PDI headquarters and used it to justify the subsequent government crackdown. The PRD activists were tried and imprisoned. Third, Megawati's ouster in 1996 decimated the PDI's showing in the 1997 election. Her supporters either abstained, spoiled their ballots, or voted for the Muslim opposition party (PPP). The initial counting showed that the PDI would win only ten seats, and there was an eleven-seat minimum to qualify for representation in the legislature. The Suharto regime faced the problem of having to "find" 60,000 votes, so that PDI could retain seats in Parliament. Otherwise, the legislature would have had only one opposition party and would have seemed even less democratic than before (MacIntyre 1999a). The cumulative effect of all three events was to convince the public of the regime's continued unwillingness to allow either greater press freedom or a gradual opening through electoral competition.

Each of these three missteps was clumsy and ultimately embarrassing for the regime. Their combined effect eroded public support, particularly among the urban middle class. Yet, although the urban middle class had grown increasingly frustrated with the lack of transparency and political openness under Suharto, this group had benefited from liberalization through rising incomes and greater availability of consumer goods. A vocal and sustained opposition movement was unlikely to develop as long as economic growth remained high.

At the elite level, both the economic technocrats and certain factions of the military had become frustrated with the accumulated wealth of the president's family and closest allies. Liberalization had encouraged multinational corporations to form joint ventures with the president's children and Chinese associates, as these ties provided access and preferential treatment for the foreign companies. The economic technocrats had lost influence with Suharto, in part as a result of their own success in fostering widespread growth, which made their skills seem less relevant to the president. Compared to the military's role in the period of state-led development in the 1970s, it was less favored in the 1990s.[15] Again, however, as long as the economy was growing rapidly, there were few options for displacing the president. What was unclear at the time was whether the economic technocrats or certain factions within the military would abandon the president if growth slowed and a mass opposition movement emerged.

ECONOMIC CAUSES OF THE 1997 FINANCIAL CRISIS IN INDONESIA

Even in early 1997, there was little reason to think economic growth could not continue indefinitely—or at least until an eventual presidential succession upon Suharto's death in office or decision not to seek another term. Indonesia's macroeconomic fundamentals were sound. The budget was balanced, inflation had dropped to around 6.5 percent, and growth had been averaging about 7 percent since the 1980s. The current account deficit was approaching 3.5 percent of GDP, with over 4 percent being a clear sign of trouble, according to Edwards (1999). Yet this deficit was lower than those of the other Association of South East Asian Nations—4 countries in 1997, or Mexico in 1994, and it was being covered by high capital inflows (McLeod 1999).

While these macroeconomic fundamentals were sound, investors' confidence in Indonesia was based on assumptions that high capital inflows would continue and the exchange rate would hold. The proximate causes for the string of devaluations that began in Thailand have been covered thoroughly elsewhere (Wade 1998; Radelet and Sachs 1998), and there is little evidence that the economic causes of the crisis in Indonesia were unique to that context (Baliño 1999). To briefly summarize economic causes of the financial crisis in Asia, the following factors tend to be identified (Wade 1998; Edwards 1999) as underlying structural weaknesses:

- large capital inflows in the context of a weak regulatory state
- excessive investment in speculative activities
- unhedged, dollar-denominated loans with very short maturity dates
- heavily managed or fixed exchange rates.

A precipitating event that led to sagging exports and exchange rate pressures throughout Southeast Asia was the fall of the yen against the dollar. After appreciating from about 230 to 80 to the dollar from 1985 to 1995, the yen began to fall in the spring of 1995 and eventually reached 147 to the dollar. Since many

East Asian currencies were linked to the dollar, this hurt the competitiveness of Asian exports in key sectors and led to growing current account deficits throughout the region (Wade 1998). Once Thailand devalued, investors lost confidence in the region and pulled out of other Asian countries in a panic. Although Indonesia's current account deficit had been lower than many other Asian countries, it was just as vulnerable to a decline in capital inflows.

Many Indonesian corporations had borrowed directly from abroad in order to take advantage of the difference between international and domestic interest rates. This type of borrowing was not well-monitored by the central bank. Thus, Indonesia's corporate debt to bank debt ratio had become the highest among East Asian countries. Sixty-five percent of all privately held Indonesian debt is held by corporations, while only 8 percent of private debt is held by private banks (EIU 1998). Much of the corporate debt was short-term, denominated in dollars, and unhedged against exchange rate fluctuations. After seeing the extreme fluctuations in the value of the *rupiah* following IMF pronouncements in October 1997, and rumors about Suharto's health in December 1997, owners of domestic firms realized how vulnerable they were to exchange rate fluctuations. Their individual decisions to sell *rupiah* played a large role in the currency's collapse (*Wall Street Journal,* 30 December 1997).

THE AFTERMATH: EXPLAINING POLICY RESPONSES IN THE FINAL YEAR OF SUHARTO'S RULE

Although the proximate economic causes of the financial crisis in Indonesia were similar to those in other Southeast Asian countries, the effects were far more severe. Indonesia had the largest drop in the value of its currency. The number of closed banks is high and corporate bankruptcies continue. Food distribution was disrupted more than in any other country at the height of the crisis. Why have the economic effects of the financial crisis been so severe in Indonesia?

First, a growing chorus of scholars has argued that the International Monetary Fund likely contributed to investor panic by insisting on bank closures and wide-ranging reforms as a condition of monetary assistance (Sachs 1998; Wade 1998; Feldstein 1998). In this view, IMF policies further eroded investor confidence and led to panic-induced withdrawals. While IMF policies were certainly misguided in some aspects, such an argument would only explain why Asian economies collectively faced large capital outflows. It would not explain why Indonesia was much harder hit than other Asian economies that had agreed to similarly designed IMF programs. Second, as mentioned above, domestic firms were quick to panic and short the *rupiah* at the first sign of political uncertainty. There is ample evidence that domestic firms were at least as culpable as foreign currency speculators in the *rupiah*'s collapse (*Wall Street Journal,* 30 December 1997). These domestic firms probably had better day-to-day knowledge of rising political vulnerabilities than foreign currency traders had.

Most importantly, Suharto's reluctance to force well-connected private banks and their related conglomerates to take a hit for their overextended borrowing was immediately apparent to domestic observers, as in the case of Suharto's second son acquiring another bank only a few days after a bank he controlled was shut down. In this view, Suharto himself did the worst damage to the Indonesian economy by wavering on IMF reforms, by allowing his children to flirt with the idea of a currency board, and by selecting in March 1998 the most personally loyal yet technocratically inexperienced cabinet of his career.[16]

While patrimonialism has long been a feature of politics in Southeast Asia, decision making based on personal relationships increased further between the period of deregulation in the 1980s and the onset of the financial crisis in 1997. These personal ties were apparent in Suharto's backpedaling on any IMF reforms that would have damaged his children's business interests or those of his close friends. During the final months of the Suharto regime, the president's policies were also markedly inconsistent and incoherent. He oscillated between cowering to the IMF and denouncing its programs as soon as new funds were disbursed. Most notoriously, Suharto's children went on a publicity campaign for a currency board, violating the terms of the second letter of intent that Suharto had just signed with the IMF. The president also made no concerted effort to explain how the new Indonesian Bank Restructuring Agency (IBRA), established as part of the second IMF agreement, would handle bank closures and recapitalizations. This lack of information kept the anxiety of domestic firms high, when in fact the establishment of IBRA could reasonably have been a signal of a more orderly program of bank closures and restructuring. Such policy flip-flops heightened investor panic (MacIntyre 1999b).

The appendix at the end of this chapter provides a more detailed account of key economic and political events in the Indonesian financial crisis. Clearly, political uncertainty often precipitated further erosions in the exchange rate.

THE INFLUENCE OF POLITICAL ACTORS AND INSTITUTIONS

One strand of the political economy literature conspicuously absent from analyses of Indonesian politics during the Suharto era is that relating to political institutions. In the past, this absence was due to the authoritarian nature of the regime. Competitive politics had not come to play a role in policy decisions, which were often reached ahead of time through consultation and consensus (Liddle 1992). Leaving out this type of analysis, however, ignores the ways in which political institutions can shape the survival strategies of even authoritarian leaders (MacIntyre 1999a).

Recently, MacIntyre (1999b) has shown how institutional variations affected the policy responses of Asian governments to the financial crisis. Building on the general veto player argument advanced by Tsebelis (1995) and the credibility-decisiveness tradeoff emphasized by Cox and McCubbins (forthcoming), MacIntyre argues that political systems with many checks and balances built into the institutional structure are "credible." This is because it is hard for leaders to change policy after they have committed to one particular policy. However, when policy change is urgently needed, as in response to an externally-induced economic crisis, these systems may experience logjams and be unable to respond to changed circumstances. A system is said to be "decisive" if one leader can respond quickly to changed circumstances. However, since that leader is not constrained in his policy responses by other domestic actors, there are no checks and balances to constrain his behavior. While leaders in decisive systems may respond quickly to changed circumstances, they may also reverse earlier policy commitments, and thus wild fluctuations in policy may occur.

A comparison between Indonesia and Thailand illustrates this point. In MacIntyre's empirical application, the Thai political system is vulnerable to logjams, since there are a large number of parties that have to form unstable coalitions in order to govern. The Indonesian system, in contrast, was one with almost no checks on the executive at the onset of the financial crisis. Suharto more or less ruled as he saw fit. As applied to Indonesia by MacIntyre (1999b), this paradigm would explain Suharto's policy flip-flops on whether to adopt a currency board, for example. In sum, Thai politicians were constrained and failed to act despite an urgent need to do so, while Suharto acted quickly but changed his policies frequently.

The institutional model employed by MacIntyre is designed to explain the extent of policy stasis or change. While it provides a useful analytical framework for explaining the swings in policy under Suharto compared to logjams in Thailand, it does not offer a complete explanation. The model does not attempt to explain why autonomous leaders sometimes pursue inconsistent rather than consistent policies. Moreover, the model was not designed to explain how societal mobilization increased in Indonesia, nor why groups that had formerly expressed latent opposition to the regime became willing to express opposition openly—even after the military began to kidnap student leaders and shoot demonstrators in early 1998.

Compared to other Asian countries such as Thailand, the Philippines, and South Korea, one of the unique features of Indonesia was that no political openings, however incremental, had occurred prior to the financial crisis. In fact, the regime had clamped down on dissent as recently as 1996, when it ousted Megawati as chairwoman of the PDI and arrested PRD activists. In the other three countries, varying levels of democratization had provided outlets for societal groups to express dissent. These incremental openings enabled interest groups to influence government policy, however weakly, an option that was unavailable in Indonesia under Suharto.

The depoliticization of socioeconomic groups in Indonesia was a notorious accomplishment of the Suharto government. Indeed, the urban middle classes and political elites did not abandon Suharto until after the economy had collapsed, unarmed students had been killed by the military, ethnic Chinese had been targeted for violence, and millions of dollars worth of property damage had been caused.

A NEW BEGINNING OR BUSINESS AS USUAL?

The final round of demonstrations prior to Suharto's resignation was triggered by the announced implementation of a condition of the third IMF agreement. The most controversial provision called for cuts in gasoline subsidies. These announced cuts were evidence that dispersed interest groups would bear an undue burden of restructuring, only weeks after the president's daughter and close allies holding large debts had been appointed to the cabinet. The ensuing demonstrations were supported by university students, a dispersed interest group, but the students' main goal was for Suharto to step down. They had no clear political alternative and did not formulate an economic plan (*FEER*, 26 November 1998). Most concentrated interest groups were silent until the collapse of the regime.

Economic recovery has been slow since Suharto's resignation in May 1998, in large part because his successor, B. J. Habibie, was tainted by close ties to the previous regime. While the transition from Suharto to Habibie followed the procedures set forth in the Indonesian constitution, it was not accepted by the public at large. To most Indonesians, Habibie was hopelessly tainted by his past association with Suharto. As long as domestic political uncertainty was high, foreign investment was unlikely to return to earlier levels, despite very high domestic interest rates. Nor would Sino-Indonesians repatriate their capital.

Habibie's government faced two difficult challenges: (1) how to address past abuses, so that the repeated protests and mass rioting would end; and (2) how to move forward with democratic political reforms. The government's failure to address either challenge well kept Indonesia in a lengthy transition period from May 1998 to October 1999. In terms of addressing past abuses, Habibie implemented a number of important policy changes. He allowed greater press freedom, granted amnesty to many political prisoners, and abided by his promises to permit election law reform and hold general elections in 1999. He was continually hampered by past events, however. His government failed to pursue allegations of corruption and human rights abuses aggressively. The new electoral system also retained several features of the old set of electoral rules, which could be expected to help the ruling Golkar party hang on to power. Among the features that were retained under the new set of electoral rules was the indirect election of the president by a legislative assembly (MPR) that consists of the mainly elected lower house (DPR) and additional appointed members. The long time lag between the general election and the presidential selection was also kept, but the presidential selection process was moved forward by three weeks when the political crisis became acute.

In the June 1999 competition for elected seats, Golkar won the second highest number of votes nationally. The party maintained a continuing presence in rural areas and the outer islands, a traditional source of strength. Further, in the distribution of appointed seats, these same areas were overrepresented relative to their populations. Thus Golkar could also be expected to receive the support of many of the representatives in appointed seats, and probably also the thirty-eight appointed military seats in the lower house. Since the president was selected indirectly, Habibie was still on track to compete closely for the presidency (Soesastro 1999), despite his lack of widespread popular support. The lengthy period between the June 1999 general election and October 1999 presidential selection also contributed to the ability of the ruling party to buy the votes of MPR representatives and engineer coalitions that would enable Habibie to retain power. It discouraged both foreign and Sino-Indonesian investors from returning to Indonesia until the political transition was resolved.

Habibie's candidacy was undone mainly because of the Bank Bali scandal. Auditors for PriceWaterhouse Coopers discovered in late July 1999 that US$80 million in economic recovery loans had been diverted to the ruling party's electoral campaign chest (*FEER,* 23 September, 30 September 1999). In the wake of this scandal, the World Bank and International Monetary Fund postponed further disbursal of loans to Indonesia in September 1999. In addition, the Indonesian attorney general announced less than ten days before the presidential selection that separate corruption investigations against Suharto and one of his sons were being dropped for lack of evidence. The combined effect of these scandals eliminated Interim President B. J. Habibie's chances for reappointment by reinforcing the widely held perception that his regime represented "business as usual" rather than a "new beginning." The Indonesian military's role in the violence in East Timor also led to widespread international condemnation during this period, though it did far less to bring down Habibie than the scandals that reinforced his strong links to Suharto. In the view of most Indonesians, Habibie represented executive turnover without a democratic transition. In an unprecedented display of legislative independence,[17] the MPR voted 355 to 322 to reject Interim President Habibie's "accountability speech," in effect a vote of no confidence.[18]

It is less obvious whether the new post-Habibie government represents "business as usual" or a "new beginning." The selection in October 1999 of Abdurrahman Wahid as president and Megawati Sukarnoputri as vice president brings to the executive branch leaders with solid democratic credentials. Both were often vocal opponents of Suharto, unlike former president Habibie. Although they have in the past been inconsistent in their policy statements regarding the student movement and the extent to which a new government should investigate past transgressions, early signs are encouraging. The full Bank Bali report has been presented to the new parliament and the corruption investigation of Suharto has been reopened. IMF lending is expected to resume shortly.

The open debate and secret balloting within the MPR that brought Abdurrahman Wahid and Megawati to power are also positive signs. On the other hand, the deals the new president had to cut to achieve power mean that past appointees retained some cabinet posts. Although the new cabinet contains many fresh faces and the fewest military appointments in years, four members served previously under Suharto or Habibie, and six members are either active or retired military officers (*Jakarta Post,* 27 October 1999). As a result, Suharto is much more likely to be pardoned than jailed, in an effort at national reconciliation.

What will be the basis for electoral politics in the new parliament? It is too early to predict whether the legislature will become highly fragmented and undisciplined, like the Thai parliament, or will develop strong party roots in society. The high number of political parties that competed (48) and won seats (21) in the June 1999 general election does not bode well for the ability of the legislature to enact new policies. Nor does the high number of parties represented in the cabinet, which resulted from backroom deals and trade-offs. This coalition building may keep the emphasis of the legislature on the type of "consensus" favored under Suharto. However, despite a large number of new parties, the main parties have historical roots in society and can be identified with specific programmatic agendas—more so than in many new democracies in which there is no earlier basis for party formation.[19] The extent to which party politics becomes institutionalized is crucial to the consolidation of democracy in Indonesia.

CONCLUSION

The two main international determinants of the economic crisis in Indonesia were the Thai devaluation in July 1997 and the collective panic of foreign investors who lost confidence in the region. The domestic determinants of the crisis were long-standing, but triggered by external events. The corruption and patronage of the Suharto regime were underlying problems that had been easy for both domestic actors and international lenders to ignore, as long as the economy was growing.[20] When the economy contracted, international lenders jumped in and attached a host of conditions to further lending, even though these conditions forced the economy into recession (Sachs 1998; Feldstein 1998). Domestic actors also became less tolerant of the Suharto regime's preferential treatment of close allies. Most importantly, Suharto failed to act consistently and coherently to restore confidence, whether by complying with IMF recommendations, or by pursuing a more controlled reform without IMF assistance.

Returning to an earlier question, are interest group demands, patronage networks, or political institutions more important factors in explaining initial policy responses to the crisis? Independently organized, concentrated interest groups had not been important actors in influencing economic policy prior to the financial crisis, and they were not early or vocal opponents of Suharto. Members of these groups were influential through patronage networks with close ties to Suharto. Dispersed interest groups were not allowed to organize, and pent-up discontent exploded following the financial crisis. In particular, students and unemployed workers became vocal opponents of the regime at great personal risk. But the students' main goal was to persuade Suharto to step down. They were not especially involved in articulating demands for specific economic policies in response to the crisis.

The enduring influence of patronage networks was apparent in Suharto's un-willingness to force close regime allies to accept financial hardship in the early stages of the crisis. Political institutions were also important because Indonesia's unique mix of military-backed authoritarianism and very limited electoral competition had prevented even incremental democratic openings prior to Suharto's resignation in May 1998. It was the closed character and institutional rigidity of the political system that finally triggered extreme political unrest and ultimately Suharto's resignation. While massive corruption had existed for decades, the decline of economic growth deprived Suharto of the dispersed interest group support he had come to expect. When the crisis broke and Suharto failed to respond coherently, the closed and rigid character of the political system forced the nascent opposition movement to emerge in a bold, highly destabilizing fashion.

Indonesia's protracted transition has shown that economic recovery is very difficult during a period of extreme political uncertainty. Both the Indonesian economy and its political institutions reached the brink of collapse at several points between December 1997 and October 1999. During this two-year period, the country confronted tremendous political and economic obstacles: panic-induced food shortages, the near collapse of the currency, widespread rioting and demonstrations, increasing separatist demands, and international condemnation for the military's role in the militia-led violence in East Timor. However, the potential for a new beginning is evident in the 1999 general election and presidential selection. As already noted, the full Bank Bali report has been disclosed to the Parliament and the corruption investigation against Suharto has been reopened.

The new government still faces a host of old problems, though. Ethnic conflict and regional demands for autonomy remain threats to the very survival of Indonesia as a nation-state. Within days of his selection as president, Abdur-rahman Wahid proposed switching from a unitary republic to a federal system of governance in order to increase regional autonomy and preserve Indonesia's boundaries. The demands of smaller Muslim parties for a role in politics are expected to increase, but the president has consistently favored the separation of religion and politics. He has also consistently tried to protect the rights of the Chinese and other ethnic minorities. Finally, the appointed military seats in the DPR are scheduled to be abolished prior to the next election, though it is not certain the military will give up its remaining thirty-eight seats. While any one of these long-simmering tensions has the potential to erupt into further violence and thereby postpone economic recovery, early market reactions to the new government are favorable. In the long run, however, development of coherent and broadly accountable economic policymaking is likely to depend on formation of a small number of ideologically consistent parties with strong ties to dispersed interest group support bases.

APPENDIX: KEY ECONOMIC AND POLITICAL EVENTS
IN THE INDONESIAN CRISIS

1997

August 14: Currency band for the *rupiah* (average value about 3,000 to the U.S. dollar) abolished; currency falls.

October 31: First IMF package announced: sixteen commercial banks closed, limited deposit insurance provided for depositors in other banks. More bank closures expected to follow.

November 31: President's second son allowed to reopen operations of one of the sixteen failed banks by assuming control of a different bank and transferring his former activities.

Early December: Suharto cancels trip abroad; rumors circulate that he suffered a stroke.

Mid-December: Deposit runs on banks, accounting for half of banking system assets.

1998

January 6: Suharto presents 1998–1999 fiscal year budget speech, which is widely perceived as out of touch with the seriousness of the economic situation.

January 8: Black Thursday. *Rupiah* free-falls to 11,000; panic-induced food buying.

January 15: Second IMF agreement; *rupiah* continues to fall; Indonesian Bank Restructuring Agency (IBRA) established and blanket deposit guarantee announced.

January 21: Suharto names B. J. Habibie as vice presidential candidate; *rupiah* falls to 16,000.

February 10–13: President's children propose currency board for exchange rate management; international lenders strongly opposed.

March 10: Suharto unanimously elected to seventh five-year presidential term.

March 14: New cabinet announced; cabinet includes Suharto's daughter "Tutut" and several close business associates, including Mohammad "Bob" Hasan.

April 4: IBRA closes seven banks and takes over seven others.

April 8: Third letter of intent signed with the IMF.

May 4: Government announces increases in gasoline prices and bus fares; riots ensue.

May 12: Military kills six students demonstrating at Trisakti University while Suharto is abroad.

May 14: Riots spread in Jakarta; thousands die; ethnic Chinese targeted for violence.

May 19: Students take over parliamentary complex; remain for three nights.

May 21: Suharto resigns; Vice President Habibie immediately sworn in as interim president.

May 22: New cabinet announced; General Wiranto rejects calls for investigation of Suharto family wealth, but Suharto's son-in-law is removed from army strategic command.

May 27: Habibie pledges elections in 1999, once new electoral laws are in place.

June 5: International lenders and Indonesian companies agree on corporate debt rescheduling.

September 30: Bank Mandiri created through merger of four largest state-owned banks; plans announced for joint government–private sector recapitalization of private banks.

October 6: Amended banking law passed, including strengthening of IBRA.

Mid-November: Protests during parliamentary consideration of electoral reforms; students killed.

1999

March 13: Government closes thirty-eight banks and IBRA takes over seven others; eligibility of nine banks for joint recapitalization with government announced.

June 7: General elections. Megawati Sukarnoputri's party, PDI-P, wins largest vote share.

July 20: Bank Bali scandal revealed by international auditors.

August 30: East Timorese vote for independence.

September: Militia-sponsored killings and looting in East Timor. Full Bank Bali report not made public. World Bank and IMF suspend loan dispersals.

October 1–6: New Parliament convenes. House and Assembly Speakers elected; continuing role for Golkar party and the military.

October 11: Attorney general drops corruption investigation of Suharto, citing lack of evidence.

October 19–20: The assembly (MPR) rejects Habibie's "accountability speech" by a 355–322 vote; Habibie withdraws his candidacy.

October 20–21: Abdurrahman Wahid elected president, Megawati vice president.

Sources: Baliño (1999); various newspapers.

NOTES

1. The Indonesian government first widened the currency band in which the *rupiah* traded in early July 1997. It then floated the currency on August 14 rather than use up its foreign exchange reserves, as Thailand had done. In October 1997, the government announced that it planned to halt large infrastructure projects.

2. At one point, the *rupiah* later fell to only 15 percent of its precrisis value.

3. The earliest signal of Suharto's unwillingness to force his children to suffer financial hardship as a result of the first IMF agreement was when one of Suharto's sons was allowed to take over a different bank only days after his Bank Andromeda was closed in

October 1997. The son then obtained another foreign exchange license and essentially transferred operations to the new bank, Bank Alfa. The currency board proposed by several of Suharto's children in February 1998, in defiance of the second IMF agreement, was another example. That proposal was ultimately dropped as a result of international pressure.

4. PKI members were blamed for the abortive coup attempt in which seven high-ranking military officers were killed. However, the full details of the relative involvement of PKI members and dissident factions within the Indonesian military in plotting the coup have yet to emerge. At that time, Indonesia had the third largest Communist party membership in the world, after China and the Soviet Union. Following the coup, the PKI was banned and most party members were executed, imprisoned, or subjected to ongoing discrimination throughout the Suharto era.

5. Comparable figures for South Korea, Thailand, Malaysia, and the Philippines ranged from 52 to 54 years for life expectancy and 28–42 percent for illiteracy (*Economist*, 3 August 1996).

6. Several members of the group studied at the University of California, Berkeley.

7. Some have argued that the early opening of the capital account was a form of insurance to ethnic Chinese businesses if they needed to exit the economy quickly, rather than a broader sign of liberalization.

8. Nonetheless, many Indonesians' incomes remained just above the official poverty line (Booth 1992; Radelet forthcoming).

9. While the Jakarta Stock Exchange was founded in 1977, the number of companies listing on the stock exchange increased dramatically after the 1988 reforms.

10. As evidence of the technocrats' frustration in trying to reform the state banks, Pincus and Ramli (1998, n. 1) and the *Wall Street Journal* (14 July 1998) cite a 1994 incident in which the technocrats leaked a list of nonperforming loans in the state banking system. It included many loans to members of the Suharto family.

11. The president often blocked economic liberalization plans in key sectors in which such reforms would damage the business interests of his children or close allies (*FEER*, 16 October 1997).

12. The competition among Suharto's children for special licenses became so intense that they were often in direct competition with each other in the same sector, particularly petrochemicals and autos. The children often engaged in bitter public feuds with each other over lucrative projects.

13. Indonesia does not have a pure presidential system because the president is not directly elected. The president is selected by a legislative assembly (MPR). Under Suharto, the MPR was composed of a mainly elected 500-member lower house (DPR)—with some seats reserved for the military—and 500 presidential appointees. Under the new electoral rules, only thirty-eight seats in the DPR are reserved for the military (scheduled to be phased out altogether), while an electoral commission now selects 200 rather than 500 appointees. There is still no direct election of the president.

14. Still worse riots were to come in 1998, following the onset of the financial crisis.

15. Suharto tried to divide the military in the 1990s by promoting "modernist" officers who favored a greater political role for Islam, while overlooking officers associated with the more traditional wing of the military. Suharto's son-in-law Lt. General Prabowo Subianto was among those associated with the rise of the modernist faction in the military, as was Suharto's successor, B. J. Habibie (Schwarz 2000; Liddle 1996).

16. Suharto named Minister of Research and Technology B. J. Habibie as his vice-presidential candidate, despite the fact that Habibie was disliked by both the army and the economic technocrats. He also appointed his eldest daughter, Siti Hardiyanti Rukmana, "Tutut," and his closest golfing buddy, Mohammad "Bob" Hasan, to the cabinet.

17. During Suharto's tenure, many important reforms were implemented by executive decree and the legislature did not reject bills submitted by the president.

18. At the end of each term in office, Suharto gave an accountability speech. The unanimous approval of this speech was sometimes cited to justify the president's consecutive terms in office. The rejection of Habibie's accountability speech led to his withdrawal as a presidential candidate only a day before the MPR was scheduled to choose a new president. After Habibie was forced to withdraw, Golkar did not field another candidate.

19. Both Vice President Megawati's PDI-P (the top vote-getter in the June election) and the National Awakening Party of President Abdurrahman Wahid (the third highest in votes) have historic roots dating back to before the only other free election in 1955. Several of the smaller Muslim parties also have roots in 1955 parties. Further, Golkar (second highest in votes) and the United Development Party (fourth highest in votes) were two of the three legal parties after 1971, along with the PDI prior to Megawati's ouster.

20. See the *Wall Street Journal* (14 July 1998) for a criticism of the World Bank's role in overlooking corruption in Indonesia.

East Asia Comparative Case Studies

7

Japan: Prosperity, Dominant Party System, and Delayed Liberalization

Eric C. Browne and Sunwoong Kim

In the mid-1980s the prognosis for Japan, the world's second largest economy, was uniformly optimistic, with expectations that its superior competitiveness would soon result in its replacing the United States as the world's leading economy (Vogel 1986). Indeed, the confidence of Japanese business and industry leaders allowed them to chide Americans openly for pursuing outdated business models and for an unproductive and uncommitted workforce. During the 1990s, however, the picture has changed dramatically. Japanese economic growth rates have fallen to levels substantially below those of the United States, Germany, and other advanced economies.

Since the collapse of the "bubble economy" of the late 1980s, Japan's economy has been stagnant, recording an annual growth rate averaging about 1 percent. By 1998, the growth rate of Gross Domestic Product (GDP) had actually turned negative. Although the growth rate recovered in the first quarter of 1999 to reach 2 percent, this increase is attributable mostly to the launching of massive public works projects financed by government deficits that amounted to more than 10 percent of GDP in 1999. At the same time, private consumption and investment remained depressed, and in the second quarter, the growth rate in GDP dropped back to 0.2 percent. Overall, by mid-1999 a healthy dose of skepticism remained about whether the Japanese economy was on the road to recovery.

What happened to Japan? Why has Japan, once one of the most dynamic economies on earth and still the largest creditor nation in the world, been unable to recover from prolonged recession? In this chapter we address this issue from a political economy perspective, focusing our analysis on the interaction of the actors and institutions that have shaped economic policy decisions in Japan. In most

133

advanced capitalist democracies, governments have accepted responsibility (at least politically) for ensuring prosperity and rising living standards for their people. Japan is surely no exception to this. Indeed, between 1955 and 1993, Japan's ruling (majority) party, the Liberal Democratic Party (LDP), actively embraced this role. In collaboration with a semiautonomous state bureaucracy, large-scale business, and industrial enterprises and financial entities, it conceived and put into practice a concerted and coordinated strategy for economic recovery and development under the aegis of what is often called the developmental state.

As a form of state-sponsored capitalism, the developmental state created a system of formal and informal relationships among the major actors that by the mid-1980s had propelled the Japanese economy to the pinnacle of success, what is often referred to as Japan's economic miracle. The economic stagnation and decline in the 1990s, then, came as a shocking surprise both to Japan's trading partners and to the Japanese alike. In what follows, we shall first describe the economic crisis that has engulfed Japan in the past decade, focusing on the policy initiatives that have been implemented to deal with a worsening set of economic conditions. We then examine the political context that has conditioned the particular policy responses of elite actors as they have confronted Japan's economic crisis.

We argue that the system of relationships that came to define the developmental state, while conducive to the rapid development of immature market structures, imposed substantial rigidities and constraints on the ability of political and economic actors to adapt to the economic imperatives of global capitalism. Japan's huge middle class belatedly arose from its complacent torpor to demand greater liberalization. But its policy preferences were long obstructed by the internal divisions within the ruling LDP, combined with the absence of credible alternative parties. These institutional conditions repeatedly provided opportunities for subsidized and protected concentrated interest groups to resist change in the status quo.

JAPAN'S ECONOMIC CRISIS AND POLICY RESPONSES TO IT

At the beginning of the millennium, the economic crisis in East Asia has persisted for almost three years. However, Japan has been struggling with a seriously underperforming economy for a longer period than this. It seems to us that the particular economic problems we shall identify below are neither unusual nor without rather straightforward economic remedies. Yet there has been great reluctance among the Japanese political and economic elite to take decisive action. Rather, they have characteristically been reactive to events, and usually in minimal ways.

We begin with an overview of the events and conditions that have contributed to the onset and perpetuation of Japan's economic crisis and the policy responses that have been proposed and implemented by the government. The policy of easy credit in force during the mid-1980s resulted in the rapid appreciation of asset prices, creating the so-called bubble economy. However, by the early 1990s, when exuberant expectations of increasing asset valuation could no longer be sustained, the economic bubble burst and the Japanese economy experienced a sudden contraction. As the economy began to rebound from the recession during 1995 and 1996, the government, in a misguided and ill-timed effort to deal with mounting budget deficits, increased the enormously unpopular sales tax in April 1997. This had the immediate effect of depressing the level of aggregate demand and consequently failed to realize the expected tax revenue windfall.

Moreover, the currency crisis that erupted in Thailand in the summer of 1997 began spreading to Malaysia, Indonesia, the Philippines, and Korea. The effect of the Asian economic crisis was to plunge the Japanese economy back into severe recession: Japan recorded negative growth in 1998. In the meantime, the government tried to revive the economy with a half dozen fiscal stimulus packages totaling ¥60 trillion (US$500 billion) of public spending while pursuing a monetary policy that reduced the interest rate to near 0 percent. The economy did not revive from these initiatives. Although the government fiscal deficit and public debt grew enormously, private consumption and investment remained depressed.

It was not until April 1998 that the government began to acknowledge publicly the enormous extent to which bad loans had accumulated during the bubble period. It then started to infuse massive amounts of public money and to impose stricter supervision of the banking system under a more independent Bank of Japan. These interventions appear to have slowed (perhaps stopped) the decline in economic growth, although it is premature at this time to say whether the economy is firmly on the road to recovery.

MACROECONOMIC POLICY IN THE 1980S AND BUBBLE ECONOMY

By almost any yardstick, the period from 1960 to 1980 was one of fabulous growth for the Japanese economy. Double-digit growth rates were common in the 1960s, and slower but still robust economic growth followed. The sharp increase in the price of crude oil in 1979 interrupted the pace of growth in Japan (as elsewhere), with GDP slowing to a rate of about 3 percent per annum during the first half of the 1980s. Beginning in the last quarter of 1986, however, the Japanese economy began to accelerate its growth, reaching a sustained rate of 5 percent of GDP per year. At the time, this was the highest growth rate recorded among advanced capitalist economies.

Rather than raise the interest rate to slow economic growth and guard against inflation, the Japanese monetary authority actually lowered the interest rate in January 1986, and again in February 1987, marking a fall from 5 percent in 1985 to 2.5 percent in 1987. At this time, Japan was subjected to pressure by the United

States to lower its interest rate, since the United States found itself in the position of having to borrow to finance its twin deficits. If Japan had maintained a high interest rate, then international capital would have flown from the United States to Japan. Additionally, in order to fight the constant appreciation of the Japanese yen, lower interest rates were seen as necessary to compensate for the huge surpluses generated from trade with the United States and for the lack of imports due to Japan's market protection policies.

It was during this period of lax monetary policy that a spectacular bubble erupted in the Japanese economy. Economic bubbles occur when asset prices rise very rapidly and are propelled on the winds of speculation instead of resulting from the sober evaluation of economic and financial fundamentals. In Japan, the brunt of this speculative bubble was borne by prices on the stock exchange and in the real estate market. To illustrate, in 1985 the total market value of all the stock traded on the Tokyo Stock Exchange was about ¥169 trillion, and the total residential land value in the Tokyo area was then estimated at ¥176 trillion. By 1989, the corresponding values had risen to ¥527 trillion and ¥521 trillion, respectively. In just four years these asset values almost tripled. The bubble finally burst in 1989, when the market psychology could no longer sustain expectations of continuously rising asset values. By 1992, the total asset value of the Tokyo Stock Exchange had plummeted to ¥297 trillion, and real estate prices had declined significantly as well. Since these financial and real estate assets had provided collateral for large-scale borrowing, the sudden and sizable diminution in their value rendered much of the paper held by banks and securities houses virtually worthless.

IMPACT OF THE ASIAN CURRENCY AND FINANCIAL CRISIS ON THE JAPANESE ECONOMY

In the aftermath of the collapse of the bubble, the Japanese economy went deeply into recession. The annual growth rate of GDP sank to around 1 percent during the first half of the 1990s. The government tried to jump-start the economy by providing a number of fiscal stimulus packages totaling more than ¥60 trillion. Due in part to these fiscal packages and in part to the depreciation of the yen, the Japanese economy started to recover in 1996, and GDP achieved a growth rate of 3.5 percent. In fact, the Japanese economy was growing faster than the economies of the United States and most Western European countries. Of this group of countries, however, Japan was also most vulnerable to the Asian economic crises, since Japan's economic ties to those Asian nations were considerably greater than were those of the United States and Western European countries.

To appreciate the extent of Japanese vulnerability, we consider the following points. First, Japanese banks lent heavily in Asia. According to Goldstein and Hawkins (1988), the total value of loans made by Japanese banks to Indonesia,

Thailand, Korea, Malaysia, and the Philippines amounted to US$97 billion in June 1997. The corresponding figures for loans by German, French, U.S., and U.K. banks were US$32, $24, $24, and $16 billion, respectively.

Second, Japanese direct foreign investments in these countries were also much greater than were made by any other country in the world. Consequently, the economic recession/depression these countries have been undergoing means a smaller investment yield or a greater investment loss for the Japanese firms operating in these countries. Third, the affected Asian countries traditionally import a substantial amount of Japanese goods. The recession/depression in these countries has had the effect of reducing Japanese exports to these countries, thus decreasing the demand for goods sold by Japanese firms.

When combined with a notable slowing of domestic consumer demand, the Asian crisis has seriously crippled the Japanese economy. As noted earlier, the economic growth rate in 1998 was actually minus 2.8 percent.

THE INCREASING GOVERNMENTAL DEBT AND DEFICIT AND THE STIMULUS PACKAGES

Since the first "oil shock" of 1973, the Japanese government has run a substantial annual deficit of about 3 percent. However, in the mid-1980s the deficit began to disappear, and it actually turned into a moderate surplus during the period of the bubble economy. But when the bubble burst, the Japanese government began immediately running substantial fiscal deficits again. By FY 1998, the deficit reached nearly 7 percent of GDP. It is likely to increase again in FY 1999 due to the enactment of a large fiscal stimulus package of ¥17 trillion, announced in April 1998 (J. P. Morgan 1999).

In the face of annual budget deficits and a mounting national debt, three responses are possible: (1) change nothing and hope that there will be a fortuitous change in economic conditions, (2) curtail government spending to the point that the annual budget is balanced or in surplus (which can be used to pay down the debt), or (3) increase government spending in an effort to stimulate the level of aggregate demand and thus encourage new investment (spend the nation to surplus). As the ministry most responsible for the financial health of the nation, the Ministry of Finance has traditionally supported the second of these policy options. Given that austerity budgets tend to be unpopular, however, the MOF increasingly has engaged in practices intended to hide the extent of the deficit and debt problem while also attempting to slow budgetary growth.

As it has turned out, the effect of the MOF's conservative approach has been akin to bailing the sinking boat with a teaspoon. The deterioration of Japan's fiscal situation since 1991 has been precipitous. In FY 1996, the gross outstanding government debt was estimated at ¥240 trillion. Debt service on this amount was ¥16.4 trillion, equal to 32 percent of all tax receipts. According to a study by

Japan's Economic Planning Agency, the national debt is expected to grow to ¥540 trillion by the end of FY 1999, the current equivalent of 92 percent of GDP.

Anxiety over the fiscal health of government finance is well founded. Since 1993, Japan's trade surplus has been shrinking in yen value. On another front, the Japanese saving rate has been decreasing markedly. In 1994, the saving rate stood at a quite respectable 12.8 percent, but this figure is more than ten percentage points below where it was just two decades ago. Many observers attribute the fall of the savings rate to a declining working age population as well as to a consumption-oriented lifestyle that is becoming more prevalent. If this is true, the situation for the future is even more unpromising, since the number of Japanese working-age people (20–64 years) rose by 10.7 million over the past twenty years but is projected to shrink by 10.5 million in the next twenty years.

A fiscal stimulus package was announced in April 1998 and provided ¥17 trillion for public social infrastructure investment, housing construction, job creation programs, and so on. There were also reductions in individual income taxes, setting the maximum tax rate at 50 percent (worth approximately ¥4 trillion), and corporate income taxes, where the effective tax rate was reduced to 40 percent. The 1998 stimulus package was the sixth of its kind, the first being launched in 1992. Such government spending is intended to ignite economic growth by raising the level of aggregate demand. Overall, however, the results from fiscal stimulation have not been impressive. From the six stimulus packages that disbursed ¥67 trillion from August 1992 to September 1995, the annual GDP growth rate could only manage 1.1 percent in 1992, 0.1 percent in 1993, 0.5 percent in 1994, and 0.9 percent in 1995.

In 1996, the economy did respond to a massive stimulus infusion of ¥15 trillion (from the 1995 package), registering an impressive GDP growth rate of 3.6 percent. However, this gain was undermined the very next year when the Hashimoto government began to implement a contractionary fiscal policy. At its center was an increase in the very unpopular consumption tax from 3 percent to 5 percent, imposed in April 1997. Predictably, consumer spending abruptly and dramatically decreased, resulting in a decrease in the GDP growth rate. Since then, the level of consumer demand has remained depressed, and successive LDP governments have steadfastly resisted strong demands that the unpopular tax be rolled back.

DEVELOPMENTAL FINANCIAL SYSTEM, NONPERFORMING LOANS, AND BANK FAILURES

In order to promote the economic development of the nation, the government and bureaucracy of Japan have routinely employed the Japanese financial system as their main instrument of industrial development policy. Most notably during the period of rapid economic expansion (1950–1970), the flow of finance capital to industrial development projects fell under the direction of the Ministry of Finance (Cargill and Royoma 1992). One of the key elements of Japan's industrial development policy has been artificially low interest rates, designed for encouraging industrial investment. Low interest rates that favor the industrial sector over the household sector for credits was the main cause for the overextension of loans through the "main bank" system. In this system, the development of long-term customer relationships is regarded as being more important than objective evaluation and monitoring of loan applications.

In order to achieve these goals of the developmental state, the Japanese financial system is highly regulated and compartmentalized according to the type of financial services that may be offered. For example, an ordinary bank may provide short-term working capital for a corporate customer but is not allowed to provide long-term credit. Long-term credit is provided by long-term credit banks and trust banks.

This practice calls attention to the relationship that exists between the Japanese central bank (the Bank of Japan [BOJ]) and the agencies of government—particularly the MOF and the Ministry of International Trade and Industry (MITI)—that have assumed major economic development responsibilities. In the United States, Germany, and other industrial democracies, the central bank stands apart from the governmental structure to prevent political interference in its ability to conduct monetary policy on a sound economic basis. In Japan, until the financial reform of April 1998, the BOJ served as an agency of the Finance Ministry and has thus been subject to political direction, sometimes to the exclusion of following sound banking practices and monetary policy principles. This meant that the BOJ not only was required to approve the channeling of finance capital to projects identified by politicians as worthy but also was directed to recapitalize financial institutions that were weak or failing. Ultimately, the politicization of the Japanese finance system has undermined the authority and flexibility of the BOJ to the extent that its ability to stabilize the finance system has become doubtful (Endo 1998).[1]

Without transparent accounting procedures and disclosures, the Japanese financial system appears to provide a congenial environment for illegal and extralegal activities and practices. Such activities run the gamut from ignoring currency reserve requirements to failure to collateralize loans adequately to sweetheart loans for favored clients to embezzlement and extortion. The typical consequence of such behavior has been the steady production of nonperforming loans. One of the best examples is the *jusen* scandal.[2] Seven *jusen* made about 200 loans during the period of the bubble economy, many of which were secured by stocks or real property having a highly inflated value. Pempel (1998, 143) reports that many such loans were granted to prominent politicians and known members of the Japanese underworld. When the economic bubble burst, the *jusen* were left with US$40 billion in uncollectable loans, which were later repaid in part by the government with tax revenues.

In another celebrated example, Yamaichi, one of the "Big Four" brokerage houses in Japan, suddenly collapsed in November 1997. What was particularly worrisome was not just the fact that Yamaichi collapsed but the way it fell. It kept insisting that it was solvent, and then after collapsing it turned out to have an extra US$2 billion in hidden losses. The Finance Ministry closely monitors the securities industry, and it either knew or did not know of these off-book losses; it is unclear which prospect is more alarming (*New York Times,* 17 December 1997).

THE FINANCIAL REFORM OF 1998: "BIG BANG"

The Japanese government has been reluctant to relax (much less dismantle) the regulatory apparatus it has relied on to prosecute its economic development plans. During the 1990s, however, public disclosures of waste, fraud, and corruption, especially in the financial system, have led to mounting public pressure on the Japanese government to enact comprehensive financial reform. After years of discussion and debate, primarily within the Liberal Democratic Party, a financial reform package, commonly known as the "Big Bang," was introduced and passed in the Diet. Its implementation began on April 1, 1998.

Although the reform package seems to promise an immediate and far-reaching policy change, it actually proposes a gradual deregulation of the financial sector, taking a full three years to complete. In essence, the Big Bang calls for freer financial markets by requiring more disclosure and fewer regulations in order to promote innovation and globalization. Specific reforms that are envisaged include lifting the requirement that a certain percentage of pension funds must be invested in the Japanese economy and removing the prohibition against individuals opening bank accounts overseas without first gaining government approval. Big Bang reforms will also make it easier for Japanese citizens to buy mutual funds, both foreign and domestic, and licensing restrictions on individuals engaged in the currency exchange business are to be abandoned (*Washington Post,* 17 February 1998, 1 April 1998, 11 June 1999).

In addition, the Big Bang reforms mandate some important institutional changes. Perhaps most importantly, the BOJ has now gained independence from the Ministry of Finance and has been placed in charge of the nation's monetary policy. While extremely reluctant, the MOF finally agreed to the BOJ spin-off in order to divert attacks by reformist politicians who were alleging corruption among top ministerial personnel and condemning the ministry's role in the bad loans scandals. Since being installed as the newly appointed governor of the central bank, Masaru Hayami has pushed hard for full disclosure of the bad loans and has inaugurated an expansionary monetary policy (*Wall Street Journal,* 28 January 1999).

Finally, under Big Bang reforms the new Financial Supervisory Agency (FSA) has been launched. It is an independent institution charged with monitoring the financial institutions. With cooperation from the newly independent central bank, the FSA has been able to speed up the process of making banks dispose of their nonperforming loans. These two institutions have made inroads into the traditional and jealously guarded regulatory turf of the MOF and have begun to move the financial system toward greater transparency and public scrutiny.

Besides the institutional reforms, government has instituted the Financial Stabilization Plan, which was announced in July 1998. Under its recapitalization provisions, fifteen of the seventeen top Japanese banks will receive an infusion of approximately ¥7.5 trillion of public funds from a total of ¥25 trillion in available capital. Two major insolvent banks (the Long-Term Credit Bank of Japan and Nippon Credit Bank) have been taken into government receivership, although they have been allowed to continue to operate. A number of other smaller financial institutions, such as Hokkaido Takushoku Bank, have been dissolved.

A major goal of the legislation creating the Financial Stabilization Plan has been to facilitate the disposal of nonperforming loans by easing property auction rules and the resecuring of bad loans. The magnitude of this problem, however, should not be underestimated. By any standard, the number of nonperforming loans is staggering and has increased over time. After years of assurance that the bad loan problems were "over the peak," MOF suddenly announced that bad loans amounted to ¥77 trillion, or 3.5 times what the ministry had previously acknowledged. While something approaching the true magnitude of the problem may have been known for years by MOF bureaucrats, it has risen to more than 15.2 percent of the 1997 Japanese GDP. By contrast, the U.S. savings and loan crisis amounted to US$160 billion, or 2.7 percent of U.S. GDP (*New York Times,* 5 April 1998). Moreover, when the U.S. S&L crisis occurred, other U.S. financial sectors, particularly the larger commercial banks, were strong enough to absorb those that failed. In the case of Japan, most of the larger banks are themselves in serious need of additional capital. When coupled with the estimates of some analysts that the actual amount of bad loans might be still larger than what has already been announced by the MOF, the outlook for the short-term resuscitation of the Japanese economy seems clouded.

THE POLITICAL ECONOMY OF STAGNATION: JAPAN IN THE 1990s

In a recent book, Gerald Curtis (1999) attributes the onset and perpetuation of Japan's economic crisis to the erosion of the postwar policy consensus and the institutional relationships that supported it, what he refers to as the crumbling of the "system of '55." This system was built on a governmental decision-making process dominated by the Liberal Democratic Party, a semiautonomous and professional state bureaucracy, and a network of industry-wide interest groups (peak organizations) that were closely allied with the major political parties. The interaction of these players occurred in the context of a broad policy consensus that the efforts of state and society should be focused on the development of the economy, with the ultimate aim of achieving parity (at least) with the richest industrial nations of the world. By the 1980s this goal had been accomplished, and the Japanese found themselves in a position where the economic decisions and policies they pursued domestically could have a significant impact on the global economy.[3]

The foundation of Japan's variant of state-sponsored capitalism was patronage, protection, and paternalism. The system was one of mutual support and mutual benefit among the major actors, whereby favors in the form of regulatory policies, protectionist trade policies, government contracts and the like were commonly repaid by campaign contributions (usually to LDP factions) and other perks, or the promise of high-paying private industry employment for retiring senior bureaucrats. While such systems of mutual payoffs for the developmental elite (a.k.a. "crony capitalism") are not uncommon economic strategies in developing nations, the sociopolitical consequence is often the exacerbation of the income and status gap separating rich and poor, creating a basis for both economic exploitation and class antagonism. In Japan, to the contrary, the less advantaged (nonelite) segments of society were from the beginning made beneficiaries of the developmental state by conscious policies of inclusion.[4] In consequence, a high level of public support was maintained for the institutions and policies of the system of '55 until the end of the 1980s. It took the bursting of the economic bubble and the concurrent disclosure of a series of spectacular scandals involving high-ranking politicians and senior bureaucrats to shake public confidence in the system.

THE POLITICS OF REFORM, JAPANESE STYLE: DISPERSED INTEREST GROUP REVOLT, SLUGGISH RESPONSE

The period of the 1990s in Japan has been one in which the nation's leaders have become preoccupied with political and administrative reform. Despite the fact that most of Japan's major political parties supported electoral system reform, which was accomplished in 1994, and that the current LDP government has begun to implement a reform of the finance system, it is probably fair to say that the governing elite has not embraced the reform process enthusiastically. What has put reform on the front burner and kept it there has been an avalanche of public scandals involving a veritable army of high-ranking politicians and bureaucrats as well as leading members of Japan's economic elite. The picture painted by the Japanese media has been of a country with its finances in shambles, its politicians corrupt and inept, its civil servants compromised by big money interests, and its corporate leaders in bed with the mob.

Fueling the impetus toward reform was the behavior of Japanese voters, who punished the ruling LDP by first depriving it of its majority in the Upper House election of 1989 and, subsequently, of its Lower House majority in the 1993 election. The overwhelming majority of voters were urban dispersed interest groups, particularly middle-class groups. The proximate cause of dispersed interest group dissatisfaction with the LDP was the involvement of top LDP faction leaders (and some leaders of other parties as well) in a series of well-publicized scandals where huge sums of money were paid by private interests for business favors. Particularly damaged by these revelations were the top leaders of the LDP's most powerful faction, Takeshita Noboru and Kanemaru Shin, both of whom were forced to resign their formal leadership positions, Takeshita as prime minister and faction leader and Kanemaru as LDP vice president and, eventually, as Diet member. There ensued a struggle for control of the faction involving four of its senior members, Ozawa Ichiro, Hata Tsutomo, Kajiyama Seiroku, and Obuchi Keizo. Takeshita threw his support to Obuchi (who was supported by Kajiyama), and he became faction leader.

With the connivance of Ozawa, Hata, and their followers, the sitting Miyazawa government was immediately thereafter brought down on an opposition motion of no confidence, leading to the early calling of the 1993 election. At that point, Ozawa and Hata (with a substantial number of followers) bolted the faction and the party to fight the 1993 election under the aegis of a new opposition party, Shinseito, on a platform of electoral reform. In this they were joined by Takemura Masayoshi, who with ten former LDP Diet members formed the new party Sakigake, and by other individual LDP dissidents.

It is interesting to note that from the Upper House election in 1989 until the Lower House election of 1996, the preoccupation with reform centered on the political system rather than on steadily worsening conditions in the economy. The centerpiece of the reform agenda, changing the electoral law, was sold publicly as a way to get money out of politics and as a way to break the influence of factions. It seems clear, however, that many of the "reformers" hoped that a new election law would facilitate a partisan realignment that would allow a credible opposition to LDP predominance to emerge and succeed. Although the seven-party, anti-LDP coalition government that was installed after the LDP's defeat in the 1993 election did indeed enact a new election law, the promise of realignment has failed to materialize. Instead, the LDP, after a short period in opposition, slowly regained its position at the center of the governmental system. This was accomplished first by the LDP accepting a "junior partnership" in a three-party coalition led by the Socialists (with Sakigake as third member). When the Socialist prime minister, Murayama Tomiichi, subsequently resigned his office, the LDP assumed leadership of the government coalition, naming Hashimoto Ryutaro as prime minister. After the 1996 election dealt a crushing defeat to its coalition partners, the LDP, even though it did not command a parliamentary majority, took control of all government portfolios, while the Socialists and Sakigake remained informally allied with the government. Finally, in April 1998, shortly before the Upper House election of that year, the allies formally went into opposition, leaving the LDP alone at the helm again.[5]

If the political leadership was preoccupied with a struggle for governmental power and position, much the same could be said of many high-ranking bureaucratic agents of the state, including those entrusted with economic policy management. As architects and defenders of the developmental state and entrenched in their ministries, senior bureaucrats have doggedly resisted encroachment on their prerogatives and responsibilities. It comes as no surprise, then, that belated attempts at administrative and financial reforms emanating from the Hashimoto government after 1996 met with vigorous opposition from senior bureaucrats.

Hashimoto's proposals for administrative reform sought to weaken the power of the bureaucracy over policy implementation by drastically reducing the number of government departments and agencies. In general, the plan was to centralize the functions of dismantled bureaucratic entities in the office of the prime minister, making them more susceptible to political control, while narrowing or dispersing the competencies of the remaining government departments. Although bold in concept, Hashimoto's government reorganization reform has come to nothing, partly as a result of determined bureaucratic opposition and partly due to the failure of his own government to pursue it vigorously.

The plan to reform the financial system (the Big Bang) has, by contrast, met with some measure of success. Perhaps most notable in this respect has been the separation of Japan's central bank (BOJ) from control by the Ministry of Finance, thus ensuring an independent monetary policy. Also important has been the creation of an independent Financial Supervisory Agency (FSA) charged with monitoring the compliance of financial institutions with existing policies and regulations. (Other components of this reform package have already been discussed above.) The MOF fought these reforms when they were drafted and succeeded in narrowing their scope somewhat and slowing their implementation. It failed, however, to prevent their adoption, and the first phase of Big Bang reforms began in early 1999.

The loss of control over the BOJ and the creation of the FSA, however, must be considered a major defeat for the MOF and, by extension, for the autonomy of bureaucratic agencies in general. That it occurred at all is remarkable, given the institutional power over policy formation and implementation that is concentrated in the various bureaucratic departments and agencies. This is doubly the case with the MOF, which is generally considered to be the most powerful government ministry. We believe that the weakening of bureaucratic control, both in this case and generally, has been influenced by two major factors. First is the manifest failure of the MOF to prevent, through its power of regulatory oversight, the accumulation by banks and other financial institutions of massive amounts of uncollectable debt that must eventually be repaid with public funds. Coupled with this has been a series of recent public disclosures of senior bureaucrats being "entertained" by the private businesses and corporations over which they have regulatory jurisdiction, giving what is perhaps a little more than the appearance of impropriety. Just as scandal weakened the ability of the parties to take resolute action in the face of economic crisis, so scandal also weakened the ability of government agencies to respond appropriately to the mounting economic problems currently facing Japan.

BEYOND DISARRAY: IS THERE A POLITICAL SOLUTION TO JAPAN'S ECONOMIC PROBLEMS?

The Western model of parliamentary government suggests that prolonged policy immobilism (or deepening crisis) is addressed most directly by an alternation in power of the political elite. The expectation is that when policy failure becomes evident, those holding power will be replaced in office by an alternative government that will overcome the policy drift and incremental decision making of the outgoing government with new and forceful initiatives. This model presumes the existence of both a vital and coherent opposition to the existing government's policy regime, and unambiguous support in the greater society for effecting a change in course. Neither of these conditions appear to exist currently in Japan.

From the beginning of the postwar political system until about 1990, Japanese politics exhibited a left-versus-right orientation that reflected the tensions of the Cold War. On the left were two main parties, the Japan Socialist Party and the Japan Communist Party, each of which faithfully represented the ideological positions of similar parties in European democracies. In 1955, the LDP emerged as a conservative opposing party on the right and promptly established itself as the ruling majority party, while the Socialists assumed the role of principal opposition party. As elsewhere, the Communists were, and continue to be, a pariah to everyone.

In power, the LDP was composed of formally organized factions based on the personalities and ambitions of their leaders. With the end of the Cold War, the Japan Socialist Party lost its raison d'être and was quickly reduced (electorally) to the role of marginal political actor. With the left now unable to mount a credible principled opposition to LDP dominance, Japanese politics degenerated into a struggle among willful LDP politicians for positions of power and prominence. As we have seen, the excesses of the party leadership resulted in loss of its majority control of parliament, opening an opportunity for the emergence of a new opposition to LDP hegemony.

The Ozawa/Hata gambit to create such an opposition was premised on an appeal to the electorate that promised reform, the tangible manifestation of which was change of the electoral law accomplished by the seven-party coalition government formed by Hosokawa Morihiro after the 1993 election. Although Ozawa subsequently succeeded in uniting several of the parties that had opposed the LDP in the 1993 election, his creation, the New Frontier Party, was beset from the beginning by personal rivalries and antagonisms that prevented establishment of a coherent program of reform.

The new party's death knell was sounded with the creation of the Democratic Party (Minshuto) on the eve of the 1996 Lower House election. Led by the brothers Hatoyama (Yukio and Kunio) and fronted by the popular ex-LDP minister of health, Kan Naoto, Minshuto sought to identify reform with leadership provided by a younger generation of politicians. Their quickly organized campaign for the 1996 election effectively split the anti-LDP vote among candidates of Minshuto and the New Frontier Party. Shortly thereafter, Ozawa, who after the 1996 electoral debacle had managed to win a closely contested race for president of the New Frontier Party, dissolved the party and established the smaller Liberal Party (Jiyuto) under his personal control. Recently, Ozawa has taken his party into formal coalition with the LDP, which was led by Obuchi Keizo until his death.

Ozawa's long march into opposition and back out again is symbolic of the difficulties of establishing a coherent and credible opposition to LDP hegemony. Beyond the issue of electoral reform, neither Ozawa nor any of the leaders of opposition parties succeeded in defining a program of economic reform that transcended disagreements with the LDP on particular policy initiatives. Rather, the opposition after 1993 was, and continues to be, amorphous, and the main message that is communicated to Japanese voters is: "We're not the LDP."

If the political class has been unable to coalesce around a coherent program of economic development and change, an argument can be made that discipline can be imposed on the parties by the efforts of their organized supporters in the greater society. That is, by their financial and electoral support of various political parties, organized interest groups should be able to impose order and discipline on the debate over policy regimes and initiatives, thereby creating credible alternatives to a status quo characterized by drift and inaction. Indeed, Japanese parties have enjoyed the support of highly structured networks of inclusive interest organizations that have pressed their policy demands in the political arena. As elsewhere, the Japan Socialist Party has enjoyed staunch support from organized labor, while the LDP has benefited from its relationship with organized farmers and producer groups.

As long as the Japanese economy lagged those of Western industrialized nations, the policy consensus on "catching up" meant, essentially, that all major interests could benefit from the protectionist and paternalistic policies of the so-called developmental state. Import-competing sectors and farmers benefited from protection and subsidies. Similarly, maturing exporting sectors also relied on the protected home market and on access to subsidized credit and scarce foreign exchange. In such an environment, large peak organizations representing the interests of farmers, employers, and industrial workers could agree to support the state's developmental policies. As the Japanese economy reached parity with its Western counterparts, however, the concert of interest within these occupational categories began to break down. In particular, the exporting sectors had matured and now no longer needed the old protection and subsidies. Instead, a closed Japanese market tended to drive up costs and threaten access to the huge foreign markets that had been developed—above all in the United States (Curtis 1999, 40ff.).

As the economic interests of these groups diverged, it became more difficult to reconcile the policy preferences of their peak organizations. Given such increasing divergence of policy interests, there were two possible directions in which exporting-sector political activity could develop. Such sectors might remain within the LDP orbit, seeking to influence policy marginally from within. Or they might organize to bolt and support the newly developing political opposition, unless the LDP were to initiate more fundamental policy change. It seems that old habits die hard, for the huge and wealthy exporting sectors appear to have opted for the former, status quo strategy.

Beyond the political elites and concentrated interest groups, what remains is the mass of voters affected by current economic conditions and apprehensive about the future. Since the overwhelming majority of this group is middle class, they compose the closest Japanese approximation of a "dispersed interest group," as that term is used in this volume. The issue is whether, by expressing their dissatisfaction at the polls, they can provide the impetus for comprehensive economic reform.

Evidence that Japanese voters are seriously disaffected from their political (and bureaucratic) rulers may be seen in all elections (Lower and Upper House) from at least 1989. In 1989 and again in 1993, the LDP was deprived of its majorities in both Houses, and subsequent elections have not reversed this outcome. If the behavior of voters can be interpreted as an expression of no confidence in the leadership of the LDP, however, it does not indicate support for any alternative either. In 1996, for example, the LDP, while not gaining a parliamentary majority, was still returned as the largest party in the Lower House of the Diet, indicating that the electorate lacks confidence not only in the LDP but in the political system as a whole.

More than depriving the LDP of parliamentary majorities, the voters have expressed their dissatisfaction and apprehension by limiting their participation in the electoral process, recording record abstentions in the 1990s. This behavior supports the interpretation that Japanese voters react to the present situation with apathy and cynicism rather than outrage and anger. Perhaps the reason for this lies in the fact that, for all its waste, fraud, corruption, and mismanagement, Japan is at bottom still a prosperous and stable country. As individuals, the Japanese have maintained a remarkably high rate of personal savings, exceeding that of U.S. citizens by a wide margin. Although Japan is reported to be experiencing a serious consumer crisis of underconsumption, we find little evidence to indicate that the general public is, or has been, undergoing actual economic hardship. Instead, underconsumption actually appears to be deferred consumption, as ordinary Japanese householders prefer to save their money as a hedge against an uncertain future.

How does this pattern of concentrated and dispersed interest group mobilization and elite responses explain the long delayed, and still incomplete, policy response to economic stagnation? It appears that the desire to conserve the tremendous economic successes of the past has delayed and blunted the reformist mobilization of both mature exporting sectors and the huge middle class. However, the middle class in particular has repeatedly signaled its displeasure over the last decade, providing an opening for opposition parties to develop into serious competitors for ruling party status. Here there has been a serious failure on the political supply side. Given the limited popularity of the Socialist Party, the new opposition had to come out of the LDP itself. However, these dissident LDP elites failed to construct a coherent alternative precisely because of their origins. They proved more interested in getting and keeping a little piece of power in the short run than in offering a principled, coherent alternative to the failed economic policies of the LDP. This has allowed the LDP to coopt the opposition and make sufficient marginal reforms to retain a large measure of support from a still conservative electorate. Barring a more fundamental economic disruption, there is every reason to believe that the LDP can retain power while continuing to muddle through with marginal policy changes.

Institutionally, the internal factionalization of the LDP, combined with absence of a serious opposition outside it, has meant a large number of "veto players." They initially favored fiscal stimulus policies and blocked crucial institutional and policy changes in monetary and financial sector policies. This is a predictable pattern. Fiscal stimulus policies were conducted in a way that provided further benefits to concentrated interest groups with long-standing connections to the LDP, while the monetary and financial sector reforms threatened other such concentrated interest groups. Only after a politically dangerous defection of dispersed interest group (especially middle class) voters, sustained through a series of election cycles, did enough LDP factions give way and adopt liberalizing policies that directly targeted the main weaknesses of the economy.

CONCLUSION

The prognosis for Japan's economic health remains uncertain. The failure of the LDP's political opposition to coalesce has meant that neither the LDP nor the set of bureaucratic officeholders need fear an immediate threat to their continued control over the levers of power. Lest the government become too complacent in its position, however, it needs to reflect on the result of the most recent election for Upper House seats, held in June 1998. Preelection polling indicated that the LDP would gain substantially, perhaps enough seats to recapture its lost majority. This prediction was based on a forecasted low voter turnout of about 40–44 percent. The actual turnout, however, was a shocking 57 percent, with most of these "extra" votes going to opponents of LDP candidates. It was a crushing defeat that cost Prime Minister Hashimoto his job.

After a bitter intraparty fight, Obuchi Keizo was named as Hashimoto's successor. Obuchi, the former foreign minister, was widely viewed as the epitome of the LDP's old guard. "Cold pizza" was the way he was characterized in the press. After making the cautious appointment of the ancient former prime minister, Miyazawa Kiichi, to the post of finance minister, Obuchi saw his approval rating sink to an all-time low for new prime ministers. Little in the way of reform was anticipated and he was not expected to last. More than a year later, Obuchi was still in office. He infused a large stimulus package into the economy and implemented the first round of Big Bang reforms. International confidence in the Japanese economy is beginning to revive and capital has begun to flow in from abroad. Whether the Japanese economy has finally turned the corner, however, is too soon to say. However, with its opposition little more than a recycled shadow of itself, the LDP system continues to stagger forward.

NOTES

1. Finally, in April 1999, the BOJ tie to the Finance Ministry was severed as part of the so-called Big Bang financial reform package, and it now functions more like an independent agency of government.

2. *Jusen,* like American savings and loan companies, provide housing loans. They are affiliated with rural cooperatives and their loan activities are supervised—loosely it appears—by the MOF and Ministry of Agriculture.

3. This "coming of age" has opened a debate in Japan, and elsewhere, over the extent of their international responsibilities. While Japan does sometimes seek a greater role, for example in its desire to hold a seat on the UN Security Council, it is reluctant to overthrow the disarmament provisions of its "peace constitution," which has been a contentious issue both domestically and regionally.

4. The most obvious of such policies is the much remarked practice of guaranteeing lifetime employment which, though not actually universal, provided a large segment of Japan's working population with income security. Less remarked but quite significant in this respect is Japan's highly progressive system of income taxation, which actually exempts from taxation virtually all workers whose income does not achieve a level most would consider middle class.

5. Eventually, as a result of the return of individuals who had deserted to the opposition, the LDP regained its majority in the Lower House of the Diet.

8

South Korea: Democratization, Financial Crisis, and the Decline of the Developmental State

Uk Heo

From the early 1960s to the mid-1990s, South Korea enjoyed a phenomenal average annual growth rate of 6.6 percent (Root 1999). However, the growth of the economy slowed in the mid-1990s, and in 1997, the economy was hit hard by a foreign exchange crisis. Foreign banks pressured South Korean banks and non-bank financial institutions to pay off loans. In order to avoid default, the South Korean government requested that the International Monetary Fund (IMF) provide an emergency rescue fund. On December 4, 1997, the IMF organized a financial rescue package of US$56 billion (*Digital Chosun Ilbo,* 5 December 1997). In addition, through emergency negotiations with the Korean government, a dozen major banks around the world agreed to convert US$15 billion in short-term loans to Korean financial institutions into long-term loans (*Digital Chosun Ilbo,* 30 December 1997).

Although the foreign exchange panic had subsided by the spring of 1998, until recently the economy continued to deteriorate. The tight macroeconomic policies urged by the IMF caused interest rates to rise and many corporations went bankrupt. The unemployment rate reached the highest level ever (8 percent) and Gross National Product dropped by 6.6 percent (*Digital Chosun Ilbo,* 27 August 1998).

What caused the South Korean economic miracle to evaporate so rapidly? According to Root (1999), South Korea did not make adequate institutional and policy adjustments in response to the changing global economic environment. In particular, the government-led development approach, once successfully employed by South Korea, has been heavily criticized. In this chapter, I investigate precrisis policies, the economic and political causes of the South Korean financial crisis, and postcrisis responses.

Thus far, the causes of the financial crisis in South Korea have been studied by economists, mainly focusing on economic policies and the structure of the financial sector. However, there are two reasons that the cause of the crisis should be investigated from a political as well as an economic perspective. First, economic performance and policies have often been affected by political changes in South Korea. Moreover, the government has played a major role in South Korean economic development. For instance, political-business ties have led to the corruption that eventually led to bad loans and a sudden increase in short-term foreign debt (Goldstein 1998).

Second, in the late 1980s, South Korea began a transition to democracy. Since then, presidents and parliaments have been elected through direct and popular elections. The government legalized labor unionizations and strikes, which resulted in frequent strikes and wage increases. As a result, the price of South Korean exported goods went up and productivity declined, which reduced international competitiveness. Diminished international competitiveness resulted in declining exports, which made the South Korean economy vulnerable to external shocks (Mo and Moon 1999).

The incumbent government's policies made some effort to address these problems prior to the outbreak of the crisis, and its opposition successor implemented significant macroeconomic austerity and structural reforms in response to the crisis. I argue that these reform efforts received strong support from the urban middle classes, unorganized labor, and the agricultural sector. This relatively straightforward story, of dispersed interest groups rebelling against the negative economic consequences of subsidies to concentrated interest groups, is complicated by regional political differences and institutional conditions specific to South Korea. The successor coalition that implemented the postcrisis reforms received particularly strong regional support from the Southwestern (Chollar) and Central (Chungcheong) provinces, to an extent that far exceeds the level of support that would be predicted from the economic structure of these regions. But this was the case before and after the crisis, and so does not explain the increased overall level of dispersed interest group support for the opposition parties after the crisis. In addition, the weakness of the party system also makes policy formation highly dependent on leadership. Thus the effective opposition response to dispersed interest group demands for reform depended a lot on decisive leadership from the new president, Kim Dae Jung. The recent transition to democracy contributed to organized labor militancy and indecisive pre-election policymaking. But the moderately reformist trend of precrisis and postcrisis policy indicates a desire on the part of the dispersed interest group majority to preserve the main elements of the macroeconomically conservative, export-oriented economic policies responsible for South Korea's remarkable record of economic growth, while selectively weeding out the policies subsidizing the concentrated interest groups that have traditionally dominated the South Korean economy.

PRECRISIS POLICIES: TREND TOWARD LIBERALIZATION
SUPPORTED BY DISPERSED INTEREST GROUPS

In the late 1980s, South Korea experienced a dramatic transition to democracy, which caused many changes. One of the most important changes was replacing the indirect presidential election with a direct one (Moon and Kim 1994). The new electoral system restored competition in the political sector and became a viable means of achieving democratic changes of government (Moon 1999). As a result, in 1997, an opposition party won the presidential election for the first time.

In 1993, Kim Young Sam was elected president. Both internal and external forces pressured him to continue moves toward democracy and a more market-oriented economy begun during the first democratic administration of Ro Tae Woo. The internal pressure focused on expanding civil rights, reducing central authority and corruption, and scaling back the size, subsidies, and political power of the huge conglomerates (*chaebol*s) that dominate South Korea's economy. These measures were of course supported by long-repressed organized labor. They also drew mass support from an overwhelming majority composed of peasants, the middle classes, and unorganized labor, who resented the privileged position of the *chaebol*s under the authoritarian regime.

In response, Kim Young Sam implemented institutional reforms of economic and administrative systems. Against the business sector's opposition, financial transparency was advanced by requiring bank accounts to be held under real names. Many regulations concerning economic activities were eased or removed. In particular, the law concerning collective protest was abolished and the labor law was amended, legalizing labor unions (Cotten 1995). In addition, administrative power was gradually decentralized and transferred to local governments. With these changes, the civil society was rapidly expanded. For instance, the number of labor unions, interest groups, and financial institutions sharply increased over a short period.

In addition, Kim Young Sam attempted to break the long-lasting vicious cycle of political contributions and policy-making patronage between big business and the political leadership. He even publicly announced that he would not accept any political contributions from the business sector, which gave him strong public support at the beginning of his tenure. He also tried to reduce the economic concentration of the *chaebol*s. However, his efforts were not successful because of his increasingly lame-duck status, a scandal involving his son, and dissent from within his own party—of all the parties, the one most closely related to the *chaebol*s (Moon 1999).

The external pressure heavily focused on opening markets. The Organization for Economic Cooperation and Development (OECD) as well as the U.S. government criticized South Korea's protectionist trade policies. In addition, during the Uruguay round, South Korea was heavily criticized for restrictions on foreign participation in the financial market and on foreign commercial borrowing

(Whalley 1989). This pressure led to structural changes in the early 1990s, with Kim's globalization campaign. First, the government liberalized banking and foreign exchange regimes. The number of financial institutions and the amount of foreign borrowing increased rapidly. Somewhat ironically, the *chaebols* were fastest to capitalize on the new opportunities, starting many nonbank financial businesses and dramatically expanding their foreign borrowing (Moon 1999).

Second, in 1992, direct access by foreigners to the share market was allowed for the first time. Between 1993 and 1995, three principal changes to regulations governing long-term capital flows were implemented: (1) the limit on foreign ownership of a company's stock was raised to 15 percent; (2) companies were allowed to get loans from international banks for the purposes of financing capital goods imports (both directly and through authorized Korean banks); and (3) constraints on the ownership of foreign currency deposits were eased (Smith 1998, 76). These changes generated increased international portfolio investment. For example, in 1993, only 5.8 percent of Korean stocks were owned by foreigners, but this number increased to 14.6 percent in 1997 (Korean Stock Exchange 1999).

In addition, the Kim administration attempted to change the structure of the national economy with two major reform bills. The first one was a labor reform bill submitted to the National Assembly in 1996 (*Digital Chosun Ilbo,* 4 December 1996). The bill aimed to provide a more flexible labor market by eliminating lifetime employment and allowing layoffs. It was an attempt to respond to the rapidly rising wages and declining competitiveness of Korean companies by providing them with a more competitive labor market. However, with strong opposition by labor unions and the opposition party, the bill was stalled in the National Assembly until the end of 1996. Because the opposition party did not participate in the vote, the government was forced to retreat and reopen discussion of the bill later (Heo and Kim 1998).

The second legislative effort was a financial reform bill that was submitted to the National Assembly in August 1997 (*Digital Chosun Ilbo,* 23 August 1997). With this bill, the government attempted to restructure the financial sector. There were two important changes included in the bill. First, the government tried to consolidate the supervision of commercial banks and merchant banks. Second, the government attempted to make the Bank of Korea more independent of the government. The financial reform bill did not pass until after the crisis broke out (Heo and Kim 1998).

DEVELOPMENT OF THE FINANCIAL CRISIS

South Korea started showing signs of economic decline in 1996 (Smith 1998). For instance, industrial output growth slowed from an annual growth rate of 14 percent in 1995 to 10 percent in 1996. The growth of manufacturing sales declined from 20 percent in 1995 to 10 percent in 1996 (Smith 1998, 67). In 1996, twenty of the thirty largest *chaebol*s showed poor profitability. (Corsetti et al. 1998, 6) Corporate bankruptcies were soon followed by bankruptcies of financial institutions. In 1996 alone, the stock market fell by 35 percent (Smith 1998, 67), and about 50,000 workers in manufacturing industries alone lost their jobs (*Digital Chosun Ilbo,* 3 March 1997). In addition, overall South Korean foreign debt increased during that period. In particular, the share of short-term loans in the total foreign debt went up by 59 percent in a year (*Dongailbo,* 4 February 1998). The current account deficit in 1996 also increased to US$23.1 billion, or 4.8 percent of GDP (Smith 1998, 67).[1]

In January 1997, the Hanbo Steel Manufacturing Company, which had become one of the thirty largest companies in the 1990s, collapsed under US$6 billion in debts. It was the first bankruptcy of one of the leading Korean *chaebol*s in a decade. It was followed by the collapse of Sami Steel Corporation and Kia Motor's request for bankruptcy protection. The impact of Hanbo's bankruptcy on the South Korean economy was huge because of a political scandal involving large-scale bribery and kickbacks. The scandal started in the early 1990s when Hanbo expanded its facility. Hanbo bribed many politicians in order to receive excessive loans without securing collateral or submitting its business plans for proper examination. As Hanbo collapsed, the lending process was investigated amid much political controversy.

On July 2, 1997, the Bank of Thailand announced a managed float of the *baht* and called on the IMF for "technical assistance." In October, the Hong Kong stock market crashed (*Digital Chosun Ilbo,* 10 April 1998). These two external shocks had a large impact on South Korean share markets for three reasons. First, South Korean financial organizations had lent a total of US$173 million to Thailand's finance companies by the end of August 1997 and US$92 million could not be guaranteed by the Thai government (*Digital Chosun Ilbo,* 1 October 1997). Thus some financial institutions were expected to struggle. Second, since 34 percent of South Korean exports went to Southeast Asian countries, a significant decline in exports was expected (*Digital Chosun Ilbo,* 4 June 1999). Thus investors started selling their stocks. Third, foreign investors were concerned about the fallout from the worsening situation in Southeast Asia (*Digital Chosun Ilbo,* 10 April 1998).

The political instability brought on by the Hanbo scandal, the collapse of big companies, and the external shocks combined to increase South Korea's country risk. The British magazine *Euromoney* reported that South Korea dropped from number 22 in March 1997 to number 27 in September, and to number 30 by December. On June 24, 1997, Moody's Investor's Service downgraded the credit of South Korean government-invested organizations and banks. The Standard and Poor's credit rating also went down for a number of banks in South Korea (*Digital Chosun Ilbo,* 2 October 1997).

This decrease in credibility caused foreign portfolio investment to dry up, which had a direct impact on exchange rates. For instance, one U.S. dollar bought

890.5 South Korean won in July 1997. However, the exchange rate went up to 1,025.6 Korean won in November, 1,484.1 in December, and 1,706.8 in January 1998 (Bank of Korea 1999). Many financial institutions experienced severe difficulties in paying off foreign loans because of the quick jump in exchange rates. Many industries were also impacted. The South Korean government then intervened to control exchange rates. However, the government's foreign exchange reserves were not large enough to control the exchange rate. Foreign currency reserves fell from US$33.7 billion in June to US$24.4 billion in July, and US$20 billion in November (*Digital Chosun Ilbo,* 4 December 1997).

CAUSES OF THE FINANCIAL CRISIS

The immediate economic causes of the capital flight–induced financial crisis were a massive increase in short-term foreign borrowing and unexpectedly inadequate foreign currency reserves, in a context of deteriorating economic performance. Although excessive short-term borrowing was facilitated by a recent liberalization of South Korean regulations on capital inflows, the sources of deteriorating economic performance were primarily political. These were three major factors. Most fundamentally, South Korean development was based on politically influenced lending to a small number of gigantic, export-oriented *chaebol*s. The *chaebol*s relied on massive amounts of debt to fuel their expansion, and the wave of financial difficulties indicates that the borrowed funds were invested in increasingly risky activities. Because of their huge size, the firms believed that the government would bail them out of any severe financial difficulties. Second, democratization spurred a wave of labor organization, strikes, and rapid wage increases. Third, the immature parties of the new democracy hesitated to force the painful process of firm restructuring and stronger oversight of lending practices.

Short-Term Loans

As many economists pointed out, the immediate cause of the crisis seemed to be the excessive dollar-denominated short-term loans and the shortage of foreign exchange reserves (*New York Times,* January 8, 1998). For example, according to a report to the National Assembly by the Ministry of Finance and Economy, long-term foreign debt increased by US$2.4 billion to US$46.1 billion, while short-term debt jumped by US$3.2 billion to US$64.2 billion from December 1996 to March 1997 (*Digital Chosun Ilbo,* 1 October 1997).[2] This increase of short-term loans is even more striking when the ratio between short-term loans and foreign exchange reserves is considered. According to Radelet and Sachs (1998), the ratio of short-term loans to foreign exchange reserves in South Korea increased from 1.623 in June 1994 to 2.073 in June 1997.

If the economy was growing, this would not have been a problem because foreign creditors would have rolled over the credits (Goldstein 1998). However, this did not happen because a number of *chaebol*s collapsed and Kim Young Sam's lame-duck presidency was wracked by political scandal. This changed credit market increased demand for dollars and drove the exchange rate very high.

Interest Rates

One of the reasons for an increase in short-term loans and overall debt was the interest rate differential between South Korea and the rest of the world. In the 1960s and 1970s, South Korea pursued export-led industrialization to promote its economic growth. To this end the government created several export-supporting systems: the setting and monitoring of export targets, allocation of credit for export purposes, and the maintenance of an export-friendly tax and trade system (Rhee et al. 1984; World Bank 1987). In order to prevent excessive credit expansion and attendant inflation, lending for other purposes was subjected to higher rates of interest.

In addition, the government emphasized self-financing for infrastructure investment. In order to attract domestic savings for this purpose, the government pursued a high interest rate policy, which continued into the 1990s (Kim and Leipziger 1998). The government owned most major banks and possessed large shares in many private banks and thus had great control over interest rates and the allocation of credit. Since domestic interest rates were higher, South Korean banks and their subsidiaries found it profitable to borrow money in the international market and lend it to the domestic borrowers (Heo and Kim 1998).

International Capital Flows

In the 1960s, foreign investment was eschewed because it was thought to threaten national sovereignty (Whalley 1989). To this end, many regulations were put in place to constrain foreign capital inflows. However, in the 1990s, with the globalization campaign, financial markets were opened.

With this change, foreign capital flowed in. However, in 1997, foreign portfolio investment started drying up because of political and economic instability. According to the Bank of Korea, foreign investors in the stock market withdrew investments worth US$1.969 billion from August to November 1997 (*Digital Chosun Ilbo,* 7 February 1998). This exodus of foreign capital led to a foreign exchange crisis.

Lack of Accounting Transparency

Before the crisis broke out, the Bank of Korea attempted to halt the local currency's slide against the dollar. Sentiment about South Korea was negative. However, after an IMF investigation, IMF managing director Michel

Camdessus said that South Korea would be spared from any kind of financial crisis (Roubini 1998). This misjudgment was caused by lack of accounting transparency. There have been two types of accounting problems in South Korea. The first type is nontransparent accounting of foreign exchange reserves. A large portion of South Korean foreign exchange reserves was deposited to its bank subsidiaries in other countries and then lent to Korean companies and used for business expansion. In other words, there was a difference between perception and reality in the total amount of foreign exchange reserves. Thus foreign exchange was not available when needed to meet the demands of international creditors (Heo and Kim 1998).

The second type of accounting problem concerns the loans obtained by the overseas branch subsidiaries of domestic companies. Many South Korean companies have overseas branch subsidiaries and they obtained loans. Due to the lack of accounting transparency, however, the Bank of Korea did not count this type of debt as foreign debt. For instance, after the IMF bailout, the Ministry of Finance and Economy announced that South Korea had US$153 billion in debt as of December 20, 1997 (*Digital Chosun Ilbo,* 29 January 1998). After debt of US$32.4 billion held by overseas branch subsidiaries of domestic companies was found, the total debt of South Korea announced by the Ministry of Finance and Economy increased to US$186.8 billion as of the end of 1997 (*Digital Chosun Ilbo,* 26 February 1998). When claims were made for all these debts, the Bank of Korea had to use its reserves to meet the claims. This misled the Bank of Korea with respect to foreign exchange reserve preparation. In other words, due to the lack of accounting transparency, the foreign exchange problems prior to the crisis were underestimated.

Bad Loans and the Role of the Government in the Financial Sector

According to Choi (1991), the Korean system of government-led, *chaebol*-dominated economic development led to flawed lending practices. Although enterprises were privately owned, management was shared between the government and the owners, and the government implicitly guaranteed the loans of the huge firms. According to Goldstein (1998), South Korea had too much "connected lending"—lending to bank directors, managers, and related businesses. Risk control by screening projects and monitoring corporate performance was minimal (Smith 1998). Therefore, financial institutions became vulnerable to external shocks that restricted their access to new credit.

Corruption within the Korean bureaucracy also played a role in poor lending practices. Since the government intervened in private sector business decision making, bureaucrats' power went beyond their legal authority (Lee 1997). This corrupt side of the Korean bureaucracy is captured in a poll by the Political-Economic Risk Consultant of Singapore. According to a poll of 300 international businessmen in Asia, the South Korean bureaucracy was the second worst in terms of efficiency and the fifth most corrupt among twelve Asian countries (*Digital Chosun Ilbo,* 8 March 1998; *Hankuk Ilbo,* 1 April 1998).

In sum, lending practices were not commensurate with business risks. Since the government was often involved, both creditors and depositors assumed that the government and the Bank of Korea would bail them out if problems arose (Goldstein 1998).

The Labor Movement and Higher Wages

As South Korea became more democratized in the late 1980s, the government legalized labor unions. Because political pressures had been building, wage increases became a primary issue between the labor and management. South Korea started experiencing frequent strikes, which eventually decreased productivity. According to the *World Labor Report 1997–1998,* workdays missed as a result of strikes and lockouts increased from 64,000 in 1985 to 4,487,000 in 1990. From 1990 to 1996, the average lost workdays by strikes per 1,000 workers in South Korea was seventh in the world (*Digital Chosun Ilbo,* 5 April 1998). In the 1990s South Korea has had the second most lost workdays due to labor strikes in Asia (International Labor Organization 1999).

Since the mid-1980s, frequent labor strikes caused South Korean labor costs to rise significantly. Despite the fact that increases in labor costs have exceeded productivity gains since 1987, wage increases continued (Root 1999). For instance, real average monthly earnings in manufacturing grew by an average of 7.8 percent per year between 1992 and 1996 (Smith 1998). These increased labor costs led to higher prices for exporting goods, which in turn reduced international competitiveness. Considering that South Korea owed its economic success to cheap, high-quality labor, these labor problems were critical for economic performance.

Political Instability

During the 1960s and 1970s, the authoritarian South Korean government maintained a relatively stable political system. Although there were some antigovernment protests, the nation generally focused on economic development. However, as the nation became democratized in the 1990s, political instability increased. In 1997, the dampening effect of political instability on economic performance in South Korea was assessed the highest among the twenty-four OECD countries (*Digital Chosun Ilbo,* 13 October 1997).[3]

The political instability in South Korea prior to the crisis came from two internal conflicts: (1) political party conflicts due to the lack of a stable and institutionalized party system and (2) intrabureaucratic conflicts between the Ministry of Economy and Finance and the Bank of Korea (Smith 1998). The party conflicts occurred because of the short history of South Korean democracy. Since South Korean political culture focuses on a few key leaders, political parties have been led by powerful individuals allied in short-term coalitions. For this reason, parties lacked developed policy positions and were more interested in short-term political gains rather than national interests or long-term goals. Politicians have also attempted to discredit the president and the policies of the government for electoral gain, which often resulted in myopic policies (Mo 1999).

For example, when Kia Motors sought bankruptcy protection, the opposition party proposed to nationalize the company. This is because Kia was based in Chollar province, where the opposition party is strongly supported. Since the presidential election was near, myopic political concerns were more important than national economic concerns. For the same political reason, the government was also hesitant to let Kia go bankrupt (*Joongang Ilbo,* 27 October 1997). This nationalization policy led international investors to be suspicious of the government's ability and willingness to control risky lending and investment practices, and to force restructuring of poorly performing firms—adding to the exodus of foreign investment (*Digital Chosun Ilbo,* 10 April 1998).

Bureaucratic infighting became significant in the vacuum created by the lame-duck presidency. The financial reform bill—creating an independent central bank and seeking to improve supervision of financial institutions—failed to pass in the National Assembly because of an intense public turf battle between the once dominant Ministry of Economy and Finance and the newly independent Bank of Korea. Since Kim Young Sam's term had less than a year remaining and he was hurt by the Hanbo scandal, the president failed to use his leadership to resolve the conflict. This delay further sapped investor confidence in the economy.

POSTCRISIS POLICIES: CONTINUED LIBERALIZATION SUPPORTED BY DISPERSED INTEREST GROUPS

Right after the IMF bailed out South Korea, in December 1997, the presidential election was held. Kim Dae Jung, a long-time dissident and opposition leader, was elected president. A coalition government was formed between Kim Dae Jung's National Congress for New Politics, based heavily in the less developed Southwest (Chollar province), and Kim Jong Pil's United Liberal Democrats, based heavily in the Center (Chungcheong province). By contrast, Kim Young Sam's Grand National Party is based heavily in the more industrialized Southeast. Because of these strong regional loyalties, swing voters are more concentrated in the North around the capital, Seoul.

During his campaign, Kim Dae Jung announced that he would renegotiate the IMF bailout program. However, after he came to office, he complied with the IMF prescriptions, which included a tight fiscal budget and high interest rates. The IMF also recognized that extensive banking and credit reforms are a necessary condition for Korean economic recovery. Thus the South Korean government began restructuring the financial sector by cleaning up nonperforming loans. In 1998, the government set up the Korea Asset Management Corporation to acquire nonperforming loans. In the process, a number of financial institutions were forced into bankruptcy. Under government pressure, banks started making loans conditional on more objective analysis of borrowers' cash flow prospects (Root 1999). A large portion of the government's shares in some banks have been sold to the private sector, and many publicly owned companies have been privatized.

*Chaebol*s have also been pressured to reform by the government. Throughout the previous high-growth period, *chaebol*s had expanded their businesses and moved into unrelated sectors. For example, several *chaebol*s moved beyond their core businesses in steel, automobiles, shipbuilding, electronics, and telecommunications into leisure businesses such as hotels and golf courses. In the process of expansion, *chaebol*s received favored credit allocation, which led to unusually high debt-equity ratios. After the crisis, they were pressured to refocus their businesses and reduce debt. *Chaebol*s started selling some subsidiary companies, closing down inefficient businesses, and laying off workers to improve productivity (Root 1999). Moreover, the owners (large shareholders) of *chaebol*s have been forced to contribute their private assets to pay off debts, in order to take responsibility for their business management failures. Thus Lee Kun Hee of Samsung and Kim Woo Jung of Daewoo have been recently forced to give up some of their private assets to improve the financial situation of their groups.

Although the new coalition government has moved ahead with *chaebol* restructuring, financial sector reform, and labor market reform, it has not questioned the orthodoxies of macroeconomic stability and export-oriented development. This reflects a consensus among all three major parties and their mass bases on conserving the components of the old policy regime that, in the space of little more than one generation, turned South Korea from a shattered peasant society into a relatively wealthy industrial powerhouse.

Since South Korea was bailed out by the IMF, the South Korean economy has been characterized by three "highs" (unemployment, won-dollar exchange rate, prices of goods) and three "lows" (growth, stock market index, and investment). With the IMF conditionality, the South Korean government let a number of nonbank financial institutions go bankrupt and sold the First and Seoul Banks. The financial and industrial sectors are suffering the pain of restructuring. These structural reforms have helped restore investor confidence. As a result of that, the Korean stock market has recovered to a precrisis level of 950 (*Digital Chosun Ilbo,* 21 July 1999). The exchange rate of the Korean won against the U.S. dollar has been relatively stable at around 1,200 won. Based on these economic indicators, South Korea seems to be on the right track to recovery.

Despite the government's efforts to restructure the manufacturing and financial sectors, the Big Five *chaebol*s—Hyundai, Samsung, Daewoo, LG, and SK—are still strong. In fact, *chaebol*s now dominate credit allocation in the nonbank sector, although the government recently has been trying to change the picture.

Domestic competition for credit has decreased (Root 1999). Although Daewoo has recently been reported to be reforming its structure to focus only on trade and the automobile industry, it will be critical to restructure the *chaebols* if another crisis is to be avoided in the future (*Digital Chosun Ilbo,* 20 July 1999).

There are three other hurdles in the way of economic reform and recovery. First, labor unions have been strongly resistant to restructuring. Although the economy has been slowly recovering from the crisis, many business companies still need to reduce costs and need more flexibility in labor markets. Since this kind of labor policy is new to many Korean workers, however, resistance has been strong. Because of this unpopularity, the government has continued to allow political considerations to block economic reforms.

Another hurdle is corruption. Recently revealed political scandals rooted in corruption and local political-business ties have reduced public support for the government (*New York Times,* July 20, 1999).[4] Since local autonomy brought elections into local politics, local business and politicians have developed ties based on mutual interests. Most causes of the crisis discussed earlier derived from political-business ties and corruption. The same phenomenon is slowly developing at the local level.

The last hurdle is political instability. The current government is based on a coalition between Kim Dae Jung's NCNP and Kim Jong Pil's United Liberal Democrats, and there have been disagreements between the two parties. Recently, there has been speculation about creating a new party combining the two parties, along with some defectors from the opposition Grand National Party (*Digital Chosun Ilbo,* 20 July 1999). But the party system continues to be dominated by strong personalities, without the discipline imposed by institutionalized parties with strong traditional policy platforms. Considering the importance of the government's role in completing economic reforms and recovery, political instability could be a critical factor.

CONCLUSION

In this chapter, I have discussed precrisis policies, the causes of the financial crisis, and postcrisis policies in South Korea. Rapid increases of short-term loans, international capital flows, and a lack of accounting transparency were the immediate causes of the crisis. However, political factors, such as government-sponsored lending practices, labor reforms, frequent strikes and increased wages, and political instability, have played more fundamental roles in causing the crisis.

Just prior to the crisis, Kim Young Sam's government made some significant efforts to impose financial and structural reforms, as well as to advance political decentralization and liberalization. Nevertheless, some crucial reforms were postponed in order to avoid alienating important constituencies in the run-up to elections. In response to the crisis and the associated surge in dispersed interest group support for reform of traditional policies favoring the *chaebol*s, Kim Dae Jung's new coalition government has imposed painful macroeconomic stringency and structural reforms. The liberalizing direction of precrisis and postcrisis reforms reflects the trend in dispersed interest group preferences under democracy, a combination of resentment at the power and privileges of the *chaebol*s, with a desire to conserve the economic achievements of the old regime. However, an accommodating liberal policy response is threatened by weak parties and hence is dependent on continued leadership by figures such as Kim Dae Jung.

One of the theoretically interesting points to be inferred from the South Korea case concerns the impact of democratization on economic policy. Thus South Korea's new democracy has produced some instability and uncertainty by unleashing organized labor and by postponing crucial financial and structural reforms in the run-up to new elections. On the other hand, South Korean voters are overwhelmingly conscious that the salutary drives to increase political and economic freedoms and discipline the *chaebol*s should not be allowed to undermine the foundations of the nation's economic dynamism. In the long run, therefore, democratization may spur liberalizing reform and improve economic performance. Above all, democratization has provided a political environment more favorable to implementing much needed structural economic reform measures (Lew 1999). The recent financial crisis and recession may be the short-term price that South Korea has to pay for the long-term benefits deriving from democratization.

NOTES

1. South Korea's current account deficit in the past three decades has been 1–2 percent of GDP (Smith 1998).

2. Even after rollover negotiations in New York after the IMF bailout, the amount of short-term loans to be paid remains US$89.9 billion (*Digital Chosun Ilbo,* February 26, 1998).

3. Of 1,000 people in top management in companies in the Asia-Pacific region, 44 percent blamed politicians for inviting the economic crisis in South Korea (*Far Eastern Economic Review,* January 22, 1998).

4. The governor of Kyonggi province and his wife have been indicted for taking bribes to stop the closure of Kyonggi Bank for excessive nonperforming loans. Several cabinet members' wives have also been accused of similar lobbying in exchange for bribes.

9

Taiwan: Sustained State Autonomy and a Step Back from Liberalization

Alexander C. Tan

The speculative attacks on Southeast Asian currencies that began in July 1997 led to a number of attacks on the Taiwanese currency (new Taiwan dollar, or NTD). While the *baht,* peso, *ringgit, rupiah,* and *won* collapsed under the pressure of "hot money" movements, Taiwan's currency was subject to a controlled 20 percent depreciation—from NTD33 to US$1 to NTD27 to US$1. Since that depreciation in late 1997, the new Taiwan dollar has stabilized at a rate of NTD33 to US$1.

Currency depreciations of the magnitude seen in late 1997 exact heavy tolls on an economy. In Thailand, Malaysia, Indonesia, South Korea, and to some extent the Philippines, they have been followed by corporate bankruptcies, employee layoffs, high inflation, and negative growth rates. Of course, these economic problems complicated the already fragile political situation in many East Asian countries. In South Korea, the "embarrassment" of having to go to the International Monetary Fund (IMF) for a bailout may have contributed to Kim Dae Jung's victory in the presidential election. In Indonesia, the economic crisis led to the downfall of long-ruling President Suharto and to the subsequent social unrest.

Interestingly, Taiwan escaped the financial crisis without the problems its neighbors experienced.[1] How did Taiwan avoid the disaster that befell its fast-growing neighbors? A cursory examination points to Taiwan's strong macroeconomic fundamentals in the years leading up to the crisis (Kuo and Liu 1999). To a certain extent, we can also attribute Taiwan's successful handling of the crisis to adept technocrats (Perng 1999). However, in-depth analysis of Taiwan's condition suggests that economic fundamentals and able bureaucrats provide only partial and more proximate explanations.

165

These explanations raise more basic questions about Taiwan's economic policy regime. What were the policies that placed Taiwan's economy in such a strong position? Why were these policies adopted? Why were precrisis institutions and policies reaffirmed and even strengthened by the crisis, rather than—as often occurred elsewhere—weakened or destabilized? In this chapter, I suggest that institutional and interest group explanations can help inform our understanding of Taiwan. Specifically, I argue that we can attribute Taiwan's "fortune" to an institutional setting that nourished a specific type of political economy. This political economy is characterized by the dominance of small and medium-sized enterprises (SMEs). This makes for weak concentrated interest groups, particularly weak capital and labor in the traded sector, and for a state that is best described as "autonomous." As long as policy making by the autonomous state continues to be associated with high and stable growth rates, the agricultural sector and dispersed middle class and labor groups in the urban service sector have little reason to mobilize against government economic policy. With the recent transition to democracy, this record of economic performance has become increasingly important in sustaining state autonomy and state technocrats' chosen policy regime. Together, the weakness of concentrated interest groups and the autonomy and effectiveness of the economic technocracy make possible swift implementation of often painful policy choices with minimal economic and political repercussions. This capability for swift and effective adjustment was once again on display in Taiwan during the financial crisis of 1997–1999.

In the next section, I briefly examine the precrisis setting. I then discuss the economic policy choices adopted as the crisis unfolded and after the crisis. Following this discussion, I examine the lessons that Taiwanese authorities have taken away from the crisis. In the fourth section, Taiwan's fortunate position is explained in terms of the nature of its autonomous state. It is this autonomous state and its associated interest group structure that in large part explain the policies adopted before, during, and after the crisis.

THE SETTING AND THE RESPONSE: ORIGINS AND CHARACTER OF THE MAINLANDER REGIME, SME INDUSTRIAL STRUCTURE, AND CAUTIOUS ECONOMIC MANAGEMENT

Taiwan's macroeconomic fundamentals in the years leading up to July 1997 have been described as rock solid (*Economist*, 18 October 1997, 72). Taiwan had large current account surpluses, a low foreign debt ratio, strong exports, low inflation, and huge foreign exchange reserves. Looking at table 9.1, one is left with the impression that Taiwan's economic performance remains strong. Though the performance for 1999 was noticeably weaker than in years past, there was no deflation or collapse of the economy.

Table 9.1 Taiwan Economic Summary

	1999	1998
Total GDP (US$bn)	271.5	257.1
Real GDP growth (%)	3.9	4.8
GDP per capita (US$000)	12.28	11.74
Inflation (% change in CPI)	1.6	1.1
Unemployment rate (%)	3.3	3.1
Foreign exchange reserves (US$bn)	88.0	86.0
Budget balance (% of GDP)	−6.0	−6.5
Current account balance (US$bn)	3.9	3.9
Exports (US$bn)	115.9	112.3
Imports (US$bn)	109.6	106.4
Trade balance (US$bn)	6.3	5.9

Source: Financial Times, 12 October 1998.

In order to understand how well Taiwan responded during the Asian financial crisis, a brief review of the economic policy regime of the Kuomintang (KMT) government is necessary. Taiwan's strong macroeconomic performance in the past forty years has been a well-researched topic in both the economics and political science literatures. After losing the mainland, the KMT government moved to Taiwan without any strong power base.

The KMT's failure to carry out effective land reform on the mainland and the consequent loss of peasant support were crucial sources of the communist victory. The KMT government was determined to not let history repeat itself on Taiwan. In the 1950s, Taiwan carried out a highly successful land reform program. Land reform was combined with a comprehensive agricultural development program, including the establishment of farmers' cooperatives, an agricultural credit system, and price supports and subsidies. The land reform and agricultural development program have given the government strong support among the island's peasantry (Moody 1992, 47).

Concurrent with the development of agriculture, early government economic policy used high tariffs to encourage import substitution and the buildup of a heavy industrial base. Because of the large capital investment required, Taiwan's heavy industrial base was dominated by state-owned enterprises. This phase of economic development did not last long, partly due to prodding by U.S. aid officials and partly due to the realization among Taiwan's economic policy makers that reliance on the island's small domestic market could not sustain rapid economic growth. Therefore, Taiwan soon adopted an export-oriented economic development path.

At the early stage of export promotion, Taiwan's export companies produced labor-intensive products to take advantage of Taiwan's abundant labor. Instead of producing under their own brand names, Taiwanese export manufacturers are mainly original equipment manufacturers (OEM) producing export goods as subcontractors. The goods produced rely heavily on imported materials and generally bear the brand names of foreign companies. Due to the conservative nature of banking policies in Taiwan, companies are generally constrained by limited access to capital.[2] This limited access to capital has contributed to an industrial structure that is dominated by SMEs. This decentralized industrial structure, and the highly competitive market it fostered, also served the political interests of the ruling elite. Not only did decentralization of the industrial structure help in lessening the potential threat to KMT power, but more importantly, the growth of thriving SMEs enabled the KMT to expand its social support base in the cities, much as the land reform and agricultural development program had enabled it to do in the countryside (Chu 1999).

As Taiwan's comparative advantage in labor-intensive production declined over time, old labor-intensive traded sector industries were gradually replaced by capital-intensive traded sector industries, nontraded service industries, and later, traded sector knowledge-based industries. Yet Taiwan's industrial structure remained decentralized and dominated by SMEs throughout the period. The dominant position of the SMEs in Taiwan's industrial structure is more obvious when compared to other newly industrialized countries (NICs), for example, South Korea. Recent data on the scale of conglomerates in the South Korean and Taiwanese economies are displayed in table 9.2.

As shown in table 9.2, Taiwan's top ninety-six conglomerates do not dominate domestic production, accounting for only 31.7 percent of gross national product (GNP). In South Korea, on the other hand, the top fifty firms accounted for 93.8 percent of the country's GNP. More recent data show that 98 percent of all registered companies in Taiwan can be considered SMEs. These companies account for 52 percent of total production output and 78 percent of the jobs on the island (Chu 1999, 2).

As a result of its export promotion development strategy, Taiwan industrialized rapidly. Yet although it "became industrialized, it did not become proletarianized" (Moody 1992, 48). In fact, undergirding Taiwan's economic success is a "fluid class structure" that tends to "inhibit the growth of independent [political] movements" (Chu 1999, 5). This is particularly so for as long as government policies produce high and stable economic growth.

As theorized in orthodox development economics, the growth and development of the manufacturing sector eventually led to the growth of the service sec-

Table 9.2   Comparison of Korean and Taiwanese Conglomerates, 1983

	Korean Top 50	Taiwan Top 96
Total sales (US$bn)	68.32	16.48
Percentage of GNP	93.80	31.70
Firms/conglomerate	11.04	4.76
Workers/firm	1500.00	444.00

Source: Fields 1995.

tor as well. In particular, the financial service industries expanded to cater to the island's cash-rich clientele and, more importantly, to the ever increasing role of Taiwan as a financier and investor in the region. To strengthen Taiwan's increasing regional financial and economic importance, the government began to develop Taiwan into an "Asia-Pacific regional operations center."

As part of the plan to set up this Asia-Pacific regional operations center, Taiwan's authorities set their sights on creating a regional financial center in Taipei. The economic stimulus behind this initiative is that a highly developed and competitive financial sector will help advance the capital-intensive industrialization of Taiwan. To achieve the objective of developing a regional financial center, Taiwan's financial industry was envisioned as becoming increasingly integrated into regional and world financial markets through deregulation, liberalization, and modernization of Taiwan's financial markets. The Central Bank of China (CBC, Taiwan's central bank) was given overall responsibility to develop the financial center. However, within the executive yuan (cabinet), the Ministry of Economic Affairs (MOEA) and the Ministry of Finance (MOF) are considered the more enthusiastic proponents of the plan (*Economist,* 25 April 1998, 72). The plans to liberalize Taiwan's financial markets were set in motion in January 1995.

Before the onset of the Asian currency crisis, several liberalization initiatives were under way or at least being planned for the near future. Some of these measures included (1) completely liberalizing capital movements by the year 2000; (2) fully liberalizing derivative transactions and active trading of nondelivery forward currencies; (3) increasing the volume and scope of business of offshore banking units (OBUs); (4) enlarging the scale of the domestic financial markets by encouraging the development of new financial products and inviting foreign banks to establish a presence in Taiwan; (5) privatizating state-owned financial institutions; (6) raising the ceiling on foreign ownership in locally listed companies; (7) fostering institutional participation in the stock market; and (8) liberalizing futures transactions (Taipei Economic and Cultural Office 1999a, 1999b). But by July 1997, the onset and diffusion of the international financial crisis resulted in a response that can be considered "a step back" from liberalization.

How did the authorities respond to the currency crisis? To answer this question, it is important to note that in Taiwan, the Central Bank of China has primary responsibility for setting monetary policy. The CBC consults with the Ministry of Finance. But because of the more political nature of cabinet appointments in the MOF, and because of memories of the damaging hyperinflation that occurred shortly before the ruling KMT moved to Taiwan, the CBC has been given greater responsibility for monetary policy and general regulatory oversight of the financial sector. During the recent financial crisis, the CBC thus played a more significant role relative to other executive yuan branches.

As the international financial crisis spread like a wildfire, the CBC took countermeasures to prevent Taiwan from being overrun. The initial inclination of CBC officials was to protect the Taiwan dollar from speculative attack by spending some of its huge foreign exchange reserves to stabilize the currency. By mid-October 1997, the CBC decided to preempt currency speculators by allowing the Taiwan dollar to depreciate by 12 percent and then later, depreciate again, up to a total of 20 percent. At NTD33 to US$1, CBC officials believed that the currency had depreciated far enough. Further depreciation would be likely to unnecessarily increase inflation and reduce domestic purchasing power.

From this encounter with "globalized" capital, CBC officials pointed to the flow of short-term capital ("hot money") as the primary source of uncontrolled currency fluctuation. To stabilize the currency, the CBC carried out several "strong arm" measures that have proven effective in stabilizing the Taiwan dollar and halting currency speculation. These measures included (1) halting new issues of Taiwan dollar-denominated bonds by multilateral institutions such as the Inter-American Development Bank and the Asian Development Bank; (2) limiting availability of Taiwan dollar short-term loans to foreign banks branches in Taiwan; (3) delaying authorization of foreign currency-denominated mutual funds; (4) introducing administrative hurdles to cut the turnover of interbank lending by 50 percent; (5) by May 1998, banning nondelivery forward contracts; and (6) requiring reporting of all outward and inward remittances in excess of US$1 million to the CBC.

The immediate objective of these measures is to keep the Taiwan dollar out of reach of foreign currency speculators and to prevent capital flight. Along with these measures the CBC also carried out an easy money policy to make Taiwan dollar-denominated loans available for Taiwanese companies. The CBC also lowered banks' reserve ratio requirements, while simultaneously stepping up oversight of commercial bank lending practices.

Economically, these measures have helped stabilize Taiwan's currency and economy since the onset of the crisis. Taiwan has an enviable status of being among the few countries in the region to register a positive economic growth rate in 1997 and 1998. Economic forecasts for 1999 are generally good as well. Politically, the adept handling of the crisis and the successful stabilization of the economy have brought the ruling KMT added political capital.

Nonetheless, the countermeasures implemented during the crisis and the months following it represent a step away from the liberalization and internationalization of Taiwan's financial industry. In fact, in the end the new measures resulted in regulation and restrictions more strict than at the start of liberalization in January 1995.

THE LESSONS LEARNED

What lessons were learned by Taiwan's economic technocrats? Why were these the lessons learned, and why were the technocrats supported by the government? Although some analysts believe that this is the "wrong lesson" (*Economist,* 25

April 1998, 72), CBC officials now believe that the Asian financial crisis can be blamed on the reckless financial liberalizations of Taiwan's neighbors. As a result, the CBC wanted to slow down the process of liberalization and even turn back the clock a bit. In a speech to bankers and industrialists in Manila, CBC governor Perng Fai-Nan—not a big fan of liberalization—touted Taiwan's countermeasures, regulation of the financial industry, and strict oversight of banks as ways of stopping unwanted influence of "global" capital.

Within Taiwan's financial industry, foreign banks were targeted as prime "suspects" of fueling speculative money flows.[3] As a result, the CBC has stepped up its monitoring of foreign banks by sending routine bank examiners, making NTD-denominated loans more difficult to get for already NTD-cash strapped foreign banks, and increasing bureaucratic red tape on foreign currency transactions in excess of US$5 million.[4] In sum, these new measures intensified CBC regulation of the financial industry and of the economy generally.

The countermeasures implemented during the crisis and the months following it represent a step away from the liberalization and internationalization of Taiwan's financial industry. A number of financial liberalization policies or plans have been halted or reversed. These actions include stopping the privatization of state-owned commercial banks where the government is the largest shareholder; reimposing monitoring of capital movements to and from Taiwan; closing down the currency futures market; using administrative and disciplinary measures to control "unruly" currency traders; targeting foreign bank operations for restrictions; canceling new licenses for bridge financing; and forcibly merging financial institutions.

These restrictions and reregulations of "speculative" fund movements imposed heavy costs on some producer groups. Nondelivery forward contracts were the only hedge mechanism in Taiwan. Banning them has taken a toll on both exporters and importers by making these companies vulnerable to currency fluctuations. Some large Taiwanese companies have cut back or put on hold their regional expansion plans until other Asian economies stabilize (*Economist*, 24 January 1998).

But the costs associated with the government's financial countermeasures have not created a strong political backlash from the affected groups. Why? To understand why relative political harmony was maintained, we have to turn our attention to the institutional and interest group structure of Taiwan's political economy.

THE POLITICAL BASIS OF THE AUTONOMOUS STATE: WEAK CONCENTRATED INTEREST GROUPS AND PERFORMANCE-BASED DISPERSED INTEREST GROUP SUPPORT

Prevailing explanations of Taiwan's fortunate circumstances have focused on economic factors, namely, the country's industrial structure, its strong economic fundamentals, and the policy choices adopted during the crisis (Kuo and Liu 1999; Lee 1999; Perng 1999; Wang 1999). Taiwan's economy is dominated by small and medium-sized enterprises. SMEs rather than the big conglomerates account for most of the country's GNP.

SMEs are thought to be more flexible in response to fluctuations in the international economy, having the ability to adapt their production to changing market trends and conditions. Past economic policy has helped these firms establish a strong competitive position. The policy response to the crisis improved their competitiveness with a controlled devaluation while staunching any tendency toward significant capital flight.

This proximate economic explanation notwithstanding, no study has posed the following, more fundamental political question about the 1997–1999 crisis: How and why was Taiwan willing and able to make the relevant policies before the crisis, and in response to it? It is important to address this question by looking at the institutions that have governed Taiwan, and how they have conditioned relevant interest groups and state actors.

History matters. Institutions matter too. When the ruling KMT established a government-in-exile in Taiwan, part of the historical baggage it carried was its gross economic mismanagement of Republican China. Since 1949, this poor management has been a stigma that KMT authorities have worked hard to get rid of. Consequently, the KMT has staked the legitimacy of its regime in Taiwan on the performance of the economy—not, at least initially, on how legitimately its political institutions represent the people of Taiwan.

To consolidate power in Taiwan, the KMT mainlander elites discouraged the concentration of wealth by implementing a comprehensive land reform and by encouraging a decentralized industrial structure. These policies prevented the

Table 9.3   Taiwan's Top Ten Business Groups, 1991

Business Group	Sales (US$m)	Assets (US$m)	Employees
Formosa Plastics	6,687	9,529	45,548
China Trust	3,228	12,191	14,008
Linden	5,638	12,109	33,015
Shin Kong	3,511	7,263	30,950
Far Eastern	2,475	5,890	15,884
Hualon	2,458	3,913	17,459
Evergreen	1,849	3,638	7,053
Yue Loong	2,580	1,946	10,693
Yuen Foong Yu	1,464	6,170	5,781
Overseas Trust	818	11,395	1,613
Total	30,708	74,044	182,004
% GNP	17	41	
% Total workforce			12.6

Source: Fields 1995.

overconcentration of rural and urban wealth and therefore limited challenges to its political power. They also gave the KMT the ability to cultivate and maintain support in rural areas, while helping to keep traded sector capital and labor politically weak. The preference for a decentralized industrial structure, evidenced by the dominance of the SMEs, has been balanced by a dominance of state-owned enterprises in key industries (e.g., finance and heavy industries). Preventing the rise of strong concentrated interest groups while fostering the growth of the SMEs across all sectors has helped the KMT to "broaden its social base" (Chu 1999, 11–12). In particular, it has allowed the KMT to create a reservoir of political support among dispersed interest groups in the burgeoning cities (i.e., among the middle classes and unorganized urban labor). With concentrated economic power in check and a strong base of support among the peasants, the middle classes, and unorganized labor, KMT mainland elites have dominated the political sphere and staked their legitimacy on economic performance.

The focus on economic performance and the delineation of the economic sphere from the political sphere is reflected in the island's industrial structure and autonomous, technocrat-driven political institutions. It is important to try to explain why, outside of strategic sectors directly controlled by the state, KMT efforts to maintain control over the urban traded sector took the form of keeping the state at a distance from SMEs. This is not the only possible strategy. In South Korea, for example, state influence was maintained by cultivating direct subsidy and patronage relations with a small number of conglomerates, giving rise to an unusually concentrated industrial structure. Taiwan's separation of the political and economic sphere and the associated SME-based industrial structure largely reflects an ethnic cleavage between "mainlanders" and "islanders."

Except for a few natives, the people of Taiwan are descended from Chinese on the mainland. The distinction between "mainlanders" and "islanders" is not so much one based on kinship, language, or religion, as one denoting when one's ancestors arrived in Taiwan. Mainlanders generally migrated to Taiwan from the end of World War II until 1949. The political sphere was totally dominated by the mainlanders until democratization began in 1988, while the economic sphere was left to the islanders. Taiwan's mainlander ruling elites ensured that the economy functioned well, but outside of a few strategic sectors they did not attempt to control its development directly. In return for this economic freedom, the political sphere was to be left to the mainlanders. Since the political sphere was not designed to be pluralistic and open to participation by society at large, Taiwan's political structures and organizations long reflected a fundamental disconnect between civil society and government. Interestingly, the replacement of the KMT old guard by islanders in major state and party leadership positions, beginning in 1988, has not substantially altered this "disconnected" relationship between civil society and government. How is this continuity across a potentially disruptive change in regime type to be explained?

SME capital and labor peak associations are not strong enough to influence national economic policy making. The high turnover and mobility of these companies do not allow for the development of coherent policy positions or lobbying organizations. This partly explains why the government can afford to stand
aside and allow companies to fail even during a crisis. The regime's institutions
that originally established a disconnectedness between civil society and the state
and fostered the decentralized industrial structure have thus resulted in an autonomous state and economic technocracy with the ability to respond rapidly and
effectively to economic crisis. As long as economic policy continues to maintain
high and stable economic growth, the peasants, the middle classes, and unorganized urban labor have not questioned the legitimacy of the existing economic policy regime and its associated political institutions.

This can be seen in the institutional consequences of the recent trend toward
political liberalization and democratization. These institutional changes have
tended to increase the legitimacy of the regime without substantially altering
the autonomy of the state and the policy formation process in the economic
sphere. Thus most of the changes in Taiwan's political institutions have altered
the form of political representation and eliminated redundancies in existing
governing structures.[5] The major parties agreed on these constitutional
amendments and institutional reforms. However, key economic policy-making
institutions, such as the executive branch and particularly the economic and finance bureaucracies, remain intact and in some cases strengthened. These
changes in political institutions have thus not qualified the autonomy of the
economic technocracy. Instead, by bolstering the legitimacy of the broader political regime, they have solidified it.

Why is this so? The popularity of opposition parties in Taiwan is not based on
an alternative economic policy vision. Rather, it is a product of the ethnic cleavage in general and the national identity issue in particular. To the extent that the
regime is still perceived as dominated by mainlanders, it has an inherent legitimacy shortcoming regardless of its economic performance. At the same time,
though, due to the limits of the politics of ethnicity, the opposition parties were
not easily able to break the KMT's hold on power. This is due to continued strong
economic performance, combined with the increasingly representative character
of political institutions. Thus the opposition's inability to exploit the recent economic crisis to their advantage underscores the low saliency of economic policy
cleavages, as well as the general consensus among the major political parties that
the government technocrats should continue to play a key role in the country's
economic policy making.[6]

During the crisis, the ability of Taiwan's economic policy makers to effectively
respond with strategic capital market interventions, including increased barriers
to capital outflows, reflects the autonomy of the regime and its economic technocracy. Continued autonomy amid democratization is based on the decentralized
nature of the industrial structure and the associated political weakness of concen-

trated interest groups, combined with a strong performance record yielding broad political support from dispersed interest groups. Unlike many other countries affected by the financial crisis, this made for a political and institutional environment that left Taiwan's technocrats free to implement policies aimed at protecting their successful economic model against the swirling waters of international economic uncertainty.

CONCLUSION

At the outset of this chapter I posed the following questions: How did Taiwan avoid the Asian currency crisis? Why was Taiwan able to make the difficult policy choices it eventually carried out? In addressing these issues, I argued that while Taiwan's macroeconomic fundamentals are strong and its technocrats are able, Taiwan's ability to avoid the crisis and adopt difficult policy choices can be attributed to the institutions of its political economy—specifically, the creation of an effective autonomous state and of an interest group structure consistent with maintaining such a state.

This autonomous state and technocracy reflect the choices that were made in Taiwan's development history and eventually shaped its political economy. The dominance of the small and medium-sized enterprises and the regime's control of key economic policies and resources resulted in a political economy characterized by weak domestic concentrated interest groups and performance-oriented dispersed economic interest groups. As a result, the autonomous economic technocracy was able to adopt tough crisis response measures with relative swiftness and with little or no political resistance.

In the year after the collapse of the bubble economies in East and Southeast Asia, Taiwan has continued to carry out a conservative approach to monetary policy. This conservatism is reflected in the cautious approach to further liberalization of the financial markets—a liberalization initiated in the hope of establishing a regional financial center. The policies undertaken by Taiwanese monetary authorities to curb speculation and stabilize the currency and the economy represents a "step back" from financial liberalization. Nonetheless, guaranteeing the stability of its own economy and encouraging investment in neighboring countries represented a small step forward toward ensuring that Asia will not remain in the economic cellar for long.

NOTES

1. While there was decline in some key economic indicators such as exports in late 1998, Taiwan continues to maintain a strong trade balance, current account surplus, and budget surplus. More importantly, East Asian economies have rebounded since early 1999.

Since approximately 50 percent of Taiwan's trade is with Asian countries, such a rebound strongly benefits Taiwan's economy.

2. Banking practices in Taiwan are considered conservative by foreign bankers doing business on the island. In general, loans to private companies are extended only on a fully secured basis. That is, collateral worth as much as the loan is required before a loan can be approved.

3. Taiwan's foreign bankers were summoned by CBC officials and told to exercise restraint in providing their views on the local currency's future market price.

4. The CBC and the MOF restrict establishment of new branches by Taiwan's foreign banks. Due to this handicap, foreign banks in Taiwan cannot avail themselves of the large local deposit base to serve as reservoirs for highly profitable business loans. Without the large deposit base, foreign banks are forced to borrow in the interbank local currency capital market. The interbank market generally carries higher interest rate costs. In the months after the crisis, the CBC singled out several foreign banks and penalized them with a higher interest rate on their overnight NTD loans. CBC administrative measures were successful in cutting the daily transactions in short-term NTD loans by all commercial banks by as much as 40 percent.

5. Some of the more important changes were made in late 1996. These include adding a popularly elected presidency, thus supplanting the old parliamentary system with a presidential one; increasing the number of legislators; abolishing the Taiwan provincial government (to eliminate administrative redundancies, since the provincial and national governments oversee almost exactly the same territory); and reducing the functions of the National Assembly (which is an electoral college rather than a legislative body).

6. This point was strongly emphasized to me by an opposition legislator (Legislator Cheng Pao-ching, personal interview by author, 24 July 1999). The March 2000 victory of an opposition presidential candidate was achieved on the basis of a split within the KMT combined with the ethnic cleavage, not on the basis of any serious dissatisfaction with the economic policy regime. Thus the new president has not called for any significant economic policy changes.

I gratefully acknowledge the support of University of North Texas Faculty Research Initiation Grant #34920

IV

Latin America Comparative Case Studies

10

Mexico: Crises and the Domestic Politics
of Sustained Liberalization

Aldo Flores Quiroga

Mexico's 1994 economic crisis has been regarded as the first crisis of the twenty-first century.[1] The Mexican economy seemed an unlikely candidate to be struck by the unprecedented volume of short-term private capital outflows that we have now come to associate with the new integrated financial world. Here was an emerging market following a nearly exemplary economic reform, pursuing for the most part consistent macroeconomic policies yet suffering a speculative attack severe enough to send it in its deepest economic contraction since the 1930s.

The most important casualty of this economic downturn was the country's financial system. Buoyed by the positive expectations deriving from the market reforms Mexico implemented during the preceding decade, private banks expanded credit to levels not seen in a long time. The coincidence of this credit expansion with the onset of the economic crisis set the conditions for a massive bank failure, which was partially averted thanks to the joint help of foreign aid for economic stabilization and domestic measures to protect public savings.

On the other hand, the recovery and expansion of the Mexican economy has not been seriously disrupted by the international financial crisis of 1997–1999. Capital flight did not develop as it had in 1994, although that scenario was being replayed in much of the developing world, including Brazil.

What explains the Mexican crisis of 1994? Why was the Mexican economy subject to speculative attacks despite implementation of an economic reform widely regarded in policy and financial circles as appropriate? What policies triggered the outflow of capital from Mexico? How did Mexican institutions respond to this crisis? And how did this response affect Mexico's performance amid the international financial crisis of 1997–1999?

Much has been written to explain the economics of the 1994 crisis, but less is understood about its politics. In this chapter I present a political–economic explanation for the choice of the institutional and policy regimes before and after the 1994 crisis. One message is that the institutional structure emerging from the 1994 crisis is part of a longer, gradual process of institutional reform in which Mexico has been immersed since the debt crisis of 1982. The exposition will therefore describe and explain institutional changes in Mexico since 1982, showing how they explain the policy choices leading to the 1994 crisis as well as the institutional transformation it generated.

The argument explains policy choices primarily as an outcome of redistributive struggles, first, between Mexico's autonomous state and the private sector and second, within the private sector. The primary struggle within the private sector has been between sectors producing for the domestic market and sectors producing for the international market. Regarding the former, it explains how the income losses and asset expropriations resulting from the 1976 and 1982 crises triggered a campaign by Mexico's private sector to regain control of productive assets through privatization of state-owned enterprises and to constrain the president's discretionary power over policy making through democratization and deregulation.

Regarding the distributive struggle within the private sector, the main proposition is that the liberalizing direction of economic policy after 1982, which entailed shifts in income distribution, was largely determined by the demands of the politically influential sector of producers with trade and financial ties to foreign markets. These sectors were relatively more concentrated than the sectors producing mostly for the domestic market, a situation that, by reducing the costs of collective action, made them more politically influential. They have also benefited from a like-minded series of still highly autonomous presidential administrations. Policy adjustments therefore reflected their preferences for free trade and capital market liberalization.

There has been a similar split among the peasants, middle classes, and unorganized labor. The 1994 elections and polls anticipating the 2000 elections have demonstrated that there is no majority of these groups in favor of a return to the highly interventionist policies that led to the 1976 and 1982 crises. On the other hand, there is a split between those who favor continued liberalization and those who would like to moderate these policies with a strengthened social safety net and a less ambitious liberalization drive. As would be expected, support for liberal policies is stronger among the middle classes than among the peasants and unorganized labor. However, there is also a pronounced regional character to the division. In the export-oriented North, the primary opposition to the ruling PRI (Institutional Revolutionary Party) is the liberal PAN (National Action Party). In the more home market–oriented Center and the more rural South, the primary opposition is the more interventionist but increasingly moderate PRD (Party of Democratic Revolution).

The discussion in this chapter is structured in four parts. In the first I describe the nature of the 1994 crisis and its impact on Mexico's economic policy and institutional design. In the second I explain Mexico's economic policy and institutional choices before the crisis. In the third I explain economic policy and institutional reforms after the crisis. Finally, I conclude by outlining the main findings.

THE CRISIS OF 1994 AND ITS IMPACT ON MEXICAN ECONOMIC POLICY AND INSTITUTIONS

Mexico's financial crisis started on 20 December 1994, when, under severe currency trading pressures, its central bank—the Bank of Mexico—announced its decision to increase the band of fluctuation of the Mexican peso by 15.26 percent. This announcement triggered a large-scale speculative attack, pushing the exchange rate to reach the ceiling of the band and drastically reducing the Bank of Mexico's foreign reserves.[2] Five days later Mexican financial authorities had no option but to abandon the mixed exchange rate mechanism (crawling peg with a band, or crawling band) they had been operating for three years as part of the broader strategy adopted in 1987 of using the exchange rate as a nominal anchor. The outcome was a sharp exchange rate devaluation in only one day, from an average of NP3.4 to NP5.1 per US$1.

The devaluation, in conjunction with the failure by Mexican economic authorities to implement complementary fiscal and monetary adjustments, resulted in a high level of uncertainty and economic dislocations. Interest rates on short-term government bonds immediately jumped 15 points to 31 percent, skyrocketing to 80 percent by the first quarter of 1995. Output contracted almost 10 percent and close to a million workers found themselves unemployed during the first quarter of 1995.

The triple squeeze of the devaluation, higher interest rates, and output/employment contraction forced many Mexican debtors to suspend payments on their loans, in turn creating the stage for bank failures. Nonperforming loans as a share of total lending of commercial banks increased from 10 percent in 1994 to 16 percent in 1995, and reached 30 percent by 1997—not counting those loans absorbed by the government-run deposit insurance fund.[3] In 1999 the financial costs of this bank failure were estimated at 20 percent of GDP (*El Economista,* July 2, 1999). Only four out of the eighteen main Mexican banks were able to avoid bankruptcy.

It would take a rescue package of US$52 billion concerted by U.S. financial authorities with international financial institutions to stabilize the foreign accounts and, six quarters later, return output to its precrisis level. Nevertheless interest rates remained above 50 percent until the summer of 1996, while bank credit showed no clear sign of expanding. A final solution to the banking crisis, described below, was reached more than four years later, in January 1999, after heated domestic debates and a restructuring of Mexico's banking system.

ECONOMIC FACTORS BEHIND THE CRISIS

What explains the punishment Mexico's economy received in response to the announcement of a modest increase in the band of fluctuation of the exchange rate?[4] The list of factors—some of them mutually interacting—identified by the literature[5] include the following:

1. Real exchange rate overvaluation
2. Excessive current account deficit
3. Excessive reliance on private short-term capital inflows
4. Insufficient information on central bank foreign reserves
5. Excessive domestic credit creation
6. Inefficient oversight of financial transactions
7. Excessive fiscal expansion
8. Higher levels of investment risk deriving from political events

In general, there is disagreement over the degree to which exchange rate overvaluation, domestic credit creation (including money supply expansion), and insufficient information on central bank foreign reserves contributed to the collapse of the peso. There is less disagreement over the negative impact that the choice of financing the relatively large Mexican current account deficit—close to 8 percent of GDP—with short-term private foreign investment had for the sustainability of the foreign accounts. There is agreement that the fiscal deficit was not a fundamental factor in generating the crisis. And there is agreement that increased political risk, combined with short-term foreign borrowing and fast capital market liberalization in an underdeveloped financial institutional framework, overwhelmed the Mexican government's ability to minimize the propagation of the adverse effects of exchange rate devaluation to the banking system.

The debate over the degree of real exchange rate overvaluation is perhaps the most controversial and centers on measurement issues and interpretations of magnitude and duration. To take two representative examples, for Dornbusch and Werner (1994) the real exchange rate, measured with relative price indices, was overvalued by 30 percent since at least 1993. For Gil-Díaz and Carstens (1996) that conclusion is not warranted, since real exchange rate indices they calculated using labor costs indicated a depreciating rather than an appreciating trend. Moreover, assuming the validity of the overvaluation hypothesis, they question its importance in the context of Mexican economic history.

Regarding credit and monetary indicators, it is now apparent that the choice of Mexican authorities to sterilize political risk–induced capital outflows by expanding the money supply (M2) in order to keep interest rates constant put additional pressure on the foreign accounts. As international reserves fell, Mexican policy makers increased the volume of short-term borrowing (long-term borrowing was scarce) in the form of dollar-denominated bonds known as Tesobonos. Essentially, through 1994 they covered the loss of US$16 billion in international reserves (from a total of US$28 billion) with US$28 billion in Tesobonos. This decision proved to be crucial for the unraveling of their economic strategy, for the large current account deficit of 8 percent of GDP was thus financed with unstable short-term capital. Given the "right" conditions, such as those occurring in December 1994, such vulnerability could encourage a speculative attack.

When these factors interacted with uncertainty about the level of the central bank's reserves at the moment in which the band of exchange rate fluctuation increased, investor apprehension increased. By the time the Bank of Mexico withdrew from the exchange market, total reserve losses amounted to US$20 billion.

Regarding the impact of the crisis on the banking system, there is close to a consensus around the perspective that the decisive steps Mexican authorities took to liberalize the financial sector in the four years preceding the crisis encouraged unwise banking and oversight practices. Between 1990 and 1993 Mexican banks were privatized and allowed to set borrowing and lending interest rates according to market forces. But not all banks were sold to investors with experience in the financial sector or clean business histories. Few banks were capitalized properly after being purchased, and none was required to hold a minimum amount of reserves of at least 8 percent. In addition, the Mexican government backed bank deposits completely while neglecting careful oversight of banking transactions (Gil-Díaz and Carstens 1997, 190). This generated well-known moral hazard problems that contributed to extreme risk exposure by banks. When interest rates increased after the devaluation, borrowers found themselves unable to service their debts, banks were swamped with nonperforming loans, and the financial system was threatened with collapse.

ECONOMIC STRATEGY AND INSTITUTIONAL
REFORM AFTER THE CRISIS

The crisis impacted both Mexico's policy stance and institutional structure. In the short term, emergency measures were applied to contain the crisis. The government negotiated with business representatives and labor leaders to form an accord to overcome the economic emergency. This involved a tightening of monetary creation, strict control of public spending, limits on price increases to imported-input price increases, and wage adjustments of 12 percent despite the projected inflation rate of 19 percent for 1995.[6] Funds from the rescue package concerted by U.S. authorities, around US$22 billion, were used in 1995 to repurchase Tesobonos, which were entirely liquidated by early 1996.

Significantly, none of the measures taken to combat the crisis reversed the market reforms implemented during the preceding decade (discussed below). Trade barriers did not increase, exchange controls were not imposed, and privatization of more state-owned enterprises continued. This approach reinforced the trend toward reducing state participation in the economy and presidential discretion across a large set of policy areas.[7]

A positive by-product of this economic strategy was that it helped Mexico come out of the crisis faster than it had in previous ones and avoid falling prey to the world financial crisis of 1997–1999. With low trade barriers and secure access to Mexico's main trading partner—the United States—through the North American Free Trade Agreement, the devaluation resulting from the 1994–1995 Mexican crisis helped to increase Mexico's exports threefold and maintain growth rates above 3 percent after 1995. Thanks to the Mexican government's decision to keep a lid on the fiscal deficit at or below 1 percent of GDP, combined with the choice of a free-floating exchange rate regime, speculation against the Mexican peso during the 1997–1999 crisis was relatively mild when compared to that experienced by Brazil or Argentina. This is not to say that Mexico did not experience dislocations resulting from the 1997–1999 crisis.[8] But relative to the Latin American norm, Mexico weathered the event relatively unscathed.

The response to the banking crisis worked along four fronts: the conversion of nonperforming loans into public debt, the provision of dollars to the banks to fulfill their financial obligations, bank recapitalization, and the creation of debt-relief mechanisms. Nonperforming loans were exchanged for bonds by Mexico's version of banking insurance, and the fund was then operated by the Ministry of Finance to back bank deposits, known as FOBAPROA (for Fondo Bancario de Protección al Ahorro).

In December 1998 a new law was enacted to replace FOBAPROA with a relatively more independent Institute for Bank Savings Protection (IPAB, Instituto de Protección al Ahorro Bancario). Besides taking over FOBAPROA's role as an insurer of deposits, IPAB was assigned the task of auctioning the assets that fell under bank control as a result of the nonperforming loan crisis, and it took over a number of financial oversight and regulation obligations. In accordance with the law that created IPAB, no person associated with the operation of FOBAPROA, including the governor of the central bank, was allowed to belong to the board of IPAB. Notably, members of opposition parties became part of its board. This composition of its governing body is expected to help in making IPAB's decision-making process more transparent.

EXPLAINING ECONOMIC POLICY CHOICES PRIOR TO THE CRISIS

The choice of the policy regime associated with the Mexican crisis of 1994 is best understood by referring to, first, the institutional structure and events surrounding two earlier Mexican crises of 1976 and 1982 and, second, the domestic political and international environments between 1992 and 1994. Both the 1976 and 1982 crises are significant because they provided Mexicans with the lessons that to date explain and justify the thrust of their country's institutional and economic reforms. The domestic political and international environments of 1992–1994 were dominated by debates and negotiations over ratification of the North American Free Trade Agreement, as well as impending presidential elections. These elections imposed constraints on macroeconomic policy making that were extremely difficult for the sitting administration to overcome, thereby contributing to the onset of the crisis.

POLITICAL INSTITUTIONS, 1920–1994: CONCENTRATED BUT ROTATING PRESIDENTIAL POWER

Formally, Mexico's political system is presidential, with a clear separation of executive, legislative, and judicial powers. Between the 1920s and 1994, however, the separation of these three branches of government was more virtual than real, due to the convergence of three factors: (1) strong electoral dominance of Mexico's largest party, the PRI; (2) a long tradition of PRI candidate selection based on the method of "unity candidates"; and (3) constitutional rules forbidding reelection. These three factors created a hegemonic party system with a highly centralized power structure controlled by the executive.

The strong electoral dominance of the PRI meant that a PRI candidate won in practically every election, at every level of representation or branch of power. The PRI, which was formed by the winning factions of the Mexican Revolution (1910–1917), encompassed at the outset almost every point on the ideological spectrum and confronted few if any nationally organized opposition parties. Opposition began to grow during the 1940s, when dissatisfied PRI notables left it to organize the parties of the right and the left. Electoral dominance also resulted from less than transparent electoral practices that, whether they were needed to assure victory or not, secured an electoral advantage for the PRI.

Traditional candidate selection rules in the PRI gave the sitting president the privilege of choosing the PRI's presidential and gubernatorial candidates and, should he wish, the candidates for nearly every other electoral position. This was done to avoid the possibility that an internal electoral contest in the PRI for candidate selection might split the party's support base into irreconcilable camps. Mexican presidents thus influenced directly or indirectly the choice of congressional and local candidates, the appointment of top administrative officials, and the appointment of justices and magistrates for the Supreme Court.

Naturally, such an influence over the selection of elected and appointed officials provided the president with strong agenda-setting powers. Anyone who opposed the approval of a bill or a nomination sent by the president to Congress

faced the possibility of not landing a government job after his term in office concluded, as long as the current president was still in control of the executive. Thus
most bills and nominations proposed by the executive tended to obtain the approval of legislators, in effect eliminating the separation between executive and
legislative powers. Added to the absence of central bank independence from executive control until 1993, this resulted in economic management practices in
which Mexico's budgetary and monetary policy decisions between 1920 and the
1980s were, to a great extent, the president's own.

   This fusion of executive and legislative powers did not evolve into a rigid
policy-making structure, however, owing to the constitutional curb on reelection.
Limiting reelection had the effect of reshuffling the lower house of Congress
every three years and the Senate and executive every six. As a consequence, centralization of power in the PRI and the executive did not restrict political representation to one particular ideology or one particular generation. Every three
years a new congressional election was held and an entirely new set of politicians
filled the floors of the lower chamber. Every six years a new Senate and president
were elected, with the latter bringing a new set of individuals to fill cabinet posts.
These three-and six-year overlapping cycles assured power sharing among the
members of the PRI's three main sectors—labor, peasants, and popular (middle
class). Equally important, they provided the space for policy flexibility. New
presidents could sway policy in directions opposite to those chosen by their predecessors with relative ease, since they controlled the PRI and commanded Congress. Certainly, such flexibility opened questions about the credibility of the investment regime at any point in time, but as explained below, until the 1970s this
problem was not serious enough for a large share of Mexicans to support reform
of their country's political institutions.

THE LEGACY OF THE CRISES OF 1976 AND 1982:
CHANGING INTEREST GROUP PREFERENCES

It was under this institutional structure that Mexico's economic crises of 1976 and
1982 took place. The 1976 crisis was a watershed because it ended, in a very disruptive way, a twenty-two-year-long economic expansion within the framework
of import-substituting industrialization (ISI). Most analysts locate the origin of
the crisis in the economic policies of President Luis Echeverría Alvarez
(1970–1976). During his mandate he attempted to address the structural deficiencies of ISI antiexport bias, shortages of intermediate goods, and raw materials needed for the production of final goods, polarized income distribution by undertaking an ambitious public investment program financed with foreign loans.
Unchecked by congressional restraints on budgetary outlays, and in control of the
central bank, the Echeverría administration's deficit-spending policies ended up
worsening the current account, increasing foreign indebtedness from around

US$4 billion to US$22 billion, increasing annual inflation from an average of 3 percent to 14 percent, and producing a balance of payments crisis in late 1976. As a consequence, economic authorities had to abandon the fixed exchange rate regime in operation since 1954, in effect devaluing the Mexican peso 100 percent, and implement an IMF-sponsored adjustment program.

The adversities of this economic scenario were compounded by President Echeverría's political approach to containing the crisis, which increased private sector distrust toward political institutions. Besides increasing trade barriers and imposing exchange controls, in a strange last-minute gesture of "revolutionary" solidarity with the peasants of Mexico's northwestern state of Sonora, he decreed the expropriation of lands from wealthy agricultural families whose property had recently been invaded.[9] The president's single-handed ability to assault private property rights was an unwelcome event, providing the private sector with a significant call to action for an institutional reform. Things would have to get worse (as explained below) for a widespread mobilization by the private sector and civil society sufficient to transform Mexican institutions.

Six years later the administration of José López Portillo (1976–1982) replicated, but on a much higher order of magnitude, the dislocations associated with the 1976 crisis. The discovery of substantial oil reserves under Mexican territory changed the fundamental assumptions supporting the design of the economic adjustment program adopted at the end of the Echeverría administration. Simply put, with rising oil prices, and with the Mexican oil industry under state control, the budget constraint of the Mexican government was relaxed. Public finances ceased to preoccupy the experts, and attention shifted instead to using the expected revenues derived from oil exports to subsidize industrial development, much as the Echeverría administration had. Public spending financed with foreign loans exploded along with domestic credit, overheating the economy and resulting in a real appreciation of the currency. As oil prices began their retreat from a peak of $34 a barrel in July 1981, this economic program proved untenable.

By the end of 1982 the Mexican economy entered a destabilizing phase that forced its government to devalue the peso by more than 100 percent (from 24.5 to 57.6 pesos per dollar), declare a moratorium on its foreign debt payments (then totaling close to US$86 billion), and implement, again, an IMF-sponsored adjustment program. To complicate matters, President López Portillo tried, like his predecessor, to contain the economic and political effects of the crisis with market-unfriendly policies: exchange controls, a dual exchange rate regime with a preferential rate for "priority" imports and financial operations, license requirements on all imports, expropriation of dollar-denominated bank deposits in Mexican banks, and nationalization of the banking sector.

The moratorium on foreign debt payments and the bank nationalization were nothing short of a bombshell for the investment community. Together with the crisis and land expropriation of 1976, they provided strong indications that Mexican institutions were no longer able to credibly commit to protect property rights

and fulfill their financial obligations. Particularly worrisome was the bank nationalization. It not only put Mexico's financial sector in the government's hands
but also threatened to transfer huge quantities of real productive assets into
state control as well. Many of the banks owned equity in industrial firms, and at
the time of the bank nationalization it was unclear if the banks alone were being
expropriated.

Significant domestic pressures for institutional and economic reform were triggered by the unwelcome consequences of an institutional structure that (1) permitted two consecutive presidential administrations an unchallenged implementation of expansionary macroeconomic policies, (2) resulted in two crises in the
balance of payments in less than six years, and (3) culminated, in the same short
time span, in assaults on private property and sharp currency devaluation. On the
institutional side, demands increased for a clear definition of the state's economic
role, for limits on presidential discretion, and for electoral transparency. On the
economic side, demands surfaced in favor of a new development strategy. These
demands took shape throughout the 1980s and 1990s, as Mexicans embarked on
a gradual process of institutional reform, to date unfinished. The 1994 crisis,
while displaying some unique characteristics, seems more like an aftershock of
the more fundamental, systemic crisis of 1982.

THE POLITICS OF REFORM, 1982–1994: INTEREST GROUP CLEAVAGES AND PRESIDENTIAL POWER

The new presidential administration of Miguel de la Madrid Hurtado
(1982–1988) confronted the difficult tasks of solving the foreign debt problem it
inherited and stabilizing the Mexican economy, while maintaining political stability and an electoral majority for the PRI. De la Madrid had to do so under
strong pressure from the main losers in the bank nationalization and debt crisis—
owners of large business conglomerates, leaders of influential business lobbies,
and foreign lenders. These groups wanted a fundamental, credible shift in government behavior and economic strategy. As the costs of the crisis spread to the
rest of the country, his administration also had to face the critiques and mobilization of the middle classes, labor unions, and domestic opposition parties that
joined in a high-profile campaign to reform the existing institutional regime. As
discussed below, this reform coalition was a heterogeneous one.

The near universal agreement in the private sector that the degree of presidential discretion and the scope of government participation in the economy had to
decline motivated a strong effort to reform the electoral system in order to increase proportional representation (PR) and guarantee transparent elections.[10] In
1988 the number of PR seats increased from 100 to 200 (out of a total of 500 seats
in the lower chamber), while the executive lost control of the Federal Electoral
Institute in 1993 to the citizenry. This effort was complemented by measures to

provide independence to a number of state offices and "anchor" policies through contractual and reputational mechanisms in various areas. The Central Bank became independent in 1993. Trade barriers were limited to a maximum of 50 percent with GATT entrance in 1986, and then were set to be phased out completely with the signature of the North American Free Trade Agreement. Reduction of the executive's bureaucratic apparatus and privatization of state-owned enterprises began in 1985, while all banks were privatized between 1990 and 1993.

It is important to note that distributive struggles as much as efficiency criteria informed the institutional and economic policy choices made during this period — reduction of executive power and the implementation of a market-oriented economic stabilization program. Sectors with strong international commercial and financial ties are concentrated in the North. They benefited from not only a smaller state that protected private property but one that promoted a market-oriented economic strategy, with free trade, full capital account convertibility, deregulation, and a "realistic" exchange rate policy. These export-oriented manufacturers tended to be supported by the middle classes and northern, export-oriented farmers. In addition, they received disproportionate support among all groups in the North.

In contrast, sectors oriented toward the domestic market, import-competing producers, and subsidized service providers preferred a smaller state that supported them with trade protection and other forms of government assistance. Even this set of producers, which preferred a less aggressive, more predictable state that would nevertheless maintain their subsidies, was split on the issue of exchange rate management. Import-competing producers benefited from an undervalued real exchange rate, but service providers, who were consumers rather than competitors of imported goods, did better with an appreciating one. These subsidized, inwardly oriented manufacturers tended to be supported by unorganized labor and home market–oriented peasants, although the latter remain more heavily influenced by the traditional PRI "machine" in the countryside. This viewpoint has received disproportionate support in the Center and South.

Outwardly oriented sectors were dominated by large business conglomerates (known as grupos, or holding companies) with stakes in a broad set of economic activities, including banks and manufacturing ventures. They had strong links to foreign investors and generated the largest share of Mexico's manufacturing exports. During the López Portillo administration they borrowed heavily in foreign currency to participate in the opportunities provided by the oil boom (Molina-Warner 1981; Maxfield 1990). They also became subject to more frequent trade sanctions from their main export market, the United States.[11] With their high exposure to foreign borrowing and their diversified portfolio they became susceptible to exchange risk and unstable investment environments, especially those reducing their international competitiveness.

A combination of conservative macroeconomic policies with a relatively undervalued exchange rate and an open economy avoided both problems. Conservative fiscal and monetary policies promoted stable inflation rates with moderate economic growth. They also facilitated foreign debt repayment by reducing the likelihood of a sharp exchange rate devaluation. A relatively undervalued (high) real exchange rate improved their competitiveness and, by extension, contributed to increased profits. A free trade strategy neither fostered protectionist pressures from Mexico's main trading partners—in particular the United States—nor increased the costs of producing inside Mexican borders.

Sectors whose production was oriented toward the domestic market, dominated by small- and medium-sized firms and including nonfinancial service providers as well as home market–oriented peasants, wanted a less extreme economic liberalization policy. To a large degree, firms in these sectors owed their existence to trade protection, government subsidies, and other forms of assistance. Since their link to the competitive international economy was primarily mediated by the country's grupos, and since their unit costs of production also tended to be higher than those of the large firms, they relied on state-owned banks, trusts, or trading companies to finance their ventures and market their products.

The main concentrated interest groups pressing in favor of both institutional reforms to constrain the president's power and market-oriented economic policies included peak business chambers, associations of exporters, and associations of international traders—all of them strongly controlled by the sectors linked to foreign markets. These included COPARMEX, the most important employer's union founded by the leaders of the grupos from the northern industrial city of Monterrey; CCE, the country's peak business chamber founded by conservative businessmen under the sponsorship of the most elitist business association, the CMHN (composed by the thirty wealthiest businessmen); CEMAI, the international affairs associate of CCE; MUSBC, the main binational association of large Mexican and U.S. corporations; CONACEX, the representative of 140 large Mexican firms that in 1982 generated 40 percent of Mexico's exports;[12] and ANIERM, the importers and exporters association.[13]

Sectors oriented toward the domestic market relied on the two largest industrial chambers, CANACINTRA and CONCAMIN; on some regional manufacturer associations; and partially on labor unions to pressure against an abrupt transition to an open economy. But their front was not uniform, and they could not count on the constant mobilization of peasants or nonunionized workers to support their policy positions. CANACINTRA represented a large set of firms of every size, but mostly small and medium-sized, based in Mexico City and central Mexico, which sold most of their output in the domestic market. It expressed an unequivocal opposition to trade liberalization, although not to privatization. CONCAMIN, the national confederation of all chambers of manufacturers, to which CANACINTRA belonged, was not an ardent supporter of trade liberalization, but it did not oppose it either. Labor unions were split, not exactly according to the dividing lines of industry but to their ties to the government. The peak labor confederation, CTM, opposed liberalization in principle, but, being a part of the PRI's coalition, expressed its willingness to discipline itself and support whatever the government's choice. A competing confederation, also a member of the PRI, known as CROC, openly supported liberalization (Flores Quiroga 1998).

Who commanded a political advantage ex ante? This is a difficult question to answer, but three things are clear: the promarket reform camp was more concentrated (in the industrial and geographical sense); it had closer ties to the economic team of President de la Madrid; it had a competitive although not overwhelming level of support among peasants, unorganized labor, and especially middle class groups; and it counted on the sympathy of its foreign creditors, who conditioned financial assistance for stabilization and growth on the adoption of similar policies. On the other hand, the sector oriented toward the domestic market was less concentrated, did not dominate broader public opinion to an extent that delegitimized liberal policies, and did not share the same clout with the president's team and foreign creditors.

By 1985 the relative pressure of the promarket camp mounted significantly. At the same time evidence began to indicate that the standard IMF medicine used since 1982 (contractionary fiscal and monetary policies combined with sharp devaluation) would not work and that falling oil prices would continue to make it difficult for Mexico's government to equilibrate its fiscal and foreign accounts. Confronted with the reality that in three years neither economic stabilization nor a return to growth had developed, and with the domestic balance of power tipping in favor of the outwardly oriented sectors, Mexico's government decided to embark on a new economic strategy. It combined structural reform—liberalization, privatization, deregulation—with stabilization.

Between July 1985 and December 1988 nontariff barriers to trade disappeared, the maximum tariff declined from 100 to 20 percent, Mexico joined GATT, and privatization of state-owned enterprises began. In 1987 a new stabilization program using the exchange rate as a nominal anchor was adopted, in response both to the lessons learned in the previous stabilization attempts and to the growing pressures of labor unions for an end to inflation. This was the beginning of "pacted" stabilization, as government officials, business representatives, and union leaders jointly agreed on the steps to achieve inflation control.[14] Although the unions have strong links with the PRI, their support for the stabilization pacts also indicated a desire to avoid the long-term inflationary consequences of past interventionist policies.

President Carlos Salinas de Gortari (1988–1994) took power at this point with a program emphasizing continuity of the market reforms. The 1994 elections showed the split discussed above. The more interventionist-oriented PRD remained far from a majority, indicating that a clear majority had no desire to return to the policies that had produced the 1976 and 1982 crises. On the other hand, the reform bloc was itself split between more and less enthusiastic liberalizers. This division was most marked within the PRI itself and those who supported it. Nevertheless, President Salinas pushed forward with liberalization.

In its first year his administration focused on two objectives: reducing the debt burden and attracting foreign capital. The first objective was achieved with a debt reduction package under the Brady Plan.[15] The second objective was pursued with the bank privatization, the liberalization of domestic and international financial transactions, the elimination of limits to foreign direct investment in most economic sectors, and, most notably, the negotiation of the North American Free Trade Agreement (1990–1993).

In response to the positive expectations generated by these developments, foreign capital poured into the Mexican economy, increasing from a total of US$16.8 billion in 1991 to US$33.3 billion at the end of 1993. Close to 80 percent of this capital consisted of portfolio investments, easily reallocated outside Mexico at the touch of a computer button.

FROM STABILITY TO UNCERTAINTY AND CRISIS, 1993–1994

By 1993 substantial ground had been covered to stabilize and reform the Mexican economy. The approach of using the exchange rate as a nominal anchor proved successful in bringing down inflation to less than 20 percent, although at the cost of appreciating the real exchange rate. But economic growth rates showed no signs of improving significantly—they stayed below 1 percent. This motivated some observers to wonder if it was time to try a modest adjustment of the exchange rate, even at the cost of higher inflation.[16] The thinking was that this measure would ease pressure on the current account while providing some space for economic growth.

However, the bad memories of the inflationary 1970s and 1980s, the success of the anti-inflation program, and the new domestic political and international imperatives of the Salinas administration gave few indications that a devaluation was appropriate at that moment. Was it clear that inflation would not return in Mexico as it had done in other countries' stabilization attempts? Would workers accept more inflation after experiencing a real wage drop of more than 50 percent during the past ten years? Were banks—which had just been privatized and bought with foreign loans and had extended credits in domestic currency to unprecedented levels—in a condition to deal with the consequences of a devaluation? As Mexico attempted to attract foreign capital and negotiated the North American Free Trade Agreement, was it wise to provide signals of economic instability? Would not Mexican firms compete better in NAFTA if Mexico's inflation rate was kept the same as that of the United States?

The answers to these questions seemed negative. Rather than run the risk of losing labor support and investor confidence, or of setting Mexican firms at a competitive disadvantage (should the domestic inflation rate fail to be contained) once NAFTA entered in full operation, Mexico's government chose to extend the economic program that had worked so well in reducing inflation. The extra effort could be rewarded with high economic growth under price stability. Thus in the absence of any shocks and in the presence of optimistic expectations for the future of the Mexican economy, foreign capital kept pouring in.

In the fourth quarter of 1993 what seemed a reasonable decision turned into a straitjacket. The hurdle of NAFTA ratification by the U.S. Congress had been passed in November, but now presidential elections were less than a year away — 7 July 1994. Devaluing the exchange rate at that moment would not bring good news to the PRI's presidential candidate, since real wages were still 50 percent lower than in 1982 and workers and peasants, who composed an important base of support for the PRI, could express their disapproval of the devaluation at the ballot box. Moreover, investors who borrowed in foreign currency to participate in the market reforms of the Mexican economy, including the new bankers, would suffer direly from a devaluation.

In the ensuing months a series of political events interacted with the upcoming elections to scare investors away. On 1 January 1994, a peasant uprising in the southern state of Chiapas made everyone aware that not all of Mexico's South agreed with NAFTA or the program of structural reform.[17] On 9 March the president of BANAMEX, Mexico's largest bank, was kidnapped. On 23 March, PRI presidential candidate Luis Donaldo Colosio was assassinated. The three events triggered capital outflows that, unless stabilized, would increase the cost of domestic borrowing, slow the economy, and complicate the presidential election.[18] Thus the nominally independent central bank's decision to increase M2 and sell Tesobonos to replenish international reserves.[19]

After the election passed and the new PRI candidate Ernesto Zedillo Ponce won with a historically low vote of 47 percent, a window of opportunity opened to devalue the currency. But President Salinas de Gortari decided against it. Why?

Two factors seem to explain his choice: the end of his mandate was only four months away and the central banks' international reserves were at a substantial US$20 billion. It was unclear if an administration with only four months in office commanded the credibility necessary to devalue its currency without scaring investors. No one knew for sure if President-elect Zedillo would support the implementation of adjustment measures. Few could tell if Mexico's secretary of finance, Pedro Aspe, the architect of the stabilization program and debt-relief strategy, or someone on his team with comparable clout in financial circles, would remain in his post once Zedillo took office. The only clear thing was that in the past the presidents that devalued at the end of their administration — Echeverría and López Portillo — lost a tremendous amount of prestige both inside and outside Mexico. In such a perspective, and counting on what seemed at the time to be sufficient international reserves to combat a possible run on the peso, the Salinas administration took a wait-and-see stance. Avoiding a devaluation, it sought to calm investor worries about domestic economic and political stability by announcing, on 24 September, the signing of a pact for welfare, stability, and growth with business leaders and labor representatives.

A few days later, on 28 September, the PRI second in command, Mario Ruiz Massieu, was assassinated, triggering yet another round of capital outflows. Now the space for exchange rate adjustment was even narrower, since President Salinas had two months left in office. As investor nervousness continued to rise, the economic teams of President Salinas and President-elect Zedillo met on November 20 — ten days before the transfer of presidential power — to discuss the possibility of implementing some economic adjustment measures, including a widening of the band of fluctuation of the exchange rate. But they concurred that an administration with ten days left in office would not command the credibility necessary for a successful economic adjustment, so they decided to wait for the start of the new administration.[20]

When President Zedillo took office on December 1, 1994, a clear understanding of the exchange rate situation existed. Now the problem was how an administration still struggling to gain political control of the country and develop an economic reputation could devalue in an orderly way. As became apparent, it could not. The 15 percent increase in the band of exchange rate fluctuation, coupled with the lack of complementary macroeconomic measures, with uncertainty about the level of Mexico's international reserves, and with the climate of political uncertainty, proved too destabilizing.

ECONOMIC POLICY AFTER THE CRISIS

As already noted, the 1994 crisis revealed the shortcomings of liberalizing capital accounts soon after trade liberalization and of relying too heavily on private commercial banks for adequate risk coverage. It also confirmed the suspicions of many that the lack of transparency in the process of privatization resulted in the allocation of financial assets to individuals without banking experience or transparent legal records. A new effort at reforming the financial structure was therefore launched, focusing on two pressing problems: (1) the protection of banking deposits and (2) the development of effective mechanisms of financial oversight.

At the outset the solution seemed straightforward: rely on FOBAPROA to exchange nonperforming loans owned by banks with government bonds in order to facilitate their recapitalization and guarantee the protection of the public's savings. The logic was that the share of nonperforming loans would begin to decrease as the economy recuperated, thereby reducing the government's own financial burden.

But when growth returned, it was concentrated in the exportables sector, which had contracted most of its loans in foreign currency with foreign banks. As production in the nontradables sector remained stagnant, more loans became nonperforming, bank troubles increased, and FOBAPROA support requirements skyrocketed. By 1996 it was clear that few banks would survive. The only way to bring the financial system back to health was to transform FOBAPROA's portfolio into public debt (at that moment calculated at US$70 billion, or 16 percent of GDP), sell at a discount the assets seized by banks, and allow a higher level of foreign investment in banks (increased from 30 to 49 percent). This was the proposal the Zedillo administration sent to Congress. Its centerpiece was the creation of another fund, managed under executive control, to replace FOBAPROA.

Such a solution, however, proved politically explosive and impracticable in the short term. The electoral reforms allowed a new majority to control the lower chamber of Mexico's legislature, composed of the PRI's opposition to the left (PRD) and the right (PAN). The new majority was unwilling to approve a piece of legislation that increased the burden on taxpayers, rewarded financial corruption, and failed to contemplate clear measures to avoid repeating the FOBAPROA blunder. They therefore refused to approve the executive's proposal unless a new mechanism supervising both the financial sector and its regulators was created outside the exclusive control of the executive.

This refusal caused negotiations between the Mexican executive and legislative powers to drag on from March to December 1998. As evidence that the financial costs of the bailout increased every second without an agreement and that this situation put economic stability at risk, the PAN, which drew most of its support from the middle classes and the Mexican right, broke ranks with the left and backed the conversion of bank debt into public debt in exchange for a commitment to create a new institution—the relatively more independent IPAB described earlier. The other significant condition was the exclusion of the central bank governor from the board of IPAB. This institutional reform represented yet another addition to the trend begun in 1982 of reducing the president's discretion.

As already noted, the fiscal and monetary stringency and continued pursuit of structural reforms and integration with the U.S. economy were decisive in minimizing the fallout of the 1997–1999 international financial crisis.

CONCLUSION: PAST EXPERIENCE AND SUSTAINED SUPPORT FOR LIBERALIZATION

The domestic determinants of, and response to, Mexico's financial crisis of 1994 lie in the political realignment that occurred after the debt crisis of 1982. The 1982 crisis put in evidence the Mexican government's inability to commit credibly to protect private property and pursue a sound macroeconomic policy. A presidency unconstrained by institutional checks and balances spent beyond the state's budgetary capabilities, nationalized banks, expropriated dollar-denominated bank deposits, imposed exchange controls, blocked free importation of foreign goods, and implemented other market-interfering policies.

Such a redistribution of income and assets from the private to the public sector produced a generalized demand for curbs on presidential discretion. This demand targeted both political and economic institutions. On the political side, there was a broad consensus across Mexican society in favor of measures to guarantee transparent electoral processes, provide greater representation of minorities in Congress, and secure the separation between judicial, legislative, and executive powers. On the economic side the private sector as a whole also concurred in the demand for a smaller state apparatus as a way to reduce the president's discretionary spending powers and regain productive assets lost during the crisis.

But there was also a significant split over the course of economic policy. Sectors whose production was oriented toward the domestic market—mostly composed of protected and subsidized small and medium-sized firms—were reluctant to reduce trade barriers and eliminate the agencies that channeled subsidies to them. These sectors tended to be supported by home market–oriented peasants and unorganized labor, especially in the Center and South. Sectors oriented toward the international market—composed of large industrial and financial conglomerates and associated with foreign capital—also relied on government subsidies, but their trading activities were endangered by trade protection, and their financial clout had been substantially reduced with the bank nationalization. They therefore preferred a more market-friendly economic strategy. These sectors tended to draw support from the middle classes and export-oriented farmers, and disproportionately from all groups in the North.

Eventually, the greater industrial and geographical concentration of the sectors oriented toward international markets and their greater access to government policy makers provided them with a political advantage over the dispersed inwardly oriented sectors. Like the latter, they were able to mobilize significant electoral support among dispersed interest groups (middle classes, unorganized labor, peasants). Economic policy therefore turned away from emphasis on government assistance and began to rely on freer markets to determine resource allocation.

These institutional and economic changes made Mexico more attractive to foreign capital but undermined the basic regulatory capabilities of financial authorities. A simplistic assessment of the ability of financial markets to avoid moral hazard problems in conjunction with an inadequate legal framework resulted in insufficient and ineffective oversight of financial transactions. In 1994–1995, combined with an increasingly vulnerable exchange rate policy based on a nominal anchor, these factors generated Mexico's deepest economic contraction since the 1930s.

The response to the 1994 crisis reinforced, rather than reversed, the trend in favor of market reforms and reduced executive discretion. The program of trade liberalization, free convertibility, and deregulation continued. Monetary and financial regulatory institutions were taken outside the direct control of the executive. The maintenance of these free market reforms, coupled with the pursuit of a disciplined fiscal and monetary policy, helped Mexico substantially avert an Asian- or South American-style crisis in 1997–1999. While this economic approach did not shield the economy completely, economic growth did not come to a halt during this period. In the 2000 elections, there was continued support for the liberal path, but the old division between more cautious and more ambitious liberalizers persisted. This pattern of public opinion has led the PRD to move toward the center, but the internal division within the PRI and its mass base persists.

Transition to democracy produced myopic preelection macroeconomic policies that contributed fundamentally to the 1994 crisis. However, both liberalizing economic policies and democratization itself were implemented as a result of a backlash against the interventionist policy–induced crises of 1976 and 1982. This helps explain why the 1994 crisis did not produce its own strong backlash, this time against liberalizing policies. A clear majority of dispersed interest groups maintains memories of the economic debacle of the late 1970s and early 1980s. In the 2000 elections, it appears that Mexican democracy will maintain the liberal economic policy regime, since sufficient numbers of those who have not yet benefited from liberalization—particularly among unorganized labor and home market–oriented peasants in the Center and South—still harbor dark memories of the interventionist past and its high inflation.

NOTES

1. The phrase is attributed to Michel Camdessus, managing director of the IMF.

2. When President Zedillo took office, Mexico had international reserves of US$12.5 billion (down from US$28 billion at the beginning of the year). After the crisis, less than a month after President Zedillo took office, reserves fell to US$6.2 billion.

3. By some estimates, adding this total would represent nearly 80 percent of loans, or US$70 billion.

4. Calvo and Mendoza (1996) referred to the Mexican episode as one of "petty crime and cruel punishment."

5. See, for example, Dornbusch (1993), Dornbusch and Werner (1994), Sachs, Tornell, and Velasco (1995), Gil-Díaz and Carstens (1996), and the readings in the volume edited by Edwards and Naim (1997).

6. These measures, announced on 3 January 1995, were complemented in 9 March with a more strict action program for the reinforcement of the Unity Accord to overcome the economic emergency.

7. For reviews of these reforms, see the series edited by Fondo de Cultura Económica (1988, 1994).

8. The contraction of the Asian economies resulted in a lower demand for world oil and thus falling oil prices. Mexico's main export commodity is oil and the oil industry is state owned, so a fall in oil prices implied a fall in state revenues—on the order of US$2 billion per year. Such a shock required adjusting domestic public spending to keep the fiscal deficit in check, which in turn helped to forestall expectations of a devaluation and rampant inflation. The adjustment was politically controversial but was eventually accepted. Nevertheless, the central bank's inflation objectives of less than 15 percent in 1997 and 1998 were not met.

9. Much like the land expropriations of the Cuban revolution and of Chile under Salvador Allende, this one occurred after a group of peasants invaded private landholdings.

Rather than expel them or apply the law strictly, President Echeverría opted to decree the expropriation of these lands. See Mayer and Sherman (1994).

10. More congressmen elected through proportional representation added a consensual aspect to legislative choices. Transparent elections increased the likelihood of a PRI electoral loss, providing more access to the opposition to government posts and probably checking PRI behavior by the mere threat of removal.

11. On the nature of United States–Mexico trade relations, see Weintraub (1984, 1989, 1990).

12. See *El Financiero* (December 16, 1983). Most prominent names belonged to this association.

13. Some of these interest groups had begun expressing their discontent with the evolution of Mexican economic policy already in late 1981, making calls to stop the aggregate demand expansion that was generating greater inflation and real appreciation of the currency, which reduced the profitability of export ventures. After the bank nationalization COPARMEX and CCE organized the Mexico in Freedom movement, which, in addition to its vehement opposition to the nationalization, repeated these groups' views: the need for a clear demarcation of the areas of influence of state and private firms; the relevance of fiscal and monetary discipline; the need for a realistic exchange rate policy; the importance of greater support to private sector firms through the construction of infrastructure, development funds, tax breaks, direct subsidies, and other types of aid; their interest in a new, stable, and predictable business environment; and the need for effective checks and balances inside the government. Large firm owners themselves were not necessarily involved in the public struggles to redefine economic policy, but these organizations, which they founded or influenced, were indeed involved in such activities. A sample of the numerous statements and opinions expressed by Mexican business leaders in these forums can be found in the newspaper *Excélsior* (October–November 1982). See also Hernández Rodríguez (1988).

14. For a discussion of Mexico's economic stabilization programs between 1982 and 1992, see Lustig (1992) and Aspe (1993).

15. A history of Mexico's foreign debt and its negotiation is presented in Moreno Uriegas and Flores Caballero (1995).

16. See the account of this debate by Edwards (1997), in which the recommendations of Dornbusch to increase the rate of depreciation to 120 pesos to the dollar were among the most relevant.

17. Mexico's southern states (Chiapas, Oaxaca, Guerrero, Michoacan) are predominantly rural and rank at the lowest end of the income, health, and literacy scales. They are also the least integrated into international markets.

18. For a review of the timing and size of these capital outflows, see Mancera (1995). In that article the president of the Bank of Mexico also defends the government's response.

19. Mexico's central bank became independent at the end of 1993, with a mandate to preserve the purchasing power of the currency. Yet its director's close alliance with President Salinas and the PRI led it to behave in accordance with the executive's interests.

20. See the account of these talks by Pedro Aspe in the newspaper *Reforma* (1995).

11

Brazil: Political Institutions and Delayed Reaction to Financial Crisis

Jeffrey Cason

Hoping against hope, Brazilian economic policy makers thought that they could avoid the worst of the Asian financial crisis. They seemed to succeed for quite some time, but in the end, internal politics undid them: the currency was sharply devalued in January 1999 and a sharp recession followed. The recession also threw other countries in Latin America into turmoil, particularly those that with Brazil are part of the Southern Common Market (Mercado Común del Sur—Mercosur).[1]

Brazil has survived, as has Mercosur. But Brazil's delayed reaction to the Asian financial crisis laid bare the problems that Brazil has in reacting to external shocks in the context of its recent turn to market-oriented policies and its stabilization efforts. Domestic politics get in the way of the best-laid economic adjustment plans. And these politics are not about to disappear, even if their effects can be mitigated. The chief problems facing Brazil when it is confronted with such adjustment include a long-standing tradition of antirecession coalitions among Brazilian business, in the exporting as well as the import-competing sectors; a political party system that is, by the most generous estimates, undisciplined; and a federal system that gives a great deal of leeway to state governments.

This general argument will be advanced in four steps. After laying out the need to look concretely at Brazilian domestic politics to understand what happened after the onset of the Asian crisis, I will briefly review Brazil's tortured history with stabilization attempts, pointing to some of the key problems that made stabilization so late in coming. After setting the stage in this way, I will outline what actually happened in Brazil when it reacted to the spreading Asian crisis. Then I will move to a more specific discussion of Brazilian politics and the obstacles that the executive faced when it tried to confront the spreading crisis. In particular, I will focus on Brazilian institutions that made adjustment difficult even in the face of strong reformist mobilization by dispersed interest groups: the Brazilian party system and the Brazilian federal system. Both of these institutional arrangements make it extraordinarily difficult for Brazilian politicians to carry out rapid and effective adjustment to outside shocks.

DOMESTIC POLITICS AND THE INTERNATIONAL ARENA

One of the premises of this book is that one cannot understand the effects of the Asian financial crisis without focusing on domestic politics. In many analyses that have been spawned by the recent international financial crisis, the concern has been with international financial "architecture" and how it broke down during the crisis. Indeed, much attention has been focused on the mistakes that international actors made in understanding the global financial crisis and its implications (Garten 1999), and there is a great deal of disagreement about what can be done to create a new international architecture that will head off crises in the future. It is probably too much, however, to hope that international changes can head off such crises; domestic politics are stubborn when it comes to the way they face the international ebbs and flows of capital. Garten (1999, 80) acknowledges this: "Local politics are crucial. In retrospect, Wall Street and Washington now realize the overwhelming role that domestic politics played in frustrating crisis management." In other words, there's only so much that an international architecture can do.

Nevertheless, economists wish that domestic politics could be overcome when it comes to the effects of a globalized financial system, focusing on whether or not developing countries should adopt capital controls in order to head off the kinds of crises that have occurred recently. For example, Edwards (1999) argues that in fact capital controls in Brazil or other countries cannot stem the sort of currency crisis that Brazil experienced, and to a certain degree he is right: no matter how stringent the controls might have been, the crisis probably could not have been avoided. He also notes that having capital controls in place often leads to policy experimentation, which only leads to more problems. Certainly, some Latin American policies in the 1980s — in response to the debt crisis — make this point quite clearly. This does not necessarily mean that developing countries should free up capital accounts completely. Rather, the main point is that the politics of handling domestic adjustment in Brazil overwhelmed any technical fix that policy makers might have designed.

Edwards and other economists would advise policy makers to follow prudent macroeconomic policies to head off any crisis. And this is true enough. But the real question is, When countries fail to follow prudent macroeconomic policies, why do they do so? Here is where an understanding of the politics behind any crisis is absolutely crucial. It is not enough to simply blame "wrong-headed" politicians who do not have the "political will" to impose painful adjustment; indeed, imposing painful adjustment may sometimes be politically impossible. Politicians sometimes face circumstances that make it extraordinarily difficult for them to do what they know they need to do.

Indeed, it is somewhat axiomatic that Brazil's domestic politics led to its problems; as Garten (1999) notes, "The Brazilian package of late 1998 was, of course, designed to be preventative, and it faltered because of domestic politics." This is the conventional wisdom, and it is correct. The question then becomes, What is it about domestic politics that led to Brazil's reaction to the crisis and the eventual need to devalue? In the following sections I address this question directly.

AVOIDING AND CONFRONTING ADJUSTMENT IN BRAZIL: BROAD CONCENTRATED INTEREST GROUP SUBSIDIES AND DISPERSED INTEREST GROUP SUPPORT FOR LIBERALIZATION

Any discussion of Brazilian stabilization and adjustment must begin with the Real Plan, which was introduced in July 1994. Before this stabilization plan, Brazil had experienced a plethora of failed stabilization programs, beginning with the Cruzado Plan that was introduced in 1986, and continuing through the Collor Plan of March 1990. In each plan, inflation dropped substantially immediately after the plan was adopted, but then it began to creep up again. It seemed that Brazil was condemned to repeat a sad history: price freezes followed by rapidly accelerating inflation.

This particular modus operandi was rooted in domestic politics, as numerous analysts have pointed out. Lal and Maxfield (1993, 27) note the historic difficulty that Brazilian governments have had in implementing stabilization programs, as organized labor and, most importantly, industry, consistently pushed growth-oriented policies, "even at the cost of inflation." This, combined with relatively weak financial control mechanisms of the state and relatively weaker political power of financial capital, led to consistent inflation and the political difficulty in imposing stabilization.

It should also be noted that a wide spectrum of Brazilian business benefited from inflation. In many other Latin American countries, there was substantial conflict between exporting and import-competing traded sectors. The import-competing sectors formed a part of populist coalitions pursuing protectionist and interventionist policies that damaged the international competitiveness of exporting sectors. However, Brazil was quite different in this regard, largely because of a substantial export promotion program that was begun in the mid-1960s (Cason 1993; Shapiro 1997; Cason and White 1998). The export promotion program gave enormous subsidies amounting to more than 60 percent of the point-of-departure value of exports during some years in the 1970s (Baumann and Moreira 1987, 484). In effect, subsidies were provided to a large swath of business, in part to maintain business support for the military regime in power between 1964 and 1985 (Martins 1986).

This simultaneous promotion of exports and import substitutes is not unknown in Asia (Bradford 1990; Wade 1991) and has shown rather impressive results in that region. In an important sense, however, the Brazilian version of simultaneous export promotion and import substitution was different. Whereas the Asian countries focused their export-promotion policies on particular industries, the Brazilian version was indiscriminate. All industrial exporters were able to access the subsidies, and this lack of selectivity made the policy extraordinarily expensive as time went on and more and more firms successfully entered foreign markets.

In other words, the pro-growth coalition in Brazil was not just one that focused on import-substitution, as is commonly assumed. Brazilian developmentalism (see Sikkink 1991), while initially largely an import-substitution regime, came to include the promotion of exports in the 1960s. Both import substitution and export promotion set a pattern for relations between industrialists and the state, in favor of expansionist policies. Major costs of this pro-growth strategy, with its concomitant provision of subsidies to industrialists, were higher budget deficits and inflation. This inflation continued to accelerate during the 1970s and 1980s. Although exporters frequently complained about exchange-rate policies that made their products less competitive on foreign markets, Brazil engaged in (usually) controlled minidevaluations of the currency during this period, which made the expansionary policies easier to live with.

Indeed, until the Real Plan, industry opposed antiinflation efforts that undermined growth, surprising many outsiders. Lal and Maxfield (1993, 38) cite a report of *Institutional Investor* in the early 1980s, which notes that "the imperative of continued growth—even at the expense of inflation—is accepted by a surprising number of Brazilian businessmen." This stance was not particularly surprising to those acquainted with Brazilian development strategy in the postwar period. There were consistent attempts to cool down inflationary pressures in the second half of the twentieth century, but they were usually opposed by industrialists. The most sustained effort to control inflation came after the military coup of 1964, which was preceded by an inflationary spiral and increasing political conflict. This stabilization effort by the military-led government succeeded in bringing down inflation temporarily, but by the late 1960s, expansionary policy was again the rule (Skidmore 1988), and from that point on, even the military government could not come up with a coherent stabilization plan. Generally speaking, inflation advanced, aided by a price and wage indexation policy that made it easier to live with.

This changed, however, with the adoption of the Real Plan. Although this plan did not tie the hands of the state as much as the Argentine convertibility plan when it came to making economic policy, it was quite limiting. The Argentine plan in effect castrated the state and eliminated monetary policy (completely) and fiscal policy (to a significant extent) as policy tools. The Real Plan was less severe in this regard, but it still substantially limited what the state could do, even in the face of pressure from industrialists to change course. In effect, it tied the Brazilian currency to a rather stable exchange anchor and thus handcuffed the state. Indeed, the state did move away from any sort of industrial policy with this plan, much to the frustration of industrialists.

Kingstone (1998) notes how the Real Plan, and the preoccupations of the government with stabilization, made any sort of long-term development strategy nearly impossible. The plan did in fact stop inflation, but it also left business without any chance of getting coherent and pro-growth policy implemented. Industrialists were facing a new world in which the imperative of stabilization was primary. Given the resulting pressure for fiscal and monetary austerity, the state found it quite difficult to direct any sort of coherent industrial policy. It should also be noted that, beginning with the Collor Plan (introduced in 1990), the economy was opened substantially, which also made the adoption of industrial policy more difficult.

In addition, the Real Plan, although successful in bringing down inflation, had its own problems. It relied on very high interest rates to attract foreign capital. This raised debt burdens at all levels of government, which in turn contributed to the crisis. The response to the Asian crisis (and the Russian fallout) was to raise interest rates even higher, fueling the problem. In a sense, the Brazilian stabilization solution was resting on a house of cards. If fiscal, monetary, and exchange rate policies were not reconciled, then the house would collapse.

How was the stabilization handled politically? It would appear to be impossible in Brazil, given the long-standing resistance to this sort of change. But there was a certain exhaustion when it came to the political economy of inflation. Weyland (1998) points out that, remarkably, Latin American voters in the 1990s supported neoliberal reform, which was quite contrary to expectations about how (populist) Latin American politics operated. There clearly was a constituency for stabilization. In terms of the analysis offered in this volume, dispersed interest groups were exhausted by the inflationary process and were willing to vote for politicians who promised to tame inflation. Current President Fernando Henrique Cardoso, who oversaw the implementation of the Real Plan when he was finance minister, was the Brazilian politician who fit this bill.

Given Brazil's long and exhausting history of inflation, the time was ripe for a political appeal based on a candidate's anti-inflationary credentials. After all, who enjoys hyperinflation? The fear of moving back to the bad old days of great instability—especially in a country like Brazil that had experienced so many failed stabilization plans—undoubtedly made this change electorally feasible. In this sense, Brazil was somewhat similar to Argentina (under Ménem) and Peru (under Fujimori). In those two cases, however, the politicians who carried out stabilization plans had not included them in their campaign platforms. In the Brazilian case, Cardoso was elected in large part because he had stopped inflation, while simultaneously (and this is important in Brazil) continuing economic expansion.

Indeed, what Weyland (1998) calls the "rescue hypothesis"—politicians who stop inflation acquire leverage for making reformist changes—appears quite relevant in Brazil. He concludes that it is not necessary, at least in the initial stages of reform, to offer compensating economic benefits for those who suffer from the costs of adjustment. Brazil was rescued from inflation with the Real Plan. Since it was successful, and since it appeared to be the only way out from hyperinflation, it was difficult to move in a different direction. It was no longer a given that inflation would lead to growth.

Interestingly enough, the new political economy of Brazil under the Real Plan has seen a reestablishment of state authority, even if this has only been in a negative way, that is, in the sense that now the state is able to ignore the demands of concentrated interest groups. It has not engaged in new industrial policy initiatives, but it has turned a deaf ear to demands. Weyland (1997–1998) argues that one of the consequences of democratization in Brazil has been the gradual recomposition of state capacity, which has allowed reform to go forward. In the early stages of democratization—the first nonmilitary government took office in 1985—clientelism and state "capture" by many feuding private interest groups predominated. But this ended in a reaction that produced a recuperation of state capacity, which eventually would have the ability to impose substantial reform. Nevertheless, as Weyland notes,

> Cardoso's precarious success is based less on lasting institutional solutions than on clever expedients (jeitinhos), such as the constant reedition of "provisional measures" and the temporary renewal of short-term fiscal adjustment plans. Thus, the Brazilian state is unlikely to overcome its longstanding weaknesses quickly. (1997–1998, 69)

This weakness became quite obvious when the Brazilian state dealt with the onslaught of the Asian financial crisis and its repercussions in Russia. Reformers in Brazil still faced substantial obstacles related to the Brazilian political system.

A major problem was that the Real Plan relied on inflows of international capital, which might or might not be forthcoming. Morais et al. (1999) and many others make the point that one of the main problems with the Brazilian stabilization plan was its reliance on these inflows of foreign capital, most of which were short-term. This strategy necessitated abnormally high interest rates to attract foreign capital. Liquidity in the international financial system was thus essential for the continued viability of the Brazilian stabilization model. But this became increasingly problematic as the Asian crisis and its aftermath dragged on. When investor confidence began to weaken, even high interest rates could not solve the problem, leading to the Brazilian devaluation in January 1999. A host of other political problems, which will be discussed below, led to this outcome.

THE ASIAN CRISIS AND ITS AFTERMATH IN BRAZIL

When the Asian crisis first hit during the latter part of 1997, there was hope that the crisis could be contained in that region. Among Latin American countries, Brazil was viewed as being vulnerable to a similar attack on its currency because of the perceived overvaluation of its currency and the difficulties that the Brazilians were having in carrying out the institutional and fiscal reforms considered necessary to consolidate economic adjustment. After the onset of the Asian crisis, Brazil increased interest rates to contain capital flight and defend the currency (the real). This seemed to work for a time. But with the Russian meltdown in August 1998, Brazilian policy makers began to think seriously about the adjustments that would be necessary to avoid an assault on the currency.

The need to adjust was complicated, however, by the fact that Brazil was facing a presidential election in October 1998, in which President Cardoso was standing for reelection. He was the first president after military rule to do so, based on a constitutional amendment passed in 1997 that allowed reelection. Some have argued that the political resources put into securing reelection wasted valuable capital that would have been better used securing economic reforms (Flynn 1999). There is certainly some truth in these allegations, and the Russian crisis occurred at a dangerous time for the president, who had less than two months remaining until the election.

The strategy at this time was to sit tight, raise interest rates, and hope that Cardoso would be reelected so that he could put into effect a new adjustment package that would contain the crisis. When Cardoso was reelected in October, the stage was set for a new set of reforms to confront the crisis head on.

The problems were serious, indeed. The budget deficit in 1998 amounted to 7 percent of GDP (Flynn 1999), the currency remained overvalued, and interest rates were sky high. These high interest rates were a particular problem for the government's fiscal balance because the cost of financing public debt was sensitive to changes in these interest rates. Each time the government raised interest rates to defend the currency, it increased its own borrowing costs, further driving up the budget deficit. The lack of inflation made this problem obvious, since governments could no longer rely on inflation to hide the disequilibrium in government accounts.

Though Cardoso was reelected in the first round of voting on October 4, 1998, he waited until after the second round of elections (for governors who had not won in the first round) to announce the new package to confront the fallout from the international financial crisis. On October 28, three days after the second round of elections, the government announced a new fiscal adjustment package that aimed to reduce the budget deficit by $28 billion reais (US$23 billion), with the majority of this adjustment coming via tax increases (*Folha de São Paulo,* 29 October 1998). The new policy stance also came with a rise in interest rates to above 40 percent, extraordinarily high in a country that was experiencing, at the time, single-digit inflation. The new Cardoso government hoped to reduce the budget deficit by increasing taxes on financial transactions, social security contributions by business, and other taxes. It also planned to reduce expenditures through structural reforms in public administration and social security. All together, these measures would reduce the government deficit to 3.6 percent of GDP (*Folha de São Paulo,* 14 November 1998). It was indeed a somewhat ambitious agenda, and one that some analysts thought should have been carried out earlier, pointing to "time wasted, for political purposes, during Cardoso's first presidency, to slackness in curbing public spending and to a lack of bite in tackling urgent issues much sooner" (Flynn 1999, 292). The new agenda, at any rate, was quite comprehensive.

At the same time that the Cardoso economic team was elaborating this fiscal adjustment package, it was engaging in negotiations with the International Monetary Fund for a stabilization package. When this package was announced on November 13, there was some hope that Brazil could in fact deal with the crisis and continue to defend the currency, which continued to be the main goal. Of course, the provision of the foreign funding was meant to head off crisis by giving the Brazilian government credibility. Alas, credibility comes from a complex interaction between economic and political factors and, politically, what matters most is what happens domestically. And so, when the fiscal adjustment package was met initially with substantial opposition, there was concern that this part of the deal would break down.

Flynn (1999) attributes the lack of domestic political support for the stabilization program to domestic political resistance.[2] This resistance came from governors upset at having to live within tighter budgets; politicians upset about not having been consulted about the plan; and business upset that the plan was not likely to bring down interest rates quickly enough, worrying that it would only lead to continued recession. As noted above, there has been a consistent antirecession bias in Brazilian economic policy making. To the extent that this new fiscal package would impose a recession, there was likely to be resistance to it. After all, Brazil had not experienced a recession since 1992, the last year of Fernando Collor's government, and this new package of policies quite explicitly promised one. In this sense, it could be argued that political credibility was weak.

Nonetheless, a number of the reforms proposed in the postelection period were approved by the Congress, and it seemed that Brazil might be able to continue to defend its currency. But on December 2, the Congress rejected one of the key measures of the adjustment package, pension reform. Although passing this reform would not have substantially cut the budget deficit, the vote was viewed with alarm. As Flynn notes,

This crunching defeat echoed throughout the international financial community, questioning the political capacity of the Cardoso government to meet the demands of its own Fiscal Stability Program of 28 October and the requirements of the IMF package of 13 November. The government tried to play down the significance of defeat of a measure which would have accounted for R$2.5 billion of the R$28 billion which it wanted to save. (1999, 299)

But small issues can be big politically, especially when the entire world is watching.

This point was driven home a few days after the new Cardoso government was inaugurated in 1999. On 5 January, former president Itamar Franco (now governor of the state of Minas Gerais) announced that his state government would place a moratorium on debt payments to the federal government, and he encouraged other states to do the same. The debt had already been renegotiated, on quite favorable terms. But Franco was making a political statement of displeasure with the government's economic policies, and it was clear that Brazil faced many political problems that could not be swept under the rug with a new fiscal program.

A bit more than a week after Franco's announcement, and following increasing capital flight, the Brazilian government announced that it was no longer going to defend the real. With the lessons of previous currency collapses in Asia fresh in the minds of policy makers and the IMF, the government finally admitted the obvious. It decided that it would be foolish to continue to defend a currency that was likely to have to undergo devaluation; it would make no sense to waste more precious foreign currency reserves, as some Asian countries had done. As a result, Brazil floated its currency, which resulted in an immediate and severe devaluation. Briefly, the rate reached over 2 reais per dollar, whereas the rate in late 1998 had been around 1.20 reais to the dollar. As of late 1999, the rate is in the 2 reais per dollar range. The old game was up.

THE POLITICS BEHIND THE BRAZILIAN CRISIS: DIVIDED POLITICAL POWER AND DELAYED ADJUSTMENT

That is the story of what happened. But why did it happen? Obviously, political factors were at the root of this crisis. The Brazilian government was trying to defend the currency as part of its anti-inflationary stance, even though its currency was substantially overvalued, as was widely recognized. In effect, policy makers basically used interest rates to try to defend the currency. In the process, they gave up many of the traditional policy instruments—monetary and fiscal expansion, including targeted industrial policy—that the Brazilian state had used to promote development. This did not go unnoticed in business circles. Although state capacity had been reconstructed, to some degree, with the Real Plan, it also was weakened, in the sense that it did not have nearly as many policy instruments at its disposal. With economic stabilization, different business sectors applied pressure for policy change, but the state said consistently that its hands were tied—that there was nothing it could do, given the priority assigned to fighting inflation. The Real Plan was embraced initially because it promised an end to inflation; indeed, this can be considered one of the great achievements of the plan. At the same time, it was a move away from Brazil's traditional developmentalist policies, which included a strategy of industrial development. In the end, the Real Plan was somewhat precarious. As long as fiscal and other reforms lagged, it depended on relatively high interest rates and the continued inflow of foreign capital. When this capital dried up and left, there was no choice but to devalue.

Fortunately for the Brazilian economy, inflation, while increasing, has shown no signs of returning to pre–Real Plan levels. Much to the relief of policy makers, some of the inflation demons seem to have been exorcised, and the economy appears to be improving after the adjustment caused by the devaluation. But in the end, politics could not be eliminated from the economic policy-making process and continue to determine what is and is not possible. In the remainder of this chapter, I will focus on two key issues that affect economic policy making in Brazil: the party system and the federal system. Any understanding of past or future economic reforms must be viewed through these two lenses.

Indeed, Brazil's state has recuperated some strength but at the same time faces a great many institutional problems. As Weyland (1997–1998) points out, many of the old concentrated interest groups—those subsidized by previous state-directed developmentalism—have been discredited. President Cardoso has managed to appeal above them to get some of his reforms passed. There were some successes in these efforts, even though not enough was done to head off the effects of the financial crisis. The reforms have led to a situation in which interest groups as commonly conceived do not have the power that they once had in the Brazilian political economy. Because they have been discredited and because the forces of the international political economy make their appeals less than persuasive, Brazil has tended to follow a rather orthodox response to the crisis. Thus neoliberalism—broadly understood, even if it is now an epithet hurled at those who are unwilling to do anything beyond reducing government deficits and running a sound macroeconomy—has made significant inroads among Brazilian politicians (Power 1988). But even if neoliberal ideology were to triumph completely, neoliberal reforms face many obstacles in Brazil. Most of them are institutional.

In Brazil, the main political causes of the financial crisis were in fact the difficulty of actually carrying out any institutional reform in the country. When it became obvious that the needed reforms would not be undertaken, the attacks became more severe. Even after the crisis hit in January 1999, it was difficult for the Brazilians to make the changes that many thought were needed. In this sense, what it illustrates about the domestic political economy is the enormous inertia of Brazilian institutions. Even an economic crisis cannot readily change these institutional patterns.

The primary institutional obstacles relate to a lack of institutionalized parties and to federalism. As Mainwaring (1999) notes, Brazil has extraordinarily weak parties for the most part, which makes it difficult for any president to generate consistent support for a particular economic program. Politicians frequently change parties, and they do not necessarily follow the directions of the leadership in the party to which they belong. They respond to many different pressures emanating from constituents, local interests, and political ambition, and Brazilian electoral law has done little to force them to behave more "responsibly." This was illustrated in the December 1998 congressional rejection of pension reform.

One of the principal problems facing any Brazilian president is that, given the fragmented nature of the party system, he must count on a coalition of multiple parties that are themselves undisciplined. In its center-right alliance, Cardoso's own Brazilian Social Democratic Party, which holds less than 20 percent of both houses of Congress, counts on the support of the Liberal Front Party (PFL) and the Brazilian Labor Party. The Party of the Brazilian Democratic Movement also usually supports the government, though there are no guarantees that it will. Nor are there guarantees that other coalition members will support any given initiative.

Beyond this party fragmentation and lack of party discipline, Mainwaring (1999, 69) notes that "despite the centralizing efforts of [former President Getulio] Vargas (1930–45) and the military regime, Brazilian politics retains a federalism and localism that are exceptional in Latin America." What this implies is that even when there are national efforts to change policy or deal with crises, the best-planned efforts can be undermined by local, nonfederal politicians. This is precisely what happened when the crisis hit with full force in January 1999. Itamar Franco did not have to worry about what national political leaders would tell him when he decided to declare a moratorium on his state's debt payments to the federal government.

The Cardoso government has attempted to place greater restrictions on state and local governments when it comes to their draw on federal resources. But as Fleischer (1998) points out, one of the consequences of the redemocratization of Brazil and its writing of a new constitution was to make the federal government's finances even more tenuous. It increased the fiscal obligations of the national state and increased the amount of tax revenues that have to be transferred to state and local governments. This in itself makes the imposition of real reform problematic and makes it even more difficult to impose austerity when international conditions might dictate that this is the best response. In this sense, Brazil's federal system has made adjustment much more difficult than is the case in most other developing countries. This has greatly complicated a whole host of reforms that might bring federal state finances under control. State and local governments can rebel, and have resources to rebel, when it suits their political or economic interests.

It should also be noted that the Real Plan contributed to the pressures faced by regional interests. In the past, they, just like the national government, had been able to finance their activities through inflationary financing. But this would no longer be possible if inflation disappeared (Selcher 1998). In this sense, stabilization, and its effects on state and local governments, contributed to the devaluation that was carried out in early 1999.

The democratization process in Brazil has also contributed to the problems of federalism. According to Weyland,

> Brazil's gradual regime transition, which avoided direct presidential elections for a long time, exacerbated this shift in power from the national to the subnational governments. From late 1982 to late 1989, elected state governors faced a president who lacked the legitimacy bestowed by direct popular election. This democratic deficit made it more difficult for the central government to resist pressure from state governors and city mayors to grant them more power and resources. (1997–1998, 73)

There is a further complicating issue in this regard. As noted above, President Cardoso expended a great deal of political capital in his effort to secure the possibility of his reelection. Part of the deal that ensued was that other executive officeholders could be reelected as well, at both the state and local level. This has the effect of entrenching those state and local office holders and, in the end, makes any sort of reform to Brazil's federal system even more difficult (Selcher 1998).

To put it differently, Brazil's state fragmentation makes it difficult to engineer change. As Selcher points out,

> Brazil has become a federal state that is increasingly difficult to manage. A fragmentation of localized interests characterizes its political process, seriously hindering the building of broader coalitions necessary for a national perspective or sense of national interest in the political class and for a truly national politics. (1998, 25)

Therefore, it becomes difficult to conceptualize and implement reform in such a system, and dealing with something like the fallout from the Asian crisis is extraordinarily difficult.

Despite the fact that many issues may be of national concern, and may cry out for national answers to the problems, Brazil faces the fact that these national issues are always filtered through regional lenses (Selcher 1998). What this means is that legislators can be pressured by the president to carry out reforms, but they will still often remain loyal to regional interests. Any alliance with the president to pursue a particular policy is only temporary and can shift, depending on circumstances and local interests.

CONCLUSION

Brazil is not facing a catastrophe in its public finances, and it is not going to fall off a cliff due to the fallout from the Asian financial crisis. But Brazil does face serious obstacles when it comes to dealing with international financial shocks. Primarily, these obstacles are related to institutional deficiencies. Brazil's democracy is now safely consolidated. Shifting dispersed interest group preferences have created a policy impetus toward liberalization and macroeconomic orthodoxy. But significant institutional constraints still remain, particularly when it comes to Brazil's ability to react quickly to the pressures of an increasingly globalized economy. This became quite clear when the pronouncement of an individual state governor led to a currency crisis that set off a devaluation and created serious problems with Brazil's Mercosur trading partners.

Given Brazil's constitutional and institutional framework, it is unlikely that these problems will be resolved in the short term. It is rather difficult to imagine how they could be. As Brazil navigates a world in which financial capital can move quickly, institutional constraints on domestic political responses will continue to play a crucial role.

NOTES

1. Because of the Brazilian devaluation, its partners in Mercosur—Argentina, Paraguay, and Uruguay—were suddenly much less competitive in the Brazilian market. This led some observers to claim that the regional grouping was in mortal danger.

2. Flynn (1999) gives an impressive blow-by-blow description of the Brazilian response to the international financial crisis, and interested readers should turn to it for more detail.

12

Argentina: The Political Economy of Stabilization and Structural Reform

Walter Molano

In the 1990s, Argentina became known as a paradigm of neoliberal policies. President Carlos Ménem was lauded for his ideological zeal in implementing radical economic reforms. Yet how much of his behavior was motivated by ideology? How much of it was spurred by political necessity? In this chapter I argue that President Ménem was a political entrepreneur who used the Convertibility Plan for expedient purposes to mobilize untapped social forces. I argue that the old division of the exporting sector, mainly composed of agricultural exporters, along with much of the nontraded sector urban middle class, against the import-competing sector, mainly consisting of import-substitution industries and organized labor unions, along with nontraded sector unorganized labor, was broken by the negative effects of protracted economic instability and hyperinflation. The rapid stabilization of the Argentine economy through the Convertibility Plan allowed the formation of a new coalition that broke the grip of groups that traditionally dominated Argentine politics. The pivotal group in this realignment was unorganized urban labor. The coalition pushed through important political and economic reforms. Unfortunately, the new political power was not used to consolidate the reforms and allow the Argentine economy to enter into a sustainable path of development and growth. Specifically, the government did not push through the labor market reforms needed to ensure the sustainability of the Convertibility Plan. Instead, the government focused its resources on amending the constitution and securing a second presidential term.

THE 1980S: ECONOMIC DISASTER AND LIBERALIZING REACTION

Argentina suffered severe political and economic crises during the 1980s. The combination of the debt crisis, an evaporation of international credit, and the

213

transition to democracy was highly destabilizing (Damill and Frenkel 1990). The end of military rule was initiated by the humiliating rout of the Argentine expeditionary forces during the Malvinas/Falklands War. National elections were held in October 1983, and Raul Alfonsín of the Radical Party won with 51.7 percent of the vote. The national elections, however, resulted in a divided government. The Radical Party controlled the presidency and the Chamber of Deputies, while the Peronists controlled the Senate. At the same time, the fledgling democracy faced increasing demands from the traditional Argentine power groups, including the military, labor unions, and industrialists.

In April 1987, renegade military officers launched the first of a series of coup attempts to overthrow the civilian government. These officers were protesting the treatment of senior military leaders during the postdictatorship human rights trials. Although the rebellion was put down, there were two more uprisings within six months (Canitrot and Sigal 1992). The Alfonsín administration also faced intense pressure from the labor unions. Between 1984 and 1989, the country was paralyzed by thirteen general strikes calling for higher wages and better working conditions. Economic and political instability led to loud protests from the business community. The national industrial organization (UIA) and the national farmers association (Sociedad Rural) openly criticized the Alfonsín government. In addition, they also made demands on the government. The industrialists called for more protection, while the agricultural community called for higher subsidies.

The government was forced to make concessions to these groups in order to hold the country together. However, these concessions raised the fiscal deficit. The monetizing of the deficit led to higher inflation rates, a faster devaluation of the currency, and more economic distress. By July 1989, the Argentine economy was spinning out of control. It was entering hyperinflation. Wholesale and retail prices went up 200 percent in a single month and consumer prices surged 3,079 percent for the year (Eichengreen 1995). The use of indexation helped preserve the real wages and savings of more organized workers in the greater Buenos Aires area, but the high inflation rate was very hard on the urban poor and rural community. Consequently, the Alfonsín administration found itself politically isolated in both the urban and rural arenas. Even the Radicals' own candidate to the 1989 presidential elections disavowed the government's economic program.

In 1989, the Radicals lost the presidential elections. Victory went to the Peronist candidate, Carlos Ménem. He was the former governor of the province of Rioja. Ménem was largely unknown in the greater Buenos Aires area. He had campaigned heavily in the provincial areas and toured the country in his so-called Ménem-mobile. Surprisingly, given the traditional urban labor base of the Peronists (Collier and Collier 1991), his victory was bolstered by the rural vote. Soon after the presidential elections, the economic and political situation took a turn for the worse. There were talks about another military coup attempt. President Alfonsín was afraid that he would not be able to hold the country together until the December inauguration and that the country would slip back into military rule. Therefore, Alfonsín decided to relinquish office five months ahead of schedule.

Ménem's presidential campaign rhetoric had suggested a return to statist policies. Many economists feared that the new government would only exacerbate the economic crisis. However, Ménem surprised the country when he entered office. Instead of naming a traditional Peronist to lead the economic team, he appointed Miguel Roig as economy minister. Roig was a senior executive from Bunge y Born, one of the largest agricultural exporters in the country. His appointment was a sign that the new government would break with its traditional allies and align itself with the exporting community. But Roig died only six days after taking office. By this time, the administration had come under intense criticism from its traditional allies, and Ménem drifted back to a more Peronist approach.

During the next year, the government employed a variety of heterodox policies. The government increased protectionism by levying higher tariffs and increasing subsidies. The power of the labor unions was enhanced. Fiscal and monetary mismanagement fueled inflationary expectations. The government implemented price and wage controls to artificially maintain downward pressure on prices. The results were disastrous. Investment and productivity plunged. Investor confidence was shattered and hyperinflation returned. Social unrest was rampant and there were rumors of another military coup. Eventually, the government lost control of the situation. A wage–price spiral exploded into an annualized inflation rate of 20,594 percent by March 1990, and Argentina entered one of its most grim historical episodes.

The return of hyperinflation led to a breakdown of order. Supermarkets were looted. Many wealthy Argentines moved their families out of Buenos Aires and took their money out of the country. By the summer of 1990, an estimated $3 billion in Argentine holdings were moved to Uruguayan banks. Ménem was quickly realizing that the narrow interests of traditional Peronist constituencies, such as organized labor, import-substituting industries, and the military, would prevent the stabilization of Argentina. Faced with the possibility that traditional Peronist policies would push the country into chaos, Ménem decided to try a new tack.

In April 1991, President Ménem appointed Domingo Cavallo as economy minister. Cavallo was a Harvard-trained Ph.D. and the former foreign minister. His first action was to centralize economic decision making. He took charge of the Ministries of Finance, Trade and Investment, Economic Programming, Agriculture, Public Works, Energy, Transportation, and Communications. In order to staff this new "super" ministry, Cavallo brought in a team of technocrats from his economic think tank located in Córdoba, the Fundación Mediterránea. Under his command, the new team moved to stabilize the economy. His first action was to implement an exchange rate stabilization program called the Convertibility Plan.

POLITICAL STRATEGY: APPEAL TO DISPERSED INTEREST GROUPS, ESPECIALLY UNORGANIZED LABOR

Before discussing the Convertibility Plan, I shall examine the shift in political strategy that occurred in 1991. The return to a more liberal economic policy approach has raised many questions, including, Did Ménem betray his political party and allies? A close look at the political development and campaign rhetoric of Carlos Ménem shows that he was not a traditional Peronist. His campaign speeches in 1988 and 1989 did not focus on organized labor. They centered on social justice. His language promised aid to the poor instead of aid to workers (Canitrot and Sigal 1992). It is important to remember that Ménem hailed from the province of Rioja and not the urban environment of Buenos Aires. Therefore, the lack of commitment to traditional Peronist allies, such as organized labor and import-substituting industries, allowed him to look for new economic policies that would stabilize Argentina, without betraying his political ideology.

Furthermore, it is important to stress that Ménem was a consummate political pragmatist and entrepreneur. He was always searching for ways to achieve his ultimate goals—economic prosperity for the rural poor and self-promotion. Yet Ménem also knew the distinction between political tactics and political strategy. An example of this pragmatism occurred even before Cavallo was appointed economy minister. It occurred in 1989 when the government tried to privatize the state-owned telephone company, ENTEL (Molano 1997).

The privatization of ENTEL promised to generate a major windfall for the government. The state-owned company was obsolete and a powerful drag on the fiscal accounts. However, it was a very valuable concession that foreign telephone companies were anxious to acquire. In addition to generating revenues, the privatization of ENTEL would result in a complete revitalization of the entire telecommunications sector. In other words, the privatization of ENTEL was a win-win situation for the government. The Alfonsín administration understood this situation very well. In 1988, it attempted to sell ENTEL to Telefonica de Espagña. However, the unions and industrialists led by the Peronists blocked the sale.

The next year, the new Ménem administration realized the immense potential of selling the company. Therefore, it decided to launch another privatization attempt. However, the government faced stiff opposition from the same groups that had blocked the sale the year before. Faced with opposition from within his own party, Ménem decided to appease the leadership of the groups while going after the factions that opposed the transaction. For example, the government decided to give 10 percent of the company shares to ENTEL workers. At the same time, the union leadership was given complete discretion over the disbursement of the shares. Opposition to the privatization quickly faded away and the sale was completed in 1990. Hence political and economic necessity drove Ménem to implement whatever tactics were necessary to achieve his ultimate goals.

Such a pragmatic approach is not so surprising for a developing country in the midst of a highly competitive political transition. Unlike more developed countries, in which strong institutions (e.g., a judiciary, central bank, and regulatory supervisory agencies) can ensure economic stability during a period of political change, many of these institutions were rendered ineffective by the military regime and the transition to democracy. This phenomenon has been recorded in many other countries, such as Indonesia and Russia. As a result, political leaders were often forced to adopt pragmatic policies that flew in the face of ideology or traditional policies.

THE CONVERTIBILITY PLAN AND STRUCTURAL REFORMS

The launch of the Convertibility Plan in April 1991 marked a major shift in Argentine economic policy. The plan was based on a currency board type of monetary arrangement. The plan fixed the exchange rate, assured full currency convertibility, and underpinned that assurance by backing 100 percent of the monetary base with the central bank's international reserves. Tying the monetary base to the available international reserves prevented the central bank from printing money to cover the fiscal deficit. This gave immediate credibility to the government's intent to control budget deficits. A change in the monetary base had to be met by a corresponding change in international reserves. The result was a mechanism that ensured monetary accountability. The change in monetary base would lead to a change in interest rates, thus creating a self-correcting mechanism. The introduction of the Convertibility Plan also coincided with a liberalization of the current and capital accounts, thus allowing capital to enter the country.

Cavallo implemented several major initiatives to sustain the new monetary arrangement. He started with reforms to improve the fiscal accounts. The fiscal measures included a simplification of the tax system, implementation of a value-added tax (VAT), privatization of the social security system, and the reform of the tax collection agency (DGI). The reforms produced rapid results. The proceeds from the VAT rose from 3.3 percent of GDP in the first quarter of 1991 to 6 percent of GDP in the fourth quarter, to an average of nearly 7 percent of GDP in 1992. Revenues of the nonfinancial public sector increased from 17.5 percent of GDP in 1990 to an estimated 25.1 percent in 1992. Capital account receipts, including privatization proceeds, increased from 0.6 percent of GDP in 1990 to nearly twice that level in 1992. In 1992, the government posted a primary budget surplus of 2.2 percent of GDP, thus exceeding a target set by the IMF.

There were also major trade initiatives, including a simplification of the tariff structure, elimination of quantitative import restrictions, and economic integration with Brazil through Mercosur. Virtually all export taxes were eliminated. The import tariff structure was simplified and tariffs were slashed to an average rate of 20 percent from the previous rate of 35 percent. Finally, the government took measures to increase foreign investment. Foreigners were granted equal legal status to domestic investors. Most restrictions on invest- ments and capital repatriation were removed. The administration deregulated many sectors of the economy and privatized most of the state-owned compa- nies. The results were impressive. Argentina's inflation rate dropped from over 20,000 percent year-on-year in 1990 to an annual rate of 3.8 percent year-on- year by September 1994. In 1996, Argentina posted the lowest inflation rate in the world—0.054 percent. The economic stagnation of the 1980s gave way to a robust growth rate of 8.9 percent in 1991.

In response to reports of rising deficits, the Argentine peso came under pres- sure for a short period of time in November 1992. But the government abided by the precepts of the Convertibility Law and sold dollars to the market to defend the peso. For a short while in November and early December, peso liquidity was tightened to raise peso-denominated interest rates by suspending swap operations against government bonds and dollars. With the resolute central bank response, those speculating against the government's political willingness to preserve the peso–U.S. dollar parity quickly retreated. Subsequently, the government an- nounced several measures to gradually increase peso–dollar substitutability, in- cluding the introduction of dollar checking accounts. Steps were also taken to allow all transactions, except for the payment of wages and taxes, to take place in dollars. Equally important, reserve requirements on demand deposits were re- duced and banks were permitted to satisfy them in either pesos or dollars. Col- lectively, all these measures made the peso more of a substitute for the dollar and enhanced the credibility of the Convertibility Law.

EXCHANGE RATE STABILIZATION PROGRAMS:
THE PERILS OF PARTIAL REFORM

Although the Convertibility Plan was introduced as a way to instill monetary and fiscal responsibility, it was an exchange rate stabilization program. In other words, the program was designed as a rapid means to reduce the high rate of in- flation, but with some dangerous side effects. The two main characteristics of ex- change rate stabilization programs are (1) fixing the exchange rate as the nomi- nal price anchor and (2) liberalizing trade in order to maintain competitive price pressure on the tradable goods sector. Uribe (1995) showed that pegging the ex- change rate generates new confidence in the government's willingness to exercise fiscal and monetary discipline. This boost in credibility was clearly evident in Ar- gentina. In 1991, when the Convertibility Plan was introduced, the Argentine stock market rose 432 percent year-on-year.

Exchange rate stabilization programs are often associated with a strong influx of imported goods. These goods help put downward pressure on the prices of domestic goods, thus helping to suppress the inflation rate. The quick stabilization of consumer prices and the real appreciation of the currency provide workers with a rapid increase in real wages. The elimination of the so-called inflation tax often explodes into a consumption boom that attracts further inflows of foreign goods. The pent-up demand for durable goods exacerbates the increase in consumption. Unfortunately, the decline in the inflation rate is not instantaneous. Therefore, there is a lag in the decline in real wages and prices. The result is a real appreciation of the currency and a subsequent disequilibrium in the balance of payments.

In addition to the disequilibrium in the external accounts, developing countries usually develop problems in the fiscal accounts. The stabilization of the economy often leads to the recognition of many unfunded liabilities, such as state debts and pensions. This recognition is often an important step in gaining credibility and legitimacy among domestic and international political and economic groups. The result is that the initial fiscal reforms often fall short of bringing government spending in line with expenditures.

Foreign investors usually finance the shortfall in the external and internal accounts. Initially, most of the investment is in the form of foreign direct investment (FDI). These inflows take advantage of the recently liberalized markets and privatization programs. As the economy stabilizes further and gains credibility, the inflows are complemented by portfolio capital inflows in the form of equity, domestic, and international bond placements. A steady stream of capital inflows results in a gradual dependence on foreign resources. These flows are sustainable as long as international investors are willing to finance the gap or until the country implements radical (often painful) economic reforms to regain international competitiveness. This creates a high degree of vulnerability to external shocks and reversals in the flow of international capital.

Several economic studies have looked at exchange rate stabilization programs. Kiguel and Liviatan (1992) and Vegh (1992) identify a three-part pattern that begins with the real appreciation of the real exchange rate, an investment/consumption boom, and deterioration of external accounts. Mendoza and Uribe (1996) built a model replicating the behavior of major macroeconomic variables during an exchange rate stabilization program. The model showed that the programs usually come under intense pressure four to five years after their inception. It seems that the initial success of the program creates a sense of complacency that distracts policy makers from implementing further economic reforms. The accumulation of debt, widening of external deficits, and appreciation of the real exchange rate usually comes to a head and forces the government to make a major adjustment to the exchange rate. This usually takes the form of a large devaluation that often results in an uncontrolled overshooting of the exchange rate. Although exchange rate stabilization programs are used to bolster credibility, the subsequent complacency of policy makers eventually erodes trust and leads to a new crisis.

Exchange rate stabilization programs can be successful in temporarily stabilizing economies, but they do not solve the structural problems that contribute to the price instability. Policy makers should use exchange rate stabilization programs as a means of buying political goodwill to implement other economic reforms to sustain price stability. The subsequent reforms often force the economy onto a path of deflation in order to realign the real exchange rate. Unfortunately, governments can become extremely vulnerable during this phase. The deflationary process can be very painful for key political groups, such as farmers and urban producers of goods and services. Certain costs, such as taxes and interest rates, remain fixed during the deflationary phase and other costs, such as rents and wages, are slow in adjusting. The result can be dangerously destabilizing. Friedman (1992) showed that a powerful deflationary episode between 1934 and 1936 was one of the major factors that undermined the regime of Chiang Kai-shek. Furthermore, the realignment of relative prices can also be a very lengthy process. The realignment of relative prices in the United States took fourteen years to complete in the deflationary period following the Civil War.

Exchange rate stabilization programs can produce quick economic results. Given the fragile political and economic environment of the early 1990s, the programs enjoyed widespread appeal in Latin America. Members of the lower income strata, particularly unorganized labor groups, received real wage increases and access to luxury items, often in the form of imported goods. The economic boom pushed up President Ménem's popularity. In 1993, President Ménem moved to capitalize on his increased popularity by seeking a second term. Although the Argentine constitution prohibited reelection, President Ménem struck an agreement with the major political parties to amend the constitution and allow reelection. In 1994, a national assembly approved the constitutional reform. Under the revised constitutional rules, the winner had to secure at least 45 percent of the vote, or 40 percent of the vote and a 10 percent lead over the next contender. In order to gain approval for the amendment, President Ménem agreed to the coparticipation (sharing) of new federal taxes with the provinces. This set the stage for the elections scheduled for 1995. It also set the stage for a deterioration of the fiscal accounts during the second half of the 1990s.

THE POLITICS OF INCOMPLETE REFORM

The economic team led by Domingo Cavallo took important steps to enhance the sustainability of the Convertibility Plan. However, the reforms were far from complete. First, the government was forced to recognize several important liabilities, such as provincial bank debt and pension obligations. The government was initially able to hide these shortfalls because of its aggressive privatization program. The Ménem administration privatized $39.6 billion in state assets during its term. Although 57 percent of the flows were in the form of debt swaps, the remainder was in cash. These inflows began to decelerate by the end of his first term, thus creating a new set of problems for the government.

The second reform left on the sidelines was that of labor markets. The use of the Convertibility Plan removed the flexibility needed to meet external supply shocks. This was a major consideration for Argentina, given the importance of agricultural exports. Argentina needed to implement more flexible labor laws in order to regain the competitiveness it had lost due to the real appreciation of the currency. Given the fixed exchange rate regime, a flexible labor code would allow the economy to adjust to external shocks, thus enhancing the sustainability of the economic program. However, labor market reform was very controversial in 1994 and 1995. Argentina was starting to suffer from a rising rate of unemployment. A combination of enterprise restructuring, external shocks, and an overvalued exchange rate pushed the unemployment rate higher. Labor reform would have eventually reduced the unemployment rate. Armed with the assurance that labor forces could be reduced whenever needed, firms would have hired more Argentines. But organized labor preyed on fears that the labor reforms would force them onto the unemployed rolls or into lower-paying jobs.

The Mexican devaluation of 1994 and the subsequent crisis sent a powerful shock wave through the Ménem administration. The crisis led to the worst recession in Argentine history. Banks were on the verge of collapse as Argentines took their money out of the country. Many commentators blasted the president and the economic plan. President Ménem needed some quick organized support if he was to win the elections. The support came from the labor unions. Backed by the CGT labor confederation and the traditional Peronist vanguard, President Ménem swept the opposition. Not surprisingly, such political weakness meant making concessions to organized labor, including postponing labor market reforms for the rest of the term.

After the elections, the fiscal and labor situation took a turn for the worse. Ménem's reelection had engendered greater confidence from foreign investors. Although the stock of saleable state companies had dwindled by 1995, the government plugged the fiscal hole by turning to the international bond market. The result was a sharp increase in the external debt load. The debt burden was ignored because the country experienced a sharp expansion rate in 1996 and 1997. However, it loomed larger in 1999 when the economy entered into the deepest recession since the 1930s.

There were also setbacks on the labor front. As a concession to organized labor during the presidential elections, Ménem appointed Erman Gonzalez as the labor minister. Gonzalez was an old-time Peronist party member and a close ally of organized labor. Under his command, the government introduced a new labor code that dismantled some of the flexibility that had been implemented by the Cavallo economic team. Gonzalez remained in office until six months before the elections, when he was forced to resign over a scandal involving unusually high pension benefits that he had received. By this time, it was of course too late to implement new labor market reforms before the elections. Given the difficult economic conditions, Ménem also felt that he could not do without organized labor support after the elections. The labor market reforms were postponed again.

The absence of the labor reforms became evident again in 1999 when Brazil, Argentina's largest trading partner, came under intense pressure. In January 1999, the Brazilian central bank was forced to devalue the currency by over 30 percent in real terms. Argentine exports to Brazil plunged by more than 46 percent in March 1999. The Argentine economy entered into an immediate recession. The agriculture lobby, Sociedad Rural, and the industrial lobby, Union Industrial Argentina (UIA), increased their criticisms of economic policy. They demanded compensation for the economic crisis. Instead of fully addressing the problem by liberalizing the labor code and improving fiscal performance, the government turned to the international financial community to float more debt. Although the international community accommodated Argentina's initial requests, the support appears to be finite.

CONCLUSION

The Convertibility Plan was successful in stabilizing the Argentine economy and restoring growth. The political and economic distress caused by years of hyperinflation had been sufficient to break the gridlock of entrenched interest groups, such as organized labor and import-substituting industries. By making tactical concessions to strategic individuals or groups, President Ménem, who had no political allegiance to these groups, was able to push through many important economic reforms. However, a danger in using an exchange rate stabilization program is a tendency to front-load many of the benefits of lower inflation. Dangerously destabilizing problems can develop unless the government follows through with the reforms needed to sustain the programs. The intent of the Convertibility Plan was to improve macroeconomic conditions and generate sufficient political goodwill for the government to follow through with deeper fiscal and labor reforms. Unfortunately, the government did not fully follow through. Instead, Ménem pushed for a constitutional amendment to allow for his reelection. The difficult economic conditions in the run-up before and after the 1995 elections forced Ménem to put off crucial labor market reforms in order to retain the support of the Peronists' traditional organized labor constituency. This decision was very costly because it sowed the seeds for the economic crisis of 1999. There is a danger that these economic difficulties will be blamed on the liberalizing turn in general, rather than on the combination of liberalization with the vestiges of traditional populism. Such a development could lead to increased defection of pivotal unorganized labor groups and a renewed populist policy cycle. However, recent memories of hyperinflation under populist policy regimes make this unlikely.

V

Central and Eastern Europe Comparative
Case Studies

13

Poland, Hungary, and the Czech Republic: National Identity and Liberalizing Consensus

Shale Horowitz

652 P33 P34

F32 G10 G20

What happened in the more advanced postcommunist countries of east-central Europe during the world financial crisis of 1997–1999? There was a financial crisis in the Czech Republic but not in Poland or Hungary. In fact, the Czech crisis of May 1997 preceded the outbreak of the East Asian crisis in Thailand in July 1997. Bouts of international capital flight emanated from a deepening East Asian crisis in October–November 1997, the Russian crisis of August 1998, and the Brazilian crisis of January 1999. All three countries suffered from inconstant international portfolio investment and depressed stock markets. But market responses in general—particularly including direct foreign investment and domestic investment—closely tracked the most significant differences in economic policy making and economic performance. That is, they correctly rewarded Poland and Hungary, and punished the Czech Republic.

What were the main patterns of economic policy making in the years leading up to the crisis? Along with Slovenia, these three countries were the leaders in making the massive macroeconomic and structural reforms necessary in moving from plan to market. Prices were freed to guide resource allocation, and hitherto prohibitive barriers to international trade and domestic private sector entry were lifted. In principle, state sector firms were to be privatized and forced to compete on an equal footing with other firms, both foreign and domestic. In practice, the most crucial differences between the three countries were in banking sector reform and regulation and, less significantly, in privatization methods, securities markets regulation, and exchange rate policy.

In Poland, the central political position of the Solidarity trade union slowed the initial process of privatization, but the early Balcerowicz program compensated with massive cuts in fiscal subsidies and with strict bad loan-workout regulations in the banking sector. Firms thus faced "hard budget constraints" on both the fiscal and credit fronts from the beginning. In the Czech Republic, a hard budget constraint was imposed on the fiscal side but not on the banking sector side. The new Czech government sought to follow a "German model," in which a few dominant commercial banks hold large stakes in industrial conglomerates and use due lending diligence to monitor performance and guide restructuring. The large Czech commercial banks ran investment funds that attracted controlling proportions of shares distributed under the two mass voucher privatization schemes. Most crucially, they made large loans in an effort to consolidate Czech conglomerates that could compete with the dominant European firms in sectors such as heavy engineering, heavy transport equipment, and chemicals. Hungarian policies fell in between. There was an initial "Czech" phase. Although Hungary imposed strict financial regulation of most firms, selected larger firms viewed as "strategic" or promising at first attracted large subsidies on the fiscal side, and large loans on the banking side. When these early Czech-style efforts faltered, policy did an about-face. Fiscal subsidies largely ended, and the entire commercial banking sector was sold off to tight-fisted foreigners.

What institutional and policy changes occurred in response to the international financial crisis of 1997–1999? The crisis did not seriously affect Polish and Hungarian economic performance. The crisis did not, therefore, spur any significant institutional change. Much as if no financial crisis had occurred, Polish and Hungarian economic policies developed with their characteristic rhythms. Hungary pushed on with its established policy of selling as many "strategic" assets as possible to foreigners. Once again led in economic policy making by the decisive Leszek Balcerowicz, Poland embarked on a furious new round of innovative structural reforms. Poland and Hungary maintained crawling peg exchange rate regimes and continued to reduce the rate of depreciation as economic performance improved. The Czechs, on the other hand, grudgingly changed. The May 1997 financial crisis led the government to reevaluate the role of banks—in particular to follow the Hungarian example—and to upgrade hitherto lax securities market regulation. Exchange rate policy shifted from defending a fixed exchange rate to managing a floating rate with an eye on the current account balance. Although Vaclav Klaus's center-right government resigned over a campaign finance scandal, it was fatally weakened by the economic turmoil. A caretaker government led by central bank head Josef Tosovsky deepened the financial sector reforms. Interestingly, the June 1998 Lower House parliamentary elections and the November 1998 Upper House elections maintained majorities for the Czech center-right. Only the latter's internal divisions allowed the center-left Social Democrats to form a new government. The Social Democrats are continuing with the banking and securities markets reforms initiated in 1997 by the Klaus government, albeit with a similar lack of enthusiasm.

How are these variations in economic policy to be explained? Variation in the size of concentrated economic interest groups does a poor job of explaining economic policies. The three countries pursued similarly ambitious economic reform policies in the initial postcommunist period. Yet concentrated interest groups losing from market reform—particularly heavily subsidized sectors such as agriculture and inefficient heavy industry—were largest in Poland and smallest in the Czech Republic. Such interest groups were also most well organized in Poland and least well organized in the Czech Republic. And relative to past and present would-be structural reformers in the rest of the world, such interest groups were extremely large in all three countries. In all three cases, it is necessary to explain the strength and persistence of support for radical reforms with predictably painful short-term consequences.[1] The most extensive and politically decisive support came from dispersed interest groups, particularly labor and the middle classes in the urban service sector. But there were also significant defections from concentrated "loser" interest groups such as heavy industry and agriculture.[2] To add to the puzzle, in the most recent round of elections, the better-performing Polish and Hungarian governments were ejected (September 1997, May 1998), whereas the poorer-performing Czech government received a vote of confidence (June 1998).

Both for dispersed interest groups with weaker economic policy preferences, and for defecting members of concentrated groups with strong status quo economic interests, widely held national identities offer the most plausible explanation for this pattern of support. These national identities viewed the communist era as an alien and baneful deviation from the previously established "true paths" of national potential. Postcommunist countries with established historical memories of precommunist political and economic "golden pasts," often reinforced by memories of precommunist and communist-era struggles for national survival, were more likely to look beyond the short-term costs of market transition to the shared goal of future national revival. In the late 1980s, by far the most attractive model for actualizing such commonly perceived latent national potentials was market democracy within the Western European family of nations—because it was perceived to reconcile the main long-term goals of national autonomy, protection from external threats, and economic prosperity.[3] By contrast, the East Asian model of authoritarian technocracy was tainted by its "all-too-Soviet" political methods. In Poland, Hungary, and the Czech Republic, the strength of voters' and elites' initial reform consensus has been shown by their patience in the face of deep postcommunist transitional recessions, as well as subsequent difficulties in Hungary in 1995–1996 and in the Czech Republic in 1997–1999. It is also reflected in the relative conservatism of center-left parties and governments. The main economic policy differences—particularly in banking sector regulation—are best explained by varying technical assessments of reformist government elites.[4]

Because the reformist consensus in favor of market democracy is so strong, variations in specific forms of democratic political institutions have had little role to play. Despite considerable variation, both across countries and over time, in the strength of presidencies, the structure of legislatures, and the nature of electoral and party systems, strong reformist consensus produced broadly similar policy demands from electorates, as well as similarly responsive policy outcomes from ruling governments and leaders. Political institutions might have mattered more if the electorate had been more indecisive and impatient.[5] Democratic political institutions per se provided scope to implement the reformist consensus. But they did not create this consensus.[6] In other words, only a dictatorship run by status quo–oriented elites would likely have been able to forestall ambitious and committed market reforms in these three countries.

In all three countries, political leadership has played a significant role in specifying important unconstrained means of pursuing broader economic policy objectives. These details have had strong effects on economic performance and have thus fed back into subsequent economic policy making—if not so unambiguously into subsequent electoral outcomes. Balcerowicz's decisive and wise early leadership allowed Poland to avoid the early policy errors made in Hungary and the Czech Republic. Gyula Horn's realistic assessment of Hungary's parlous economic condition in early 1995 produced unusually prompt and effective corrective policies. On the other hand, Klaus's stubborn refusal to admit his early errors delayed policy corrections in the Czech Republic, setting the stage for the financial crisis and Klaus's own fall from power.

The following case studies of Poland, Hungary, and the Czech Republic survey the main economic policy developments before and during the international financial crisis, and discuss the relative explanatory power of different political explanations of these developments. Economic policy is outlined in its macroeconomic and its microeconomic (or structural) dimensions. The main potential explanatory factors are then discussed: economic structure and the associated relative size of concentrated interest groups opposed to reform; political institutions, party systems, and political leadership; and national identities and the associated influence on economic policy preferences, especially among dispersed interest groups. The relative importance of these explanatory factors is then evaluated in an analytical narrative of political outcomes and economic policy developments. It is argued that the most important factors have been market-friendly national identities and, to a lesser but still significant extent, political leadership. Concentrated interest groups have played secondary roles, and political institutions have functioned primarily as permissive intervening variables.

POLAND

Economic Policy

In 1989, Poland became the first postcommunist country to embark on ambitious "shock therapy" economic reforms in making the transition from a planned to a market economy. The main initial policies were rapid and near complete liberalization of prices and trade, along with macroeconomic stabilization. After a large initial devaluation, the zloty exchange rate was pegged to a basket of currencies. Later a crawling peg exchange rate regime was adopted, in which the monthly rate of depreciation has fallen progressively over time. Until 1994, wages were controlled by a tax on increases above an agreed ceiling. Poland's initially massive foreign debt burden was made more manageable by early debt renegotiations and has fallen dramatically since 1994. Fiscal deficits have been relatively high, at 6.7 percent of GDP in 1991–1992 and at around 3 percent of GDP in other years.

Privatization of small enterprises was completed rapidly. However, strong Solidarity union influence in the factories made medium and large privatizations subject to employee and management approval—a provision not eliminated until August 1996. As a result, medium and large privatization has been quite slow, with the dramatic private sector growth generated overwhelmingly by new business start-ups. Large, heavily unionized sectors such as coal and steel remain in state hands. On the other hand, a "hard budget constraint" was imposed rapidly and lastingly on state sector firms. Government subsidies were cut dramatically in 1989–1992, and more slowly thereafter. Strict lending regulations have made for a relatively low level of commercial bank lending, with only about 18–20 percent of GDP outstanding in loans to enterprises in 1994–1997. An unusually effective bank restructuring dramatically cut nonperforming loans from 28.7 percent in 1994 to 10.4 percent in 1997. Recapitalization of state-owned commercial banks was linked to effective bad loan-workout programs, keeping costs to a remarkably low 3 percent of GDP. Bank privatization has been slow but has occurred with significant foreign ownership participation. This trend has accelerated with large bank privatizations in 1997–1999. Strict regulation and slow privatization has slowed the development of securities markets, but the stock market has developed more strongly since 1997 with a rash of new medium and large firm privatizations.[7]

Restructuring in industry has been significant, with a dramatic fall in its share of output matched by a dramatic rise in productivity. Unemployment rose rapidly to 16 percent in 1994 and dropped below 10 percent by 1998. The deep transitional recession of 1990–1991 was followed by a rapid and sustained recovery, which reached 5–7 percent annual growth rates in 1994–1998. Growth was export led to 1995 but driven by high levels of investment thereafter—with Poland increasingly overtaking Hungary as the main destination of direct foreign investment in east-central Europe. In the face of ballooning pension costs in 1989–1996, a July 1997pension reform partially privatized social security—standing to significantly reduce the fiscal burden and increase savings in the future. Since September 1997, the new Solidarity Electoral Action (AWS)-Freedom Union government hasembarked on a series of ambitious structural initiatives. Beyond some small spending and tax cuts, these initiatives include downsizing of the coal, steel, and defense sectors, accelerated privatization of large state-sector firms, bureaucratic streamlining and regional decentralization of government, reform of education financing, and creation of an internal market in health care. Despite some depression of stock market prices and weakness in Russian export markets, Poland has been relatively impervious to the international financial instability of 1997–1999.[8] An initial public offering of shares in the main Polish phone company pointedly went ahead in the teeth of the Russian crisis, the zloty has remained strong, and DFI continues to explode (Balcerowicz et al. 1997; *Business Central Europe,* April 1997–April 1999; EBRD 1994, 32–33, 165; EBRD 1997, 189–192, 231; EBRD 1998, 182–183, 223; Sachs 1993).

Explanatory Factors

In terms of economic structure, Poland had the largest agricultural sector and the largest unsalvageable heavy industrial sectors of the three countries. Moreover, in the Solidarity trade union, Poland had by far the most powerful labor organization, concentrated in "losing" heavy industrial sectors such as coal and steel (EIU 1996; OECD 1997, 127; World Bank 1996, 175, 214–215; World Bank 1997, 220–221, 236–237; World Bank 1999, 192–3, 212–213).[9]

The first, still partially rigged elections of June 1989 were held for a single member district-based bicameral legislature. After Solidarity's crushing victory, the Lower House elections were shifted to a proportional representation (PR) basis, and a directly elected, veto-wielding presidency was established for Solidarity leader Lech Walesa. The two main parties or party nuclei have been Solidarity and the reformist successor to the Communist Party, the Democratic Left Alliance (SLD). The Solidarity parties have been beset by internal factionalism. The main formations are a group of more loosely allied social conservative or Christian Democratic parties, and the smaller but more unified, socially and economically liberal Democratic Union (later Freedom Union). The SLD has dominated the center-left, often in alliance or coalition with its smaller, communist-era satellite party, the agrarian Polish Peasant Party (PSL). Initially the Solidarity parties were overshadowed by the proud and erratic (even, his enemies argued, semiauthoritarian) figure of Walesa. After the SLD's moderate and statesmanlike leader Aleksander Kwasniewski defeated Walesa in 1995, Balcerowicz emerged from among the Democratic Union's old-bull intellectuals as the main luminary of the center-right.

Polish national identity has been steeled in the fires of past political tribulation. The long fall from imperial greatness culminated in the division of the Polish state among the Prussian, Austrian, and Russian empires. The reborn interwar state was once more divided, its elites being massacred as a matter of policy, by Nazis and Soviets. After World War II its borders were brutally moved westward by Stalin. Under communism, Poland showed the most consistent active resistance to Soviet rule. Protest or reform movements mushroomed in 1956, 1968, 1970, and 1976, and culminated with the development of Solidarity in the 1980s.

Although Solidarity began as a trade union, it quickly developed into a microcosm of Polish society, adding religious, agrarian, and urban intellectual and professional wings. Solidarity's unifying ideological mission was to smash the Soviet-imposed system and to move Poland irreversibly onto a westward path consistent with national autonomy and renewal of national greatness.

Explanation of Political Outcomes and Economic Policy Developments

The results of the June 1989 election, supposedly rigged to enable the Communist Party to retain veto power, were one indicator of the strength of reform-nationalist momentum. Solidarity won all but one of the freely contested Senate seats and all the freely contested Lower House seats. It successfully campaigned for reformists in other parties and, contrary to all expectations, was able to form the government. Radical market transition policies—which became known as the Balcerowicz plan after the young finance minister—were implemented in December 1989. Such radical transition policies had never been attempted anywhere and were pursued for over a year into the trough of a massive recession. The Solidarity leadership was making a conscious effort to radically reorient Poland's political and economic destiny. Citing the precedent of West Germany's postwar miracle, Prime Minister Tadeusz Mazowiecki told Balcerowicz that he was "looking for [his] Erhard." Perhaps more remarkably, in October 1991 elections that returned Solidarity to power, the public ratified this leap into the unknown in the midst of the downturn. As already noted, Balcerowicz's policies were stalled mainly in the area of privatization, as Solidarity's legacy of workplace organization led to an employee–management veto on privatization—predictably stalling most medium and large firm privatizations.

By 1993, the Polish economy was in its second year of recovery. Solidarity's defeat in the September elections was due to internal divisions—a fratricidal war between Walesa and Solidarity intellectuals, largely over whether Poland's future was Catholic and conservative or secular and liberal. Along with high thresholds for representation in the PR system, this put the SLD and PSL in power with a combined vote of around 35 percent. Even then, SLD leader Kwasniewski was only able to bring his party back from the wilderness by his studied moderation and his declared respect for the basic political and economic reforms of the preceding Solidarity governments. Although Kwasniewski campaigned for slightly higher fiscal outlays to cushion the shock of transition, and although he did little to advance Solidarity's legacy, he crucially made no serious effort to restore large fiscal subsidies or soft credits to Poland's still huge state sector. This moderation, combined with Walesa's dogged interference with his administration, allowed Kwasniewski to defeat Walesa in the November 1995 presidential elections. All this time, the dividends of Balcerowicz's policies—especially compared with other postcommunist countries—continued to grow and his legacy became ever more irreversible politically. Following the more aggressive Hungarian

Socialists, the SLD government even made modest advances toward selling Polish banks to foreign investors and passed a fiscally important pension reform.

In September 1997, the social conservative Solidarity Electoral Action coalition won the elections and formed a government with Balcerowicz's liberal Freedom Union. Continuing AWS internal divisions have left economic policy largely under Deputy Prime Minister Balcerowicz's control. Although Poland's economic performance by this time hardly required such support, it would be hard to imagine someone more likely than Balcerowicz to reassure domestic and international investors about the future. In addition to the expected fiscal and monetary measures to guard against a deterioration of the current account, Balcerowicz has pushed ahead with politically sensitive structural reforms of heavy industry and the state (Balcerowicz 1995, chaps. 14–17; East and Pontin 1997, chap. 2; Michta 1997; Millard 1994).

By comparison with all other countries that have embarked on massive structural reforms, Poland's record is impressive. In terms of the relatively backward, inefficient structure of production and the unmatched prestige and organization of Polish independent trade unions, in terms of the early internal divisions of the main political reform movement and the scope given them by the strong separation of powers in its reformed political institutions, Poland should have been a slower, less decisive reformer than either Hungary or the Czech Republic. While national identity was decisive in all three countries, it overcame greater obstacles in Poland. Poland's huge agricultural sector and state sector industries were to an unusual extent forced to fend for themselves, the latter even while remaining in state hands. The Solidarity trade union was absorbed and domesticated by the larger national movement that grew out of it. Despite the often bitter animosities that grew up among Solidarity leaders, their allegiance to the national cause always constrained their egos and their specific policy disagreements. Just as importantly, the national movement converted the left as well as the right, thus guaranteeing the early policy legacy against any severe setbacks. On top of this reform–nationalist consensus, Poland was lucky to have in Balcerowicz an astute leader of the technical specifics of reform. His leadership may have spared Poland from the financial policy errors committed in Hungary and the Czech Republic. By the same token, the reform consensus in Poland was strong enough that, as in Hungary or the Czech Republic, such mistakes would almost certainly have been corrected sooner or later.

HUNGARY

Economic Policy

Hungary's first postcommunist government, like Poland's, immediately instituted a rapid and nearly complete liberalization of prices and trade, along with macroeconomic stabilization. Unlike Poland, Hungary made no serious effort to restructure its huge communist-era foreign debt. Fiscal deficits have been relatively high, especially in 1992-1995. To avoid overvaluation amid relatively high inflation, Hungary adopted a crawling peg exchange rate regime. Output began to recover in 1993, but 1993–1994 saw continued large fiscal deficits and a significant current account deterioration. The large foreign debt burden made such current account deficits unsustainable. Fiscal austerity, wage restraints, and structural reforms in 1995 forced significant restructuring and brought down the current account deficit. The GDP growth rate accelerated to 4–5 percent from 1997. The rate of devaluation fell from 1.9 percent in 1995 to 1 percent in August 1997 to 0.6 percent in 1999, on the strength of improved competitiveness and sharp foreign debt reduction.[10]

Small privatization was completed rapidly. From the outset, medium and large privatization policy targeted large strategic investors on a firm-by-firm basis. It was believed that such a slow, piecemeal approach was justified by the external direction and investment likely to come with large outside investors. In the context of the overall reform package, this policy has attracted by far the largest DFI inflows per capita in east-central Europe—until the recent surge into Poland, by far the largest inflows even in absolute terms. Enterprise performance has been clearly superior in foreign-owned firms. But then what happened to firms as long as they remained in state hands? Hungary imposed strict bankruptcy rules, and there is evidence of hard budget constraints in the early surge of unemployment to 12.3 percent in 1992. However, the hard budget constraint was also compromised significantly on an ad hoc basis. In 1992 the state made large investments in a number of large "strategic" enterprises, and as late as 1994 large commercial banks continued to make large soft loans to many medium and large enterprises. Most of these investments turned out to be bad. To date, bank recapitalizations have cost around 10 percent of GDP, despite a level of credit outstanding—at somewhat less than 20 percent of GDP—similar to that of Poland. Large-scale bank recapitalizations in 1992–1994 culminated in the decision—as part of the March 1995 austerity plan—to sell the large commercial banks to foreign owners. In April 1997, a partial privatization of the pension system significantly reduced long-term fiscal burdens and promises to stimulate savings. By 1999, most significant assets in industry and banking have been privatized to strategic investors, a high proportion of them foreign. Although Budapest's once high-flying stock market has been brought back to earth by the bursts of international capital flight from emerging markets, domestic and foreign direct investment has remained robust (*Business Central Europe*, April 1997-April 1999; EBRD 1994, 26–27; EBRD 1997, 173–175; EBRD 1998, 170–171, 217; Frydman et al. 1997).

Explanatory Factors

Hungary's economic structure was among the most advanced in the communist world, though somewhat less so than that of the Czech region of

Czechoslovakia. Agriculture formed a relatively small share of output and employment, and industry had a significant specialization in relatively capital-intensive sectors such as electronics, machinery, transport equipment, and chemicals. Moreover, late-communist market socialism experiments gave many firms valuable management expertise and experience competing in foreign markets. Organized labor encompasses about one-third of the workforce and is particularly strong in the public sector (EIU 1997; OECD 1997, 127; World Bank 1996, 175, 214–215; World Bank 1997, 220–221, 236–237; World Bank 1999, 192–193, 212–213).

The postcommunist unicameral legislature is elected approximately equally by PR and by single-member districts. The presidency is a weak and largely ceremonial post. The Hungarian party system is dominated by a loose center-right with both Christian Democratic and more socially and economically liberal factions, and by the reformed communist Socialist Party on the center-left. The center-right has been more organizationally weak and changing, partially due to relatively weak and indecisive leadership, and partially due to a relatively small Christian Democratic constituency. There is also a strong socially liberal, economically welfarist center party—the Free Democrats—founded by communist-era dissident intellectuals. Compared to the Polish party system, the Hungarian spectrum is further to the left on both economic and social issues. Moreover, the Free Democrats are doctrinally closer to the Socialists than to the center-right, a notable contrast with Poland's Democratic Union/Freedom Union. While leadership has been weak on the right, the Hungarian Socialists have until recently been ably led by Gyula Horn, a moderate, pragmatic, and statesmanlike figure much like Poland's Kwasniewski.

Hungary's sense of national greatness is rooted in its ethno-linguistic distinctiveness, in its mythic barbarian-warrior past, and more recently in its co-dominant position within the Austro-Hungarian Empire. Hungarians have been aggrieved by the post–World War territorial losses that left huge numbers of their kin under Romanian, Czechoslovakian, and Yugoslavian rule. They are keenly aware of their precommunist political, economic, and cultural achievements, and they feel themselves to be an elite people amid the Slavic sea of Eastern Europe. Hungary famously challenged Soviet rule in 1956, suffering a brutal invasion and repression. On the other hand, the development of the Hungarian party system reflects the relatively liberal, economically reformist character of the post-1956 period. Like similarly liberal Slovenia, Hungary did not develop a monolithic nationalist popular front to slay a relatively orthodox communist party. The Hungarian communists cautiously but actively promoted the demise of the Soviet system in east-central Europe in 1988–1999. Moreover, most Hungarians felt that they had already come a long way along the road to a market economy and initially did not feel the same urgent need for a massive structural transformation that was felt in Poland and the Czech Republic.

Explanation of Political Outcomes and Economic Policy Developments

Despite the early organization of the centrist Free Democrats, the more strongly anticommunist Hungarian Democratic Forum (MDF) and allied center-right parties handily won the March-April 1990 elections. Although the MDF implemented serious market reform policies, its leader, Jozsef Antall, publicly emphasized compromise. Although this may have been in tune with public sentiment, it did not adequately prepare the public for the inevitable deep transitional downturn. It also facilitated excessively expansionist fiscal policies and selective subsidies and soft credits that threatened the viability of the recovery in 1993–1994. The Socialists duly won the May 1994 elections, initially adopting similar economic policies. But by early 1995, growth was stagnating and an unsustainably large current account deficit had developed. In March 1995, Horn's Socialists bit the bullet. They imposed fiscal austerity and decisively ended soft lending by rapidly selling off the commercial banks to conservative foreigners. After two years of difficult restructuring, the current account and debt burden had improved dramatically, and GDP growth accelerated to a 4–5 percent annual pace. Tired Hungarians nevertheless ejected the Socialists in favor of Viktor Orban's Young Democrats (Fidesz) in the May 1998 elections. After Antall's 1993 death and the MDF's disastrous 1994 election performance, Fidesz ultimately emerged as the newly dominant center-right party. Much as the Socialists initially continued the MDF's fiscal and structural policies until crisis impended in 1995, Fidesz has continued the Socialists' fiscal and structural policies initiated in 1995. The Hungarian party system continues to be ideologically moderate. Its electorate and parties are driven by a consensus on convergence to Western European political and economic norms, but one pursued through pragmatic responses to opportunities and obstacles instead of inspiring and controversial crusades (East and Pontin 1997, chap. 3; Pittaway and Swain 1994; Tokes 1997).

The unquestioned westward orientation of Hungary's political spectrum is rooted in the Hungarian self-image of an advanced nation seeking its place within the Western European family. On the other hand, the division, moderation, and relative weakness of the center-right are rooted in the relatively liberal and reformist character of the post-1956 communist regime. If the moderate reformist consensus contributed to indecisive leadership during the first center-right postcommunist government, it also contributed to the Socialists' realistic and decisive response to economic deterioration in 1993–1995. The specific form taken by democratic political institutions does not appear to have had a significant impact on these outcomes.

THE CZECH REPUBLIC

Economic Policy

As in Poland and Hungary, early market reform policies in the Czech Republic involved a rapid and nearly complete liberalization of prices and trade, along with macroeconomic stabilization. Unlike Poland and Hungary, foreign debt was very low, and fiscal deficits were kept virtually nonexistent. From 1991 until May 1997 the koruna was fixed against a basket of foreign currencies. There was a rapid recovery from the transitional output shock, with accelerating growth in 1993–1995. Unemployment remained at remarkably low 3–4 percent levels. Rising wages and foreign investment inflows helped fuel a rapid current account deterioration in 1996, leading to a run on the koruna and a devaluation of approximately 15 percent. Restructuring policies have since produced a recession and a marked improvement in the current account. In an effort to prevent a repetition of the previous overvaluation, the koruna has been floated and at times purposefully held down by interest rate cuts.

The major flaws in the initial market reform program were in the related areas of banking sector regulation and corporate governance. Medium and large enterprise privatization occurred mostly through two mass voucher distributions. Most shares were put under the management of investment and privatization funds (IPFs), usually owned by or affiliated with the large commercial banks. Large shareholdings also continued to be owned by the government-controlled National Property Fund. Government policy was to use commercial bank lending to organize restructuring and consolidation of larger enterprises. The objective was to make the firms competitive without unduly sacrificing the large preexisting capital stock, and without selling the "crown jewels" to foreigners at bargain basement prices. Unfortunately, the commercial banks had neither the expertise nor the political will to force difficult reorganizations. Instead, the large loans they extended all too often delayed restructuring until it became clear that they could not be repaid. Meanwhile, firms lacked dominant shareholders outside the bank-related IPFs and did not need to go to outsiders for financing. This was exacerbated by weak legal protection for minority shareholders, as well as poor transparency and low levels of liquidity in the equity market. The situation was a recipe for pie-in-the-sky corporate empire building, and for corrupt asset stripping and misuse of funds, depending on management proclivities and the prominence of the given firm.

Again, all of this reflected the fact that the state maintained control over the large commercial banks. They consciously promoted their use by political appointees to pursue visions of a "German model." This resulted in heavy lending to enterprises (67.9 percent of GDP in 1994, falling to 56.0 percent in 1997), large bad loan portfolios (bank recapitalizations have already cost 18 percent of GDP and it is estimated that another 10 percent will have to be spent), and delayed restructuring. The Skoda auto works, the great success story of Czech industry, was one of the few large enterprises sold early on to a foreign investor—in this case Volkswagen. More typical are the stories of "crown jewels" such as the heavy engineering firm Skoda-Plzen, the heavy transport equipment maker CKD, and the chemical maker Chemapol, whose asset bases and credit lines were wasted on ambitious diversification efforts. If they had been sold to large Western multinationals, they would have been focused on their most viable core operations and used as export bases. Instead, direct foreign investment and foreign portfolio investment were discouraged by lack of opportunities and low transparency. The 1997 run on the koruna finally put an end to the open credit lines, forcing unemployment over 8 percent. Fiscal austerity, plans to follow Hungary in selling the big commercial banks to foreigners, and efforts to protect minority shareholders and bring greater transparency and liquidity to equity markets have only gradually restored investor confidence. Resistance to selling the "jewels" to foreigners persists, and with it lingering suspicions that the reforms may well be compromised. Thus the international financial crisis has further weakened an already chronically depressed stock market and has been matched by sluggish domestic and direct foreign investment (*Business Central Europe*, April 1997–April 1999; EBRD 1994, 22–23; EBRD 1997, 164–166; EBRD 1998, 182–183, 213; Frydman et al. 1997).

Explanatory Factors

The Czech part of late-communist Czechoslovakia had an unusually large specialization in industry. This industry was the most capital-intensive in the postcommunist world, specialized in chemicals, machinery, heavy transportation equipment (trucks, rail equipment, trams), and heavy engineering. Unlike most communist-era capital-intensive investment, this specialization was broadly consistent with Czech comparative advantage and was largely viable with suitable structural reforms. On the other hand, the agricultural sector was even smaller than that of Hungary. In terms of purchasing power parity indices, the Czech region was far wealthier than Hungary (not to speak of Poland). Among postcommunist countries it was rivaled only by tiny Slovenia. Organized labor has been weak, even relative to Hungary (EIU 1995; OECD 1997, 127; World Bank 1996, 175, 214–215; World Bank 1997, 220–221, 236–237; World Bank 1999, 192–193, 212–213).

The old Czechoslovak state had two federal chambers and two separate republic (Czech and Slovak) chambers. The split into two separate states occurred in January 1993, whereupon the old Czech republic chamber became the legislature of the new Czech Republic. Elections to all of these legislatures have been by PR. In October 1995, a Senate was added, elected by single-member districts. The presidency is weak and mostly ceremonial. The Czech party system has been strongly right leaning. The popular front Civic Forum's dominant successor was Vaclav Klaus's Civic Democratic Party (ODS), which enunciated a remarkably pure free market ideology of the West German social-market type. The neo-orthodox Czech Communist Party has been slow to reform itself in line with the electorate and thus has been supplanted as the dominant left party by Milos Zeman's moderate Social Democrats. The charismatic Klaus has consistently overshadowed the rest of the country's political leaders.

Czech national identity is rooted in the long-standing economic achievements and political travails of Bohemia and Moravia. In the interwar period, independence was coupled with resilient democracy and economic performance. Like Hungarians, Czechs feel themselves to be a more advanced people than other Eastern European ethnic groups, including the Slovaks. During the communist period, the famous Prague Spring effort to democratize and break out of the Soviet sphere was brutally repressed.

Explanation of Political Outcomes and Economic Policy Developments

After the popular front Civic Forum and its Slovak sister's victory in the June 1990 elections, Klaus spearheaded the ambitious Czechoslovak economic reforms. Again, the most unusual features were the mass voucher privatization and the commercial bank-led, state-backed industrial policy. The apparent success of these policies in holding down unemployment was a factor in the June 1992 election victory of Klaus's ODS, vis-à-vis the rest of the center-right as well as the center-left, and in Czech resistance to Slovak nationalist demands to water down the economic reforms. In 1995, a surge of foreign investment exacerbated the effects of slow restructuring and rapidly rising wages, producing a severe current account deterioration. Fiscal tightening and belated moves toward a Hungarian-style bank restructuring in 1996 were insufficient to prevent the May 1997 koruna devaluation. A fresh deepening of fiscal tightening and structural reform efforts in June did not markedly improve the situation, largely because Klaus's continued defense of his policies called into question the credibility of the reform efforts. A weakened Klaus was forced to resign over a campaign finance scandal in November. Central bank head Tosovsky led a government of experts in the run-up to the June 1998 elections. Remarkably, Klaus's ODS did just as well as Zeman's Social Democrats, and smaller center-right parties continued to hold the balance of power. Rather than provide an opening for his regicidal rivals on the right, Klaus decided to support a minority Social Democratic government. Zeman's policies have differed little from the crisis-era Klaus policies. Zeman has extracted a small increase in the fiscal deficit, but he has been indecisive about pushing forward planned commercial bank privatizations or forcing the distress sale and breakup of Czech national champions such as Skoda-Plzen and Chemapol (Bugge 1997; *Business Central Europe,* April 1997–April 1999; East and Pontin 1997, 76–109; Olson 1997).

Czechs strongly believed that communism prevented them from having freedom and a standard of living comparable to that of Austrians or West Germans, and they were resolved to adopt the political and economic institutions they believed were necessary to erase these shortfalls. National identity was strongly oriented toward market democracy. Czech democracy had already proven itself in the interwar period, and Czech economic excellence had long been established. Of course, it is also true that the favorable economic preconditions—the small agricultural sector and sophisticated industrial sector—made for weak concentrated interest groups opposed to reform. Note that the advanced economic heritage feeds in at both levels, making for weaker concentrated interest groups opposed to reform and raising the expectations and the resolve of dispersed interest groups for the process of long-term structural reform efforts. The independent importance of the national identity factor is indicated not only by more purely politically motivated reformist identities such as those of Poland and the Baltic States but also by the Czech electorate's patient reaction to the May 1997 crisis and the subsequent recession. By being subject to subsidies and poor management for so long, Czech industry lost much of its early lead and became more resistant to structural reform than it was in the early postcommunist period. Even among dispersed interest groups, Klaus's policy errors would have been expected to produce a leftward shift—even if only in support of a moderate left party such as the Social Democrats. Yet, relative to the outcome of the June 1992 elections, the Czech electorate did not budge an inch leftward. It remained convinced of the rightness of the initial direction of market reform, albeit somewhat confused about what had gone wrong and what needed to be done to rectify the situation. This confusion has been exacerbated by Klaus's refusal to admit his errors. His continued leadership may have played a secondary role in steeling the electorate's ideological convictions, but it is difficult to accept that such leadership alone could account for such remarkable political stability in the face of economic turbulence. Again, there is little evidence that the specific form of democratic political institutions had a large impact on the course of economic policy making. Despite having to form coalition governments, Klaus was able to control most specifics of the economic policy-making agenda until recently. Even a more powerful and independent presidency would probably at most have affected only less central, primarily fiscal components of his reform package.

CONCLUSION

It has been argued that reformist national identities were generated by collective memories of precommunist "golden pasts," reinforced by traditions of collective resistance against alien rule and repression. These reformist national identities singled out democratic political institutions and market economic institutions because—in the present historical period and relative to rival, more authoritarian and interventionist models—these offered the most plausible means of achieving the collective goals of national autonomy, security, and cultural and economic revival. The resulting reformist consensus in favor of an irreversible break with the communist past singled out a rapid transition to a market economy as a necessary condition—alongside political democratization and a westward geopolitical and economic reorientation. Therefore it has also functioned as a reliable error-

correction mechanism, as misconceived components of the initial economic reform package began to undermine the success of the larger economic transition.

Thus all three countries chose "shock therapy" transition policies. Center-left
as well as center-right parties and governments accepted the general goal of rapid
market transition. Where flawed banking sector and other policies threatened the
success of the overall transition, governments of both left and right—the Hungarian socialist government of Horn, the Czech ODS government of Klaus, the
Czech caretaker government of Tosovsky, and the Czech Social Democratic government of Zeman—initiated or persisted with important corrective policies
rather than use the difficulties to try to overturn the overall reformist program. It
must be emphasized that this ideological consensus operated not only through periodic voting constraints but also as a self-imposed constraint on elites in power.
There is no evidence in any of the three countries of parties or leaders appealing
to public opinion in order to take power, only to use this power to adopt economic
policies sharply at variance with what was promised. On the contrary, ideological principles have dominated intraparty leadership selection, interparty political
competition, and the policy-making process. The reformist ideological consensus
has thus acted as a constraint on institutional and leadership peculiarities that
might otherwise have seriously impeded and compromised market reform efforts.

The reformist political consensus has been a vital anchor in the stormy sea of
international financial markets in 1997–1999. By virtually ruling out both a fundamental backlash against market reform and any serious political instability or
violence, and by supporting relatively prompt and reliable corrective policies, it
has placed a high floor under downside economic risk. Despite some volatility in
portfolio investment, enduring confidence of domestic investors and international
direct investors has kept economies buoyant where competitiveness has been improving (Poland and Hungary), and relatively resilient where competitiveness has
shown some deterioration (the Czech Republic).

The recent collapse of the communist system and the reformism of national
identities have made Polish, Hungarian, and Czech economic policy choices highly
convergent and "forward looking," that is, based on consensus theoretical ideals as
opposed to specific past performances of rival parties and leaders. This might be
expected to change as memories of the "heroic" early postcommunist period fade
and as a reasonably stable and adequately performing successor regime takes hold.
On the other hand, there is little evidence that this has happened yet. In the second
and third rounds of postcommunist elections, the simple backward-looking electoral rule of advanced industrial democracies—that growth leads to reelection and
recession doesn't—has been violated in seven of the eight cases.[11] Decisively large
numbers of voters have continued to look ahead in an effort to guard their cher-
ished national ideals instead of focusing more exclusively on how their own short-
term prospects have been developing in the recent past. This has tended to keep
like-minded leaders in control of the main parties competing for power.

NOTES

1. For example, Przeworski (1991) predicted that large transitional recessions would render ambitious market reforms politically infeasible.

2. Along with Yugoslavia, Poland was unique in Eastern Europe and the former Soviet Union in having a mostly smallholding, uncollectivized agriculture. Polish smallholders were more self-sufficient and less heavily subsidized than the Polish collective farms. There is a corresponding voting difference. Regions dominated by smallholders have been much more likely to vote for Solidarity and its successor parties (Raciborski 1996).

3. That such goals were best served by market democracy is of course to a large extent historically contingent. During the last interwar "rebirth" of these countries, the international economic, military, and even ideological environments were much less hospitable to market democracy.

4. These variations were possible largely because in 1989–1991 there was as yet no optimal policy consensus in these areas in the Western economics profession, among Western governments, and among international financial organizations such as the IMF and World Bank.

5. Particular forms of democratic political institutions arguably had more independent influence on governmental and policy outcomes where postcommunist electorates were more indecisive and impatient, as, for example, in Bulgaria, Romania, and Russia.

6. Hellman (1998) has argued that democracy per se has produced more ambitious market reforms in the postcommunist countries. The argument here is that reformist national identities strongly influenced adoption of both democratic political institutions and ambitious and committed market reforms.

7 Most notable was the June 1997 listing of the National Investment Funds, which hold controlling stakes in a large number of medium and large firms via a mass voucher privatization scheme.

8. At around 10 percent of exports at the time of the Russian crisis, Poland was two to three times more dependent on the Russian market than were Hungary and the Czech Republic.

9. One such sector, shipbuilding, was the birthplace of Solidarity.

10. The current account deficit fell from 9.4 percent of GDP in 1994 to 2.2 percent in 1997, and external debt fell from 46 percent of GDP in 1994 to 25 percent in 1997.

11. With economies deteriorating, incumbent center-right governments won elections in Poland in October 1991, in Czechoslovakia in June 1992, and in the Czech Republic in June 1998. With economies improving, incumbent governments lost elections in Poland in September 1993 and September 1997, and in Hungary in May 1994 and May 1998. If we do not count the September 1993 Polish election as a loss (because the center-left won a majority of seats without winning a majority of votes), that makes seven of eight election outcomes in defiance of the "normal" pattern.

243- 63

14

Russia: Entrenched Elites Ride Out the Crisis

Peter Rutland

052133
F32 P21
P34
G20 G10

The Southeast Asian crisis of 1997 had a delayed but substantial impact on Russia, triggering a devaluation and debt default in August 1998. This event showed that Russia had come a long way from its Soviet past and was now an integral part of the global capitalist economy. It also confirmed that integration is a risky business, bringing increased exposure to fluctuations in world commodity and capital markets.

The crisis triggered much angst among Western governments, which woke up to the fact that all was not well with the Russian transition. But once the dust had settled, the impact of the crisis on Russia's political and economic institutions was surprisingly muted. It caused some reshuffling within the political and financial elites but did not change the basic trajectory of developments in the country since 1991.

Post-Soviet Russia has an authoritarian political system with formal democratic institutions, very strong presidential leadership, a fragmented party system, and a weak ideological framework. The economic policy pursued since 1991 has been generally forward looking, but usually with a very short time horizon and often driven by the venal interests of a narrow circle of decision makers and their cronies. Surprisingly radical steps were taken in the direction of market reform in chaotic 1992, but since then progress toward further liberalization has been slow and episodic. The relatively weak impetus for a return to greater state intervention imparted by the August 1998 crisis was deflected with relative ease by the strong presidency.

INTRODUCTION: CONCENTRATED AND DISPERSED INTEREST
GROUPS AND POLITICAL INSTITUTIONS

The key contours of Russian political economy were shaped long before 1998. The crisis merely served to highlight the system's existing features. The August crisis was the most serious since the collapse of the ruble in October 1994 ("Black Tuesday") but did not presage any fundamental systemic changes.

Politically, Boris Yeltsin had succeeded in creating a powerful presidential system of rule by the end of 1993. This gave the government a high degree of autonomy from political and economic groups in society, enabling it to ride out crises with a high degree of impunity. Some individual leaders were jettisoned, but the real levers of power did not change hands.

The numerous subsidy-seeking industrial and farm lobbies inherited from the Soviet system had already been bludgeoned into political powerlessness by the twin shocks of Soviet collapse in December 1991 and price liberalization in January 1992. Federal revenues fell to 10 percent of GDP, and these lobbies were scrambling for a share of a vanishing pie. Soft bank credits bought them some time in 1992–1993, but tightening control over the money supply from 1994 left them high and dry.

The key new interests were the private banking groups that emerged out of the wreckage of the Soviet economy and became major players in Yeltsin's Russia. Although they thrived under market reform, they continued to depend on state favors. They grew rich from sweetheart deals as state assets were privatized, and from the granting of beneficial licenses to import highly taxed goods like alcohol and tobacco. The big money was made through the export of metals, oil, and gas (with access to the state-owned export pipelines granted through a nontransparent quota system). The new bankers built up media empires that they used to help Yeltsin win reelection in 1996.

The August crisis slowed the onward march of the oligarchs and strengthened the hand of the state apparatus (especially the security structures, that is, the men with guns). Many of the financial oligarchs were weakened or ruined by the debt default and devaluation, while the energy lobby suffered from falling oil prices in the wake of the Asian crisis. However, oil prices soon rebounded, and the oligarchs likewise showed considerable staying power, rallying forces in the December 1999 parliamentary election behind new prime minister Vladimir Putin.

In a pluralist democracy, the financial oligarchs would have faced a more serious political challenge from the Soviet-era industrial and agricultural interests, whose workers made up a large share of the electorate. However, Yeltsin's superpresidential system and the tight control over the mass media prevented these antimarket social interests from coalescing at the ballot box.

Ideological factors should also be taken into account, especially among dispersed interest groups such as the urban middle classes and the expanding number of urban poor. People were voting not just on the basis of their economic interests but also in keeping with their perceptions of what kind of political system they wanted to see in Russia. The majority of Russians wanted to live in a forward-looking, Western-style society, rather than try to turn the clock back to the Soviet years.

The August crisis caused an inflationary surge and a steep decline in living standards, on the order of 20 percent.[1] Yet this did not cause an upsurge of popular protest. There are two main reasons for this. One is that repeated crises and dashed hopes over the previous decade had numbed popular capacity for mobilization. If the August storm cloud had burst out of a clear sky, people would have run for cover. Having been drenched by daily downpours for a decade, the average Russian hardly bothered to open his or her umbrella. The other reason was that the main alternative policy regime involved a sharp turn back to a Soviet past that remained broadly discredited—both politically and economically—among dispersed interest groups.

The political will for a limited shift to a more centrist or statist economic policy was clearly present in Russian society—and certainly in the Russian Parliament—in the immediate aftermath of August. But given the nature of Yeltsin's superpresidential regime, the Kremlin was able to keep proposals for constitutional reform and greater economic intervention at arm's length. It simply sat out the postcrisis months with only modest course corrections in economic policy.

In the next section I briefly review post-Soviet Russia's initial political and economic conditions and then explain how Yeltsin's early political decisions produced a strong presidency, compromised market reforms, and created a corrupt new elite interested in perpetuating these compromises. In subsequent sections I describe the compromised reforms and show how they fed into the August 1998 economic crisis. Yet this crisis brought little change to economic policy or political institutions. In the concluding section I show that this was due to a combination of significant residual opposition to a return to the Soviet past, fortified behind the institutional defenses of the strong presidency.

THE SOVIET LEGACY: DISPERSED AND CONCENTRATED INTEREST GROUP PREFERENCES

The Ideological Politics of Post-Soviet Russia

By 1989, four years of abortive reform under the leadership of Mikhail Gorbachev had wrecked the control systems of the socialist economy without creating any effective new mechanism in its place. Russia saw open worker unrest for the first time in eighty years, as coal miners struck to protest empty store shelves. Nationalist unrest in the Baltic and Caucasus Republics was another headache for Gorbachev. The country was held together by massive foreign loans (amounting

to $80 billion) while Gorbachev pleased Western lenders by allowing the disso-
lution of the Soviet empire in Central and Eastern Europe. The Soviet budget collapsed as republic governments refused to pay taxes to the federal center. The
year 1991 saw the collapse of not only the centrally planned economy but also the
communist political system and the multinational empire it sustained. Russia
faced a triple transition—to market, to democracy, and to nation-state.

Suddenly, the leaders of the fifteen republics of the Soviet Union found
themselves at the head of sovereign states, facing the daunting task of building new political and economic systems from scratch. Most of them seized
upon at least the idea of market reform: they had lost their ability to manage
their economies and had little choice but to embrace the market system being
urged on them by the West.[2] Note, incidentally, that choosing a national leader
was not an immediate problem: the republic leaders who were already in
power when the Soviet Union collapsed stayed on as presidents of the newly
independent states. They included Boris Yeltsin, who was elected president of
the Russian Federation in June 1991.

The primary utility of market reform in 1991 was more political than economic. It provided a sense of purpose and direction. It gave the governments a
policy agenda to follow, as well as a rhetoric of legitimation with which to appeal
to their citizens for support. It also opened the door to potentially billions of dollars of Western aid, loans, and investment. Behind the rhetoric of a brighter future for all, marketization also gave the more self-serving incumbent elites a
chance to enrich themselves.

The main claim to legitimacy of the new postsocialist regimes in Eastern
Europe was the reclaiming of a suppressed national independence and identity.
The situation in Russia was complicated because Russian national identity was
closely intertwined with patriotic feelings for the now deceased Soviet state.
In 1990–1991 Boris Yeltsin and the democrats started using the symbols of
Russian nationalism against Gorbachev and the Soviet state. After 1991 the
Communist Party of the Russian Federation tried to use Russian nationalism
mixed with nostalgia for the Soviet Union to mobilize opposition to Yeltsin's
reforms. However, Yeltsin was the man who had created the new sovereign
Russian state by challenging the Soviet leadership. In contrast to the communists' Soviet nostalgia, Yeltsin argued that he was building a forward-looking
Russia, one that would join the international community of nations as a partner of the United States and as a democratic and capitalist country. Hence market reform was particularly important to Yeltsin's political image. The political advantages of a forward-looking economic strategy sustained Yeltsin in
power despite the fact that GDP fell for seven straight years and reform produced few concrete benefits for the average Russian. Vladimir Lenin's dictum
that "politics is the ABC of economics" seems to hold true also for the transition from socialism to capitalism.

The Specificity of the Soviet Economy and the Structure Of Concentrated Interest Groups

The Soviet economy of 1991 differed structurally from any other on the planet. For seventy-five years the Soviet economy had been built up according to the logic of central planning, with its objectives of national security and social transformation. It was heavily militarized, with from 25 to 40 percent of industry devoted to military production. Industrial location was based on the strategic decisions of central planners with scant regard to production costs. What would happen when such an economy was exposed to the forces of supply and demand? The concentrated interest groups opposed to market reform were unusually large and the market transition was an unusually difficult one.

Russia's vast oil and gas reserves gave Moscow options that most other post-socialist states did not possess. Energy exports generated $40–50 billion a year, accounting for more than half of Russia's export earnings and a quarter of federal revenues. This energy wealth might have been used to cushion the shock of transition by providing for a more generous social safety net and much needed infrastructure and a lower tax burden. But for political reasons it turned out to have a strongly negative impact. It encouraged myopic, rent-seeking behavior by Russian elites and discouraged them from embracing full-blown economic liberalization. They kept control of energy reserves out of the hands of foreign investors— not realizing that Western companies would simply look elsewhere (Nigeria, Venezuela, etc.) rather than accept the terms the Kremlin was prepared to offer. Inside Russia, the state gas monopoly, Gazprom, used export revenues to subsidize domestic producers and consumers, creating a mini–planned economy. Gazprom used its subsidized deliveries as an excuse to avoid paying taxes and as an opportunity to build political alliances with regional elites.

In many countries, the concentration of wealth that comes with oil has bolstered authoritarian regimes and corrupt elites, and has stymied the development of competitive markets and civil societies. Post-1991 Russia fits this pattern. This might have been prevented or minimized by more decisive and forward-looking early leadership, especially since Russia inherited a more developed and diverse economy than is typical of petro-states. But it was not to be.

THE POLITICAL AND INSTITUTIONAL CONTEXT FOR REFORM, AND ITS EFFECTS ON POLICY AND ELECTORAL OUTCOMES

In Eastern Europe, the democratic political systems that were introduced after 1989 were primarily parliamentary rather than presidential. In most of those countries (including Hungary and the Czech Republic), the presidents are elected indirectly, by the Parliament. Even where the presidents are directly elected (as in Poland and Croatia), they have only limited powers (to delay legislation, to call for referenda, and in some cases to dissolve Parliament). Governments are formed by the parties that win parliamentary elections, and they fall when they lose parliamentary support or are defeated in elections. In most countries broad democratic coalitions won the first wave of parliamentary elections in 1990 and set about market reform. There was a broad social consensus on the need to build a democracy and market economy, and there was no sharp polarization between the friends and foes of change. On the contrary, when reformed ex–communist parties won power in Poland and Hungary in elections in 1993 and 1994, they continued the reform programs of their liberal predecessors.

In Russia, the political system evolved in a quite different direction and displayed a lot more continuities with its socialist predecessor than was the case in East Europe (Shevtsova 1999). In the Russian Republic the legislature (Congress of People's Deputies) and executive (President Boris Yeltsin) were elected before the collapse of the Soviet Union (in March 1990 and June 1991, respectively). Yeltsin and the Congress were united in opposition to Soviet President Mikhail Gorbachev and his efforts to hold together the Soviet Union. After the Soviet collapse, Yeltsin and the Congress disagreed over what sort of constitution Russia needed (presidential or parliamentary), and over how fast to push the pace of economic reform.

President Yeltsin moved into the Kremlin, recently vacated by Gorbachev, and his administration swelled to more than 7,000 officials—more than in the old Soviet Communist Party Central Committee. There was no equivalent to this presidential bureaucracy in Eastern Europe. Yeltsin refused to become the leader of a political party and call for a fresh electoral mandate for reform, claiming that as head of state he was "above" party politics. In following years the Russian legislature was treated not as source of laws and a vehicle for democratization but as an annoyance that was to be ignored or avoided wherever possible. Governments and ministers were changed at the president's whim. The central characteristic of Russia's postcommunist political system was a debilitating stalemate between the president and parliament, a deadlock that hampered the government's ability to implement policies to build a functioning market economy and an effective rule of law.

The first major rift between Yeltsin and Congress came in January 1992, when the acting prime minister, liberal economist Yegor Gaidar, initiated ambitious market reforms. Most of the economic liberalization measures had to be introduced by presidential decree—a power that Congress had voted the president on an emergency basis for one year in November 1991. Implementation of reforms was in the hands of bureaucratic institutions that were insulated from parliamentary scrutiny. They were run by cliques operating out of the presidential administration, with minimal legal or public accountability. This environment was fertile ground for corruption. In June 1992 Congress voted into law the voucher privatization program crafted by the energetic young reformer Anatolii Chubais. Chubais watered down the privatization program to accommodate the interests of the state enterprise directors' lobby, allowing workers and managers to buy a controlling block of shares in their own firm. In December 1992, when Yeltsin's emergency presidential powers expired, the Congress refused to renew Gaidar as prime minister. Instead they endorsed Yeltsin's compromise choice, Viktor Chernomyrdin, a bland bureaucrat who had headed the Soviet gas industry.

Yeltsin called a referendum in April 1993 and won a narrow majority in support of his policies. Given the privations of the preceding year, the vote in favor of continued market reform was a triumph of hope over experience. Over the summer of 1993 Yeltsin tried to engineer passage of a new constitution that would grant him broader powers. Congress resisted, and in September 1993 Yeltsin ordered the parliament to disband. This was an act that was beyond his constitutional powers (so he disbanded the Constitutional Court too). The Congress refused to go, and recalcitrant deputies were dislodged by a full-scale army assault on the parliament building—the very White House that Yeltsin had defended against the Soviet hard-liner coup attempt in August 1991.

After the bloody events of October, parliamentary elections were held in December 1993. The voters delivered a rebuke to Yeltsin by voting in a majority of communists and antiliberal nationalists. A simultaneous referendum on the new constitution passed by a narrow majority (amid allegations of vote rigging). It gave more powers to the president, creating in effect a superpresidential system. A new bicameral parliament consisted of the State Duma and the Federation Council (composed of two officials from each of Russia's eighty-nine provinces). The president has the right to nominate the prime minister, subject to Duma approval. If the nominee is rejected three times, the president can dismiss the Duma and call fresh elections—a powerful incentive for the Duma to accept his nominee. The president issues decrees over areas in which no law has been passed and has the power to veto legislation. (The veto can be overridden by a two-thirds majority of each house.)

In the Duma elections in December 1995, the Communist Party emerged as the strongest force and was able to block Yeltsin's legislative initiatives. Each fall, for example, there was a confrontation over the next year's budget. The government proposed spending cuts and a smaller deficit, while the Duma insisted on passing a budget with higher spending. In practice the government simply ignored the budget and held actual spending below the target levels.

At the beginning of 1996, with the economy shrinking for the seventh year in a row and an unresolved war in Chechnya, Yeltsin's popularity ratings were in single digits. And yet in July 1996 Yeltsin returned from political oblivion to win reelection as president over communist challenger Gennadii Zyuganov. His remarkable political recovery was due to a combination of a vigorous anticommunism campaign in the state and privately owned media and lavish pork-barrel spending, helped by a $10.1 billion, three-year loan approved by the IMF in March 1996. The communists could rely on the support of some 25–30 percent of the electorate, but their reactionary policies (the Duma foolishly passed a resolution calling for the restoration of the Soviet Union) lost them the support of centrist voters, especially among the dispersed interest groups of the big cities. Yeltsin's campaign managers painted the election as a stark choice between a communist past and a democratic future. A prominent role was played by the self-styled "seven bankers," magnates such as Boris Berezovskii who had created huge and lucrative business empires out of the Soviet collapse (*Izvestiya,* 5 January 1997). The seven leading oligarchs agreed to pool their financial and media resources to engineer a Yeltsin victory.

Some see the 1996 election as proof that democracy was consolidated in Russia. Others suggest that the election was a travesty of democracy and showed the consolidation of an oligarchic elite who had learned to stay in power through manipulating the rules of the democratic game. It had been assumed that the main barrier to reform would be opposition from groups with a vested interest in the pre-1991 system, such as communist bureaucrats and workers in state-subsidized industries and farms. However, these backward-looking elites were politically disemboweled by the rapid collapse of communism and proved totally unable to defend their interests in the transition economy. The workers in these sectors also proved politically inert despite (or perhaps because of) shattering social changes, a massive fall in living standards, and tremendous uncertainty about their future.

By 1996 it was clear that the main threat to the Russian transition came not from communist reactionaries or irate workers but from some of the very elites who were leading the charge toward the market economy. These elites hijacked the market transition and only tolerated liberalization to the extent that it lined their own pockets (Handelman 1997; Sachs and Pistor 1997). The emergence of the oligarchs slowed the development of other concentrated interest groups with a stronger commitment to genuine market reform. Their antics also discredited the reform cause and hence weakened its dispersed interest group base.

BUILDING A MARKET ECONOMY: COMPROMISED REFORM

In late 1991, with the Soviet Union disintegrating and its economic system in chaos, President Yeltsin decided to adopt the same strategy for rapid market liberalization that had been introduced in Poland in 1990. The strategy—known by its critics as "shock therapy" and more generally as the "Washington consensus"—consisted of a trinity of policies: monetary stabilization, liberalization, and privatization. Most of these policies are sensible and have proved their effectiveness in a variety of circumstances (Williamson 1993; World Bank 1996). In Russia, however, they proved inadequate to the task at hand: building a prosperous market economy out of the ruins of the Soviet system.

Stabilization meant introducing a stable currency and preventing hyperinflation (inflation of more than 50 percent per month). Given a recent past of monetary instability, the easiest way to facilitate this is to make the currency convertible and use the exchange rate as the "nominal anchor" of the stabilization program. Liberalization meant lifting restrictions on business activity, domestic and international. Price controls and subsidies should be ended. Quotas and duties on exports should be eliminated and import tariffs lowered. Free trade would reveal Russia's comparative advantage and draw foreign investment into the sectors with growth potential. Privatization meant the sale of state-owned firms in order to unleash entrepreneurship and create competitive markets (Frydman et al. 1993; Nelson and Kuzes 1994). Subsidies should stop for the remaining state enterprises (the "hard budget constraint") and loss-making firms should be forced into bankruptcy.

The reforms in east-central Europe brought inflation down and GDP growth restarted after a "transition recession" of about two years' duration. Privatization policies varied within Eastern Europe. While Hungary sold many state firms to foreign buyers, Czechoslovakia opted for a crash program of voucher privatization—in which shares were given away to citizens who bid for them with special coupons distributed to all adults at nominal cost. The scheme led to dispersed share ownership and weak corporate governance, creating many opportunities for corruption by unscrupulous entrepreneurs. But it enabled the reformist government of Prime Minister Vaclav Klaus to win reelection in May 1992. Political utility overrode economic efficiency. Russia was to adopt a version of the Czech voucher scheme—with similar results.

The Operation Succeeds, but the Patient Sickens

After 1991 Russia made some remarkable steps in the direction of a market economy, leading many international observers to proclaim that capitalism had taken firm root in Russia (Åslund 1995; Layard and Parker 1996; Shleifer et al. 1995). But inflation fell more slowly than in Eastern Europe, and the transition recession never really ended. The cumulative fall in GDP was greater than 40 percent—higher than during the Great Depression in the United States. Recovery only began in 1997, and then with anemic GDP growth of 0.8 percent.

Liberalization had the most dramatic initial effect. Most price controls were lifted on 2 January 1992, and store shelves quickly filled up. Controls on energy prices continued for several years, and housing and utilities remain price controlled to this day. Trade liberalization led to a flood of imports, which soon accounted for about half of all consumer spending. There was an export boom as producers switched their sales of oil and metals from the ex–Soviet republics to hard-currency markets (Davydov 1998; Tarr and Michalopoulos 1996). Among the disappointments was the slow growth in small businesses and in foreign investment (below $6 billion). Both these failings were rooted in the evils of crime, corruption, and bureaucratic regulation.

Stabilization remained elusive for some years. The ruble was made convertible into dollars, but inflation clocked 1,600 percent in 1992, wiping out people's hard-earned savings. It took three years of political infighting before the government was able to bring the money supply and budget deficit under control, with inflation falling to 130 percent (annual) by the end of 1995. From then on the ruble held its value against the dollar within the corridor announced by the central bank. However, the ruble stabilization was accompanied by the dollarization and demonetization of much of the economy. Many firms resorted to barter, which accounted for more than half of all industrial transactions by 1997. Arrears became a money substitute: arrears in paying suppliers, tax authorities, and workers. The rise of this hidden economy—something not really seen in Eastern Europe—was largely ignored by the international community until 1998. Another disturbing trend was the slump in federal tax revenues, which fell from 25-30 percent of GDP in 1989 to 10–12 percent by 1997, while federal spending was still running at 15–18 percent of GDP.

Privatization was hailed as a major victory for the reformers. Some 70 percent of productive assets were transferred out of state ownership. First, in 1990–1992 many state firms were turned into private corporations at the stroke of a pen, with their shares held by federal and regional governments or other firms. Most of Russia's 2,000 commercial banks were created in this manner, as was the gas monopoly Gazprom. Second, in 1992 citizens were given vouchers to bid for shares in state enterprises. Workers and managers could acquire a majority of the shares in their own firm, which differed from the Czech model. More than 70 percent of firms chose the buyout, and in these cases control was typically concentrated in the directors' hands. Third, privatization through cash sales began in 1994. The government did not want to sell to foreign investors, but Russian buyers lacked capital. So in 1995 the privatization tsar Anatolii Chubais decided to swap shares in a dozen leading oil and metals companies in return for loans from Russian banks. The transactions reeked of corruption: the firms were sold at bargain prices to bidders chosen in advance. The loans-for-shares scheme enabled the Moscow-based banks to take control of some of the major revenue-generating assets of the economy, such as the Norilsk Nickel mine.

On the Brink of Success?

By 1997 the rudiments of a capitalist economy were in place in Russia, and Yeltsin's reelection victory seemed to show that the reform leadership was firmly in control. In spring 1997 Yeltsin tried to restart the reform momentum that had faltered during his electioneering in the first half of 1996 and ill health in the second. He appointed Anatolii Chubais and Boris Nemtsov, the youthful governor of Nizhnii Novgorod, as first deputy prime ministers. They launched a "second liberal revolution."

However, their efforts to cut spending to close the yawning budget deficit were blocked by the barons who controlled the energy industries: they resisted the proposed increases in taxes and utility prices. Meanwhile, the oligarchs vied for control over the remaining spoils in the state sector, such as the telecom company Svyazinvest and the last state-owned oil companies. The reformers also faced a recalcitrant State Duma, which blocked the new laws needed to move forward with market reform: laws to revise the tax system and introduce a new civil code, to allow land sales, and to permit production sharing in the energy sector for foreign investors.

Liberal hopes were raised in March 1998, when Yeltsin fired Viktor Chernomyrdin, premier since December 1992, fearing that he was developing presidential aspirations. Yeltsin replaced him with Sergei Kirienko, a thirty-five-year old political unknown and ally of the liberal Nemtsov. Kirienko was soon overwhelmed by the daunting task of dealing with the delayed aftereffects of the Southeast Asian financial meltdown—and with a domestic financial crisis of Russia's own making.

A HOT AUGUST

During one intense week in August 1998, the shaky edifice of financial stabilization in Russia was shattered. On 17 August, payments on most categories of international and domestic government debt were suspended, and the exchange rate floor was lowered from six to nine rubles to the dollar. Panicked individuals tried to change all their rubles for dollars, and the financial system froze up. Imports plunged and domestic prices surged by 40 percent within a month. By 7 September the ruble had fallen from six to twenty-one to the dollar. The August crisis was caused partly by the contagion effects of the 1997 Asian crisis and partly by policy errors coming from the Russian government. Chief among these were the decision to fix the exchange rate at too high a level and the government's resolve to finance the budget deficit through international borrowing.

An Increasingly Overvalued Ruble

In July 1995 the Russian government committed itself to maintaining the ruble within a "corridor" of 4,300–4,900 rubles to the dollar.[3] Inflation ran at 130 percent in 1995. Even after the switch to a more flexible "inclined corridor" in July 1996, the ruble appreciated against the dollar by 30 percent in real terms. But tighter monetary policy pushed inflation down to 22 percent in 1996 and 11 percent in 1997.

All told, this put the exchange rate at a rather high level—50 percent of the dollar purchasing power parity (PPP), rising to 70 percent of PPP by 1998 (Popov 1998). (In contrast the Chinese yuan is set at about 20 percent of PPP.) The "strong" ruble lowered the cost of imports and fueled the emergence of a consumer middle class. But it priced Russian manufacturers out of export markets and exposed them to fierce import competition. Russia was not competitive in finished goods like autos at any price. But her semifinished industries such as steel, paper, and chemicals were potentially competitive.

The IMF thought that the exchange rate was defensible, given that Russia was running a current account surplus of about $15 billion each year, thanks to its oil and gas earnings. The ratios of external debt to GDP and of annual repayments to export earnings (each around 15–25 percent) were also manageable. However, signs of trouble began to appear even before the Asian crisis broke. In July 1997, for the first time in a decade, Russia's current account slipped into deficit, due to a leveling off in export earnings. Some economists, not to mention exporters, issued increasingly strident calls for a devaluation of the ruble.

Neither a Borrower nor a Lender Be

The second error that led to the August crash was the 1995 decision to finance the federal deficit through borrowing—at the urging of the IMF, which extolled the virtues of "non-inflationary deficit financing" over printing more money (Treisman 1998). But by 1997 the federal government was collecting a mere 10 percent of GDP in taxes while spending about 15 percent of GDP. The Achilles' heel of Russia's "crony capitalism" was tax collection. Liberalization made it easier for firms to hide earnings from the tax man—especially export earnings. As a result, even after monetary stabilization was achieved, fiscal balance remained elusive. The "fat" had already been cut from the budget—procurement of new arms had dropped to almost zero, for example—so spending could only be cut through delaying payments in federally funded wages and social benefits. This was politically risky, since the recipients had the ability to vote and to protest.

The deficit was financed through the sale of treasury bills (in Russian called GKOs). About half of GKOs were bought by foreigners, attracted by the high rates of return. GKO nominal rates averaged 63 percent in 1996, falling to a low of 26 percent in mid-1997. There was concern at the mounting pile of GKO debt, which reached 50 percent of GDP. Tax collection had still not improved, so new GKOs were issued to pay off previous bonds, in what critics called a "pyramid scheme."

The Impact of the Asian Crisis

The effects of the Asian financial meltdown on Russia were twofold. First, it caused a flight from emerging markets (including Russia) by international investors. Partly this was driven by fear and partly by the desire to cash out gains in Russia to compensate for losses in Southeast Asia. Second, the global recession that followed the Asian crisis caused a slump in commodity prices. Oil fell from $18 a barrel in December 1997 to $11 a barrel by the end of 1998. This was a severe blow to Russia, which relied on oil for nearly half its export earnings.

Each $1 per barrel fall in the oil price cost the government an estimated $1 billion in lost revenue (out of annual receipts of $30 billion).

Increasing uncertainty caused GKO rates to rise. By June the stock of GKOs was about $40 billion, of which half were held by foreigners or by Russian banks—for the latter, typically with money borrowed abroad. Interest payments accounted for 30 percent of federal expenditure, and the government found it hard to sell GKOs even at rates in excess of 100 percent. In July 1998, to reduce exposure to a possible ruble devaluation, the government converted $6.4 billion of GKOs into Eurobonds at 15 percent interest, denominated in dollars. However, that still left $11 billion of GKOs falling due by the end of September.

Fearful that a ruble devaluation would cause panic, the IMF approved a $22.6 billion aid package on 20 July, including $4.8 billion in cash. The IMF insisted on emergency spending cuts and tax increases to bring the deficit below 3 percent of GDP. The IMF loan did not calm investor fears—although it did enable most Western banks to liquidate their GKO holdings. Then came a fateful 13 August letter from George Soros to the *Financial Times,* saying that devaluation was inevitable. The ruble crashed.

AFTER AUGUST: INSTITUTIONALIZED STABILITY

In the wake of the ruble devaluation and debt default alarmists predicted complete economic collapse—hyperinflation, the breakdown of food supplies, the introduction of rationing—which could trigger anything from a fascist coup to the resurrection of communism. Even sober observers foresaw efforts to reintroduce more state planning, including price controls, the suspension of ruble convertibility, and the renationalization of enterprises. In the end, none of these dire scenarios played out. The overall effect of the crisis was to cause a long overdue correction in the ruble exchange rate, to puncture the power of the bank oligarchs, and to cause a revival of demand for Russian products.

The ruble slipped from 6.2 to the dollar on 16 August to 22 to the dollar at year's end, where it stabilized. The financial freeze caused a sudden drop in imports and the effective collapse of the commercial banking sector. Russian banks had borrowed about $10 billion to finance GKO purchases: the crash plunged them into insolvency.[4] People with accounts in commercial banks that folded lost all their deposits. Seventy-five percent of savings were in the state-owned Sberbank, but even those lost three-quarters of their value due to inflation. Most people kept a large proportion of their savings in dollars under the mattress, and these canny savers were unaffected by the crisis.

Imports fell by about half in the four months following August. Consumers switched to domestic products, causing industrial production to rise 10 percent in the fourth quarter. Exports were expected to rise after the deep devaluation of the ruble. Inflation hit 38 percent in September but fell to 4.5 percent in October, 5.7

percent in November, and 11.6 percent in December—showing that Moscow did not turn on the printing presses. Inflation eased to 8.5 percent in January and 3.8 percent in February.

By September 1999 industrial production had risen 18 percent above the September 1998 trough, and 7 percent above the same month in 1997 (*Russian Economic Trends,* October 1999). In the first seven months of 1999 Russia ran a $15.6 billion foreign trade surplus. GDP growth for 1999 was 1.8 percent, the best since the collapse of the Soviet Union. The government was even able to cut the backlog of state wage arrears from 2.1 months average delay in January to 1.3 months in April (*Itar-Tass,* 25 May 1999). The stock exchange (RTS) plunged 85 percent in dollar terms in 1998. But it rose 27 percent in the first two months of 1999 and 85 percent by the year's end, reversing the loss of the previous year.

The crisis altered the relationship between Moscow and the international financial community—ironically strengthening the former at the expense of the latter. The devaluation dispelled the illusion that the IMF's previous policies had been working. The Russian government felt emboldened to reintroduce export tariffs on oil, which they had reluctantly abolished at the IMF's behest in 1996. The debt default bought time and increased Russia's bargaining leverage. Russia had $17 billion in interest and principal falling due on its international loans in 1999: a sum the government would not pay. As Russia was "too big and too nuclear" to allow a formal default, the IMF agreed to a new $4.5 billion loan in June 1999—to be used solely to repay IMF loans falling due in 1999. Negotiations with the Western banks holding frozen GKOs dragged on for months. Some banks settled for the meager terms that Moscow was offering—equivalent to less than 5 cents on the dollar—in the hope of winning more Russian business in the future.

Russia's recovery was helped by the rebound in the world oil price, which doubled by the end of 1999. The new oil export tariff raised $1.5 billion (6 percent of federal revenues) in the first half of 1999, enabling the government to run a primary budget surplus of 3 percent of GDP by the summer of 1999. This was a radical turnaround from the fiscal crisis of the previous summer.

Political Fallout Muted

The August crash forced the resignation of Premier Kirienko and his replacement by former spy chief Yevgenii Primakov. Initial fears of a radical transformation in the political system, with social upheaval and perhaps even an attempted return to communism, proved unfounded. In fact, the overall impact of the crisis was to reinforce rather than undermine Russia's basic political institutions. Some individual careers were damaged or boosted by the crisis, and some financial circles rose while others fell. But the crisis did not open the political system to any significant new political actors. One January 1999 poll indicated that "as a result of the crisis [Russia's] political regime, strange as it may be, not only did not grow weaker but even grew stronger" (Byzov and Petukhov 1999). While 49 percent of poll respondents reported a "very significant" fall in living standards, very few took part in any political activity, and by 47 to 39 percent still supported the idea of a market economy.

After Kirienko resigned, the Duma twice rejected Yeltsin's initial nominee to replace him, Viktor Chernomyrdin. On 11 September Yeltsin appointed Foreign Minister Yevgennii Primakov as prime minister, a choice eagerly approved by the Duma. Primakov appointed some former communist apparatchiki: Viktor Gerashchenko returned to head the central bank and former planning chief Yurii Maslyukov became first deputy prime minister for economic policy. But young reformers still occupied about half the ministries, and there was no reversal in government policies with respect to stabilization and market reform.

The August crisis and subsequent change of government served to reinforce constitutional procedures and weakened President Yeltsin vis-à-vis the parliament. But the communists were not able to exploit the crisis to dislodge Yeltsin from power. The crisis shifted the balance of power within the executive branch, weakening the oligarchs and strengthening the "power ministries" (defense, interior, and Federal Security Service). This seems to be the most lasting political consequence of the August crisis. Not only Primakov but both his successors as premier came from the security organs. Yeltsin fired Primakov in April 1999, fearing that the wily ex-diplomat was becoming too popular and that he might launch anticorruption investigations aimed at Yeltsin's inner circle. Yeltsin replaced Primakov with interior minister Sergei Stepashin. Stepashin in turn was fired in August 1999 for failing to stop Chechen attacks on Dagestan. Yeltsin replaced Stepashin with the forty-seven-year old Vladimir Putin, the head of the Federal Security Service and a fifteen-year KGB veteran who had never been elected to public office. Putin was enthusiastically confirmed by the Duma.

The three postcrisis prime ministers did not reverse the course of economic and domestic policy pursued by their predecessors. The main change came in foreign policy: they hardened their rhetoric toward the United States. But this had more to do with NATO's air war against Yugoslavia than the 1998 financial crisis. Another possible consequence of the resurgence of the security apparatus was the launching of offensive operations against Chechnya in August 1999. However, the immediate cause of the Russian assault was attacks by Chechen militants on neighboring Dagestan.

Public support for Russian military action against the Chechens surged in the wake of the as-yet-unsolved bombing of apartment buildings in three Russian towns in September, which killed roughly 300 citizens sleeping in their beds. Russian forces launched a bombing campaign against the rebel republic, followed by a ground invasion. Vladimir Putin's popularity soared as the public rallied behind the youthful, energetic, and decisive premier, who stood in sharp contrast to the ailing President Yeltsin. A political bloc hastily formed to nominate candidates who supported Putin in the December 1999 parliamentary elections—the Unity bloc—did surprisingly well, finishing in second place behind the communists, with 23 percent of the vote in the national party list race.

Still, it came as a great surprise when Yeltsin announced his resignation as president on 31 December 1999—and nominated Putin as his acting successor. The resignation meant that the presidential elections were brought forward from the scheduled June 2000 to March 2000, and Putin coasted to easy victory in the first round. Putin's first step as acting president was to sign a decree granting immunity from criminal prosecution to Yeltsin and his immediate family, leading cynics to suggest that Putin was beholden to the oligarchs who were keen to protect the Kremlin "family"—and their own fortunes.

The August 1998 crisis also seemed to reinforce the shift in power from federal to regional leaders. This trend began with the declarations of sovereignty by ethnic republics in 1991–1992 and was strengthened once regional governors started to be directly elected (from 1996 on). In summer 1997 the Federation Council—composed of the heads of the executive and legislative branches in each of Russia's eighty-nine provinces—refused to allow Yeltsin to dismiss the controversial governor of Primorskii krai in the far east. Another important victory for regional interests came in April 1998, when parliament passed—over Yeltsin's veto—a law transferring 33 percent of the stock in the electricity monopoly UES to regional governments.

Some governors tried to use the August crisis as an excuse to introduce price controls and restrictions on the export of goods from their region. Within a few weeks such efforts proved unwise and unnecessary. Some regional bosses also managed to renationalize local enterprises that became insolvent after the crisis. The Primakov government tried to reach out to regional leaders: eight governors were invited to join the national cabinet. The new budget for 1999 gave regions the option to levy a regional sales tax of up to 5 percent (Petkov and Shklyar 1999). But these changes were incremental rather than revolutionary, and the decentralizing trend predated the August crisis. Also, in contrast to Primakov, Premier Putin has taken a tougher line on regional autonomy, so some of the post-August gains may be rolled back.

THE RUSSIAN CASE IN COMPARATIVE PERSPECTIVE: INTEREST GROUP COALITIONS AND POLITICAL INSTITUTIONS

There are some interesting parallels between Russia and other countries that have experienced financial crises in the wake of market liberalization, from Asia to Latin America. But Russia also has distinctive features: a strong pro-reform presidency undertaking a historic social transformation and facing weak and disoriented opposition groups.

In Russia the political consensus for reform was weak but positive. The bureaucratic capacity to implement reform was weaker still, leading to much frustration. Surprisingly, many potentially powerful interest groups inherited from the Soviet system failed to prevent the adoption of reform policies—partly because the president felt able to ignore, bribe, or threaten the parliament. However, these interests were often able to block the implementation of reforms. Relatively simple policies that were easy to execute at the national level were successfully adopted, while more complex or demanding reforms failed to take root. Reforms that required doing less of something (e.g., printing money or controlling prices) were easier than reforms that required doing something positive (such as building effective corporate governance or a reliable court system).

One might have expected the Asian crisis to have greater impact in Russia than in Eastern Europe—given that the political consensus for reform was weaker in Russia, and given Russia's dependence on price-sensitive energy exports. Despite the dramatic collapse of the ruble in August 1998, the aftershocks of the Asian crisis did not cause fundamental changes in either the course of economic policy or the exercise of political power in Russia.

Dispersed Interest Group Coalitions

Experience in other countries suggests that the urban middle classes can be a significant factor magnifying the impact of international financial crises. Sharing diverse and dispersed interests—as opposed to the concentrated interests associated with specific industrial lobbies—they are usually politically quiescent and poorly organized. However, an exogenously induced crisis, such as an exchange rate collapse, may trigger their political mobilization. A loyal urban middle class is key to building a successful pro-reform coalition.

In Russia the middle class was politically passive before and after August 1998—despite the fact that the crisis dealt a serious blow to their current living standard and confidence about the future. One of the most puzzling features of Russian politics since 1991 has been the political apathy of the middle class, and of the Russian people in general. Eight years of falling GDP has generated a small number of "winners" from the market transition and a large number of "losers." There are perhaps 1–2 million "New Russians" earning more than $2,000 a month, a precarious middle class of 5–10 million earning more than $500 a month, and a sea of more than 80 million poor making ends meet as best they can, spending more than half of their income on food. Most of the middle class have remained supportive of the market reforms, voting for Yeltsin in the 1993 referendum and 1996 election. The communists are supported by a solid 25 percent of the electorate (White et al. 1997). But other discontented voters are just as wary of the communists as they are of the government. In elections they either abstain or register a protest vote for one of the charismatic nationalists, such as Vladimir Zhirinovsky or Aleksandr Lebed.

The urban poor include many members of the Soviet-era middle class—educated, urban white-collar employees. Their lifetime savings were wiped out by the 1992 hyperinflation, and many of them work in public sectors (education, health, defense) decimated by budget cuts. Despite paying a heavy price in lost income and jobs, these people have not mobilized against market reform. Some would say this shows the persistence of an authoritarian political culture under which the Russian people—and especially the "service classes" employed by the state—dutifully obey their rulers. Optimists would say it is because they have a long-term, forward-looking perspective, similar to the ideology of "national renewal" that helped forge reform coalitions in east-central Europe. Recognizing the failure of the Soviet system, they want to build a better Russia for the sake of their children. Despite the slump, there were some improvements in the life of the middle class since 1991, such as increased personal freedom, freedom to travel abroad, and the right to buy their state-owned apartment at a bargain price. The experience of 1992 planted in the middle classes a deep fear of hyperinflation, something that could help explain their willingness to support Yeltsin's reform policies. The events of August 1998 can also be seen as validation of this inflation-phobia hypothesis, since the postcrash government maintained fairly tight monetary policy.

After the surprises and shocks of the past decade, the Russian people, poor and middle class alike, have developed their own urban survival economy and seem to have been able to ride out the August crisis with relative impunity. Perhaps they have become so disillusioned by the criminalization of the Russian political elite and the artificial polarization between Yeltsin's government and the communist Duma that they have simply abandoned hope in collective, political solutions to their problems.

Concentrated Interest Group Coalitions, Trade Policy, and Subsidies

Foreign trade liberalization was a crucial component of the Russian transition. Since 1992 foreign trade as a proportion of GDP has more than doubled. In 1998, exports stood at around $70 billion and imports $60 billion, making up one-third of GDP. This trade boom was partly due to the dismantling of most barriers to imports and exports, but also to the sharp decline in domestic GDP. A fall in trade with Eastern Europe and the ex-Soviet republics was balanced by an increase in trade with the West.

Export-oriented industries clearly benefited greatly from liberalization of trade—as well as from the slackness of tax collection. Most of the benefits were siphoned off by the corporate elites: few of the proceeds from exports found their way back to the communities that produced them. For example, even the oil sector was not immune to the arrears in wage payments that plagued Russian industry after 1994. So it is hard to find evidence of broad concentrated interest group coalitions based around export industries.

Restrictions on imports were also radically reduced, with the average tariff barrier falling to around 12–15 percent by 1994—relatively low by international standards. Russian producers were hurt by the opening to imports, which were more competitive in terms of quality, price, and general attractiveness. This applied to all sorts of goods, from food to tractors to airplanes. Just about the only sector able through political lobbying to maintain high tariff barriers was automobiles, where tariffs stayed at the 40–50 percent level even until 1999. Domestic auto production maintained its 1991 level, although truck sales fell by two-thirds as their mainstay clients (farmers and the army) ran out of cash.

Despite suffering from trade liberalization, these domestic manufacturers were unable to mobilize politically to reverse the policy. This is testimony to the centralized, authoritarian character of the post-1991 political system and the closed nature of the policy-making elites. The industrialists were still able to exert influence at the regional level, but the trade and exchange rate regime was a nationally determined policy.

Most of the politically tough issues regarding trade liberalization had been settled long before the August crisis. One puzzle is why the exporters were not more successful in pushing for an earlier devaluation of the ruble instead of waiting for the crisis to force this change. It seems that monetary policy was insulated from the wealthy and powerful energy lobby. It was jealously guarded by the autonomous central bank and Finance Ministry, which listened more to the IMF than to any domestic actors. These financial agencies lost some autonomy after August, having been held responsible for the mismanagement that brought about the crisis.

The entire Soviet economy was built around the principle of state subsidies, creating a gigantic, nationwide constituency for handouts after 1991. The very fact that there were so many claimants made it easier for the government to say no: the cupboard really was bare. It was cold turkey for the military-industry complex, which accounted for about 25 percent of the Soviet-era economy. State orders for their products fell by 90 percent. True, many sectors benefited from indirect subsidies in the form of tolerated arrears in taxes and energy bills. But only farmers and coal miners had any success in winning direct subsidies (if not from the budget, then through soft bank credits or a share of international loans). The miners won some concessions because they were still able to mount effective protests—blocking train lines in May-June 1998, for example. The farm lobby was able to mobilize rural voters and was the only economic sector to have its own party (the Agrarians) in the Duma. But subsidies to farmers fell from 10 percent of GDP in Soviet times to less than 2 percent after 1992.

CONCLUSION

The August crisis exposed the deep institutional flaws of Yeltsin's Russia: the centralization of political power, its potential for instability, and the continued presence of a powerful security apparatus. It challenged naïve assumptions about Russia's progress toward a prosperous and stable market economy. However, the crisis did not usher in any radical structural changes in Russia's political economy. It forced a severe but overdue devaluation of the ruble, which helped revive domestic manufacturing industry. It weaned the government off its previous overreliance on borrowing to plug the gaps in the budget. But it did not shift policy in the direction of protectionism and increased subsidies. It caused the government to fall and strengthened the influence of the security ministries while weakening the power of the financial oligarchs. But it did not dislodge Boris Yeltsin from the Kremlin or lead to any fundamental shift in the presidential system of government he had fashioned.

The dispersed interest groups that supported Yeltsin from the beginning have become increasingly disillusioned but are little disposed to turn back the clock. The crisis also weakened the financial-industrial oligarchs that grew fat on Yeltsin's compromised reforms. But the Soviet-era concentrated interest groups had been weakened tremendously by August 1998. Most importantly, the strong presidency made it difficult for them and their parliamentary supporters to push through significant institutional or policy changes in response to the increasing popular disillusionment and the weakened position of the financial-industrial oligarchs.

This situation has remained unchanged during the subsequent political rise of Prime Minister Putin in 1999–2000. Putin was an acceptable successor because he appeared to be a winner and because he seemed likely to insulate Yeltsin's Kremlin circle from future political retribution. The strong performance of his new party, Unity, and his first-round victory in the presidential elections following Yeltsin's resignation did not reflect a resurgence of support for either reform or for the status quo. Both the Communist Party and (even more so) the center-right reform parties remained widely unpopular, as did Yeltsin himself. Putin's economic policy platform remained as enigmatic as those of other centrist nationalists attempting to fill the electoral vacuum, for example, Primakov's. In fact Putin declined to publish a specific electoral platform at all, confining himself to issuing a vague "letter to the Russian people." He also refused to take part in debates with the other presidential candidates. Putin's victory occurred because of his decisive military intervention in Chechnya, which provided Russia's bruised and battered national pride with a welcome respite from repeated humiliation, and not because voters expected him to come up with policies capable of tackling Russia's pressing economic problems.

NOTES

1. Data on economic performance are taken from the quarterly and monthly reports of *Russian Economic Trends*, published by the Working Center for Economic Reform in Moscow.

2. The only presidents who openly rejected market reform and proclaimed their own path were Islam Karimov (Uzbekistan), Saparmurad Niyazov (Turkmenistan), and Alyaksandr Lukashenko (Belarus).

3. In January 1998 the ruble was redenominated: 1,000 old rubles became one new ruble.

4. For example, Menatep Bank lost control over Yukos, the second largest oil company, when it defaulted on a $236 million loan backed with Yukos shares (*Wall Street Journal*, 31 May 1999).

Appendix

Economic Indicators

EXPLANATORY NOTES FOR COUNTRY TABLES

GDP growth and inflation are annual rates of change. Fiscal balance is annual government budget surplus or deficit as a share of GDP. Current account balance is an annual surplus or deficit as a share of GDP. Total debt refers to the total value of debt outstanding, and this is shown as a share of GDP. (In the case of Japan, a large net creditor, the figure is for assets rather than debt.) Debt service refers to annual payments, and the latter are shown as a share of exports of goods and services. Except for Japan, the figures are those most recently available from the World Bank. We thank Natasha Rodriguez for making them available to us. Dashes indicate that data is not yet available for 1999 or not available for earlier years. Japanese statistics are derived from data available on the Economic Planning Agency and Ministry of Finance Web sites: <http://www.epa.go.jp> and <http://www.mof.go.jp>. For similar data on Taiwan, also a large net creditor, see table 9.1.

SHORT-TERM DEBT/RESERVES

Short-term debt obligations are those due within a year. All years are as of the end of December, except for 1999, for which the latest available data are as of the end of June. Joint BIS-IMF-OECD-World Bank short-term debt categories are liabilities to banks, debt securities issued abroad, and nontrade bank credits. The first and second categories may overlap, so a high estimate of short-term debt is

265

obtained by summing all three categories, and a low estimate by summing only
the first and third. These high and low estimates are then divided by holdings of
international reserve assets. The latter include monetary authorities' holdings of
foreign exchange, reserve positions at the IMF, and holdings of SDRs, and exclude gold reserves. Source: <http://www.oecd.org/dac/debt/htm/backsum.htm>.

Table A.1   Argentina Economic Indicators

	1996	1997	1998	1999
GDP growth	5.53	8.11	3.90	−3.50
Inflation	−0.05	−0.46	−2.02	−2.00
Fiscal balance	−1.94	−1.46	−1.37	−4.98
Current account balance	−2.38	−4.11	−4.94	—
Total debt/GDP	31	38	—	—
Debt service/Exports	39.61	50.34	58.77	—
Short-term debt/Reserves				
High	1.70	1.58	1.64	1.91
Low	1.45	1.34	1.43	1.73

Table A.2   Brazil Economic Indicators

	1996	1997	1998	1999
GDP growth	2.80	3.20	0.15	0.00
Inflation	17.24	7.85	3.65	9.00
Fiscal balance	−2.56	−2.65	−5.48	−9.65
Current account balance	−3.14	−4.07	−4.49	—
Total debt/GDP	26	23	—	—
Debt service/Exports	41.71	63.47	73.61	—
Short-term debt/Reserves				
High	0.95	1.12	1.15	1.07
Low	0.77	0.99	1.01	0.97

Table A.3   Czech Republic Economic Indicators

	1996	1997	1998	1999
GDP growth	3.82	0.32	−2.33	—
Inflation	9.65	6.51	10.96	—
Fiscal balance	−0.38	−1.37	−1.42	—
Current account balance	−7.41	−6.06	−1.88	—
Total debt/GDP	42	40	—	—
Debt service/Exports	8.42	14.14	15.28	—
Short-term debt/Reserves				
High	—	—	—	—
Low	0.41	0.60	0.64	0.48

Table A.4 Hungary Economic Indicators

	1996	1997	1998	1999
GDP growth	1.34	4.60	5.10	—
Inflation	21.17	18.44	14.19	—
Fiscal balance	0.81	−1.83	−4.39	—
Current account balance	−3.72	−2.15	−4.81	—
Total debt/GDP	62.00	52.00	—	—
Debt service/Exports	41.28	29.78	27.29	—
Short-term debt/Reserves				
High	0.61	0.71	0.86	0.76
Low	0.49	0.50	0.65	0.49

Table A.5 Indonesia Economic Indicators

	1996	1997	1998	1999
GDP growth	7.84	4.69	−13.21	0.23
Inflation	8.65	12.58	73.07	17.17
Fiscal balance	1.11	−0.53	−3.32	−5.57
Current account balance	−3.55	−0.79	4.90	3.92
Total debt/GDP	64.00	62.00	—	—
Debt service/Exports	35.85	30.62	34.73	—
Short-term debt/Reserves				
High	2.06	2.32	1.20	0.98
Low	2.02	2.27	1.14	0.94

Table A.6 Japan Economic Indicators

	1996	1997	1998	1999
GDP growth	5.1	1.6	−2.5	0.3
Inflation	−2.0	0.6	−2.4	−0.7
Fiscal balance	7.1	5.8	8.6	10.0
Current account balance	1.4	2.2	3.2	2.5

Total assets/GDP	20.7	24.4	26.7	—

Table A.7   South Korea Economic Indicators

	1996	1997	1998	1999
GDP growth	6.75	5.01	−5.84	—
Inflation	3.89	3.15	5.32	—
Fiscal balance	0.02	−1.66	−4.23	—
Current account balance	−4.42	−1.71	12.64	—
Total debt/GDP	—	33.00	—	—
Debt service/Exports	8.64	7.99	12.49	—
Short-term debt/Reserves				
High	2.20	3.25	0.82	0.74
Low	2.01	2.96	0.63	0.59

Table A.8   Malaysia Economic Indicators

	1996	1997	1998	1999
GDP growth	8.58	7.50	−7.50	−1.70
Inflation	6.84	3.35	9.10	1.42
Fiscal balance	1.05	2.52	−1.46	−5.91
Current account balance	−4.56	−4.78	12.69	6.96
Total debt/GDP	52.00	48.00	—	—
Debt service/Exports	8.96	7.45	8.72	—
Short-term debt/Reserves				
High	0.49	0.80	0.43	0.31
Low	0.48	0.77	0.42	0.30

Table A.9   Mexico Economic Indicators

	1996	1997	1998	1999
GDP growth	5.15	6.76	4.80	3.40
Inflation	30.74	17.73	13.97	15.90
Fiscal balance	−0.42	−1.27	−1.72	—
Current account balance	−0.66	−2.07	−4.06	−2.91
Total debt/GDP	44.00	37.00	—	—
Debt service/Exports	35.42	33.07	20.80	—
Short-term debt/Reserves				
High	1.73	1.18	1.06	0.99
Low	1.46	0.98	0.97	0.92

Table A.10 Poland Economic Indicators

	1996	*1997*	*1998*	*1999*
GDP growth	6.00	6.82	4.80	—
Inflation	18.71	14.00	11.70	—
Fiscal balance	−2.38	−1.26	−2.40	—
Current account balance	−0.96	−3.01	−4.34	—
Total debt/GDP	31.00	27.00	—	—
Debt service/Exports	7.51	6.67	10.68	—
Short-term debt/Reserves				
High	—	—	0.28	0.33
Low	0.22	0.22	0.27	0.33

Table A.11 Russia Economic Indicators

	1996	*1997*	*1998*	*1999*
GDP growth	−3.40	0.90	−4.62	1.30
Inflation	44.19	16.48	11.60	56.28
Fiscal balance	−8.86	−7.89	−8.02	−5.49
Current account balance	2.33	0.62	0.45	8.65
Total debt/GDP	25.00	27.00	—	—
Debt service/Exports	6.71	6.40	12.14	—
Short-term debt/Reserves				
High	2.40	2.55	2.36	2.03
Low	2.40	2.55	2.34	1.96

Table A.12 Thailand Economic Indicators

	1996	*1997*	*1998*	*1999*
GDP growth	5.52	−1.25	−9.42	3.32
Inflation	4.03	2.97	8.73	2.18
Fiscal balance	2.23	−0.60	−2.71	−0.50
Current account balance	−7.91	−6.16	9.16	8.06
Total debt/GDP	56.00	61.00	—	—
Debt service/Exports	12.60	15.45	19.12	—
Short-term debt/Reserves				
High	1.31	1.62	0.97	0.77
Low	1.29	1.61	0.95	0.74

Bibliography

Acuña, Carlos. 1993. "Politics and Economics in the Argentina of the Nineties." Buenos Aires: CEDES mimeo.

Adams, Charles, et al. 1998. *International Capital Markets: Developments, Prospects, and Key Policy Issues*. Washington, D.C.: International Monetary Fund.

Akira, Suehiro. 1989. *Capital Accumulation in Thailand, 1855–1985*. Tokyo: Centre for East Asian Cultural Studies.

Akrasanee, N., K. Jansen, and J. Pongpisanupichit. 1993. *International Capital Flows and Economic Adjustment in Thailand*. Bangkok: Thailand Development Research Institute.

Alexander, Arthur. 1998. *Japan in the Context of Asia*. Washington, D.C.: Johns Hopkins University, SAIS Policy Forum Series, 2 September.

Andaya, Barbara W., and Leonard Y. Andaya. 1982. *A History of Malaysia*. London: Macmillan.

Asian Business. December 1998.

Aslund, Anders. 1995. *How Russia Became a Market Economy*. Washington, D.C.: Brookings Institution.

Aspe, Pedro. 1993. *Economic Transformation the Mexican Way*. Cambridge: MIT Press.

Australia, Government of. 1995. *Overseas Chinese Business Networks*. Canberra: East Asia Analytical Unit, Department of Foreign Affairs and Trade.

Balcerowicz, Leszek. 1995. *Socialism, Capitalism, Transformation*. Budapest: Central European University Press.

Balcerowicz, Leszek, Barbara Blaszczyk, and Marek Dabrowski. 1997. "The Polish Way to a Market Economy, 1989–1995." In *Economies in Transition: Comparing Asia and Europe*, edited by Wing Thye Woo, Stephen Parker, and Jeffrey D. Sachs, 131–60. Cambridge: MIT Press.

Baliño, T. J. T., et al. 1999. *Financial Sector Crisis and Restructuring: Lessons from Asia*. Washington, D.C.: International Monetary Fund.

Bangkok Bank Monthly Review. February 1979–December 1993.

Bangkok Post. 6 August 1997–30 September 1998.

Bank of Korea. 1999. <http://www.bok.or.kr>.

Bank of Thailand. 1992. *Fifty Years of the Bank of Thailand: 1942–1992*. Bangkok, Thailand: Bank of Thailand.

Baumann, Renato, and Heloiza C. Moreira. 1987. "Os Incentivos às Exportações Brasileiras de Produtos Manufaturados—1969/85." *Pesquisa e Planejamento* 17, no. 2: 471–90.

Becker, Gary S. 1983. "A Theory of Competition among Pressure Groups for Political Influence." *Quarterly Journal of Economics* 98: 371–400.

Blake, Charles Henry, II. 1992. "Social Pacts, Labor Relations, and Democratic Consolidation: Argentina in Comparative Perspective." Ph.D. diss., Duke University.

Boileau, Julian. 1983. *GOLKAR: Functional Group Politics in Indonesia*. Jakarta: Yayasan Proklamasi/Centre for Strategic and International Studies.

Booth, Anne. 1992. "Income Distribution and Poverty." In *The Oil Boom and After: Indonesian Economic Policy and Performance in the Soeharto Era*. Edited by Anne Booth. Singapore: Oxford University Press.

Bradford, Colin. 1990. "Policy Interventions and Markets: Development Strategy Typologies and Policy Options." In *Manufacturing Miracles: Paths of Industrialization in Latin America and East Asia*. Edited by Gary Gereffi and Donald L. Wyman. Princeton: Princeton University Press.

Bresnan, John. 1993. *Managing Indonesia: The Modern Political Economy*. New York: Columbia University Press.

Bridge News. 4 February 1999.

Bugge, Peter. 1994. "The Czech Republic." In *Political Parties of Eastern Europe, Russia, and the Successor States*, edited by Bogdan Szajkowski, 149–173. London: Longman.

Business Central Europe. April 1997–April 1999. London: Economist Group.

Business in Thailand. June 1974–July 1976.

Byzov, Leontii, and Vladimir Petukhov. 1999. "August Shook Pockets but Not Heads." *Obshchaya Gazeta* 7, 18–24 February.

Calvo, Guillermo, and Enrique Mendoza. 1996. "Petty Crime and Cruel Punishment: Lessons from the Mexican Debacle." *American Economic Review*, May, 170–175.

Calvo, Guillermo, and Carlos Végh. 1994. "Inflation Stabilization and Nominal Anchors." In *Approaches to Exchange Rate Policy: Choices for Developing and Transitional Economies*. Edited by Richard C. Barth and Chorng–huey Wond. Washington, D.C.: International Monetary Fund.

Campos, Jose Edgardo, and Hilton L. Root. 1996. *The Key to the Asian Miracle: Making Shared Growth Credible*. Washington, D.C.: Brookings Institution.

Canitrot, Adolfo, and Silvia Sigal. 1992. "Economic Reform, Democracy, and the Crisis of the State in Argentina." Buenos Aires: Instituto Di Tella mimeo.

Cargill, Thomas F., and Shoichi Royama. 1992. "The Evolution of Japanese Banking: Isolation to Globalization." In *Emerging Challenges for the International Financial Services Industry*. Edited by J. R. Barth and P. F. Bartholomew. New York: JAI Academic.

Cason, Jeffrey. 1993. "Development Strategy in Brazil: The Political Economy of Industrial Export Promotion, 1964–1990." Ph.D. diss., University of Wisconsin.

Cason, Jeffrey, and Gregory White. 1998. "The State as Naïve Entrepreneur: The Political Economy of Export Promotion in Brazil and Tunisia." *Policy Studies Journal* 26, no. 1: 46–68.

Chaiyasoot, Naris. 1993. "Commercial Banking." In *The Thai Economy in Transition*, edited by P. Warr, 226–64. Cambridge: Cambridge University Press.

———. 1995. "Industrialization, Financial Reform, and Monetary Policy." In *Thailand's Industrialization and Its Consequences*, edited by M. Krongkaew, 160–82. New York: St. Martin's.

Choi, Dong Kyu. 1991. *The Government in the Age of Rapid Growth*. Seoul: Korea Economic Daily Press.

Christensen, S. R., and J. Bamrungchatudorn. 1996. *Property and Bad Debt: Getting Deeper into the Red*. Jardine Fleming Industry Report, December.

Chu, Yun–han. 1999. "Surviving the East Asian Financial Storm: The Political Foundation of Taiwan's Economic Resilience." Paper presented at the 1999 annual meeting of the American Political Science Association, Atlanta, Georgia.

Cole, David C., and Betty F. Slade. 1996. *Building a Modern Financial System: The Indonesian Experience*. Cambridge: Cambridge University Press.

Collier, Ruth Berins, and David Collier. 1991. *Shaping the Political Arena: Critical Junctures, the Labor Movement, and Regime Dynamics in Latin America*. Princeton: Princeton University Press.

Corbett, Jenny, and David Vines. 1998. *The Asian Crisis: Competing Explanations*. CEPA Working Paper Series 2, 7. New York: New School for Social Research.

Corsetti, Giancarlo, Paolo Pesenti, and Nouriel Roubini. 1998. *What Caused the Asian Currency and Financial Crisis?* <http://www.stern.nyu.edu/~nroubini/asia/AsianCrisi.pdf>.

Cotten, James. 1995. *Politics and Policy in the New Korean State*. New York: St. Martin's.

Cox, Gary W., and Mathew D. McCubbins. Forthcoming. "The Institutional Determinants of Economic Policy Outcomes." In *Structure and Policy in Presidential Democracies*. Edited by Stephan Haggard and Mathew D. McCubbins. New York: Cambridge University Press.

Cristensen, Scott R., et al. 1997. "Thailand: The Institutional and Political Underpinnings of Growth." In *Lessons from East Asia*, edited by Danny M. Leipziger, 345–386. Ann Arbor: University of Michigan Press.

Crouch, Harold. 1996. *Government and Society in Malaysia*. Ithaca: Cornell University Press.

Curtis, Gerald L. 1999. *The Logic of Japanese Politics: Leaders, Institutions, and the Limits of Change*. New York: Columbia University Press.

Damill, Mario, and Roberto Frenkel. 1990. "Malos Tiempos: Argentina en la Decada de los Ochenta." Buenos Aires: CEDES mimeo.

Davydov, Oleg. 1998. *Inside Out: The Radical Transformation of Russian Foreign Trade, 1992–1997*. New York: Fordham University Press.

Deyo, Frederic C., ed. 1987. *The Political Economy of the New Asian Industrialism*. Ithaca: Cornell University Press.

Digital Chosun Ilbo. 4 December 1996–20 July 1999. <http://www.chosun.com>.

Dixit, A. K., and Victor Norman. 1980. *Theory of International Trade*. Cambridge: Cambridge University Press.

Dixon, C. 1996. "Thailand's Rapid Economic Growth: Causes, Sustainability, and Lessons." In *Uneven Development in Thailand*, edited by M. J. G. Parnell, 28–48. Brookfield: Avebury.

Doner, Richard, and Anek Laothamatas. 1994. "Thailand: Economic and Political Gradualism." In *Voting for Reform: Democracy, Political Liberalization, and Economic Adjustment*, edited by S. Haggard and S. B. Webb, 411–52. New York: Oxford University Press.

274   *Bibliography*

Doner, R., and A. Ramsay. 1999. "Thailand: From Economic Miracle to Economic Crisis." In *Asian Contagion: The Causes and Consequences of a Financial Crisis*. Edited by Karl D. Jackson. Boulder: Westview.

Doner, R., and D. Unger. 1995. "The Politics of Finance in Thai Economic Development." In *The Politics of Finance in Developing Countries*, edited by Stephan Haggard and Chung H. Lee, 93–122. Ithaca: Cornell University Press.

Dongailbo. 4 February 1998. <http://www.dongailbo.co.kr>.

Dornbusch, Rudiger. 1997. "The Folly, the Crash, and Beyond: Economic Policies and the Crisis." In *Mexico 1994: Anatomy of an Emerging–Market Crash*. Edited by Sebastian Edwards and Moises Naim. Washington, D.C.: Carnegie Endowment for International Peace.

Dornbusch, Rudiger, and Alejandro Werner. 1994. "Mexico: Stabilization, Reform, and No Growth." *Brookings Papers on Economic Activity* 1.

East, Roger, and Jolyon Pontin. 1997. *Revolution and Change in Central and Eastern Europe*. Rev. ed. London: Pinter.

EBRD [European Bank for Reconstruction and Development]. 1994. *Transition Report 1994*. London: EBRD.

——. 1997. *Transition Report 1997*. London: EBRD.

——. 1998. *Transition Report 1998*. London: EBRD.

Economist. 3 August 1996–29 August 1998.

Edwards, Sebastian. 1997. "Bad Luck or Bad Policies? An Economic Analysis of the Crisis." In *Mexico 1994: Anatomy of an Emerging–Market Crash*. Edited by Sebastian Edwards and Moises Naim. Washington, D.C.: Carnegie Endowment for International Peace.

——. 1999. "A Capital Idea? Reconsidering a Financial Quick Fix." *Foreign Affairs* 78, no. 3: 18–22.

——. 1999. *On Crisis Prevention: Lessons from Mexico and East Asia*. <http://www.anderson.ucla.edu/faculty/sebastian.edwards/>.

Edwards, Sebastian, and Moises Naim, eds. 1997. *Mexico 1994: Anatomy of an Emerging–Market Crash*. Washington, D.C.: Carnegie Endowment for International Peace.

Eichengreen, Barry. 1995. *International Monetary Arrangements for the Twenty-First Century: Integrating National Economies: Promise and Pitfalls*. Washington, D.C.: Brookings Institution.

EIU [Economist Intelligence Unit]. 1995. *Country Profile: Czech Republic, Slovakia, 1995–96*. London: EIU.

——. 1996. *Country Profile: Poland, 1995–96*. London: EIU.

——. 1997. *Country Profile: Hungary, 1996–97*. London: EIU.

——. 1998. *Country Report: Indonesia*. 4th quarter. London: Economist Intelligence Unit.

Endo, Yukihiko. 1998. "Can the 'Big Bang' Cure the Ills of Japan's Financial System?" *NRI Quarterly*, Summer, 20–37.

Far Eastern Economic Review. 27 May 1972–30 September 1999.

Far Eastern Economic Review Asia Yearbook. 1995–1996.

Feldstein, Martin. 1998. "Refocusing the IMF." *Foreign Affairs*, March–April, 20–33.

Fields, Karl J. 1995. *Enterprise and the State in Korea and Taiwan*. Ithaca: Cornell University Press.

Fischer, Bernard, and Helmut Reisen. 1993. *Liberalising Capital Flows in Developing Countries: Pitfalls, Prerequisites, and Perspectives*. Paris: Organisation for Economic Co–operation and Development.

Fischer, Stanley. 1998. "In Defense of the IMF." *Foreign Affairs,* July–August, 103–106.

Fleischer, David. 1998. "The Cardoso Government's Reform Agenda: A View from the National Congress, 1995–1998." *Journal of Interamerican Studies and World Affairs* 40, no. 4: 119–136.

Flores Quiroga, Aldo R. 1998. *Proteccionismo versus librecambio: La economía política de la protección comercial en México, 1970–1994.* Mexico: Fondo de Cultura Económica.

Flynn, Peter. 1999. "Brazil: The Politics of Crisis." *Third World Quarterly* 20, no. 2: 287–317.

Folha de São Paulo. 29 October 1998–14 November 1998.

Fondo de Cultura Económica. 1988. *Cuadernos de renovación nacional.* Edited series. Fondo de Cultura Económica.

———. 1994. *Una visión sobre la modernización de México.* Edited series. Fondo de Cultura Económica.

Frey, Bruno. 1984. *International Political Economics.* New York: Basil Blackwell.

Frieden, Jeffry. 1991. *Debt, Development, and Democracy: Modern Political Economy and Latin America, 1965–1985.* Princeton: Princeton University Press.

Friedman, Milton. 1992. *Money Mischief: Episodes in Monetary History.* New York: Harvest.

Frydman, Roman, Andrzej Rapaczynski, and Joel Turkewitz. 1997. "Transition to a Private Property Regime in the Czech Republic and Hungary." In *Economies in Transition: Comparing Asia and Europe,* edited by Wing Thye Woo, Stephen Parker, and Jeffrey D. Sachs, 41–102. Cambridge: MIT Press.

Frydman, Roman, et al. 1993. *The Privatization Process in Russia, Ukraine, and the Baltic States.* Budapest: Central European University Press.

Garten, Jeffrey. 1999. "Lessons for the Next Financial Crisis." *Foreign Affairs* 78, no. 2: 76–92.

Gerschenkron, Alexander. 1989. *Bread and Democracy in Germany.* Ithaca: Cornell University Press.

Gil–Díaz, Francisco, and Agustín Carstens. 1997. "Pride and Prejudice: The Economics Profession and Mexico's Financial Crisis." In *Mexico 1994: Anatomy of an Emerging–Market Crash.* Edited by Sebastian Edwards and Moises Naim. Washington, D.C.: Carnegie Endowment for International Peace.

Goldstein, Morris. 1998. *The Asian Financial Crisis: Causes, Cures, and Systemic Implications.* Washington, D.C.: Institute for International Economics.

Gomez, Edmund T. 1991. *Money Politics in the Barisan Nasional.* Kuala Lumpur: Forum Publications.

———. 1999. *Chinese Business in Malaysia.* Surrey, U.K.: Curzon.

Gomez, Edmund T., and K. S. Jomo. 1997. *Malaysia's Political Economy: Politics, Patronage, and Profits.* Cambridge: Cambridge University Press.

Gourevitch, Peter. 1986. *Politics in Hard Times: Comparative Responses to International Economic Crises.* Ithaca: Cornell University Press.

Hadiz, Vedi R. 1994. "Challenging State Corporatism on the Labour Front: Working Class Politics in the 1990s." In *Democracy in Indonesia: 1950s and 1990s.* Monash Papers on Southeast Asia 31. Edited by David Bourchier and John Legge. Clayton, Australia.

Haggard, Stephan. 1990. *Pathways from the Periphery: The Politics of Growth in the Newly Industrializing Countries.* Ithaca: Cornell University Press.

Haggard, Stephan, and Robert R. Kaufman. 1992a. *The Politics of Economic Adjustment: International Constraints, Distributive Conflicts, and the State*. Princeton: Princeton University Press.

———. 1992b. "The Political Economy of Inflation and Stabilization in Middle–Income Countries." In *The Politics of Economic Adjustment: International Constraints, Distributive Conflicts, and the State*, edited by Stephan Haggard and Robert R. Kaufman, 270–315. Princeton: Princeton University Press.

Haggard, Stephan, and Steven B. Webb. 1995. *Voting for Reform: Democracy, Political Liberalization, and Economic Adjustment*. Oxford: Oxford University Press.

Hale, David D. 1997. "The Markets and Mexico: The Supply–Side of the Story." In *Mexico 1994: Anatomy of an Emerging–Market Crash*. Edited by Sebastian Edwards and Moises Naim. Washington, D.C.: Carnegie Endowment for International Peace.

Handelman, Stephen. 1997. *Comrade Criminal: Russia's New Mafiya*. New Haven: Yale University Press.

Hellman, Joel S. 1998. "Winners Take All: The Politics of Partial Reform in Postcommunist Transitions." *World Politics* 50, no. 2: 203–234.

Heo, Uk, and Sunwoong Kim. 1998. "The Political Economy of Financial Crisis in South Korea: Failure of the Statist Development Paradigm." Paper presented at the Midwest Conference on Asian Affairs, Milwaukee, Wis., September 25–27.

Hernández Rodríguez, Rafael. 1988. *Empresarios banca y estado: El conflicto durante el gobierno de José López Portillo, 1976–1982*. Mexico: FLACSO–Miguel Angel Porrúa.

Hewison, Kevin. 1985. "The State and Capitalist Development in Thailand." In *Southeast Asia: Essays in the Political Economy of Structural Change*. Edited by Richard Higgott and Richard Robison. London: Routledge & Kegan Paul.

———. 1989. *Bankers and Bureaucrats: Capital and the Role of the State in Thailand*. Yale University Southeast Asia Studies, Monograph Series 34. New Haven: Yale University Press.

IMF [International Monetary Fund]. 1998. "Statement by the Hon. Dato Mustapa Mohamed, Governor of the Fund and the Bank for Malaysia, October 7, 1998." IMF Press Release no. 45, 6–8 October.

———. 1999. *World Economic Outlook and Policy Responses to the Global Slowdown*. <http://www.imf.org/external/pubs/ft/weo/1999/01>.

International Labor Organization. 1999. *World Labor Report*. <http://www.ilo.org/public/english/80relpro/publ/wlr/97/index.htm>.

Iskander, Magdi, et al. 1999. "Corporate Restructuring and Governance in East Asia." *Finance and Development* 36: 1. <http://www.imf.org/external/pubs/ft/fandd/1999/03/iskander.htm>.

Izvestiya. 5 January 1997.

J. P. Morgan. 1999. *Asian Financial Market*, 29 January.

Jakarta Post. 27 October 1999.

Jansen, Karel. 1997. *External Finance in Thailand's Development: An Interpretation of Thailand's Growth Boom*. New York: St. Martin's.

Japan Economic Planning Agency. 1998. *Outline of Emergency Economic Package*. <http://www.epa.go.jp>.

———. 1999. *The Japanese Economy in 1998: A Review of Events and Challenges for the Future*. <http://www.epa.go.jp>.

Johnston, R. B. 1991. "Distressed Financial Institutions in Thailand: Structural Weaknesses, Support Operations, and Economic Consequences." In *Banking Crises: Cases and Issues*. Edited by V. Sundararajan and Tomás J.T. Baliño. Washington, D.C.: International Monetary Fund.

Joongang Ilbo. 27 October 1997. <http://www.joongang.co.kr>.

Juro, Hashimoto. 1997. "Corporate Structure and the Japanese Economy." In *The Political Economy in Japanese Society*. Edited by Banno Junji. Oxford: Oxford University Press.

Khoo Kay Jin. 1992. "The Grand Vision: Mahathir and Modernisation." In *Fragmented Vision*. Edited by Joel S. Kahn and Francis Loh Kok Wah. Honolulu: University of Hawaii Press.

Kiguel, Miguel, and Nissan Liviatan. 1992. "The Business Cycle Associated with Exchange Rate Based Stabilization." *World Bank Economic Review* 6: 279–305.

Kim, Kiwhan, and Danny M. Leipziger. 1998. "Korea: A Case Study of Government–Led Development." In *Lessons from East Asia*. Edited by Danny M. Leipziger. Ann Arbor: University of Michigan Press.

Kingstone, Peter. 1998. "Corporatism, Neoliberalism, and the Failed Revolt of Big Business: Lessons from the Case of IEDI." *Journal of Interamerican Studies and World Affairs* 40, no. 4: 73–95.

Korea Stock Exchange. 1999. <http://www.kse.or.kr>.

Korea, Government of. 1998. *Letter of Intent of the Government of Korea, May 2nd, 1998*. <http://www.imf.org>.

Krugman, Paul 1999. *The Return of Depression Economics*. New York: Norton.

Kuo, Shirley W. Y., and Christina Y. Liu. 1999. "Taiwan." In *East Asia in Crisis: From Being a Miracle to Needing One?* Edited by Ross H. McLeod and Ross Garnaut. London: Routledge.

Kwan, C. H. 1998. "Asia's Currency Crisis and Its Implications for the Japanese Economy." *NRI Quarterly*, Spring, 20–37.

Lal, Deepak, and Sylvian Maxfield. 1993. "The Political Economy of Stabilization in Brazil." In *Political and Economic Interactions in Economic Policy Reform: Evidence from Eight Countries*. Edited by Robert H. Bates and Anne O. Krueger. Cambridge: Blackwell.

Laothamatas, A. 1992a. *Business Associations and the New Political Economy of Thailand: From Bureaucratic Polity to Liberal Corporatism*. Boulder: Westview.

———. 1992b. "The Politics of Structural Adjustment in Thailand: A Political Explanation of Economic Success." In *The Dynamics of Economic Policy Reform in South–east Asia and the South–west Pacific*, edited by Andrew MacIntyre and Jayasuriya, 32–49. Kuala Lumpur, Malaysia: Oxford University Press.

Layard, Richard, and John Parker. 1996. *The Coming Russian Boom*. New York: Free Press.

Lee, Yeon–ho. 1997. *The State, Society, and Big Business in South Korea*. London: Routledge.

Leeahtam, Pisit. 1991. *From Crisis to Double Digit Growth*. Bangkok, Thailand: Dokya.

Leijonhufvud, Axel. 1981. *Information and Coordination: Essays in Macroeconomic Theory*. New York: Oxford University Press.

Lew, Seok–Jin. 1999. "Democratization and Government Intervention in the Economy: Insights on the Decision–Making Process from the Automobile Industrial Policies." In *Democracy and the Korean Economy*. Edited by Jongryn Mo and Chung–in Moon. Stanford: Hoover Institution Press.

Liddle, R. William. 1992. "Indonesia's Democratic Past and Future." *Comparative Politics* 30: 443–62.

———. "The Islamic Turn in Indonesia: A Political Explanation." *Journal of Asian Studies* 55 (August): 613–34.

Lijphart, Arend. 1969. "Consociational Democracy." *World Politics* 21, no. 2: 207–25.

Lustig, Nora. 1992. *Mexico: The Remaking of an Economy*. Washington, D.C.: Brookings Institution.

MacIntyre, Andrew. 1994. "Power, Prosperity, and Patrimonialism: Business and Government in Indonesia." In *Business and Government in Industrialising Asia*. Edited by Andrew MacIntyre. Ithaca: Cornell University Press.

———. 1999a. "Institutions and Investors: The Politics of the Financial Crisis in Southeast Asia." Paper presented at American Political Science Association annual meeting, Atlanta, Georgia.

———. 1999b. "Political Parties, Accountability, and Economic Governance in Indonesia." In *Democracy, Governance, and Economic Performance: East and Southeast Asia in the 1990s*. Edited by Jean Blondel, Ian Marsh, and Takashi Inoguchi. Melbourne: Cambridge University Press.

Mackie, Jamie. 1992. "Changing Patterns of Chinese Big Business in Southeast Asia." In *Southeast Asian Capitalists*. Edited by Ruth McVey. Ithaca: Cornell Southeast Asia Program.

———. 1999. "Indonesia: Economic Growth and Depoliticization." In *Driven by Growth: Political Change in the Asia Pacific Region*. Edited by James W. Morley. Armonk, N.Y.: M. E. Sharpe.

Magee, Stephen P., William A. Brock, and Leslie Young. 1989. *Black Hole Tariffs and Endogenous Policy Theory: Political Economy in General Equilibrium*. Cambridge: Cambridge University Press.

Mainwaring, Scott. 1999. *Rethinking Party Systems in the Third Wave of Democratization: The Case of Brazil*. Stanford: Stanford University Press.

Makin, John H. 1996. "Japan's Disastrous Keynesian Experiment." *Economic Outlook*, December. Washington, D.C.: American Enterprise Institute.

Malaysian Department of Statistics. 1999. *Population Figures*. <http://www.jaring.my/isis/merc/gemc.html>.

Martins, Luciano. 1986. "The Liberalization of Authoritarian Rule in Brazil." In *Transitions from Authoritarian Rule: Latin America*. Edited by Guillermo O'Donnell, Philippe Schmitter, and Lawrence Whitehead. Baltimore: Johns Hopkins University Press.

Maxfield, Sylvia. 1990. *Governing Capital: International Finance and Mexican Politics*. Ithaca: Cornell University Press.

McLeod, Ross H. 1999. "Indonesia." In *East Asia in Crisis: From Being a Miracle to Needing One?* Edited by Ross H. McLeod and Ross Garnaut. London: Routledge.

Mean, Gordon P. 1991. *Malaysian Politics: The Second Generation*. Singapore: Oxford University Press.

Mendoza, Enrique, and Martin Uribe. 1996. "The Syndrome of Exchange Rate–Based Stabilization and the Uncertain Duration of Currency Pegs." *International Finance and Discussion Papers* 548 (April). Washington, D.C.: Board of Governors of the Federal Reserve System.

Michta, Andrew. 1997. "Democratic Consolidation in Poland after 1989." In *The Consolidation of Democracy in East–Central Europe*, edited by Karen Dawisha and Bruce Parrott, 66–108. Cambridge: Cambridge University Press.

Millard, Frances. 1994. "Poland." In *Political Parties of Eastern Europe, Russia, and the Successor States*, edited by Bogdan Szajkowski, 313–42. London: Longman.

Mo, Jongryn. 1999. "Democratization, Labor Policy, and Economic Performance." In *Democracy and the Korean Economy.* Edited by Jongryn Mo and Chung–in Moon. Stanford: Hoover Institution Press.

Mo, Jongryn, and Chung–in Moon. 1999. "Epilogue: Democracy and the Origins of the 1997 Korean Economic Crisis." In *Democracy and the Korean Economy.* Edited by Jongryn Mo and Chung–in Moon. Stanford: Hoover Institution Press.

Molano, Walter. 1997. *The Logic of Privatization: The Case of Telecommunications in the Southern Cone of Latin America.* Westport, Conn.: Greenwood.

Molina Werner, Isabel. 1981. "El endeudamiento externo del sector privado y sus efectos en la economía mexicana." *Comercio Exterior* 31, no. 10: 1140–47.

Montes, Manuel. 1998. *The Currency Crisis in Southeast Asia.* Singapore: Institute of Southeast Asian Studies.

Monthly Bulletin. Bank of Thailand. February 1972–December 1979.

Moody, Peter R. 1992. *Political Change on Taiwan.* Westport, Conn.: Praeger.

Moon, Chung–in. 1999. "Democratization and Globalization as Ideological and Political Foundations of Economic Policy." In *Democracy and the Korean Economy.* Edited by Jongryn Mo and Chung–in Moon. Stanford: Hoover Institution Press.

Moon, Chung–in, and Young–cheol Kim. 1994. "A Circle of Paradox: Development, Politics, and Democracy in South Korea." In *Democracy and Development: Essays on Theory and Practice.* Edited by Adrian Leftwich. Cambridge: Polity.

Morais, Lecio, Alfredo Saad Filho, and Walter Coelho. 1999. "Financial Liberalisation, Currency Instability, and Crisis in Brazil: Another Plan Bites the Dust." *Capital and Class* 68: 9–14.

Moreno Uriegas, María de los Angeles, and Romeo Flores Caballero. 1995. *Evolución de la deuda pública externa de México.* Mexico: Castillo.

Murphy, Ricardo López, and Fernando Navajas. 1996. "Domestic Savings, Public Savings, and Expenditures on Consumer Durable Goods in Argentina." November. Buenos Aires: Fundación de Investigaciones Económicas Latinoamericanas (FIEL).

Muscat, R. J. 1994. *The Fifth Tiger: A Study of Thai Development Policy.* Armonk, N.Y.: M. E. Sharpe.

Muscat, Robert J. 1995. "Thailand." In *Financial Systems and Economic Policy in Developing Countries,* edited by Stephan Haggard and Chung H. Lee, 113–39. Ithaca: Cornell University Press.

Nelson, Lynn, and Irina Kuzes. 1994. *Property to the People: The Struggle for Radical Economic Reform in Russia.* Armonk, N.Y.: M. E. Sharpe.

New Straits Times. 26 July 1998.

New York Times Online. 13 September 1999. <http://www.nytimes.com>.

New York Times. 17 December 1997–5 April 1998.

Nijathaworn, Bandid, and Madee Weerakitpanich. 1987. "Economic Fluctuations and Stability of the Commercial Banking System." Bangkok, Thailand: Thammasat University Symposium Paper.

Nikkei Weekly. 27 September 1999.

Nukul Commission Report. 1998. *The Commission Tasked with Making Recommendations to Improve the Efficiency and Management of Thailand's Financial System: Analysis and Evaluation on Facts behind Thailand's Economic Crisis.* Bangkok, Thailand: Nation Multimedia Group. English translation.

OECD. 1997. *Agricultural Policies in Transition Economies: Monitoring and Evaluation, 1997.* Paris: Organization for Economic Cooperation and Development.

Olson, David. 1997. "Democratization and Political Participation: The Experience of the Czech Republic." In *The Consolidation of Democracy in East–Central Europe*, edited by Karen Dawisha and Bruce Parrott, 150–96. Cambridge: Cambridge University Press.

Olson, Mancur, Jr. 1965. *The Logic of Collective Action: Public Goods and the Theory of Groups*. Rev. ed. New York: Schocken.

Otker, Inci, and Ceyla Pazarbasioglu. 1995. "Speculative Attacks and Currency Crises: The Mexican Experience." IMF Working Paper 112. Washington, D.C.: International Monetary Fund.

Pasuk, Phongpaichit. 1990. *The New Wave of Japanese Investment in ASEAN*. Singapore: Institute of Southeast Asian Studies.

Pempel, T. J. 1997. "Regime Shift: Japanese Politics in a Changing World Economy." *Journal of Japanese Studies* 23, no. 2: 333–62.

Perng, Fai–nan. 1999. "How the Republic of China ROC Has Responded to the Asian Financial Crisis and the Implications of the International Cooperation for Regional Economic Security." *Economic Review* 308: 1–7.

Persson, Torsten, and Guido Tabellini. 1990. *Macroeconomic Policy, Credibility, and Politics*. Chur: Harwood Academic Publishers.

———. 1994. *Monetary and Fiscal Policy*. Vol. 2, *Politics*. Cambridge: MIT Press.

Petkov, Radoslav, and Natan Shklyar. 1999. "Regional Responses to the August Crisis." *Transitions*, March.

Phongpaichit, Pasuk, and Chris Baker. 1995. *Thailand: Economy and Politics*. Kuala Lumpur: Oxford University Press.

———. 1998. *Thailand's Boom and Bust*. Chiang Mai, Thailand: Silkworm.

Pincus, Jonathan, and Rizal Ramli. 1998. "Indonesia: From Showcase to Basket Case." *Cambridge Journal of Economics* 22: 723–34.

Pittaway, Mark, and Nigel Swain. 1994. "Hungary." In *Political Parties of Eastern Europe, Russia, and the Successor States*, edited by Bogdan Szajkowski, 185–245. London: Longman.

Popov, Vladimir. 1998. "Will Russia Achieve Fast Economic Growth?" *Communist Economies and Economic Transformation* 10, no. 4: 421–29.

Posen, Adam S. 1999. *Implementing Japanese Recovery*. Washington, D.C.: International Economics Policy Briefs, Institute for International Economics 99–1.

Power, Timothy J. 1998. "Brazilian Politicians and Neoliberalism: Mapping Support for the Cardoso Reforms, 1995–1997." *Journal of Interamerican Studies and World Affairs* 40, no. 4: 51–72.

Przeworski, Adam. 1991. *Democracy and the Market: Political and Economic Reforms in Eastern Europe and Latin America*. Cambridge: Cambridge University Press.

Przeworski, Adam, and Fernando Limongi. 1993. "Political Regimes and Economic Growth." *Journal of Economic Perspectives* 7, no. 3: 51–69.

Raciborski, Jacek. 1996. "An Outline of the Electoral Geography of the Polish Society." In *Political Sociology and Democratic Transformation in Poland*, edited by Jerzy J. Wiatr, 29–54. Warsaw: Wydawnictwo Naukowe Scholar.

Radelet, Steven. Forthcoming. "Indonesia's Implosion." *Harvard Asia Pacific Review*. <http://www.stern.nyu.edu/~nroubini/Asia.homepage.html>.

Radelet, Steven, and Jeffrey D. Sachs. 1998. "The East Asian Financial Crisis: Diagnoses, Remedies, and Prospects." *Brookings Papers on Economic Activity* 1: 1–90.

Rajan, Ramkishen S. 1998. "The Japanese Economy and Economic Policy in Light of the East Asian Financial Crisis." New York: IPS Working Paper 2. <http://www.stern.nyu.edu/ ~nroubini>.

Rhee, Yung Whee, Bruce Ross–Larson, and Gary Pursell. 1984. *Korea's Competitive Edge: Managing the Entry into World Markets*. Baltimore: Johns Hopkins University Press.

Robinson, D., Yangho Byeon, and Ranjit Teja with Wanda Tseng. 1991. *Thailand: Adjusting to Success, Current Policy Issues*. Occasional Paper no. 85. Washington, D.C.: International Monetary Fund.

Rodrik, Dani. 1998. "Who Needs Capital–Account Convertibility?" In *Should the IMF Pursue Capital Account Convertibility?* Edited by P. Kenen. Princeton; International Finance Section of Princeton University.

Rogowski, Ronald. 1987. "Trade and the Variety of Democratic Institutions." *International Organization* 41, no. 2: 202–23.

———. 1989. *Commerce and Coalitions: How Trade Affects Domestic Political Alignments*. Princeton: Princeton University Press.

Root, Hilton L. 1996. *Small Countries, Big Lessons: Governance and the Rise of East Asia*. New York: Oxford University Press.

———. *The New Korea: Crisis Brings Opportunity*. Santa Monica: Milken Institute.

Roubini, Nouriel. 1996. "Japan's Economic Crisis." <http://www.stern.nyu.edu/~nroubini>.

———. 1998. *Chronology of the Asian Currency Crisis and Its Global Contagion*. <http://www.stern.nyu.edu/~nroubini/asia/AsiaChronology1.htm>.

Ruangsun, Thanapornpan. 1976. "Commercial Banks: Leech of the Thai Society?" *Social Sciences Review* 12, no. 16: 30–56.

Russian Economic Trends. August 1998–October 1999. Moscow: Working Center for Economic Reform.

Sachs, Jeffrey. 1993. *Poland's Jump to a Market Economy*. Cambridge: MIT Press.

———. "The IMF and the Asian Flu." *American Prospect* 37 (March–April): 16–22.

Sachs, Jeffrey, and Katarina Pistor. 1997. *The Rule of Law and Economic Reform in Russia*. Boulder: Westview.

Sachs, Jeffrey, Aaron Tornell, and Andres Velasco. 1995. "The Collapse of the Mexican Peso: What Have We Learned?" NBER Working Paper 5142. Cambridge, Mass.: National Bureau of Economic Research.

Schwarz, Adam. 2000. *A Nation in Waiting: Indonesia's Search for Stability*. 2d ed. Boulder: Westview.

Selcher, Wayne A. 1998. "The Politics of Decentralized Federalism, National Diversification, and Regionalism in Brazil." *Journal of Interamerican Studies and World Affairs* 40, no. 4: 25–50.

Shamsul, A. B. 1994. "Religion and Ethnic Politics in Malaysia." In *Asian Visions of Authority*. Edited by Charles F. Keyes, Laurel Kendall, and Helen Hardacre. Honolulu: University of Hawaii Press.

Shapiro, Helen. 1997. "Análisis de las políticas de promoción de exportaciones de Brasil." *Integración y Comercio* 1, no. 3: 73–98.

Shevtsova, Lilia. 1999. *Yeltsin's Russia: Myths and Reality*. Washington, D.C.: Carnegie Endowment.

Shleifer, Andrei, Maxim Boycko, and Robert Vishny. 1995. *Privatizing Russia*. Cambridge: MIT Press.

Siamwalla, Ammar. 1997. "Can a Developing Democracy Manage Its Macroeconomy? The Case of Thailand." Unpublished manuscript.

Sikkink, Kathryn. 1991. *Ideas and Institutions: Developmentalism in Brazil and Argentina*. Ithaca: Cornell University Press.

Siow, Moli. 1983. "The Problems of Ethnic Cohesion among the Chinese in Peninsular Malaysia: Intraethnic Divisions and Interethnic Accommodation." In *The Chinese in Southeast Asia*. Edited by Linda Y. C. Lim and L. A. Peter Gosling. Vol. 2, *Identity, Culture, and Politics*. Singapore: Maruzen Asia.

Skidmore, Thomas. 1988. *The Politics of Military Rule in Brazil, 1964–85*. New York: Oxford University Press.

Skully, Michael. 1984. "Financial Institutions and Markets in Thailand." In *Financial Institutions and Markets in Southeast Asia*, edited by Michael T. Skully, 296–378. London: Macmillan.

Smith, Heather. 1999. "Korea." In *East Asia in Crisis: From Being a Miracle to Needing One?* Edited by Ross H. McLeod and Ross Garnaut. London: Routledge.

Smith, Peter H. 1997. "Political Dimensions of the Peso Crisis." In *Mexico 1994: Anatomy of an Emerging–Market Crash*. Edited by Sebastian Edwards and Moises Naim. Washington, D.C.: Carnegie Endowment for International Peace.

Smith, William. 1991. "State, Market, and Neoliberalism in Post–Transition Argentina: The Ménem Experiment." *Journal of Interamerican Studies and World Affairs* 33: 45–82.

Soesastro, Hadi. 1999. "The 1999 Election and Beyond." *Bulletin of Indonesian Economic Studies* 35: 139–46.

Stepan, Alfred, and Cindy Skach. 1993. "Constitutional Frameworks and Democratic Consolidation: Parliamentarism vs. Presidentialism." *World Politics* 46 (October): 1–22.

Summers, Lawrence. 1999. "Japan and the Global Economy." Address delivered at National Press Club, Tokyo, 26 February.

Sundaravej, T., and Prasarn Trairatvorakul. 1989. *Experiences of Financial Distress in Thailand*. Washington, D.C.: World Bank.

Tachi, Ryuichiro. 1993. *The Contemporary Japanese Economy: An Overview*. Tokyo: University of Tokyo Press.

Taipei Economic and Cultural Office, Information Division. 1999a. *Background and Strategies for Developing Taiwan as Regional Financial Center.* <http://www.taipei.org/current/crisis3.htm>.

———. 1999b. *Financial Liberalization and Internationalization.* <http://www.taipei.org/current/crisis4.htm>.

Tarr, David G., and Constantine Michalopoulos. 1996. *Trade Performance and Policy in the New Independent States*. Washington, D.C.: World Bank.

Tokes, Rudolf L. 1997. "Party Politics and Political Participation in Postcommunist Hungary." In *The Consolidation of Democracy in East–Central Europe*, edited by Karen Dawisha and Bruce Parrott, 109–49. Cambridge: Cambridge University Press.

Treisman, Daniel S. 1998. "Fighting Inflation in a Transitional Regime—Russia's Anomalous Stabilization." *World Politics* 50: 2.

Tsebelis, George. 1995. "Decision Making in Political Systems: Veto Players in Presidentialism, Parliamentarism, Multicameralism, and Multipartyism." *British Journal of Political Science* 25, no. 3: 289–325.

Uribe, Martin. 1995. "Exchange–Rate–Based Inflation Stabilization: The Initial Real Effects of Credible Plans." *International Finance and Discussion Papers* 503 (April). Washington, D.C.: Board of Governors of the Federal Reserve System.

Vegh, Carlos. 1991. "Stopping High Inflation: An Analytical Overview." *IMF Staff Papers* 39: 626–695.

Vichyananond, P. 1994. *Thailand's Financial System: Structure and Liberalization.* Bangkok: Thailand Development Research Institute.

Vogel, Ezra. 1986. "Pax Nipponica?" *Foreign Affairs* 64 (Spring).

Wade, Robert. 1991. "How to Protect Exports from Protection: Taiwan's Duty Drawback Scheme." *World Economy* 14, no. 3: 299–309.

———. 1998. "The Asian Crisis and the Global Economy: Causes, Consequences, and Cure." *Current History,* November, 361–73.

Wall Street Journal. 30 December 1997–1 September 1999.

Wang, Heh–Song. 1999. "The Asian Financial Crisis and the Lessons Learned." *Economic Review* 308: 21–31.

Warr, P. G. 1995. "Explaining the Thai Miracle: Dragons, Planners, and Other Myths." Research School of Pacific and Asian Studies, Economics Division Working Paper.

Warr, P. G., and Bhanupong Nidhiprabha. 1996. *Thailand's Macroeconomic Miracle: Stable Adjustment and Sustained Growth.* Washington, D.C.: World Bank.

Washington Post. 17 February 1998–11 June 1999.

Weintraub, Sydney. 1984. *Free Trade between Mexico and the United States?* Washington, D.C.: Brookings Institution.

———. 1989. *Mexico frente al acuerdo de libre comercio Canadá–Estados Unidos.* Mexico: Diana.

———. 1990. *A Marriage of Convenience: Relations between Mexico and the United States.* New York: Oxford University Press.

Weyland, Kurt. 1998. "Swallowing the Bitter Pill: Sources of Popular Support for Neoliberal Reform in Latin America." *Comparative Political Studies* 31, no. 5: 539–568.

———. 1997–1998. "The Brazilian State in the New Democracy." *Journal of Interamerican Studies and World Affairs* 39, no. 4: 63–94.

Whalley, John. 1989. *Developing Countries and the Global Trading System.* Ann Arbor: University of Michigan Press.

White, Stephen, Richard Rose, and Ian McAllister. 1997. *How Russia Votes.* London: Chatham House.

Williamson, John. 1993. "Democracy and the 'Washington Consensus.'" *World Development,* 8 August, 1329–1337.

World Bank. 1987. *Korea: Managing the Industrial Transition.* Washington, D.C.: World Bank.

———. *The East Asian Miracle: Economic Growth and Public Policy.* New York: Oxford University Press.

———. *From Plan to Market: World Development Report 1996.* Washington, D.C.: Oxford University Press.

———. 1997. *The State in a Changing World: World Development Report 1997.* Washington, D.C.: Oxford University Press.

———. 1999. *Knowledge for Development: World Development Report 1998/99.* Washington, D.C.: Oxford University Press.

Yamamura, Kozo. 1997. "The Japanese Political Economy after the 'Bubble': Plus Ca Change?" *Journal of Japanese Studies* 23, no. 2: 291–332.

Yasuda, Nobuyuki. 1991. "Malaysia's New Economic Policy and the Industrial Coordination Act." *Developing Economies* 29, no. 4: 340–41.

Index

Federation Council (Russia, post-Soviet),
249, 258
Feldstein, Martin, 57
FIDF. *See* Financial Institutions
Development Fund
Filho, Alfredo Saad, 204
Finance One (Thailand), 70, 72
Financial Institutions Development Fund
(FIDF) (Thailand), 86
Financial Stabilization Plan (Japan), 141
Financial Supervisory Agency (FSA)
(Japan), 140–41, 144
First Trust Company (Thailand), 82
fiscal expansion, 42, 46; deficit financing,
42, 47–48; East Asia, 42; false
expectations of, 48–49; foreign
financing, 48–49; market expectations,
effects on, 48; private sector, effects
on, 49–50; safeguards for, 50
fiscal impulse measures, 46
Fischer, Stanley, 55
Fleet Group Sdn Bhd (Malaysia), 97
Fleischer, David, 209
Flynn, Peter, 206–7
FOBAPROA. *See* Fondo Bancario de
Protección al Ahorro
Fondo Bancario de Protección al Ahorro
(FOBAPROA), 184, 194–95
foreign debt, Thailand, 68, 70
foreign direct investment (FDI), 59, 219;
Malaysia, 93, 94, 99–102; South
Korea, 157
foreign economic policy regimes, defined, 5
Franco, Itamar, 207
free trade, 21
Friedman, Milton, 220
FSA. *See* Financial Supervisory Agency

G
Gaidar, Yegor, 248, 249
Garten, Jeffrey, 200, 201
GATT, 191
General Finance (Thailand), 72
German model, 236
Gil-Díaz and Carstens, 182
Goldste and Hawks, 136–37
Goldstein, Morris, 54, 158

Gomez, Edmund T., 98, 103–4
Gonzalez, Erman, 221
Gorbachev, Mikhail, 245–46, 248
Gore, Albert, 107
Gross Domestic Product (GDP):
Argentina, 217; Czech Republic, 236;
Hungary, 233, 235; Indonesia, 114,
117; Japan, 133, 135; Russia, 246, 251,
252, 254, 256; Thailand, 44
Gross National Product (GNP), 151
Gulf War, 67

H
Habibie, B. J., 112, 118, 123–25
Haggard, Stephan, 32
Hashimoto Ryutaro, 143, 149
Hata Tsutomo, 143
Hatibudi Nomees Sdn Bhd (Malaysia), 97
Horn, Gyula, 228, 234
Hosokawa Morihiro, 145
Hungarian Democratic Forum (MDF), 235
Hungary, 31; agricultural workforce,
38n18; agriculture, 247; dispersed
interest groups, 12–13; economic
indicators, *267;* election of president,
247; GDP, 233, 235; hard budget
constraints, 233; industry, 247; land-
labor ratios, 38n16; national identity,
234; organized labor, 233; peg
exchange rate, 233; postcommunism
policy, 232–33; precrisis policy, 226;
privatization, 233, 251; service sector
workforce, 37n4; unemployment, 233

I
IBRA. *See* Indonesian Bank Restructuring
Agency
import substitution, Brazil, 201–2
import-competing sectors, 21–22, 25
imports, 51, 113
Indochina, 66–67
Indonesia, 10–11, 34, 35, 55; agricultural
workforce, 38n18; agriculture, 114;
Chinese in, 10, 116–17; Communist
Party, 112–13; concentrated interest
groups, 10, 11, 117–18; corporate debt,
120; corruption, 10; coup, 112–13;

About the Contributors

Eric C. Browne is a professor of political science at the University of Wisconsin-Milwaukee. His Ph.D. is from Syracuse University. He is the author of many articles in well-known professional journals, such as the *American Political Science Review,* the *American Journal of Political Science,* and the *British Journal of Political Science.* His research focuses on political institutions, and much of his recent work analyzes Japan's political system.

Jeffrey Cason is an assistant professor of political science at Middlebury College in Middlebury, Vermont. He is coauthor, with Christopher Barrett, of *Overseas Research: A Practical Guide* (1997) and coeditor, with Michael Carter and Frederic Zimmerman, of *Development at a Crossroads: Uncertain Paths to Sustainability after the Neoliberal Revolution* (1998). He has published articles and book chapters on the political economy of export promotion in Brazil, economic integration in South America, and North/South relations, and was a founder and director of the Latin American Studies Program at Middlebury College. He is currently working on a project on South American integration.

W. Max Corden is a professor of international economics at the School of Advanced International Studies at Johns Hopkins University. He is a world-renowned international economist and the author of many books and articles. He received his Ph.D. from the London School of Economics. His more recent books include *Trade Policy and Economic Welfare* (1997), *The Road to Reform* (1997), *Economic Policy, Exchange Rates, and the International System* (1994), and *International Trade: Theory and Policy* (1992).

Aldo Flores Quiroga obtained his Ph.D. in political science from the University of California, Los Angeles. He is currently assistant professor at the Claremont Graduate University. He recently published a book on the political economy of Mexico's trade policy with Mexico's Fondo de Cultura Economica. His research interests include the political economy of trade and exchange rate policy in Mexico, as well as the politics of institutional change. He was born and raised in Mexico, and he has been conducting research in Mexico and interviewing prominent Mexican policy makers for a number of years.

Uk Heo is an associate professor of political science at the University of Wisconsin-Milwaukee. He is a native Korean and received his Ph.D. from Texas A&M University. He is the author of *The Political Economy of Defense Spending around the World* (1999) and the author or coauthor of articles in *American Politics Quarterly*, *Journal of Politics*, *Journal of Conflict Resolution*, *International Interactions*, *Journal of East Asian Affairs*, *Asian Perspective*, *Journal of Peace Research*, *West European Politics*, and *Korean Journal of International Studies*. His research focuses on the political economy of financial crisis in East Asia, the defense-growth nexus, and conflict theories.

Shale Horowitz is an assistant professor of political science at the University of Wisconsin-Milwaukee. He has an M.A. in economics and a Ph.D. in political science from UCLA, has taught for a year at Central European University in Budapest, Hungary, and has done research in many countries of Eastern Europe and the former Soviet Union. He is the author of book chapters and journal articles on economic policy making and democratization in the postcommunist countries. He is currently editor of *Analysis of Current Events*. His research focuses on the political economy of international trade and finance, the political economy of market transition and institutional change in the postcommunist countries, and the politics of agricultural policy.

Sunwoong Kim is an associate professor of economics at the University of Wisconsin-Milwaukee. He is a specialist in urban economics but also has strong research interests in political economy and development, particularly in East Asian countries. He received a Ph.D. in economics and urban planning from MIT in 1985. He has published many articles in well-known professional journals, including *American Economic Review*, *Journal of Political Economy*, *The Review of Economics and Statistics*, *Journal of Urban Economics*, *Journal of Regional Science*, *Regional Science and Urban Economics*, *Journal of Housing Economics*, *Journal of Housing Research*, and *Social Science Quarterly*.

James LoGerfo is an equity research associate at Bank of America Securities. He received his doctorate in political science from Columbia University in 1997. His academic interests include regime change, civil society, social movements, democratic politics, and civil–military relations. He is the author or coauthor of articles in *Asian Survey* and *Journal of Democracy* and has written a forthcoming book chapter on provincial democracy movements in Thailand.

Walter T. Molano is head of Latin American research at BCP Securities, Inc. He is responsible for all macroeconomic, financial, and corporate research. Prior to joining BCP, he was the director of economic and financial research at Warburg Dillon Read. Between 1995 and 1996, he was a senior economist and vice president for Latin America at CS First Boston. He completed his Ph.D. at Duke University and was the recipient of the Duke Endowment Fellowship, SSRC Fellowship, and Tinker Foundation Grant. Molano also holds an M.B.A. and a certificate in international law. He is a 1983 graduate of the U.S. Naval Academy. He is the author of *The Logic of Privatization: The Case of Telecommunications in the Southern Cone of Latin America*. He was ranked in the Gold Medal Category during the 1998 Latin Finance Research Olympics and as a top economist for Venezuela in 1997. Molano is a member of the Council of Foreign Relations, Latin American Advisory Council, a faculty fellow at the Yale School of Management, an adjunct professor at Columbia University, and a trustee at Duke University.

Gabriella R. Montinola is an assistant professor of political science at the University of California, Davis. She received her doctorate in political science from Stanford University in 1995. Her current research interests focus on economic development, interest representation, and the causes and consequences of political corruption. She is the author or coauthor of articles in *World Politics*, *Journal of Democracy*, *Development and Change*, *Crime, Law and Social Change*, and *Asian Journal of Political Science*.

Kimberly J. Niles is an assistant professor in the department of political science at the University of Colorado, Boulder. She received her Ph.D. from UCLA in December 1999. Her dissertation examines the role of political institutions in determining which countries adopt targeted poverty alleviation programs during economic adjustment. It includes data from sixty-four developing countries in Latin America, Asia, and Africa. Niles spent nine months in Indonesia on a National Security Education Program graduate fellowship and has also conducted field research in Brazil, Thailand, and the Philippines. She recently contributed a background paper entitled "Economic Adjustment and Targeted Social Spending: The Role of Political Institutions" to the World Bank's *World Development Report 2000/1*.

Peter Rutland is a professor of government at Wesleyan University and an associate of the Davis Center for Russian Studies at Harvard University. He has a

B.A. from Oxford University and a Ph.D. from the University of York. From 1995 to 1997 he was assistant director for research at the Open Media Research Institute in Prague. He is the author of *The Myth of the Plan* (1985) and *The Politics of Economic Stagnation in the Soviet Union* (1993). Since 1996 he has been the editor of the *Annual Survey of Eastern Europe and the Former Soviet Union*. He is currently editing a book entitled *The Rise of the Oligarchs: Business and the State in Russia*. He is also a well-known public commentator on Soviet and post-Soviet affairs.

Alexander C. Tan specializes in comparative political parties, comparative political institutions, and the political economy of East Asia and the advanced industrial democracies. Prior to joining the faculty at the University of North Texas, he was Tower Fellow at the John Goodwin Tower Center for Political Studies at Southern Methodist University. Born and raised in the Philippines, he lived and worked in Taiwan for four years, first as an economist with the Taiwan Institute of Economic Research and then as a banker with Hongkong Bank. He holds an A.B. in economics from the Ateneo de Manila University, an M.A. in economics from the University of California at Santa Barbara, and a Ph.D. in political science from Texas A&M University. His research has been published in such scholarly journals as the *Journal of Politics*, *Party Politics*, *West European Politics*, *Issues and Studies*, and the *Journal of East Asian Affairs*. His current research is on the role of domestic political institutions in the Asian financial crisis, with particular emphasis on Taiwan and Korea.

A. Maria Toyoda is a research scholar at Stanford University's Institute for International Studies and associate director of the Asia/Pacific Scholars Program. She received her Ph.D. in government from Georgetown University and holds an A.B. in human biology from Stanford University. She spent a year and a half in Osaka and Tokyo, Japan, as a Monbusho (Ministry of Education) Scholar from 1995 to 1997. Her research interests are comparative financial politics and Asian political economy. Currently, she is part of a research team comparing financial regulations in several dozen countries.